Religious Freedom and The Saffron Politics

About the Author

With masters in English literature, degree of Bachelor of Education, post graduate diploma in journalism and International Human Rights Certificate from CHRC (Canada) he has been a journalist, human rights activist and a writer. He was editor of two Catholic newsweeklies 4), and was associated with Religious News. He has written extensively on the religious conflict and politics in India. Gathia has been associated with People's Union for Civil Liberties (PUCL), Citizen for Democracy-CFD (founded by Jayaprakash Narayan).

The author has visited many countries in Europe, Asia, North America and extensively travelled in the Indian sub-continent and has keenly observed human rights, social issues and religious concerns.

Joseph Gathia has been associated with Human Rights Information and Documentation System-HURIDOCS (Geneva), International Human Rights Services-ISHR (Geneva) and OMCT-(World Organisation Against Torture (Geneva) in the early 1990s. He participated in the UN World Conference on Human Rights (Vienna, 1993), UN World Conference for Social Development (Copenhagen, 1995) and the UN Fourth World Conference on Women (Beijing, 1995).

Many institutes and universities invited him to give lectures. To mention just a few among are: The Vrij University, Amsterdam; International Institute of Social Science of Erasmus University, Rotterdam, Netherlands; KIT Royal Tropical Institute, Amsterdam, Netherlands; South Asian Centre, Monash University (Australia); Indian Institute of Mass Communication, New Delhi; Aligarh Muslim University (AMU); and McGill University (Canada) on 50th anniversary of Universal Declaration of Human Rights.

The author has penned many books: Women and Child Workers in the Unorganised Sector in India (1986); Child Labour in India (1992); Child Prostitution in India released by the Justice M.V. Venkatchelliah, Chief Justice, Supreme Court of India (Concept Publishing Company, New Delhi, 1999); *Bharat main Balika* released by Justice J.S. Verma, Chief Justice, Supreme Court of India (Concept Publishing Company, 2002); *Asia Mai Dheh Vyapar* (Hindi) (Concept Publishing Company, 2003) and Children's Rights and Well Being in India (Concept Publishing Company, 2015).

Joseph A. Gathia is currently engaged in setting up Centre for the Study of Future.

RELIGIOUS FREEDOM AND THE SAFFRON POLITICS

Joseph A. Gathia

CONCEPT PUBLISHING COMPANY PVT. LTD.
NEW DELHI-110059

ISBN-13: 978-93-86682-90-1

First Published in 2019

Published and Printed by

Concept
Since 1974

Concept Publishing Company Pvt. Ltd.
A/15-16, Commercial Block, Mohan Garden,
New Delhi-110059 (INDIA)
T: 91 11 25351460, 91 11 25351794
E: publishing@conceptpub.com; *W*: www.conceptpub.com

Many inspired and helped me to understand
meaning of religious freedom and peaceful coexistence
My mentors in journalism Frank Moraes and VJF Kulandaiswamy
late Archbishop Eugene D'Souza (Bhopal),
Archbishop Angelo Fernandes (Delhi),
Fr. James Tong SJ; Fr.John Barret SJ
Late Shri S.K.Dey, India's first Union Minister for Community
Development, Cooperation and Panchayati Raj, Socialist Surendra
Mohan, late Shri K.S. Radhakrishna of Gandhi Peace Foundation,
Archbishop Anil Joseph Thomas Couto of Delhi
Archbishop Vincent Concessao, Archbishop Emeritus of Delhi
Sr. Anfreda (Choti Maa jee) SSpS
Blessed Sr. Rani Maria Vattalil, FCC
Sr. Valsa John, SCJM

To them in gratitude
This book is dedicated.

Walk together in the path of truth without bias.
Talk to each other to enhance knowledge, wisdom
And affection without malice or hatred.
Keep working together to enhance knowledge and bliss.
Follow the path of truth and selflessness as exemplified by noble people.

—*Rig Veda (10.162.1)*

Preface

I began thinking about this book in the city of Maheshwar on the river Narmada in central India. I had gone in that area to cover problems faced by the Bhil tribal Christians of Dhar-Jhabua in Madhya Pradesh.

The principal object of the present work is to examine the rise of Rashtriya Swayamsevak Sangh (RSS), its capacity to influence public policy process *vis-à-vis* religious freedom in India. As a journalist and human rights activist, I have observed the activities of the RSS and its affiliates since mid-1970s during the Emergency days in India.

I travelled across the country from Nagaland in North East, to Tiruchi in Tamil Nadu, to the Dangs and Godhra in Gujarat, to Kunkuri in Ambikapur district (Chhattisgarh), to Kandhmal (Odisha), to Jhabua in Madhya Pradesh, to Malegaon in Maharashtra, to Adilabad in Andhra Pradesh. In all these places, I was helped by journalists working with small newspapers. I purposely visited small towns where it is still possible to discuss social issues at a small tea stall. These towns are mixture of rural thinking and urban desire to join the middle classes. It was great experience.

Like any other author writing today on this subject of this book, I have had to fall back for many of my facts on through work of eminent scholars and specialists in their respective fields. These include, Romiia Thapar, Abdul Gafoor, Abdul Majeed Noorani, Wendy Doniger, Walter Andersen, Shridhar Damle, Sanjeev Kelkar, Sebastian Kim, Ashok Chowgule, Robert Eric Frykenberg,

Shamshul Islam, Chandra Prakash Bhambhri, and others, all of whom are listed in the bibliography and more specifically acknowledged in the text.

The reason for writing this book is rooted in my experience as an editor of two Catholic Hindi weekly newspapers, which had a lasting effect. My interest in the issue of religious freedom began in 1981 when I first visited Meenakshipuram (Tamil Nadu) where large number of Hindu Dalits had embraced Islam. This incident made international headlines. Then the Catholic Bishops Conference of India's (CBCI) objection over Arun Shourie's book, *Missionaries in India: Continuities, Changes, Dilemmas* (1994) further aroused my curiosity. The debate between Hindus and Christians over religious conversion became intense when Atal Bihari Vajpayee, Prime Minister of India called for a 'national debate on conversion' in January 1999.

The large-scale resentment among Hindus over visit of Pope John Paul II to India in November 1999 further made me search why Hindu leaders strongly contest religious freedom in India. There have been several occasions when this issue surfaced in public discourse but *ghar wapsi* incident at Agra in December 2014 led me to reflect further on the theme of religious freedom in India and emerging challenges in the light of the BJP's landslide victory earlier in that year.

This prodded me to examine the impact of saffron agenda Rashtriya Swayamsevak Sangh (RSS) religious freedom in India. While much of the material, in one form or other, is obtainable elsewhere, the analysis and presentation of this material, however, abbreviated what the author has digested and interpreted over the course of the past forty years. It provides contextualization, without undemanding which it would be rather difficult to fully grasp the shape of emerging threats to the freedom of religion in India.

What sort of India do we want? What sort of Indians do we want to be? What sort of country do we want to leave behind for future generations? These questions all involve one of the most fundamental ideas of India.

This book strongly argues that government in a mature democracy should pursue policies that protect religious freedom where all religious groups should be free from the spectre of threat and persecution. My background in journalism, teaching, and human while allowing me to explore the issues of globalization and culture, ethics and development, responses to concern for environment efforts and global warming, children's well-being, religious and faith based approaches to conflict resolution and efforts to create inter-religious dialogues also facilitated observing how thoughtful and concerned people (secular and religious and caring and committed organizations (again, secular and religious) drove the best of themselves to the challenges of creating a world that is compassionate, just, and peaceful.

New Delhi
December 21, 2018

Joseph A. Gathia

Acknowledgements

Working on a book for three years make any writer beholden to a long list of people who either encouraged or excused such obsessive behaviour. My list, while long, is nowhere near as inclusive as I wish it could be, and I apologize for any names I have overlooked.

My interest in the issue of religious freedom began in 1981 when as a young journalist I visited Meenakshipuram (Tamil Nadu) where large number of low caste Hindus had embraced Islam. This incident made international headlines. This interest was renewed in 1994 with the Catholic Bishops Conference of India's (CBCI) objection over Arun Shourie's book, *Missionaries in India: Continuities, Changes, Dilemmas*. The debate between Hindus and Christians over religious conversion became intense when Atal Behari Vajpayee, Prime Minister of India called for a 'national debate on conversion' in January 1999. The large-scale resentment among Hindus over Pope John Paul II visit to India in November 1999 further made me search why Hindu leaders strongly contest religious conversion in India. There have been several occasions when this issue surfaced in public discourse but *ghar wapsi* incident at Agra in December 2014 led me to reflect further on the theme of religious freedom in India and emerging challenges in the light of the BJP's landslide victory earlier in that year.

This prodded me to examine religious freedom in India under new political scenario of realignment of Indian politics along *Hindutva* values. Yet, it seemed an ambitious task to write a book that spanned half a century. To engage with so many contemporary debates in conversion and freedom of religion. Even so, I decided to go ahead with the project.

This turned out to be a journey in exploration and discovery. This journey has been long and hard. During this journey, many people helped me who shaped my thinking and supported me in many ways, and I acknowledge the contributions they made directly or indirectly to this book.

The faces of countless men, women, and children have been before me as I wrote this book. Their lives instructed, inspired and encouraged me and deepened my conviction that good God does work, albeit in odd and surprising ways. I cannot mention their names, but many will hear in the pages of this book echo of our conversions, with sorrow and joy. I cannot thank you enough.

This journey has been long and hard. During this journey, many people helped me who shaped my thinking and supported me in many ways, and I acknowledge the contributions they made directly or indirectly to this book.

My thanks are due to my memories of the formative help, which I received during the Think Tank meetings of Archdiocese of Delhi. I wish to thank Archbishop Vincent Michael Concessao, Archbishop Emeritus (Delhi), the new Archbishop of Delhi Anil J. T. Couto, and Rev. Dr. Richard Howell of Evangelical Federation of India for their time to time public statements on the status of religious freedom in India which guided me in my work.

I owe a posthumous debt, personal and professional, to the late Archbishop Eugene Louis D'Souza, M.S.F.S. (Archbishop of Nagpur and later of Bhopal). The writings of Raimon Panikkar, pioneer of inter-faith dialogue, and protestant theologian Prof. Stanley Jedidiah Samartha greatly influenced my thinking about religious freedom. Protestant theologian, the late M. M. Thomas, the late Dr. Habil James Massey and the late Dr. K. Rajaratnam (Master of the Senate of Serampore, President of the National Council of Churches in India) opened new windows to me.

I cannot forget the encouragement and inspiration that I received from the late Archbishop Eugene Louis D'Souza, M.S.F.S. (Archbishop of Nagpur and later of Bhopal). Archbishop Eugene wrote excellent critique of the Niyogi Report and as a journalist, I had many discussions with Archbishop Eugue D'Souza, before and after his retirement. He was at Asha Niketan, Bhopal after his retirement. I mention them because today they may be a forgotten entity but they played key role in one way or other to defend religious freedom and gave message of peaceful co-existence of all religions in India. They provided perspective comments on religious freedom in the bygone era and who saw earlier than most, and with greater clarity the issues with which this book is concerned.

I would be failing in my duty if I do not thank the late Dr. R.M. Pal, the late Justice Vithal Mahadeo Tarkunde (prominent Indian lawyer, and the "Father of the Civil Liberties Movement" in India) and late Justice R. Sachar (Ex-Delhi High Court Chief Justice and the architect of the landmark Sachar report on status of Muslims in India).

Special thanks to Shri Rajendra Prabhu (former special correspondent, *The Hindustan Times*) and human rights activist Alex Tuscano (Bangalore) for commenting on some chapters of this book.

In the preparation of this book, it took many times to either read the manuscripts or comment or interact with the issue. My many debts, are both professional and personals: Rev. Dr Nirmal Minz (Bishop Emeritus of the Protestant North Western Gossner Evangelical Lutheran Church Society), Maulana Wahiduddin Khan (Islamic spiritual scholar), Shahanawaj Siddiqui (Muslim journalist), Prof. G. Haragopal (Visiting Professor in NLSIU and teachers at the Centre for Human Rights, University of Hyderabad), Rev. Dr. Dominic Emmanuel SVD, Dr. John Dayal, Fr. Suresh Mathew (Indian Currents), Marianus Kujur sj, Sr. Mary Scaria scjm (Advocate, Supreme Court of India), T.K. John sj, Francis Gonsalves sj, Sr. Nirmalini, AC Michael, Joseph Malikal (journalist), former Member of Delhi Minorities Commission, AC Michael, activists, Cedric Prakash sj, Tehmina Arora, Dr. K Mohansundaram (Associate Professor in History, Islamiah College, and Prof. Ram Punjabi, Surety Parthsarathy (Advocate, Madras High Court) and of course to writer Anto Akra. I am very grateful to all of them for their counsel and support. But, most importantly, I wish to thank my friends, Prof. Darvesh Gopal (School of Social Sciences, IGNOU), and Prof. Abdulrahim P. Vijapur (Political Science, Aligarh Muslim University) for insisting to explain the complex things in simple manner.

This book would not have been fully representative without inputs from some knowledgeable Hindus. I owe great debt to the late Shri Kuppalli Sitaramayya, Sudarshan, Sarsanghachalak, Rashtriya Swayamsevak Sangh (RSS) from 2000 to 2009, with whom I spent two days in Hyderabad learning about *Sarvadharm Sambhav*. I also owe debt to the late Dr. N.K. Trikha, and Shri Shyam Khosla (both once *pracharak* and later journalist), and Prof. Arvind Sharma (McGill University, Canada) for introducing me to the inner functioning of the RSS.

My thanks are due to the Librarians of Vidhya Jyoti (Delhi), Gurukul Lutheran Theological College and Research Institute (Chennai), Ecumenical Christian Centre (Whitefield, Bangalore), Union Bible Seminary (Pune), the Milli Gazette library, Indian Social Institute and Centre for Study of Religion and Society (CSRS), and Vivekananda International Foundation (VIF).

I am grateful to Shri Ram Madhav jee of India Foundation and important office bearer of the BJP/RSS for inviting me to India Conclave held in 2014 held at Goa. I had wonderful experience and learned a lot about the RSS.

Here I would like to make special mention of John L. Allen Jr. Vatican correspondent for the National Catholic Reporter and author of many books including 'All the Pope's Men'. I met him in 2005. Another two distinguished authors that deserve mention here are Richard Cimino and Don Lattin. They together penned book *Shopping for Faith*, which greatly enriched my understanding of emerging challenges to Christianity in the twenty-first century.

At the Concept Publishing Company Pvt. Ltd., New Delhi, Shri Ashok Kumar Mittal gave me the right kind of encouragement. Young Nitin Mittal at the Concept Publishing Company Pvt. Ltd., has remarkable grip of the issues and talking to him has been very useful in terms of appreciating the scope of the issue. My thanks to them.

My greatest debt of gratitude is to my Hindu friends and their families at Maheshwar, a small town on the banks of River Narmada, for their openness and hospitality during my stay when I was finalising the book.

I am most appreciative of all this assistance and support, but hold only myself responsible for the content of this book.

The enormous support from my family throughout was invaluable. I recall many conversions with my elder son Sanjay and younger son Akshay during which they made some practical suggestions by sharing their wonderful pleasant experiences with their Hindu friends. My wife Molly provided the moral support and read first draft of the manuscript. The years in preparation for this work would never have been possible without her support.

By the help of Holy Spirit, this journey, though long and hard has been joyful.

New Delhi
December 2018

Contents

PART IV
CONTOURS OF CONTROVERSY

PART V
CONCLUSIONS

Introduction
The Watchers at the Dawn

Let noble thoughts come from all directions. —Rig Veda

On 17th September, 2018, the RSS Sarsanghachalak, Shri Mohan Bhagwat, while addressing a three-day conclave, 'Future of Bharat: An RSS Perspective', at Vigyan Bhavan in New Delhi, touched many key issues which indirectly related to parameters of religious freedom.

The freedom to choose in a globalised world economy, which effects cultural identity has emerged as one of the biggest challenges. With phenomenon, economic growth beginning in the mid-2000s India really began to change and by 2018, it emerged as the sixth largest economy in the world.[1] In the wake of fiscal reforms in early 1990s, the national economy had expanded, in real terms, over 400 per cent. Many Indians became rich in this process and some have made to the Forbes List of super rich. The richest one per cent owns more than half of national wealth, one of the highest rates in the world. The International Monetary Fund (IMF) suggests that India, alongside China, now ranks as Asia's most unequal major economy. The economic growth has also increased gap between India's rich and the poor.

There is a strange consensus among intellectuals both right and the left about inequality and they downplay this situation. Recent IMF research has challenged the consensus that inequality harm, showing that unequal nations tend to grow more slowly and be more prone to financial instability (Crabtree, 2018). Countries driven by internal divisions are also less likely to build the kind of broad social consensus that make it easier to introduce tough structural reforms, of the type that India itself now badly needs, if it is to continue to develop economically. There is also every reason to believe that, without intervention, the gap between India's rich and the rest will keep widening.[2]

Despite such inequality, there are 1.1 billion cell phones and it is estimated that 500 million access the Internet from their mobile phones by 2018. The rapid adoption of mobile phones and the enhanced use of the Internet undermine traditional social diarchies and provide individuals and group an autonomy that is socially disrupting (Andersen and Damle, 2018). The rise of the super rich then brings us to a second issue: crony capitalization meaning collation between political and business elites to capture valuable public resources for themselves. Such situation in any country can be cause of worry as it has potential to influence the factors that control religious liberty even in a democracy.

Globally, it has been noted that, economic growth has not improved the level of religious freedom. The hope that prosperity would beget freedom and democracy has faded as well. Every year since 2006 according to Freedom House, the number of countries registering a decline in political rights has outstripped the number of registering in increase. In all, 100 countries, more than half the world's total have suffered some loss of freedom during the past ten years. The number of democracies has not changed dramatically, but repression is on the rise even in countries like Russia, that keep up the appearance of elections. Few observers argue anymore that prosperity in China will lead to democracy. They point instead to the rise of a new and increasing assertive form of authoritarianism regimes that reject democracy as a universal value while defending softer forms of political repression as expression of unique national cultures.

Debates about religious liberty often turn on the expression of religious bellies in the public sphere, set against the limits that the state imposes to maintain public order. Do religious communities have the right to open churches for public worship, and to establish schools to educate their children within their religious traditions? Can symbols of religious identify be displayed on buildings, or on bodies, when these are in the public sphere? Conceived in this manner, freedom of religion is primarily a matter of the relationship between religious communities and the state. But matter becomes complicated when non-state actors determine the contours of the religious freedom.

Hinduism is, and continues to be, one of the great religions of the world. Traditionally Hindus are tolerant and have lived with multi-ethnic communities since centuries. This tolerance has been the hallmark of Hinduism for generations. India is the world's most populous secular democracy and the Constitution of India guarantees freedom to profess, practice, propagate, and change religion without fear. However, the issue of religious freedom commands particular attention now, when the very idea of the secular state is being contested in India after the landslide victory of the BJP in 2014 Lok Sabha elections. In the twenty-first century India, freedom of religion or belief has emerged as a greater and more urgent issue than ever before due to growing religious fundamentalism which presents a major challenge to the philosophy of a plural society.

Since 2014, there has been a growing drumbeat of alarming episodes involving Hindu chauvinists, almost all of whom are staunch Modi supporters. Some have involved symbolic strikes against secularism: removing Nehru's name from school textbooks for instance, or banning works on Hinduism by liberal Western scholars, whose ideas were said to offend mainstream sensibilities. Others have features jingoistic campaigns against 'anti-national' elements from students to human rights activists, and even those who resist chanting patriotic slogans or standing when the national anthem is played in cinemas. None of this was caused directly by Modi or indeed condoned by him. But almost all these incidents were linked in one-way or another to a constellation of fanatical Hindu groups that had grown bolder after Modi's arrival, most notably the RSS whose leaders remained tied close to his government (Crabtree, 2018). The RSS is today in a position to influence the government policy as no other organization (Andersen and Damle, 2018).

There is then particular animosity directed at Islam, begging with trumped up campaigns against what was often called 'love jihad', in which Muslim men were accused of using surreptitious marriage proposals as a tool for the conversion of Hindu women. Many street names were changed in Delhi. More prominent still was a spate of violent campaigns to protect cows, which is considered sacred by Hindus. Some are involved in legal changes, for instance to tighten rule governing slaughterhouses, most of which are run by Muslims. But at their worst they developed

Islamophobia, leading to a rash of murders and lynching conducted by *gau rakshaks* (cow protectors) against those suspected of eating or selling beef (Andersen and Damle, 2018). All this lead to social tension amidst economic growth.[3]

On one hand, Narendra Modi is trying hard to make India a super power and on the other hand, these actions by non-state actors are giving different signals to the world community.

Today India is at the crossroads, therefore, it is all the more important to examine religious freedom.

Before we proceed further, let us briefly ponder over why religious freedom is core human rights.

Freedom of religion is a fundamental right and represents a major triumph of any democratic society. Respect for another person's belief is one of the hallmarks of a civilised society. It is 'one of the foundations' of democratic rights.

Article 18 (1) of the United Nations Universal Declaration of Human Rights, 1948 contains a definition echoed in many subsequent international and domestic human rights instruments. It states:

> "Everyone has the right to freedom of thought, conscience, and religion; this right includes freedom to change his religion or belief and freedom, either alone or in community with others and in public or private, to manifest his religion or belief in teaching, practice, worship, and observance."

Five characteristics of religious freedom: (i) assembling for peaceful religious activities such as worship, preaching, and prayer; (ii) speaking freely about one's religious beliefs; (iii) changing one's religious beliefs and affiliation; (iv) possession and distribution of religious literature, including sacred texts; (v) raising one's children in the religious teachings and practices of one's choice are indicator of religious liberty in any society.[4]

Under the Constitution of India, freedom of religion is a fundamental right and one has right to profess, practice, or choose his/her religion or faith.

Freedom of religion cannot prosper on its own: it requires protection of collateral rights such as freedom of thought, expression, association and of assembly. These four freedoms:

Religion (thought), Speech (expression), Association, and Assembly—are interrelated and fundamental freedoms of the individual, and essential for the exercise of all other rights. The guarantee of each is necessary for enjoyment of the other and indeed for the exercise of all human rights. Thus, freedom of expression is necessary if freedom of thought is to be exercised. In turn, freedom of expression has little meaning without the individual having freedom to think and have an opinion. The right to practise or to teach a religion includes the freedom to publish religious literature or broadcast religious programmes. If religious communities or denominations are to exist, their freedom of association is essential, as is their right to assembly for religious purposes. Freedom of expression is essential when people come together to pursue their interests through other associates, such as a trade union, political parties, or community groups. Freedom of expression is essential also to the freedom to assemble and the right to demonstrate over grievances.[5] Thus, while each freedom is distinct in theory, in practice they are interrelated and interdependent.

THE NEW ALPHABET OF RELIGIOUS FREEDOM: POINTS OF TENSION AND A CHALLENGE FOR UNIVERSALITY

Since 2001, international attention and international law has come to focus on three particularly controversial issues—(1) national security, (2) globalization and increasing consumerism, and (3) regulating religious freedom. Each of these three issues deserve further adumbration, as they are among the most hotly contested religious freedom issues today and arise particularly when religious traditions and religious believers confront each other in the current global resurgence of religion.

National Security and Religious Freedom

After 9/11 of 2001, terror attack in the US and parallel events elsewhere in the world (in India 26/11 of 2008 terrorists attack in Mumbai) have etched into everyone's understanding that there are powerful security concerns in some cases need to override freedom of religion.

In the years that followed the attacks on the World Trade Centre and the Pentagon in 2001, security discussions increasingly referred to an assumed link between religion and terrorism. One theory is that when religion is not confined to the private sphere violence will result, and that there is an actual link between some religious doctrine and acts of terrorism. There is an argument offered by some commentators that, religion should be placed under surveillance as part of an effort to prevent acts of 'terrorism'.

Such thinking has led to police raids of religious places of worship and certain minority organizations are often subjected to surveillance and searches. Furthermore, religious leaders of some religious groups have come under increased police supervision. The international migration clause recognized the need to limit freedom of religion to deal with threats to public safety and public orders. However, in many cases, this justification of additional state interference with religious freedom and other human rights has been carried much too far. It is important to remember that national security in abstract is not one of the enumerated grounds that serves permissible basis for limiting religious liberty and cannot legitimise restrictions on religious freedom or faith. Even when limitations are more rightly linked to public safety and public order issues, there is still a risk that limitation can have the unintended consequences that might fall under persecution. Great care must be taken to ensure that public safety concerns are not allowed to unduly reduce religious freedom protections.[6] The exercise of religion need not automatically be interpreted as a threat to national security.

The right to manifest freedom of religion and belief in worship, preaching, practice, and observance is fundamental to the exercise of the right in all of its scope. By limiting the right to teach religion, unless this right is derogated from in accordance with the intended provisions of international law, this right will be violated. While national security concerns are not cited as a legitimate justification for limiting freedom of religion or belief, public safety and given the broad scope of activities that could be perceived to act as threat to 'public safety', there is a risk that states will cite them to justify restrictions on religious freedom imposed for reasons tantamount to national security interest, by arguing that a religious group is engaged in political activities that endanger public safety and order.[7] Given these challenges to religious freedom and the scope for limitations, the right is currently vulnerable to violation in a new way. Most pertinent is the threat to religious equality right.

Freedom of Religion in Globalizing Future

Globalization is a complex and crosscutting phenomenon; it combines centripetal pressures—internationalism, economic integration, and interdependence—with the centrifuge, force of proliferating pluralism, especially with regard to religion and most acutely the meaning of religious liberty itself.

Global flow of capital and labour also can be more direct vehicle for religious diversity and help create political and cultural space for more religious liberty. One can see this in Arabian countries and the Gulf countries, which are now slowly opening up for non-Muslims. Although full religious freedom remains a distant dream, the demographic fact of religious pluralism along with some government accommodation of houses for public worship, demonstrates one positive effect of globalization on religious liberty.

The early enthusiastic voices for globalization promised that old rivalries, hatred, and chauvinism would dissipate as the new interconnectedness provides people a common humanity and celebrated their differences. Just as often, however, the new communication networks and economic mobility exacerbate prejudices and help create new identities that has even contributed to a diminishing of religious freedom in many parts of the world.

Another hallmark of globalization is the creation and proliferation of new technologies and modes of communication. Whereas manifested encomium of the liberating powers of technology and communication are virtually inseparable, a less acknowledged but fact that is more pernicious may be how those technologies can be used to constrict liberty, particularly religious freedom. Profound new capabilities in surveillance technology enable authoritarian and totalitarian regimes to maintain even scrutiny on virtually every word and action for both their citizens and many other visitors.

Advances in quality, efficiency, and especially accessibility of Internet based communications technologies (including video production, online networking, and mobile device delivery) are being used by religious militants to promote their perverse agenda of violence and religious intolerance. These new technologies by themselves can be enlisted for nefarious purposes.

The use of globalization's new technologies for oppression is not confined to government security services working with—and sometimes coercing—multinational companies. At the other end of the organizational spectrum are the various transnational and sub-national organizations primarily fundamentalist fanatic forces and groups who have proven remarkably adept at adapting new communications and media technologies for their own purposes of fermenting religious intolerance. Internet forums, interactive Web sites, satellite television, and especially propaganda video produced rapidly and disseminated *via* mobile phone and inerrant have all become indispensable elements in the militants' arsenal. They are employed for various purposes including recruiting new adherents to the group's cause, publicizing its views, agenda, and campaign, countering criticism and stigmatizing and even inciting violence against other religious groups or other perceived enemies. All of these actions are deeply inimical to a culture of pluralism and religious liberty.[7]

The global rise of populism poses a dangerous threat to human rights. The supporters of populism claiming to speak for "the people", treat rights as an impediment to their conception of the majority will, a needless obstacle to defending the nation from perceived threats and evils. Instead of accepting that rights protect everyone, they encourage people to adopt the dangerous belief that they will never need their rights against an overreaching government claiming to act in their name.

In this cauldron of discontent, certain politicians are flourishing and even gaining power by portraying rights as protecting only the terrorist suspect or the asylum seeker at the expense of the safety, economic welfare, and cultural preferences of the presumed majority. But, if these voices of intolerance prevail, the world risks entering a dark era. When populists treat rights as an obstacle to their vision of the majority will, it is only a matter of time before they turn on those who disagree with their agenda. Such claims of unfettered majoritarianism, and the attacks on the checks and balances that constrain governmental power, are perhaps the greatest danger today to the future of democracy and religious freedom.[8]

The rising tide of populism in the name of a perceived majority has paralleled a new infatuation with strongman rule. The thinking seems to go, why not embrace the autocrat who shows no qualms about asserting his "majoritarian" vision—self-serving as it may be—and subjugating those who disagree.[9]

The best way to counter populist trends is by vigorous reaffirmation of human rights. Governments committed to respecting human rights serve their people better by being more likely to avoid the corruption, self-aggrandizement, and arbitrariness that so often accompany autocratic rule. Governments founded on human rights are better placed to hear their citizens and recognize and address their problems. And governments that respect human rights are able to protect freedom of religion in much better manner.

Regulating Religious Freedom

Regulating religion is still a common phenomenon in the world, though the ways in which government or regimes intervene in religious matters varies widely. It is by nature a complex and multi-dimensional subject and is closely related to the legal, political, and social dynamics of each country.

Understanding this nature of relationship is of importance, since there is a common assumption, primarily along human rights activists and groups, that state regulating of religion constitutes a threat to religious freedom. The state is seen to commit an "atrocity" if it involves itself in managing the religious life of its citizens. One of the basic arguments of this is clear: for some human rights activists in many liberal states in particular, religion is a private and personal matter for each individual. Therefore, a "modern" government in a "Modern" state should accordingly maintain zero or at least minimal involvement in religious life if it is not to be seen as violating of humanity and freedom of its citizens.

Some scholars say that the state regulation of religion is not always contrary to the principles of religious freedom. In many cases, government intervention on religious activities may prevent or at least minimize the conflicts between religious groups. Some cases also have shown that due to government involvement, freedom of religion, particularly for minority groups, is preserved and protected. Nevertheless, it is also a fact that so often policies on religion are shaped by the opinion of majority groups rather than respect for basic rights, including that of religious freedom. Consequently, some policies in many countries tend to be far from "fair". In the extreme case they are "detrimental", particularly against minorities or non-mainstream groupings.

Regulating religion is not a new phenomenon as it can be traced as far back as history of human civilization itself.

Nevertheless, it is a fact that the state regulation of religion may cripple religious freedom to some degree, since there is no "clear boundary" on the extent of the state involvement in religious life, and on how particular treatment of religious groups is to be pursued by any given government. Even so, there are no clear principles on how to govern religion in international law to be found in some international documents relating to religious freedom, such as the 1965 International Covenant on Cultural and Political Rights and the 1981 Declaration on the Elimination of Religious Intolerance and Discrimination. For some observers in this field, this is one of the main gaps in existing legal framework and discourses on the extent of the state involvement in religious life (Ismalu Ropi, 2017).

THE BOOK

This book explores the way in which religious freedom (for both individual and organised collectives) is approached by the state within Indian democracy particularly after election victory of the BJP in 2014 and the RSS's growing influence on public policy process. This book examines the religious controversies such as *ghar-wapsi,* cow protection and beef controversy, saffronising of education, and the Sangh Parivar's approach towards religious minorities such as Muslims and Christians.

The aim of the book is to provide an overview of the developments in religious freedom in India after independence and promote better-informed and hopefully less acrimonious analysis by identifying the core values and experiences that underlines current ethnic tension. My goal is to inform and explain. I want to tell readers what is happening, but I also want to help them in understanding why it is happening and what importance it might have. This way of conceiving the task takes me beyond the strict objectivity of simply "recording the events", and into the more subjective realm of context, background, and consequences. This work of analysis aids readers in forming their own judgements.

The book is rooted in my experience of covering socio-economic development and ethnic tensions, and violence in the name of religion during last forty years beginning from Meenkashipuram Dalits embracing Islam in 1981 to attacks on Christians in the Dangs in 1999, to *ghar-wapsi* in 2014 to lynching in the name of cow protection in 2017 and so on.

Furthermore, I address fundamental questions regarding the connections between specific political actions and religious developments, which have direct implications on society.

The structure of this book is simple. Following this Introduction, it is divided into five parts comprising 15 chapters and ends with an Epilogue. Each chapter covers a broad field and a multiplicity of themes. In an effort to give this volume internal coherence, I have included, as an introductory chapter, my own reading of some of the common themes and used this as a basis for grouping the chapters themselves. Inevitably, the chapters themselves engage in much greater depth with these issues. Moreover, the grouping may be somewhat arbitrary since many of the chapters span more than one theme. The result may be somewhat uneasy tensions but it does at least help to keep one's feet on the ground. Each Part of this volume address a different dimension of religious freedom and conversion—historical, academic, social and political and cultural and experimental. Taken together they comprise a sustained examination of the nature and plausibility of religious freedom as well as review of its implication for future, values, politics and science and to other domains of inquiry.

PART I: THE SPRINGS OF INITIATIVE is made up of three chapters. Chapter 1 provides a brief narration of three distinguished Indians—Gandhi, Ambedkar, and Golwalkar—who affected inter-religious relations in India. By a variety of dates in the twentieth century, all these personalities can be characterized as coiled for long-range expansion. The chapter describes the Ideas left behind by them and their effect on Constituent Assembly debates. Chapter 2 deals with the debates in the Constituent Assembly and apprise the reader how the complex issues were dealt immediately after the Independence. Chapter 3 explains the Constitutional provisions and various state laws, which govern freedom of religion in India.

PART II: THE SPRINGS UNCOILED, presents review in more detail the competing conceptions of freedom of religion in relation to the Hindu religious-cultural sovereignty model stretched and the role of as a site for anxiety for secular national sovereignty. It contains chapters 4, 5, 6, and 7. Chapter 4 explains how political concern for Hindu sovereignty formed basis for the Niyogi Report (1956) which, in turn bolsters contemporary anti-conversion campaigns. Chapter 5 deals with internal discussion among Christian evangelical groups regarding change of strategy in dealing with opposition conversion activities. Chapter 6 deals with new wave of "liberation theology" and attempts by the Sangh Parivar to preserve Hindu religious identity and shifts of religious identity. Hindu nationalist activities in this period were to contain Christian spread. It also traces the remarkable transformations that took place in India in the 1980s, a period that began with the formation of the BJP after break-up of Janata Party. It charts how the VHP took a leading role in massive demonstration to foster a sense of Hindu unity, mass agitations against Muslims and Christian proselytization, and campaigns to recover mosques that were once allegedly Hindu temples. Chapter 7 narrates how the emergence of *Hindutva* forces as an effective political force in India from the beginning of the 1990s, which coincides with the restructuring of capital in the era of neoliberal globalization and the Indian state's embrace of policies of economic liberalization.

PART III: THE TWIST OF INITIATIVE, containing chapters 8 and 9 try to show how the 'age of Hindutva' seems to have been launched not into a vacuum but in the Hindu 'cow belt' of north India resulting in new challenges before religious minorities—Muslims and Christians. It traces the rise of the BJP and growing influence of the RSS affiliates in the public life. Chapter 9 traces the rise of the BJP rule (1999-2004) and again in 2014 and how the discussions on religious conversion was high on the agenda of the *Sangh Parivar* and religious minority communities frequently accuse the RSS, VHP, and other Hindu nationalist groups and individuals of intolerance, discrimination, and violence against them. This Chapter also describes the political and cultural consequences of rise of *Hindutva* supremacy on religious freedom from 2000 to 2014 until the advent of Narendra Modi on the scene. The UPA rule from 2004 to 2014 was ineffective in checking violence against minorities.

Chapter 9 deals with the phenomenal victory of the BJP in 2014 elections under Narendra Modi and subsequent political scenario. It describes religious intolerance and authorities turning a blind eye to communal violence and how India's economic aspirations appear to have overshadowed the rhetoric of the extreme Hindu right, with issues pertaining to India's future with regard to economic revitalization, infrastructure development, modernization, and globalization. Chapter 9 also describes how the BJP victory in 2014 general election bring tectonic shift of political equilibrium in Delhi from the middle of the centre ideological pinning of the Congress to the right wing brand of politics of the Bharatiya Janata Party (BJP) which rolled out a new political discourse promising to usher in a new India free from the Congress. Chapter reports that after BJP overwhelmingly won the national elections in 2014, the issue of religious freedom became more important in particular, emphasis on the role of Indian secularism in protecting the plurality of India and the guarantee of exceptional personal legislation for religious minorities, the *Sangh Parivar*, including the BJP government, have aimed to protect the Hindu.

PART IV: CONTOURS OF CONTROVERSIES containing chapter nos. 10, 11, 12, 13 and 14 shows how far the ideals of respectful pluralism and the rule of law have been threatened by religious ideology. This part deals with cow vigilantism (*gau-raksha*), forced reconversion in the name of homecoming (*ghar-wapsi*), new agenda in the education, the RSS plans to woe religious minorities and problem of illegal migrants. The subject of Chapter 10 is cow protection and beef controversy. It also describes lynching in the name of cow protection and the tension the *gau-rakshaks* have created for the Modi government and the RSS. Chapter 11 deals with controversial political issue *ghar-wapsi*, which came into prominence in December 2015 after such ceremony was performed in Agra. Chapter 12 describes recent efforts of the RSS to influence Muslims and Christians. This is new development in Indian politics. Education has been key areas of interest for the *Sangh Parivar*. Chapter 13 gives summary of what is transpiring the education field under the direction of the RSS and how this will affect minorities. Chapter 14—The NCR: Illegal Migrants—deals with the issue of un-regulated cross-border migration. Illegal migration from Bangladesh has been a problem for a long time but now in the light of Rohingya refugees this has added new dimension. The Modi government is not ready to accept non-regulated refugees who are mostly Muslims. The idea of the National Citizenship Register is briefly explained in this chapter.

PART FIVE CONCLUSIONS contains chapter 15—The Final Frontier of the Saffron Agenda. We live in an era of globalization juggernaut in which global crisis of religious liberty is emerging as one of the key issues in the twenty-first century. What is the status of religious freedom in India today? How different political parties restrict, promote, or regulate religious life? What are the emerging threats to the freedom of conscience belief, and how do they shape the frontiers of law?

India is set to grow in economic might and political power for the remainder of the twenty-first century. By some account, it has already overtaken China as the world's most populous nation; by others, the baton will pass during the next decades or two. By mid-century, more than 400 million Indians will have moved from villages to cities, in one of the largest ever-human migration. Today, in a country that is changing so quickly, what will happen to religious freedom, particularly when the RSS is emerging as policy forming non-state actor. This chapter raises the question whether India would become super power with growing chasm between rich and the poor and the large number of religious minorities being pushed to second-class citizens category. India's ambition to lead second half of the Asian century—and world's hopes for a more democratic, liberal future depends on getting this right. I have succumbed to a temptation and given a short sketch of recommendation for a possible future.

In Epilogue I, emphasis on the first higher consciousness principle and to ponder *who we are,* is as important as what we *do*. Further, I conclude with suggestions for individual and group actions to defend freedom of religion or belief in the twenty-first century. I hope that this book will provide windows of understanding in this compartmentalized world, giving us all a better idea of building stable, peaceful communities, which is central to the quest for religious freedom.

Notes

1. *Indian Express,* July 12, 2017, India becomes sixth largest economy in the world, overtakes France https://indianexpress.com Accessed on August 27, 2018.
2. Crabtree, James (2018). *The Billionaire Raj: A Journey through India's New Gilded Age,* HarperCollins Publishers, India, p. xx.
3. W. Andersen and S.D. Damle, (2018). *The RSS,* HarperCollins Publishers, India.
4. The United Nations Rapporteur on Religious Freedom has dealt with this subject in his reports. See UN doc.ECN.4/58 (1999).
5. Durham, W. Cole, Tore Sam Lindholm and Bahia Tahzib-Lie, (2013). *Facilitating Freedom of Religion or Belief: A Deskbook,* NA Brigham Young University, and Oslo, Norway, p. xxxvii.
6. Hertzke, Allen D. (2012). *Future of Religious Freedom: Global Challenges,* OUP.
7. Hertzke, Allen D. (2013). *The Future of Religious Freedom: Global Challenges,* OUP, USA.
8. Marzouki, Nadia, Duncan McDonnell, Olivier Roy (2016). *Saving the People: How Populists Hijack Religion,* C. Hurst & Company (Publishers), London.
9. Doniger, Wendy and Martha Craven Nussbaum (2015). *Pluralism and Democracy in India: Debating the Hindu Right,* New York: Oxford University Press, p. 1.

PART I

Springs of Initiatives

It is clear that we are entering a new stage in the globalized world. That stage demands careful re-study of our message and our methods. If you want the present to be different from the past, study the past.

—*Baruch Spinoza*

1

Gandhi, Ambedkar and Golwalkar on Religious Freedom

INTRODUCTION

India's political history from 1920s until the Independence in 1947 is full of intense special mobilisation that witnessed the emergence of anti-colonial movements, some of which were organized along religious communitarian-sectarian lines. The development of collective Hindu consciousness was initiated in an organised manner around 1920s. The Arya Samaj, the Hindu Mahasabha and the Rashtriya Swayamsevak Sangh—all three were active during this period with objective to establish Hindu national identity drawing inspiration from a so-called Vedic 'Golden Age'. Hindu nationalism was constructed as an ideology between 1870 and 1920s. In 1920s, Mahatma Gandhi and Ambedkar also arrived on the scene.

Any debate on freedom of religion in India during this period would not be complete without taking into accounts views of Gandhi, Ambedkar, and Savarkar-Golwalkar. Gandhi mixed politics and religion—Hindu spirituality and culture, whereas Ambedkar favoured rationality in politics. It was in this context that V.D. Savarkar and M.S. Golwalkar emerged as chief proponents of *Hindutva,* arguing that those who did not comply with Hindu culture and standards should not even have citizen's rights in an independent India. All three had different approaches to freedom of expression and worship.

Rise of Hindu Nationalism

Hindu nationalism drew upon the politics of Hindu revival

articulated by Balwantrao Gangadhar Tilak (1856-1920), the leader of the Congress extremist[1] group, whose adoration was central to the Hindu Mahasabha.

Between 1910s and 1930s, the issues like religious conversion, *shuddhikaran*, *gau raksha* (cow protection), and *stri raksha* (saving Hindu women from Muslims) drew public attention. They were challenge to the basis of the political framework with which nationalists were opposing British rule. Second, both Hindu leaders and the leaders of the Depressed Classes saw the political potential of conversion, especially as liberation from caste system. Therefore, the issue became a dominant concern for both sides in their respective struggle for freedom—from the British Raj and from the system of untouchability in Hindu society. Due to this peculiar situation, mass conversions were seen as caused by 'outsider intervening' by the missionaries for 'ulterior motives', which raised strong suspicions among Hindus.

Meanwhile, Hindu organisations in Punjab advocated an exclusive form of 'Hindu politics' and made efforts for national 'regeneration', a drive that eventually led to the establishment of the Punjab Hindu Sabha in 1909 and the All India Hindu Mahasabha in the UP in 1915. The Mahasabha had originated with the active patronage and influence of social groups, which were once the patrons of the Congress, even though it heavily depended on the support of landed and aristocratic groups, business class, and urban traders in the province. Hindu Mahasabha gained strength in the aftermath of the Moplah massacres and the Khilafat movement in the 1920s, representing an aggressive and militant anti-Muslim mobilisation in north India. Later on, the Tablighi Jamaat was formed at a time of intense rivalry between Muslims and Hindus in India. However, Tablighi Jamat rejected the use of violence and adopted to remain apolitical. The movement emphasized its peaceful and gradualist approach instead.

One important aspect of Hindu nationalists in the pre-1920s formulations was that Indian nationalism did not demarcated Muslims as exterior to the Indian nation, but within it. However, after the 1920s, Hindu nationalism began to articulate a 'homogeneous, unified India', characterized by exclusion of Muslims as 'others' and a 'threat' to the country. There were several factors behind this move; large scale religious conversion by the *Dalits* to Islam or Christianity, Periyar's Self Respect Movement, the Vaikom Satyagraha (1924) for temple entry by lower caste Hindus, British government's move in 1932 to provide a separate electorate for the Depressed Classes, Ambedkar's call to renounce Hinduism (1935), social reforms such as raising marriage age through Sharda Act, 1929 and rising female literacy which was seen as threat to Hinduism by conservative rightwing Hindus.

The concept of Brahaminic Hinduism, projected as the sole legitimate form of Hinduism, was at the root of multiple religious revivalist movements. Its political translation began mainly with Bal Gangadhar Tilak (1856-1920) who initiated the Ganapati Festival to wean away lower castes popular participation in the Muslim Muharram festival. Anti-Muslim sentiments were consistently used by Tilak to project a political methodology of consolidating the Hindus. Various Hindu ideologues have also exacerbated fears that the Islam threatened the survival of Hindu traditions.[2] Vinayak Savarkar (1883-1966), who regarded Tilak as his *guru*, and can be called the first exponent of the doctrine of *Hindutva*, brewed the combination of "Syndicated Hinduism" with nationalism. Savarkar's book '*Hindutva*: *Who is a Hindu*?' (1923) became and remains the basic text defining this political concept. After British released him from the prison in 1924, his all activities were directed against the Muslims.

The *Hindutva* according to Savarkar rests on three pillars: geographical unity, racial nature, and common culture. He further went on to elaborate the criterion for who was Hindu. According to him only those who regard India as their motherland and holy land are truly Hindu and thereby the people to whom this land belongs. This led to the automatic interpretation that Christians and Muslims, whose holy places are Jerusalem and Mecca, are not on par with 'Hindus' who therefore 'own' the country. Savarkar began to articulate the ideology of Hindu elite (*zamindars, Brahmins, raja-rajwadas*) by integrating Brahmanical Hinduism with nationalism, calling it *Hindutva* and then demonstrating the way in which a *Hindu Rashtra* could be built.[3] His key sentence was "Hinduize all politics and militarize all Hindudom."

It was at this time Mahatma Gandhi came to the national scene and his nationalism was different from religious nationalism of Tilak. Gandhi's ideas inspired large numbers of Indian masses to join the anti-colonial struggle. With the leadership of Congress slipping away from the Brahmins, with the dissatisfaction with

Gandhi's conciliatory methods and against a backdrop of a declining Brahmanic hegemony over the lower castes, the idea of an organisation representing the aspirations of the high castes took root and this gave birth to the RSS in 1925.

By this time Periyar's "self-respect movement" opposing the exploitation of the non-Brahmin indigenous Dravidian communities in modern Tamil Nadu and a new awareness in Kerala due to the influence of Narayan Guru movement had created new wave. In Maharashtra already Jotiba Phule's influence had mounted a powerful challenge from lower caste Hindus to Brahminical forces and attacked the sanctity of Vedas. Bhim Rao Ambedkar carried out their struggle. The anti-Brahmanism strand of reform movements also resulted in the fierce debate between Gandhi and Ambedkar over the issue of abolition of untouchablity in the 1930s.

The period from 1930s to 1940s is dominated by Gandhi and Ambedkar. Already before Ambedkar rose to prominence in Punjab, Mango Ram established a new religion, which he called Adi Dharma, which broke from the *bhakti path*. Equality was no longer an abstraction but something to be realised at once, by force if necessary. However, the vision of equality remained ritual and ethical rather than secular and materialistic.

From the moment that Ambedkar gained an influential seat at Round Table Conference of 1930-31 and incurred the opposition of Gandhi, the struggle against untouchability transformed. By then Ambedkar had abandoned temple entry as a fruitless and pointless exercise. However, 1930s turned out to be far from the period of political triumph that Ambedkar looked forward. His process was checkmated by Gandhi. The period from 1935 to 1950 can be seen as a belonging to solidity to the realm of secular politics an institutional avenge rather than to religious and social reform.

Below I give views on religious conversion of three personalities who influenced our thought.

Mohandas Karamchand Gandhi (1869-1948)

The study of Gandhi's ideas on religion during the period 1914-1948 presents great difficulties because of the immensity of the materials assembled in the 75 vclumes of the Collected Works. This forbidding mass of material is compounded by the enormous complexity of the various ways Gandhi's religion expressed itself.

Religion was for him not just a vague ideological background and a routine of occasional rituals. Religion was a way of life that penetrated all aspects of his private, public, and political activity. Moreover, his religious conceptions were challenged repeatedly by the formidable forces of Hindu orthodoxy, who did not accept Gandhi's religious authority. Below I give gist from various sections from the Collected Works, which I studied in detail in order to extract all the materials that related to religion.

The passage from colonial to the post-colonial period is marked by harsh reality of religious conflicts and concept freedom, justice, and equality. From the time of Gandhi's early steps in India, he countered the reality of religious exclusivism and simultaneously the possibility of inter-religious cross-fertilization. He was influenced by his mother's Satparnami teaching, his education in London, with its introduction to the *Bible*, the reading from Edwin Arnold's translation of *Bhagvad Gita*, Madam Blavatsky and the secular society; and his time in South Africa, which affected his ideas and practices.

At the time when Gandhi entered the Indian politics and took leadership, the scene was charged with unfounded hatred and criticism against Islam and Christianity and nationalism was just beginning to grow.

Formation of Gandhi's views on Conversion

In this chapter, I shall discuss how a representative Hindu approaches to the theme of 'conversion' crystallized in the life, thought and experience of Mahatma Gandhi. Because of historical and biographical consideration, I have dealt with the topic in the context of Gandhi's relations with Christianity, though the principles involved are applicable to other world religions also.

Gandhi encountered the conversion issue in three separate contexts: that of Christianity, Islam and Buddhism. Each context, it must be stressed was different from others. Gandhi's contact with Christianity came first in his own hometown, where he heard missionaries preaching aggressively to convert people. Then in London and South Africa where he himself was target of conversion. Gandhi was impressed by the social services aspect of Christianity.

The Hindu-Muslim relationship drew Gandhi's attention

almost throughout his life in India and during the Partition it was disillusioning. The communal riots occurring in the twenties, thirties and forties, that is to say when Gandhi's influence was by no means negligible, even though it ebbed and flowed, highlighted conversion as an inevitable accompaniment of the abduction of women or as inducement or threat. This image of conversion, which he acquired, was of process, which made people forcibly change their religion, and, therefore, tore them away from their own ancestral communities.

The third context, in which Gandhi faced the issue of conversion was within Hinduism, in his own community, when, in reaction to the centuries long oppression of the so-called Untouchability by caste Hindus, Bhimrao Ramji Ambedkar threatened to leave Hinduism and gave call for all *Dalits* to leave Hinduism. Conversion in this context was primarily a social issue, and one, which dealt with injustice.

While these three contexts fill out Gandhi's specific encounters with the question of conversion on a community scale that is in addition to the occasion when particular individual consulted him about whether they should convert or not, the indication he gave in his writings concerning his general attitude to this matter need to be considered.

Gandhi's writings contain both a critique of conversion and advice as to individual to follow their conscience. For example, in 1934 he writes, "God has created different faiths just as He has votaries thereof, how can I even secretly harbour the thought that my neighbour's faith is inferior to mine and wish that he should give up his faith and embrace mine."[4]

This provides a theistic ground for non-interference in another's religion. In a way, Gandhi was not against 'real conversion'. He wrote in 1934 to a Baptist in Orissa "... if a person discards his country, his custom, and his old connections and manners when he changes his religion, he becomes all the more unfit to gain a knowledge of God. When there is a real conversion, the man's heart grows...In my view your object in changing your religion should be to bring about that prosperity of your country.[5]

John Hick mentions an interesting case where an Indian from a Brahmin family had become a Christian during his student days. He writes:

> His family sent him to Gandhi, hoping that the Mahatma

> would dissuade him from this, to them, terrible step. Gandhi talked at length with the young man, questioning him carefully, and finally concluded that conversion to Christianity would be appropriate to his case, and advised him to proceed giving him his blessings."[6]

Therefore, it is not the case that Gandhi always frowned on conversion. However, he believed that one's own inner critic of change of heart and consequent transformation of daily living provides the best guide to assessment of any particular conversion.

As M.K. Gandhi became leader of the Swaraj movement and the leading figure in Indian politics, he became increasingly aware of the need for a unified national identity that could bring political momentum to fight against the British Raj. He also knew that such a national identity was not possible unless there was peaceful co-existence of the different religious communities in India. He saw conversion as a threat not only to the communal harmony but also to the very concept of the Indian nation. Therefore, he openly expressed his disapproval of conversion to Christianity.[7] Gandhi engaged in many debates on the issues with missionaries and Indian Christian leaders. In the early 1930s, as mass conversion became a 'movement', his tone on the issue of conversion was increasingly hostile and focused on the issue of the proselytizing activities of the missionaries among the 'untouchables'.

For Gandhi religion and politics were inseparable; therefore he could not regard mass conversion as a purely religious movement, as the missionaries insisted it was; but increasingly felt the potential political and communal problems that would result for his agenda. By the early 1930s, there was growing tension between Gandhi and the missionaries which eventually led to a debate between M.K. Gandhi and E. Stanley Jones, the prominent American Methodist missionary.

Gandhi and Stanley Jones on Conversion 1931

E. Stanley Jones was very influential and well respected in India through his practice of inter-religious dialogue, *ashram* living, and his interaction with educated Hindus. In his book", The Christ of the Indian Road" which was first published in 1925, Jones stressed that Christian presented a Christ to India who is not a Western import but was 'to produce Christ like character', not to Westernize India, and discerned a regeneration of Indian life through an as yet unrecognized experience of Christ (Jones, 1925).

Although Jones believed that Gandhi truly practiced the teachings of Christ, in 1926 he wrote to Gandhi to persuade him to meet and experience the 'radiant Person of Christ' for both his own sake and that of the nation. Gandhi expressed his appreciation of these sentiments and invited Jones to his *ashram* to discuss the matter further, and they remained friends and he did not accept the necessity for a personal experience of Christ.

Controversy began when Gandhi interviewed by Madras based daily newspaper *The Hindu* asked if he would favour the retention of foreign missionaries when India obtained self-government. He replied,

> If instead of confining themselves purely to humanitarian work and material service to the poor, they do proselytizing by means of medical aid, education etc., then I would certainly ask them to withdraw. Every nation's religion is as good as another is. Certainly, India's religions are adequate for her people. We need no converting spirituality (CWMG, XLV: 320).

This brought an immediate reaction from missionaries in India as well as Christians in the West who were concerned that Gandhi was advocating the prohibition of conversion but also missionaries work as a whole. E. Stanley Jones wrote an 'open letter' to Gandhi opposing the original statement. He agreed with Gandhi that missionaries should not use hospitals and schools for the purpose of proselytizing as he saw education and healing as sufficient ends in them. However, he also argued:

> ...I think it is an entirely different thing for me to share my faith with others, and if that sharing leads to moral and spiritual conversion. I believe that person so inwardly what he has experienced inwardly and to join any group where that new life, be cultivated...[I]t is a fundamental human right and a fundamental human duty to share what he finds precious in any realm... intellectual, social, moral, political and spiritual (BCCR, May 1932).

As for the statement that the 'religion of one nation is as good as another nation' he claimed that the truth is by its very nature universal, comparing it with scientific truth. He concluded that what Gandhi was demanding was the relinquishment of the right to share Christ with others, which he regarded as inherent in a Christian's spiritual make-up.

The root of Jones argument was that the Mahatma whom he regarded as 'the apostle of the new freedom', was inconsistence in using political means to limit religious freedom, which hinged on the issue of conversion, while talking about a new India which would be the embodiment of toleration. To this open letter Gandhi replied in a personal letter (CWMG XLVI: 45) in which he expressed his disappointment that Jones who he regarded as his friend, had responded without checking the accuracy of the interview report.

Later Gandhi also allowed publication of an interview with a missionary nurse in which he stated, "If I had power and could legislate, I should certainly stop them proselytizing" (*Harijan*, May 11, 1935).

While Gandhi argued against conversion by applying the principle of *swadeshi*, Jones' argument was based on human rights. They also differed over the nature of religious identity. Gandhi considered that religion was embodied in the religious heritage of one's ancestors—thus a person is born into it. Therefore, conversion to another religion was not only religious apostasy but also a denial of the self and understood as rebuff to Hindu society. Nevertheless, Jones believed that religion, like ideology or scientific facts, could be separated from one's socio-cultural heritage. It is something that the individual may decide rather than something already decided by one's socio-cultural background. While Gandhi argued for the duty of Hindus to keep the identity they were born with, Jones argued for the right of individual to select the religion of their choice. Hindus felt that under the British *raj*, the missionaries and the Christians has held an unfair advantage and could impose their religion upon the people of India. Christian and missionaries feared that the situation after independence would be reversed. Therefore, Jones sought a way of allowing conversion while maintaining Hindu identity. Jones' struggling to untangle the problem of conversion was by no means new or unique to him: it remains a recurring problem of Christian mission in India.

The debate continued when Gandhi went to England to attend the Second Round Table conference in London. During this visit in 1931, Gandhi spoke to a missionary conference where he emphasized that it was a misunderstanding of its intention to say that he would legislate to prohibit missionary activity: however, he held to his position that just as a nation has no right to impose its ideology and so the missionaries had no right to impose their religious convictions on the poor. He drew a further parallel between the British Empire and the missionary enterprise: as the Empire was meant for the benefit of its own people by exploiting the poor of India so the missionary activities to convert people were primarily in the interest of the missionaries and not out of genuine concern for the people in their need. Perhaps what Gandhi found most unjustifiable was the missionary's insistence that they knew better what the people of India needed—spiritual salvation in the form of religious conversion. What he saw as the real need, the fundamental right of his own people, was deliverance from oppression and poverty. He could not tolerate what he saw as the arrogance of the missionaries, just as he could not accept the rule of the British Raj.[8] However, this was not Gandhi's final verdict on religious conversion. We will come to this later in this chapter. First more about debate between Gandhi and missionaries.

GANDHI AND BISHOP AZARIAH (1935-1937)

V.S. Azariah, Bishop of Dronakal and Chairman of the National Council of Churches of India, Burma and Ceylon, became the "most successful leader of grassroots movements of conversion to Christianity in Asia during the early twentieth century" (Harper, 2000). Azariah and other Christian leaders were initially cautious of association with the mass conversion movements because these were politically sensitive. Nevertheless, Azariah's writings show that his attitude to mass conversion was not unfavourable and he believed that, in spite of the problems, there was a spiritual dimension to mass conversions that represented the sovereign work of God (Azariah, 1929). The most significant forum for cooperation evangelism among the Protestant Churches in India was the Forward Movement in evangelism, which was initiated by the National Council of Churches in 1932. They defined their main objective as 'evangelism', by which they meant the presentation of Christ to all Indian people with a view of their conversion. It was very much a church-centred mission, emphasizing that the church is the 'divine instrument' and that the convert should join the church to share in its privilege and responsibilities. The council issued a series of 'Calls to the church' beginning in August 1933 to mobilize its members for evangelism and a nation-wide Protestant Christian movement developed, which was supported by churches and mission organisations.

As the protestant churches engaged in full-scale evangelism especially among the Depressed Classes, the leader needed to present their views on conversion in order to counter the widespread criticism of Christian conversion by Hindu leaders. Responding to one such presentation which defined conversion as a change of heart from sin to God brought about by Christ alone, Gandhi took the opportunity to make strong attack on conversion, especially mass conversion. He declared that this definition could only be applicable to cases of individual conversion, not to the mass conversion of the 'Depressed Classes', and insisted that conversion should be left to God and no one should judge another's heart. He argued that it could not be a Christian's right to convert others because the motivation to convert others is in itself wrong. He forcefully stated his belief that:

> ...there is no such thing as conversion from one faith to another in the accepted sense of the term. It is a highly personal matter for the individual and his God. I may not have any design upon my neighbour as to his faith, which I must honour even as I honour my own. For I regard all the great religion of the world as true at any rate for the people professing them as mine is true for me...Whether they—the missionary...and we wish it or not, what is true in the Hindu faith will abide, what is untrue will fall to pieces. Every living faith must have within itself the power of rejuvenating if it is to live (*Harijan*, September 28, 1935).

In October 1935, B.R. Ambedkar, leader of the All India Scheduled Caste Federation and a renowned lawyer, made rather unprecedented declaration that he and his followers would renounce Hinduism. Indian Christian leaders, being cautious about the political nature of Ambedkar's move, did not immediately make a direct approach to him to persuade him to become a Christian. Azariah, in the third 'call to the Church' issued in January 1936, saw fit to challenge the churches in India to make a 'concentrated and definite advance in evangelism'. He stated that 'widespread and deep unrest' among the Depressed Classes was not from 'material dissatisfaction' but a response to 'deep spiritual hunger' (Azariah, 1939). At this stage, he clearly justified the church's engagement in evangelistic work among the Depressed Classes on the grounds that, although they might appear to be communally or materially motivated, the mass movements were spiritual matters.

Later, in December 1936, a Conference on the Mass Movements was held, which discussed the unrest among the Depressed Classes and the progress of the Forward Movement. In response to criticism of the motives, methods and results of mass conversion by Gandhi and others and to some Indian Christians apprehensions about the spiritual quality of the new converts, the National Christian Council justified mass conversion by terming the real motives behind the movement as 'spiritual' caused by the work of Holy Spirit. However, the motivation of the convert from Depressed Class backgrounds was still the focus of criticism from Hindus and a major concern of Christian leaders. Azariah wishes to embrace the Depressed classes, whose motives included the social and economic, but without understanding the credibility of Indian Christianity; therefore, he made a statement legitimizing 'non-spiritual' motives in conversion, which he said should not prevent converts from joining the Christian fellowship. In his letter to all the heads of churches and missions, he acknowledged a variety of motives in the mass conversion but stated:

> We are, however, convicted that underneath all appearances, there is the longing, in the generality of these groups, to flee from the superstitions and religious practise of the past, to escape from the religion which has not respected their personality and to abandon the society which has not treated them with fair justice. We believe these motives are justifiable for people to change their religion...."[9]

Susan Harper explains how, by 'recognizing their socio-political dimensions, Azariah interpreted Ambedkar's efforts for the Depressed Classes and their outcome as valid reflections of God's activity '. Azariah defended the movements not only from Biblical precedents but also 'from the particularities of the Indian situation', that is he viewed the problem of conversion 'from within the context of a culture in which the material reality was imbued with sacred significance'. This led him to develop a more subtle understanding of the motivation of mass-conversion beyond the dichotomy between spiritual and material. In a shift from his earlier approach of looking for the spiritual motive behind the other motives, Azariah now saw the completely human predicament as motivations for conversion. However, as he also stated at the time, he believed that through good discipleship of the new converts by the members of the Christian community, any 'unworthy motives' would later disappear and be replaced by 'love to the Lord Jesus'. Azariah's confidence in the ability of the Christian community to bring about a spiritual outlook in the converts was in sharp contrast to that of Gandhi, who believed in the 'non-spiritual 'motives of the community. After his son Hiralal publicly announced of his conversion to Islam on May 29, 1936 Gandhi's polemic against conversion became more forceful and by 1937 almost hysterical: he denounced it as the "deadliest poison that ever sapped the fountain of truth" (*Harijan*, January 16, 1937) and "an error which is perhaps the greatest impediment to the world's progress towards peace" (*Harijan*, January 30, 1937).

It is important to notice that Azariah recognized the source of the motivation and decision for conversion in the people themselves. In his analysis, they were motivated to convert not because of the proselytizing activities of outsiders by their own concerns. As Azariah looked towards imminent Independence, after which Indian Christians would have to live under *Swaraj*, it was important to establish that Indian Christians were not just a product of outsider's inferences but also the outcome of their own search for the new life in Christ. Gandhi, on the other hand, increasingly criticized Christian efforts to convert the Depressed Classes by saying 'the poor Harijans have no mind, no intelligence, no sense of difference between God and no-God (*Harijan*, November 28, 1936) and, in which he compared evangelizing Harijans to preaching the gospel to a cow (*Harijan*, December 19 and 26, 1936).

Gandhi portrayed the mass conversions as efforts to impose their religion by offering material and social benefits to people who did not known the consequences. However, it seems as if Gandhi was patronizing the Depressed Classes as mere objectives of conversion, who could be easily manipulated by other groups wanting to take advantage of them, and this provoked resentment from intellectuals of a Depressed Class background as well as Christian leaders.

The active mobilization of mass movements among the Depressed classes by Indian Christian leaders created tension with Hindu leaders, and the relationship between Azariah and Gandhi especially soured (*Harijan*, April 17, 1937). Harper Harrison, Secretary of the Indian Coalition Group, and also of the Gandhi-Azariah meeting at Nagpur in 1937, in his letter to Harrison, Azariah made his position clear: "Christianity has always stood for conversion, and for changing people from one society to another which means breaking with the old fellowship and joining a new fellowship", and he called on Gandhi to abandon his 'attitude of antagonism to change of religion as such' (Azariah's letter, January 17, 1937). The mediation meeting failed, as it was bound to do since the differences of view of conversation between Gandhi and Azariah were so deep, and their suspicion of each other's intensions increased. The struggle between the two was not only a personal divergence of views, but also a reflection of the stigma attached to conversion in India, as a result of its history and politics, and of the deep religious difference between Hindus and Christians.

Gandhi's suspicions about conversion meant that he tended to regard the Indian Christians community as an appendage of the missionaries and not a spiritual community.[10] Therefore, he found it difficult to accommodate the Christians as equal partners in his vision for India. Gandhi was alarmed by the fact that in the 1930s Indian Christians themselves initiated mass conversion movements among the Depressed Classes not only because of the growth caused in Christians numbers but also because of the increasing confidence of their leadership. Gandhi that he would use politica means to prevent conversion was understandable. In view of the inseparability of politics and religion in his outlook, but it was seen by Christians as a threat to exercise oppression in free India. The price of gaining political freedom from the British Raj would be that religious minorities had to conform to the Hindu majority, and therefore, conversion would be severely constrained.[11]

Within the complexity of Indian society and given the socio-economic situation of the Depressed Classes, the motives for conversion were inevitably mixed. This undermined the legitimacy of the Christian community as a whole. Gandhi saw the mass conversion movements as yet another political move by the *Harijans*. He regarded the *Harijans* as sharing a common Hindu heritage and made many attempts to 'uplift' them but underestimated their resentment at being treated as object rather than subject and their deep desire for human dignity and equality. It was ironic that the man whose confidence in the equality of his people with other nations led him to challenge the British Empire should himself take such a paternoster attitude to oppressed communities within his own nation.

The differences between Azariah and Gandhi hinged on the nature of conversion: Gandhi asserted that conversion takes place ultimately only in the spiritual realm of the individual; whereas Azariah concluded that, it also embraced socio-political realms of human community. In the Indian context—and perhaps in any context—such affine separation of motives as Gandhi's impossible. On the other hand, Azariah's attempt to legitimize socio-economic and political motives for conversion was based on the confidence that the Christian gospel would eventually lead converts into spiritual maturity and produce a transformed community—a premise that would frequently be challenged by Hindus, as I shall explain in the following chapters. Though much effort was expended in discussing motivation, it became increasingly clear that for Gandhi any change of religion was unacceptable because it contrived his ideal of an India founded on traditional Hindu values. The differing views on conversion of Gandhi, Jones, and Azariah, though conditioned by the socio-political circumstances of their time and the result of their personal convictions, also represent the particular religious traditions of each. The Hindu argument against conversion based on religious tolerance and Christian arguments for conversion as a fundamental right and a part of the essential nature of Christianity were to be characteristic of alter debates as well.

It would be wrong to conclude from this that Gandhi is opposed to conversion from one religion to another. On the contrary, he defended the rights of those who wish to change their religious allegiance to follow their inclinations in this matter. It is, in his view, a personal matter between an individual and his God. The right of conversion is not questioned. What is questioned is the kind of methods that might be employed to bring about conversions. Gandhi's reference to people being allowed to follow their own desires, provided they were old enough to know what they are doing and were not submerged by force or material inducements, is an indication of the dubious conversion methods employed by some missionaries. He approved the humanitarian work of Christian missionaries in the field of medicine and in the alleviation of the conditions of the poor. He approved also of their work in the field of education. However, he strongly disapproved of the proselytizing that went on under the cloak of humanitarianism.[12]

Mahatma Gandhi's overall position in the matter is ably summarized by Donald Eugene Smith, as followed:

> "Gandhi once wrote that the different religions were branches of the same majestic tree; all faiths are 'equally imperfect.' This great truth should preclude even the thought that another individual embrace one's own faith. Accepting this position, we can pray, if we are Hindus, not that a Christian should become Hindu, or if we are Mussalmans, not that a Hindu or a Christian should become a Mussalman, nor should we even secretly pray that any one should be converted, but our inmost prayer should be that a Hindu should be a better Hindu, a Muslim a better Muslim and a Christian a better Christian." Gandhi felt so strongly about this question that on another occasion he wrote "If I had power and could legislate, I should stop all proselytizing." Gandhi did agree, however, that "if an individual found that he could realize God better through embracing a different religion, he should have complete freedom to do so."[13]

Gandhi's comparative study of religions led him to the appreciation of the best in every tradition and to the formulation of the concept of *Sarva-dharma-sambhava;* the expression implies looking on all religions with an equal eye.[14]

Dr. B.R. Ambedkar (1891-1956)

B.R. Ambedkar was a leader, scholar, and activist of the "depressed classes" or untouchables, who are now known as *Dalits*. His books and speeches created upheaval in the Hindu society in India and abroad. His famous books are: *Who Were the Shudras?, The Untouchables—Who were they, and Why they became Untouchables and Why Go for Conversion ?*

Born on April 14, 1891 in Mhow, a cantonment town close to Indore in Madhya Pradesh, into a Mahar untouchable family from Konkan areas of Maharashtra called Ambavade, and Ambedkar's real name. Ambavadekar comes from there (he changed it into Ambedkar in 1900, when his Brahmin school teacher, impressed by his intellect and personal qualities, decided to give him his own name). Overcoming insuperable obstacles of caste prejudice, Bhim Rao Ambedkar rose to become one of the most highly educated Indian of his time, with Ph.D. from Colombia University in Political Science and further advanced work in Law and Economics at the London School of Economics. His academic achievements, however, did not exempt him from the disdain of caste Hindus. Returning to India to work in a law office, Ambedkar suffered the humiliation of clerks throwing files at him so as not to be defiled by his touch. Inflamed by these experiences, he threw himself into the uplifting of the Untouchables, not, however, by working for reform within Hinduism but by asserting the rights of untouchables to full equality before the law—what he called the only positive legacy of British colonialism. Ambedkar's uncompromising appeal to principles of political liberty overrode what might have easily been a more modest project of eliminating the civil disabilities under which untouchables suffered daily harassment.

After completing his studies, he returned to India, started a publication "Mook Nayak" in 1920, and entered in the public sphere. He advocated the need for a forum to deliberate on the injustices let loose or likely to be imposed on the *Dalits* and depressed people and to think of their future development and appropriate strategies towards it critically.

Ambedkar's earlier attitude to Hinduism was ambivalent. In the early 1920s, he had some faith in the reform within Hinduism and Untouchables changing their status through emulating higher caste practices. He gradually came to the conclusion that this process had little effect in changing the attitudes of caste Hindus. By 1927, his mind was already made up when the *Manusmriti* was burnt in his presence at a large public meeting. In 1935, he announced his decision to leave Hinduism.

He wrote:

> To get human treatment, convert yourself. Convert for being organised. Convert for becoming strong. Convert for securing equality. Convert for getting liberty. Convert so that your domestic life may be happy.[15]

Ambedkar's views on conversion underwent a gradual transformation and maturity over time. At first, he had great hopes in the work of 'high caste' Hindu reformers, but later he veered round to the conviction that *Dalit* emancipation is not possible while remaining in the Hindu fold. Moreover, that task is to be led by the *Dalits* themselves. Ambedkar declared that the *Dalits* must convert in order to liberate themselves. As long as they remain within the Hindu fold they would remain 'Untouchables', for the Hindu religion, he said, teaches that they are to be considered worst than slaves or animals. He argued that the continued cruel subjugation of the *Dalits* in India by 'upper caste' Hindus can be countered only through empowerment. Since the Hindu religion and scriptures are based on the caste system and on the stern disabilities that they impose on the *Dalits*, the search for their quest for liberation and empowerment necessarily calls for religious conversion.

Dr. Ambedkar blurred religious and political conversion, overtly looking for a more democratic religion. In a 1936 speech, which he never actually delivered due to his invitation, being rescinded after the text was disclosed—Ambedkar argues that "Caste has killed public spirit" and that "you must give new doctrinal basis to your religion—a basis that will be in consonance with Liberty, Equality and Fraternity, in short with Democracy. He did recognize "two aspects of conversion, social as well as religious; material as well as spiritual", but did not see these aspects as contradictory, certainly not as something that demanded a defensive response.

Ambedkar summarized his understanding of Gandhi on Christian mission:

> "Whatever anybody may say I have no doubt, all the Untouchables, whether they are converts or not, will agree that Mr. Gandhi has been grossly unjust to Christian Missions" (quoted in Moon, 1989). Ambedkar's perception of Christian mission comes out clearly in the following statement: "Comparatively speaking the achievements of Christian Missions are very great. No one except a determined opponent of everything Christian can have any doubt."[16]

All the same, Ambedkar was sad to acknowledge that the condition of the Untouchables did not change in spite of their conversion to Christianity. Ambedkar not only raised this issue, he also made a commendable analysis of why the Christian *Dalit's* negative status remained the same as before the conversion. The following observation of Ambedkar with regard to the *Dalit* Christians is very pertinent. He lamented that most benefit of the Christian education goes to high caste Hindus (Massey, 1995).

> "Has Christianity been able to save the convert from the suffering and ignobility, which is the misfortune of everyone who is born 'an untouchable'... I am sure the answer to... [The question]... must be in the negative. In other words conversion has not brought about any change in the social status of untouchable convert."[17]

As a pioneer, Ambedkar moved though from one objective to the other. At first he strove to reform the Untouchability, to enable them to advance within wider Hindu society (particularly *via* education), and later turned to politics in the 1930s. The parties that he founded emerged sometimes as Untouchable organisations and sometimes as the rallying points of all the oppressed. However, he did not limit his political action to party politics: he also collaborated with governments—whether they were British or Congress—in order to exert pressure from within on those in power. However, such political activity did not yield the desired results, which Ambedkar was seeking for untouchables. After this he considered the conversion, and ultimately in 1956 he changed his religion from Hinduism to Buddhism.

Ambedkar, therefore, oscillated between the promotion of the Untouchables in Hindu society or in the Indian nation as a whole;

and the strategy of a break that could take the form of a separate electorate, or a separate *Dalit* party and/or of conversion outside Hinduism. He searched for solutions, explored strategies and in doing so; set the *Dalits* on the path of an arduous emancipation through conversion.

M.S. Golwalkar (1906-1973)

After the death of Dr. Keshav Baliram Hedgewar (1889-1940), who in 1925 had founded the Rashtriya Swayamsevak Sangh or "National Volunteer Association", the BHU-trained biologist Madhavrao Sadashiv Golwalkar (1906-1973) took over as the second Sarsanghchalak, "Chief Guide of the Association", until his death.

The main self-imposed task of the Hindu Mahasabha and the RSS was Hindu "self-organization", *Sangathan*. This was the practical application of Swami Shraddhananda's book *"Hindu Sangathan, Saviour of the Dying Race"* (1924). If one book can make you understand modern Hindu activism in general, of which Hindu nationalism and a foundation of the RSS rests, it is that one, far more than *Bunch of Thoughts*. Although Savarkar outlined basic framework of *Hindutva,* it was Golwlkar who in 1939 gave the RSS the Charter it had previously lacked. He did this in his book, *Our Nationhood Defined, or We.*

The contents of *Bunch of Thoughts* remains a central part of most Sangh's ideological formation. The only book to rival it, is Deendayal Upadhyaya's *Integral Humanism* (1965), adopted as official ideology by the Jana Sangh and (after some confusion with "Gandhian socialism", finally agreed to be but another name for the same ideology) its successor body, the BJP. Golwalkar was a nationalist, and the movement he led, is known worldwide as "Hindu Nationalism" until today.

Golwalkar was greatly influenced by German romanticism and draws on a number of German writers, especially Johanna Kasper Blutschli, who argued that a nation points to birth and race and that the essence lies in its civilization, rather than in any voluntary social contacts. Bluntschli's writings together with other similar writers led Golwalkar to look at the case of India in the light of five criteria for understanding the nation: geographical unity, race, religion, culture, and language. The racial factor was most important, according to Golwalkar, and the Muslims minority posed the most severe threat by being a 'foreign body' lodged into the Hindu society, thus undermining the Hindu nation. Hinduism essence is caste. Golwalkar vigorously defends the caste system, saying that "it kept Hindus united and organized down the centuries."

Golwalkar's nationalism was a belated import of a 19th-century influence, particularly through the Italian nationalist Giuseppe Mazzini, whose political manifesto had been translated by V.D. Savarkar. Christopher Jeffrelot in his excellent study of Hindu nationalism and Indian politics seeks to trace the German sources of Golwalkar's ideology, which comes from the book "We or Our Nationhood Defined." Even if this particular text were to be removed from the Golwalkar writings, his idea of endless sacrifice of individuality in the service and love of the nation, his argument about the intrinsic superiority of Hindus over all other people, fanaticism and religious frenzy that mark all his formulations, the obsessive accent on youth and the constant harping on conspiracies against the Hindu nation are the most distinct resemblance with Fascism.[18]

Golwalkar was influenced by the thoughts of Adam Muller, a German disciple of Edmund Burke who propagated that any attempt to reduce the nation state to a set of laws or to a written constitution was doomed to failure. The only constitution of any consequence was the one that lived in the hearts of human beings.

Golwalkar clearly distinguishes Christians and Muslims from the Hindus, and describes them as mere guests *vis-à-vis* the host society, who have to ("re")-assimilate, or else accept a protected status as foreign residents, "claiming nothing, not even citizens' rights."

The Hindu nationalists' objection to religious conversion is based on the premise of *Hindutva*. This was made clear by M.S. Golwalkar in his writings:

> "...the non-Hindu people in Hindustan... adopt the Hindu culture and language, must learn to respect and revere Hindu religion, must entertain no idea but the glorification of the Hindu nation...they must cease to be foreigners or may stay in the country wholly subordinated to the Hindu nation claiming nothing, deserving no privileges, far less any prudential treatment, not even citizen's rights."[19]

He is credited with greatly expanding the RSS's presence in Indian society by creating a *Parivar* ("family") of specialized organizations, including a pan-Hindu religious platform, a trade union, a student organization, a network for tribal welfare, and a political party. This party, the Bharatiya Jan Sangh (BJS, "Indian People's Association"), founded in 1951, was a venture into explicit politics which Golwalkar agreed to against his wishes.

In such a philosophy only Golwalkar and the Sangh were true, 'real' and pure and only they knew where the good of the nation lay. The Indian nation might have been created in 1947, but for Golwalkar, Hindus were not sovereigns in that nation. His task was to liberate Hindu society and establish the ultimate *"Hindu Rashtra"*. Throughout his lifetime, he was chasing the chimera of his own creation. And the RSS still follows the same goal.

Discussion

We have three different views on religious conversion. Gandhi appears to be opposing religious conversion only if they are by allurement, fraud, or force. Ambedkar supported religious conversion as mean of liberation. Golwalkar rejected religious conversion because of nationality.

Gandhi and Ambedkar met each other at the Second Round Table Conference in 1931. Ambedkar came away from the conference still convinced that caste and capitalism were the chief enemies of the Indian people, although he continued to be a strong supporter of the movement for Indian Independence.

On October 13, 1936, Ambedkar gave a speech in the Depressed Classes Conference in Yeola which created a furore. He solemnly announced on that occasion that he would not die a Hindu and urged those he was addressing to renounce Hinduism since there was no likelihood of their fate within the Hindu community ever being better than it was. They should realize that their religious identity was a matter of choice. Behind this lay his conviction that religion should promote social justice, its concept should be governed by morality and not conflict with reason and science. Religions should never bolster up injustice and justify poverty.

Ambedkar believed in the right to religion, which included a right to change one's religion. He wrote:

> "Hinduism is inconsistent with self-respect and honour of the Untouchable is the strongest ground which justifies the conversion of the Untouchable to another and nobler faith."[20]

Ambedkar's struggle was with the question of which religion to choose. There is an interesting difference between Ambedkar and Gandhi's study of religion.

While Gandhi considered *Dalits* are incapable of discerning mentally and spiritually not fit to decide which religion was best for them, Dr. Ambedkar openly gave call to the Untouchables to change their religion. Gandhi opined that others have to decide what is good for them (*harijans*) whereas Ambedkar was in favour of decision by choice by *Dalits* themselves. Mahatma Gandhi's patronizing attitude has persisted and is embodied in post-independence anti-conversion approach by elite Hindus and Hindu political leadership.

The issue that concerns most in this discussion is that of conversion, for Gandhi and Ambedkar differences on this resemble a clash of Titans.

Some of Gandhi's contemporary *Hindutva* critics, who deplore his supposed appeasement of Muslims but applaud his courage in resisting Christian missionaries, have attempted to depict Gandhi as a firm foe of conversion.

Often it is quoted about Gandhi that "If in self-governing India missionaries kept on proselytizing by means of medical aid, education etc., I would certainly ask them to withdraw" (Sarkar, 1999:76). However, Sarkar states that the "crunch comes when we look at the entire article." Gandhi went on to add, "this is what a reporter has put into my mouth... All I can say is that it is a travesty of what I have always said and held" (Sarkar, 1999). Gandhi then offers a clarification: "I am, then, not against conversion. But I am against the modern methods of it. Conversion now-a-days has become a matter of business, like any other" (Sarkar, 1999:76).

Yet, in an interview he gave to the Reverend John Mott in 1931, he took what appears to be a contrary position. "I disbelieve in the conversion of one person by another." When, however, Gandhi was asked, "Will you under *swaraj* allow Christians to go on with their proselytizing activity without any hindrance?", he replied: "No legal hindrance can be put in the way of any Christian or of anybody preaching for the acceptance of his doctrine." Predictably, Gandhi then complicates his own argument with an observation that takes us to the heart of his position: "My effort should never be to undermine another's faith but to make him [or her] a better follower of his [or her] own faith."

In short, Gandhi's views on conversion, and on religious practice, are best encapsulated in his idea of what constitutes the 'fundamental truth of fellowship'.

The RSS was against the freedom of religious conversion. They see this as an anti-national activity. Golwalkar even advocates, militant means (*Dharma Yuddha*) to put down the anti-national activities of the 'allies' and the hostiles. This created great turmoil among the communities. Hence based on *advaita*, Gandhi wanted to synthesize all religions and cultures, and he preached equality of religions. Gandhi wanted to bring the low caste *Dalits* to the mainstream of Hindu religious tradition, by reducing social segregation, humiliation, discrimination and injustice, so that they may gain social acceptance, which was the main argument of subaltern leaders especially Ambedkar. Where Gandhi's path was one of rediscovering Hinduism, Ambedkar was one of bitterness and eventual rejection of the religion of his ancestors. Secondly, while Ambedkar was more emphatically egalitarian than Golwalkar, the latter's nationalism equally had egalitarian implications.

Several questions arise here such as whether a person has the right to convert to another faith. Would conversion to Christianity or Islam equate to less patriarchy?

Nationalism and Hinduism were linked during 1940s and this deadly combination became more fervent in the years leading up to Indian independence, notably in the rhetoric of Hindutva—a cultural identity and political posture in India. It was in this context that Savarkar and Golwalkar emerged as chief proponents of *Hindutva*, arguing, "Those who did not comply with Hindu culture and standards should not even have citizen's rights in an independent India. Gandhi saw India's pluralistically religious heritage as an assets in defining Indianness. Here is where Gandhi differs from Golwalkar. Some researchers say that Golwalkar did not object to religious conversion provided they were voluntary and not forced."[21]

CONCLUSION

The period 1920 to 1947 was marked by number of assumptions and omissions, the opening of the fresh question regarding the religious conversion.

This period was dominated by Mahatma Gandhi, Ambedkar, and extreme right wing *Hindutva* leaders (Savarkar, Hegdewar, and Golwalkar). During this period growth of the Muslim League and its demand for separate nation entirely shifted the content and tone of the discussion and 'the Muslim view' or 'Hindu politics' had become current and acceptable by the late 1940s. One major contribution of both Gandhi and Ambedkar has been what Freire calls 'concretization', education of a type which enables the learner to understand critically their own situation of oppression and to take control of their lives.

The religious conversions issue fell somewhat into the background in the late 1940s, with Communalism turned into obsessive affairs by Hindus and Muslims culminating in the partition of India in 1947. However, the issue of religious conversion has not vanished, and was suddenly revealed by a near explosion on the floor of Constituent Assembly in 1947, in the course of debates on the fundamental right to religious freedom.[22]

Notes

1. Sarkar, Sumit (1989). *Modern India 1885-1947*, New York: Palgrave Macmillan.
2. Jaffrelot, Christopher (1999). "The Hindu Nationalist Movement and Indian Politics: 1925 to the 1990s" *Strategies of Identity-building, Implantation and Mobilisation (with Special Reference to Central India)* Penguin Books India.
3. Madhok, Balraj (1986). *RSS and Politics*, Delhi: Hindu World Publications.
4. *Harijan*, April 20, 1927, p. 352.
5. Desai, Mahadev (1940). "Day to Day with Gandhi", *Navjivan*, Vol. VII, p. 196.
6. Hick, John (1989). *Gandhi Significance Today*, eds. John Hick & Lamont C. Hemped, Macmillan, p. 88.

7. Barua, Ankur (2015). *Debating 'Conversion' in Hinduism and Christianity*, New York: Routledge.
8. Majumdar, Uma (2012). *Gandhi's Pilgrimage of Faith: From Darkness to Light*, New York: SUNY Press.
9. Azariah's letter entitled "All Heads of Churches and Missions (Private Circulation)", May 1936, Box 395/43, IMC/CMC/CMS, NCCC, SOAS.
10. Chatterjee, Margaret (2005). *Gandhi and the Challenge of Religious Diversity: Religious Pluralism Revisited*, New Delhi: Bibliophile South.
11. Wilfred, Felix (2014). *The Oxford Handbook of Christianity in Asia*, Oxford University Press.
12. Richards, Glyn (2005). *The Philosophy of Gandhi: A Study of His Basic Ideas*, Routledge.
13. Rambo, Lewis R., Charles E. Farhadian (2014). *The Oxford Handbook of Religious Conversion*, Oxford University Press, p. 264.
14. Rao, Kale Seshagiri (1990). *Mahatma Gandhi and Comparative Religion*, New Delhi: Motilal Banarsidass.
15. Ambedkar, B.R., edited by Mulk Raj Anand, *Annihilation of Caste*, New Delhi: Arnold Publishers.
16. Larbeer, Paulraj Mohan (2003). *Ambedkar on Religion: A Lacerative Perspective*, ISPCK for *Dalit* Resource Centre, Tamil Nadu Theological Seminary, Madurai.
17. Shastri, Uttra (1996). *Religious Converts in India: Socio-Political Study of Neo-Buddhists*, Delhi: Mittal Publications.
18. Jafferlot, Christopher (1999). *The Hindu Nationalist Movement and Indian Politics, 1925 to the 1990*, New Delhi: Penguin Books, pp. 53-55.
19. Golwalkar, M.S. (1938). *We or Our Nationhood Defined*, Nagpur, p. 27.
20. *Hinterlands and Horizons* (2002). Lanham: Lexington Books.
21. Kohli, Ritu (1993). *Political Ideas of M.S. Golwalkar: Hindutva, Nationalism, Secularism*, Deep and Deep Publications.
22. Aktor, Mikael and Robert Deliège (2010). *From Stigma to Assertion: Untouchability, Identity, and Politics in Early and Modern India*, Copenhagen: Museum Tusculanum Press, p. 115.

2

The Debate on Conversion in the Constituent Assembly, 1947-49

Introduction

With the end of Second World War in 1945, a new phase of struggle for religious freedom dawned globally. The freedom of thought, conscience, and religion, one of President Franklin D. Roosevelt's four freedoms were enshrined in the Universal Declaration of Human Rights in 1948. Soon the doctrinal basis for religious freedom as the cornerstone of human rights and the democratic rule of law became embedded in the international tradition. Constitution of India, which came into being after lengthy discussion late in 1949, contains a section guaranteeing a range of Fundamental Rights such as right to equality, freedom of religion, and freedom from exploitation. In this chapter, we will discuss the reasons for the emergence of conversion as a major constitutional concern, and then analyse the subsequent debate in order to understand arguments in an informed manner.

I. Conversion and the Politics of *Swaraj*

As independence approached, the political centre of gravity was inevitably located in the Constituent Assembly, the body that would frame the Constitution of independent India. As Jawaharlal Nehru and S. Radhakrishnan emphasized, this would be the first test of whether the 'sovereign body' of the Constituent Assembly could define *Swaraj* in such a way as to meet the 'fundamental needs' of all the people of India regardless of their race, religion or community.

The formulation of constitution based on their ideologies of 'sovereignty, unity, order, a strong state, secularism, parliamentary democracy, economic self-sufficiency, and the need for social and economic reform' was the primary political agenda of the nationalist leaders as they faced the challenge of the new era.[1]

In this process of shaping the new India, the leaders of the nationalist movement not only had to arrange for the orderly transition of power from the British but also to channel into a common direction widely different views within the Hindu majority while keeping together the various 'minority' communities of the country. As the struggle with the British for Independence neared its close, the struggle between different communities within India became apparent—particularly between the majority Hindus and the minorities.

As far as Hindus and Christians were concerned, religious freedom was a major issue. It caused communal tension and was an obstacle to common identity. This was evident during the debate concerning the fundamental rights to be ensured in the Constitution.

The Christian community had made it clear that they wishes to be integrated into the wider Indian community in building up the nation, and they welcomed the movement towards Independence.[2] Nevertheless, there was growing fear and concern among Christians that their religious liberty would be limited under Hindu majority rule. This fear was confirmed by increasing attempts by the Hindus prior to Independence to prohibit conversion in various parts of India. Although the passing of the *Lex loci*, the Regulation Law in 1832 and the amendment of I in 1850 known as the Caste Disabilities Removal Act or the Freedom of Religion Act, the disadvantages caused by changing of religion had been largely removed in British India. This did not apply in the princely states, where Hindu or Muslim law was practised and, in the period before Independence, various restrictions concerning conversion were passed in various states. The Raigarh State Conversion Act of 1936 required that a person seeking conversion need to obtain a certificate of conversion from the authorities and disallowed preaching for the purpose of conversion. Similarly, the Patna States Freedom of Religion Act of 1942; Sarguja State Apostasy Act in 1945; the Udaipur State Anti-Conversion Act in 1946—all placed legal obstacles in the way of the 'would be' convert and the one propagating the message. These restrictions on conversion in the princely states led to anxiety among missionaries and Indian Christians that their religious freedom would be severely limited and the rights of the Christians minority ignored in independent India.[3]

While the intentions of Hindus in these states to restrict conversion were clear—and this was gaining support from most states even in British Raj. Indian Christians regarded their right of conversion as a key issue in the matter of religious freedom. At Nagpur mass meeting on Religious Freedom in November 1944, the participants passed a resolution, which emphasised that, the Christianity and the 'inalienable and unalterable right' of all Christians and that this has no political or communal motives. The joint committee of the Catholic Union of India and All India Council of Indian Christians passed a resolution in October 1945, which urged that, in the Constitution, 'the free profession, practice, and propagation of religion' should be guaranteed.

Stanley Jones, who was then the leading figure among the missionaries, expressed his concern that "where if [conversion] is not allowed there is a denial of freedom of conscience. A denial of freedom of conscience strikes at the root of individual freedom. It would be the beginning of other bondage. No free people could or would tolerate it." (Jones, 1946).

There was a growing movement among Christians to safeguard this religious freedom in the Constitution itself under the 'fundamental rights' to be included in it.

The Christian campaign then focused on the Constituent Assembly to ensure that the Christian representative in the Assembly to present their position on conversion. The National Council of Churches tenth triennial meeting in Nagpur stated that:

> Christian desire and expect that provision shall be made in the Constitution of the country that will ensure to every single individual freedom to profess, practice and propagate his or her faith, including the right to change it voluntarily, and described further that no person because of conversion should be deprived of any civil, or personal rights, not be subjected by the State to any social, or economic or legal disability because of such change in religion.[4]

Similarly, the Catholic Union of India, in its statement on fundamental rights, declared that the freedom of conscience includes 'the right to change one's religion' and the freedom of expression includes 'the right of individual or of organisation to preach, and propagate the tenements of their creed and win adherents".

In September 1946, in the midst of this discussion, J.F. Butler and S. Samuel published a 45-page booklet *"The Right of Conversion"* with the intention of justifying in a systematic way the Christian insistence on the importance of conversion. The authorities defined conversion as 'changes of faith, together with the outward expressions that such change formally involve, and efforts to promote such changes and insisted that the right of conversion, along with freedom of religious belief and expression, was an 'inherent right' based on one's sense of 'duty and integrity'. They argued that:

> Truth is universal—true and therefore good, for all: hence, when it fully grips a man, it (or what is sincerely taken to be it) grips him not only as a thing to hold, but also as a thing to spread. In addition (subject to the usual provisions about anti-social conduct) a man has a right to give due expression to so fundamental a conviction as this. This right is a universal one.

The Hindu objection to the right of conversion was forcefully presented when a conference of the heads of the various Hindu religious institutions issued a memorandum to the Constituent Assembly in December 1946—statement that established the Hindu understanding of the issue. They stated that freedom of religion should be safeguarded as a basic and fundamental need of all, not just for one particular community, and furthermore, this safeguard should be expressed in accordance with the principle of *Dharma* as embodied in the Hindu tradition and not on the basis of 'rights' as Christian insisted (*Indian Social Reformer*, December 21, 1946). They alleged that the Christian campaign of conversion was carried out by organized agencies, not with religious motives but for secular advantage, using various means including schools and hospitals, which caused disadvantages to society. Therefore, they concluded that '[s]ocial peace and political stability can best be secured by allowing cultural and religious groups to live their own life, unhampered by external interference or aggression, 'letting the people continue in the faith in which they were born' free from 'proselytizing interference'.[5]

Hindus deeply resented conversion because they saw it as something imposed by a colonial power from outside. Moreover, the conversion of Indians to Christianity was understood by the Hindu leaders not as a primarily spiritual or religious question but rather as a political and communal one, and a major disturbance to Indian society.

In the context of increasing tendencies to mass conversion among the Depressed Classes and the tribals of the hill areas, they felt that the life of the major Hindu community should be protected. Christians, however, regarded conversion as a fundamental political right of the individual and feared that, under *Swaraj,* Hindus would use their majority power to oppress them by legislating further against conversion. Therefore, they geared their efforts towards getting the Constituent Assembly's position to guarantee the fundamental right of conversion in the new Constitution. Christian of both Catholic and Protestant traditions held the view that conversion is a vital part of the Christian faith and that the Constituent Assembly's position on the right of conversion be barometer of the attitude of the new movement towards the Christian community. The sharp differences on conversion between Hindus and Christians are evident as in the following discussion of the debate in the Constituent Assembly.

II. Debate in the Constituent Assembly

The Constituent Assembly was officially inaugurated on December 9, 1946. On January 24, 1947, as part of the process of formulating the Constitution of India, the Assembly adopted the Advisory Committee in turn to set up five subcommittees including a Fundamental Rights Sub-committee and a Minorities Sub-Committee. Sardar Vallabhbhai Patel, the Chairman of the Advisory Committee and a former president of the Indian National Congress, predicted that the differences between the interests of the majority were the most difficult areas the committee would have to deal with. This turned out to be the case, largely due to the issue of conversion.

Debate on Conversion in the Advisory Committee

Conversion was initially dealt with in the Fundamental Rights Sub-Committee. There were several drafts submitted to the sub-committee on the subject of religion, but the draft articles by K.M. Munshi and B.R. Ambedkar explicitly dealt with the question of conversion. Munshi, a former Home Minister of Bombay, emphasized duties as inseparable from 'fundamental Rights' and argued that the law of the Union should be able to prevent the misuse of rights. He included in his draft a preventive measure on conversion in his section on 'The Religious and Cultural Freedom': 'Conversion from one religion to another brought about by coercion, undue influence or the offering of material inducement is prohibited and is punishable by the law of the Union.' On the other hand, Ambedkar saw the main purpose of the articles as the maintenance of 'the rights of every subject to life, liberty, and pursuit of happiness and to free speech and free exercise of religion'. His draft section on 'Fundamental Rights of Citizens' stated: 'The State shall guarantee to every Indian citizen liberty of conscience and the free exercise of his religion including the right to profess, to preach and to convert within limits compatible with public order and morality' and that there should be no compulsion to participate in any religious act. While Munshi homed in on the rights of the people who are exposed to conversion activity from which they need to be protected, Ambedkar stressed conversion as a right of each individual to exercise their free will.[6]

The meeting of the Fundamental Rights Sub-Committee on 24 March decided to take up Munshi's draft and examine it in conjunction with other drafts. After lengthy discussion, the report of the sub-committee was submitted to the Advisory Committee on April 16, 1947. This included Clause 16 on religious freedom and Clauses 22 and 24 regarding the conversion, which were subsequently the same as in Munshi's original draft.

Rights Relating to Religion

(16) All persons are equally entitled to freedom of conscience, to freedom of religious worship and to freedom to profess religion subject to public order, morality, or health and to the other provisions of this chapter.

(21) No person under the age of 18 shall be made to join or profess any religion other than the one in which he was born or initiated into any religious order involving a loss of civil status.

(22) Conversion from one religion to another brought about by coercion or undue influence shall not be recognized by law and the exercise of such coercion or influence shall be an offence.

The Minorities Sub-Committee, unlike the Fundamental Rights Sub-Committee, and the Assembly as a whole, had a significant Christian representation. There were four Christians out of 22 members including the chairperson H.C. Mukherjee. In its first meeting on 17 April this sub-committee decided to examine the draft clauses recommended by the Fundamental Rights Sub-Committee for the purpose of minority rights. In their meeting, M. Ramaswamy proposed that certain religions were 'proselytizing religion' in their doctrine, so propagation of their faith should be permitted as a fundamental right. He also pointed out that Clause 21 would result in breaking up family life in the case of parents changing their religion, and proposed that minor should be allowed to follow their parents. The Sub-amendments, therefore, recommended amendments, and relayed these to the Fundamental Rights Sub-Committee on 19 April. In these recommendations, the phrase 'the right freely to profess or, practice and propagate religion' was inserted in Clause 16 in place of 'freedom of religious worship and to freedom to profess religion'—and thus the right to propagate was recognized. However, the amendment on Clause 21 contained serious restrictions on conversions.

The conversion of minors was prohibited, except in the case of following the decision of their parents to change religion, and any conversion of an adult had to be recognized by a Magistrate. Both the Christian insistence on the right of propagation and the Hindu attempts at the prevention of conversion were thus represented in these clauses.

It then became necessary for the Advisory Committee to examine both the draft and the amendments. Regarding Clause 16, there were strong objections to the word 'propagate'. It seems that the members were not very clear on the meaning and implications of the word but they were very much aware that the Christian community strongly supported it as a vital part of their 'minority right'. Several members pointed out that the right to 'freedom of speech and expression', which has been accepted already, should cover the point presented. Munshi expressed his suspicion that this word might be intended to cover 'forced conversion involved'. Others argued that it gave biased support to the 'propagation of particular religious faiths and belief'. Nevertheless, there was also strong support of the Christian position so that the debate could not reach a consensus. The chair, therefore, took a vote on the clause and the amendment to add word 'propagate' was accepted.

In this discussion on Clause 21, the chairperson, Patel argued that it did not concern fundamental right and should, therefore, be deleted and the matter left to legislation. On the same ground, the chairperson wanted to delete Clause 22. He also thought that conversion by coercion or undue influence should be an offence against the Penal Code anyway. Mr. Frank Anthony, the President of the Anglo Indian Association objected apparently because he feared that leaving the matter to the legislature might result in more severe restrictions on conversion. Other made the point that the rights of the person who is converged by 'undue influence' should be recognized. As a result, the chair suggested retaining the sentence 'conversion from one religion to another brought about by coercion or undue influence shall not be recognized by the law', but deleting the rest of the clause. The clauses on fundamental rights finally sent by the Advisory Committee to the Constituent Assembly on April 23, 1947 included the following:

(13) All persons are equally entitled to freedom of conscience, and the right freely to profess, practice, and propagate religion subject to public order, morality, or health and to the other provisions of the chapter.

(17) Conversion from one religion to another brought about by the coercion or undue influence shall not be recognised by the law.

Much to the relief of Christians, the word 'propagate' was included as a fundamental right, and the clause on the prohibition of conversion of minors was deleted. However, Hindus were not satisfied with the results of the Advisory Committee so the debate on conversion now continued in the Constituent Assembly.

Debate on Conversion of Minors in the Constituent Assembly

On April 29, 1947, Sardar Vallabhbhai Patel presented to the

Constituent Assembly the interim report on Fundamental Rights as submitted by the Advisory Committee. Clauses 13 and 17 among the 'Rights relating to religion' generated a debate, which took place on May 1, 1947. As the Constituent Assembly discussed Clause 13, the word 'propagate' was accepted without debate. However, as the Clause 17 was presented, K.M. Munshi moved an amendment for rewording Clause 17 to read as follows: "Any conversion from one religion to another of any person brought about by fraud, coercion, or undue influence or of a minor under the age of 18 shall not be recognised by law."

Mushi's amendment was twofold: the word 'fraud' was added to 'coercion' and 'undue influence'; and the prohibition of the 'conversion of minors' was again brought in.

The debate then focused mainly on the issue of the legitimacy of the conversion of minors. Explaining the amendment with regard to "conversion of a minor", Munshi argued that the amendment would provide legal protection to minors. Munshi said, "As a matter of fact, it was proposed by one or the other Committee in some form or other, and it is the general feeling that this clause should be restored in this form,—any conversion of a minor under the age of 18 shall not be recognised by law. The only effect of non-recognition by law would mean that even though a person is converted by fraud or coercion or undue influence or be converted during his minority he will still in law be deemed to continue to belong to the old religion and his legal rights will remain unaffected by reason of his conversion. The idea behind this proposal is that very often, if there are conversions by fraud or undue influence or during minority, certain changes in the legal status take place, certain rights are lost. This will have only this effect that the rights will remain exactly the same as at the moment a person was converted by fraud or coercion or undue influence and in the case of a minor at the moment of conversion."

In short, in the case of minors being converted by fraud, coercion, or undue influence, they would still legally belong to the former religion so that their rights would not be lost.

In response to Munshi's argument, Frank Anthony proposed to add a sentence to Munshi's amendment, "except when the parents or surviving parents have been converted and the child does not choose to adhere to its original faith."

Intervening in the debate Purushottamdas Tandon (who had become the President of the Indian National Congress) stressed that 'the majority of the Assembly were against the idea of conversion, especially in the case of youth, since they are 'immature' in the legal and more aspects of life. He further argued that conversion of minors was necessarily brought about by some kind of adult influence; therefore 'under all circumstances' conversion of minor's would be invalid. He expressed his strong resentment at the Christian insistence on the right to convert minors (CAD III: 492-93).

The Hindu objection to the conversion of minors was understandable given that such conversions have many ramifications in the context of the legal and social complexity of the Indian civil laws. However, the amendment was opposed by many because of its serious problems with regard to the integrity of the family. Rev. Jerome D'Souza (a Catholic priest) opposed the amendment pointing out that this would bring to 'family authority' notwithstanding the 'legal and juridical difficulties', and supported referring it back to the Advisory Committee. Dr. Ambedkar explained the practical difficulties of the amendment, especially in the case of minors whose parents were converted. He opposed the amendments on the grounds that the earlier committees had considered the matter in great detail and came to the conclusion that the prohibition of the conversion of minors 'would lead to many disruptions, to so many evil consequences' that it 'would be better to drop the whole thing altogether'. As the debate in the Assembly could not be settled, the decision was made to referrer it back to the Advisory Committee.[7]

The debate caused great concern to the Christian community. A letter was sent to the Advisory Committee insisting that it was an 'inalienable right' that one should be 'free to choose his religion or society, without his motive being impugned by government'. The editor of NCCR regarded the proposed amendment as 'undue interference' that would harm the cause of the religious liberty (NCCR, June-July 1947: 277-78). As the discussion on the issue continued, Christians not only objected to the amendment but were also of the opinion that the whole clause itself should be deleted because they regarded the amendment as intended to 'nullify' the religious freedoms stated in Clause 13. This concern was voiced at the Annual Missionary convention in Kodaikanal at which Protestant missionaries devoted their time to discussing their role in independent India. Much of their declaration was devoted to statements of intent to cooperate with the government and serve the people of India, but they also made it clear that they would stand for the 'right of the individual to outer conversion where there is an inner conversion', with the qualifier that they had; 'no desire to build up communal power for political ends through conversion'.

The view that all religions are the same was used by L. Krishnaswami Bharati to argue for freedom to propagate. Since all religions worship the same God under different names, there can be no harm in propagation. However, K.M. Munshi argued that whatever advantages the Christian community might have had under the British; there will be no such advantage under a secular state in which everyone is treated equally regardless of their religion. He saw it as unlikely, that, any community could gain a political advantage through propagation:

> "In the present set-up that we are now creating under this Constitution, this is a secular State. There is no particular advantage to a member of one community over another, nor is there any political advantage by increasing one's fold. In those circumstances the word 'propagate' cannot possibly have dangerous implications, which some of the members think that it has."[8]

According to Jerome D'Souza, a Christian member of the Constituent Assembly, there were various attempts by the Christian members to convince the others that the phrase 'undue influence' was very vague and therefore open to abusive interpretation, and that the Christians did not intend to use conversion for political means. As a result, the Christians gained support from other members of the committee and Munshi, the main Hindu protagonist became 'sympathetic' towards the Christian position.

Eventually when Patel, the chairperson of the Advisory Committee, suggested in a committee meeting that clause 17 should be dropped, this was accepted without difficulty. Patel sent a letter along with the 'Supplementary Report' of the Advisory Committee to the President of the Assembly in which he said, 'on further consideration... the clause enunciates a rather obvious doctrine which is unnecessary to include in the constitution and we recommend that it be dropped altogether.' On August 30, the Constituent Assembly again discussed whether they would drop the clause. Although there was some opposition, Patel argued that the clause was not necessary in the list of fundamental rights since forcible conversion was not recognised by law. Finally, motion was put to vote and it was decided that the clause should be deleted altogether.

Thus, the result of the debate on conversion in the Constituent Assembly was, in as it turned out, in favour of the Christian position. The word 'propagate' was retained.

Most Christians were relieved and by the decision of the Assembly and applauded the efforts of the Christians members.[9]

Comparison of Christian and Hindu position in the debate reveal that although both side were dealing with the rights of minors their views on minors, their views on conversion were directly opposed. While Christians regarded conversion a vital to faith and religious freedom, and therefore, essentially good and right, Hindus saw conversion as something alien, a symbol of oppression and enslaving power imposed upon the people of India against their will, and therefore, essentially anvil and wrong.

The debate in the Assembly revealed two broad ideological tendencies. On one side were those Congressmen who were, like the Hindu Mahasabha and Rashtriya Swayamsevak Sangh (RSS), opposed to the very idea of conversion and therefore, did not want the word 'propagate' to be included within the Fundamental Rights. The other comprised those who were more liberal minded, aware of new developments in world public opinion and not opposed to the idea of conversion as such. But they understood it as pertaining to an 'individual' conversion. It is clear from the views of Patel and Abul Kalam Azad, this ideological current was opposed to what they called 'mass conversion' (NCCR, 1947).

In the words of another Congress leader Santhanam: "Those who drafted this Constitution have taken care to see that no unlimited right of conversion has been given. A person has freedom of conscience and, if any person converts voluntarily owing to freedom of conscience is acceptable. No restriction can be placed against this. But, if any attempts made by one religious community or another to have mass conversion through undue influence either by money or by other means, the state has every right to regulate such activity."[10]

Debate on the Propagation of Religion in the Constituent Assembly

The result of the debates in the Constituent Assembly was prepared by B.N. Rao, the Constituent Adviser as a first draft Constitution and presented to the Drafting Committee on October 27, 1947. Then the committee, headed by Ambedkar, went through it clause by clause and submitted their revised Draft Constitution to the President of the Constituent Assembly on February 21, 1948. The clause allowing the right of conversion was as follows:

> Article 19. (1) Subject to public order, morality and health and to the other provisions of this Part, all persons are equally entitled to freedom of conscience and the right freely to profess, practice and propagate religion (FIC:524).

The draft Constitution was published and the people and organizations of India had an opportunity to express their view before it was adopted by the Constituent Assembly 1948. During a session of the Constituent Assembly to approve the draft Constitution on December 3, 1948, there was again strong opposition to the word 'propagate' in the article. Tajamul Husain, a Muslim representative from Bihar argued that it was not right to permit people to propagate religion in India since religion is a private matter between a person and his God and moreover, propagating activities had become a 'nuisance'. T.K. Singh alleged that there had been abuse of freedom of religion in educational institutions, hospitals and asylums in which the Christian authorities used their position to convert vulnerable people, and he claimed in such circumstances a charge of religion was 'open' to 'suspicion'.

He also saw the debate as a clash between religions such as Christianity, which openly proselytized, and others such as Hinduism, which did not, and urged that the former should exercise 'self-restraint' (CAD VII: 820-21).

Among the Hindu respondent, Loknath Mishra was most explicit in expressing Hindu feeling on the article:

> Article 19 is a Charter for Hindu enslavement. I do really feel that this is the most disgraceful Article, the blackest part of the Draft Constitution. I beg to submit that I have considered and studied all the constitutional precedents and have not found anywhere any mention of the word 'propagate' as a Fundamental Right, relating to religion...Justice demands that the ancient faith and

> culture of the land should be given a fair deal if not restored to its legitimate place after a thousand years of suppression (CSDVII: 822-23).

He declared that it would pave the way for 'complete annihilation of Hindu culture'. He claimed that the root of the recent communal violence was the aggressive propagation of Christianity and Islam in the land of India.

Some other members who were not Christians saw no objection in keeping the word 'propagate' and stated that the Islam and Christianity could not have a monopoly on proselytism. Their reasons included the following: first, the right of conversion should not only be applicable to the Christian community but also to all communities. In particular, the right to propagate would also apply to all communities particularly, the right to propagate would also apply to Hindu culture and heritage as against other religious communities. Second, there were ample safeguards against the misuse of such rights and each state has the right to regulate such activity. Third, since the Christian community had exhibited great willingness to assimilate to the general community, they should be allowed to propagate their own religion. Fourth, the article does not give unconditional freedom, but only expresses limited toleration. T.T. Krishnamachary thus argued:

> Sir, objection has been taken to the inclusion of the word 'propagate' along with the word 'profess and practice' in the matter of religion. Sir, it does not mean that this right to propagate one's religion is relevant to any particular community or to people who follow any particular religion. It is perfectly open to the Hindus and the Arya Samajists to carry their *shuddhi* propaganda as it is open to the Christians, the Muslims, the Jains, the Buddhists and to every other religionist, so long as he does it subject to public order, morality, and the other conditions that have to be observed in any civilized government." (Krishnamachary, 1989).

He further emphasized that under the Constitution, all are equal and this equal right should be given equally to anyone to 'propagate his religion, and to convert people' if a person should be convinced that this was his 'duty towards his God and his community.'

Pandit Lakshmi Kanta Maitra pointed out that: the Indian Christian community happens to be the most inoffensive community in the whole of India", and justified retention of the right to 'propagate'. Krishanaswami Bharati also took the same stand and stated that, "so far as my experience goes, the Christian community have not transgressed their limits of legitimate propagation of religious view... It is for other communities to emulate and propagate their own religions as well."

These arguments were endorsed by K.M. Munshi who insisted that, in contrast to the past, there would be no political threat caused by conversion in independent India. He realized that this issue would have to be solved by compromise and he expressed his sympathy with Christians:

> ... it was this word that the Indian Christian community laid the greatest emphasis, not because they want to convert people aggressively, but because the word 'propagate' was fundamental part of their tenet... So long as religion to religion, conversion by free exercise of the coincident has to be recognized (CAD VII: 837-38).

Munshi's speech proved decisive and convinced most of the members although many Hindu members still tried to delete word 'propagate' and it was clear that they were not happy with the inclusion of the word. However, during the ensuing votes on each amendment, the Assembly opted to retain the word 'propagate', and it was included in the Constitution as Article 25 in the section on "The Right to Freedom of Religion." It was finally adopted by the Assembly on November 26, 1949. Thus, finally, the idea of conversion was included in the Constitution as a fundamental right despite the resistance exerted by many quarters. In addition, interestingly, this was achieved with the efforts of Sardar Patel and K.M. Munshi, leaders considered the defenders of Hindu cultural prestige and interest.

The question still arises that since the Hindus were in a majority in the Constituent Assembly, why they conceded the right to 'propagate' to the Christian minority. This cannot be fully explained as the result of the convincing arguments of Christians, or as the outcome of the campaign for religious freedom since there is no evidence of a long-term change in the Hindu attitude towards conversion. It has been argued that the Hindus accepted the word 'propagate' in a compromise with the Christians that involved the later giving up their reserved seat in the legislature. Notably, the 1935 Government of India Act, which established the categories of Scheduled Castes and Scheduled Tribes, allocated some legislative seats to these protected categories as well as to religious minorities, giving any large-scale conversion political implications.

However, if one considers the chronology of events, it is evident that the Christians expressed their confidence in the Hindu majority after the later had made provisions for the minorities in the fundamental rights. This concession to Christians appears to be what caused Christians to cooperate with Hindus in the abolition of reserved seats.

As the ferocity of the debate shows the Christians and the missionaries' optimism to view, the result of the debate did not produce mutual understanding between Hindus and Christians but instead confirmed their differing views on conversion.[11]

In the proceeding of the Constitute Assembly, and in the Christian literature during and after it, the word 'propagate' as used by Christians and Hindus was understood to include the right to seek the conversion of others. The question then arises as to why Christian used the word 'propagate' instead of 'convert' at the time of the Constituent Assembly. Throwing light on this Kim (2003) states that one reason is that the word 'conversion' was sensitive at that time so that the Christians would tend to avoid it in order to minimize the reaction from the Hindus. But, more significantly, it appears to be the case that the Christians used the word 'propagate' because they saw the right to propagate one's faith as the most fundamental right and assumed that the right of an individual to convert to another religion was guaranteed by the clause 'freedom of conscience' in the same article.

This would seem to settle the matter as the Constitution of India guarantees the right to propagate religion. However, despite the clarity of the constitutional provision, the debate on whether the propagation of religion should be permitted and, if so, on what terms continues.

At the time of the Constituent Assembly, the questions of religious freedom, developed in the West in the struggle over church-state relations was a very important part of the agenda in the Western nations. The UDHR was approved by the United Nations Assembly on December 10, 1948 and Western Christian leaders played a major role in promoting religious freedom as fundamental human right. Therefore, the Hindu suspicion that the debate in the Assembly was instigated by the wider Christian churches, which were eager to continue their influence in India after the demise of colonial rule, was not entirely unfounded.[12] However, the Indian Christian insistence on the right to conversion as a fundamental right was more directly a result of the Hindu attempt to restrict or prohibit conversion in various states prior to the Constituent Assembly.[13]

Although the campaign for the right to conversion was initiated by the Christian missionaries soon other minorities such as Muslims also joined this demand as they were convinced that the right of conversion was vital for their identity and existence, and thus they actively campaigned for this right at the time of the Constituent Assembly.

Clause 17 stated: Conversion from one religion to another brought about by coercion or undue influence shall not be recognized by law. From now on, the anti-Christian forces were to focus on this clause and carry on the propaganda in society that all conversions were in fact being affected by 'undue influence' and by denouncing Hindu gods and religion. The logic of democracy was being used to subvert a democratic right. First, public opinion was roused and mobilized to create the right atmosphere. This was followed by demand for a new legislation to curtail activities of the missionary institutions. This has provided an excellent weapon to these forces to harass, intimidate, and demoralize the Christians in general and Christian works in particular.

The clause on religious freedom as it stands today is indicative of the fact that the House was able to fight down bigotry and narrow-mindedness and while it was not in favour of conversion through compulsion, it certainly advocated freedom to profess, practice, and propagate religion.

III. Religious Freedom and the Secular State

In the Constituent Assembly debates, although the term secularism was not often used, there were frequent references to a 'secular state'. Most advocates of a secular state emphasized that it did not imply that the state was hostile to religious belief.

Moreover, a secular state was not a state that was incognizant of the importance of religious faith in Indian society; nor it zealous in inculcating scepticisms towards religious belief among its citizens. Supporting an amendment giving the President the option of taking his oath of office in the name of God, a proposal that was supported by representatives of religious minorities and incorporated into the Constitution, K.M. Munshi asserted:

> A secular state is not a Godless state. It is a state, which is pledged to eradicate or ignore religion... We must take cognizance of the fact that India is a religious minded country. Even while we are talking of a secular state, our mode of thought and life is largely coloured by a religious attitude to life... the state in India cannot be secular in the sense of being anti-religious (CAD, VII, p. 1057).

The thinking in the Constituent Assembly was largely influenced by the thinking of Mahatma Gandhi and his struggle against the British Raj. Mahatma Gandhi promoted certain approach in order to embrace different religious communities and created a common identity of India as a nation that shares traditional Indian values. For him, religious differences were unimportant and even irrelevant in his search for a common Indian identity because Hinduism was tolerant of a variety of religious beliefs and practices.

From tolerance, Gandhi moved to respect for all religions. He pleads that all religions enjoin the worship of one god who is all pervasive. Gandhi had deep mark on many of the members of the Constituent Assembly. Equal respect for all religions—*Sarva Dharma-Sambhava*—was included by Mahatma Gandhi in the eleven vows that a volunteer of non-violence movement was required to take.

Prime Minister Nehru, at the moment India became independent on August 15, 1947, addressed the Indian people and used stark phrased to describe the state of the country they had inherited and the task before them: "Our first and most immediate objective must be to end all internal strife and violence, which disfigure and degrade us and injure the cause of freedom" (Nehru, 1949). The Preamble to the Constitution, as adopted in 1949 and amended in 1976, describes not the reality of Indian life as it existed but what its authors hoped it would become. There is no mention of God or creator, but rather of the people "who give to themselves": this Constitution for a "sovereign, socialist, secular, democratic republic, assuring the unity and integrity of the nation."

For Nehru and those who followed him "secularism" was the key to ending both secessionist movement inspired by religion and the internal clashes of Hindu-Muslim antagonism. There was not much serious discussion in Parliament over socialism, democracy, or unity and integrity. However, there was fierce debate in the media and in political meetings over secularism and this debate continues. The first draft of the Constitution had said all citizens were to have the right "to freely profess and practice religion", but Christians and Muslims demanded that a third right be added "the right to propagate religion. Propagating or proselytizing, they insisted, was a fundamental requirement of their faiths. That right was accepted unwillingly and it has remained a source of tension. The debate has often turned violent, as militant Hindu have argued that leaving Hinduism and accepting Islam or Christianity is to become denationalised through adherence to foreign religion—indeed, they argue, it is to betray India."[14]

Legal Limits on Religious Conversion in India

During the Independence struggle, it was Nehru, Jinnah, and Subhas Chandra Bose who maintained that it was wrong for religion to interfere in politics. From 1920 onward, Nehru's view that all human enterprises should be delivered from religious dominance became more apparent. He understood that the destruction of religious superstition by secularism was the only means for a peaceful India. Nehru looked at secularism as a great cementing force of the diverse people of India. Secularism had to displace the religious outlook if people of India were to live and grow together in unity and fraternity.[15]

Nehru represented the Western form of secularism whereas Gandhi stressed on the equality of all religion and religious pluralism. While Mahatma Gandhi and Maulana Azad spoke of secularism from the perspective of religion, Pandit Nehru was the first in the subcontinent to accept Western concept of secularism (Masud, 2007).

Thus, there have been mainly two sets of views among the Hindus regarding secularism in India. One view is that secularism in India can only be possible with the adoption of pluralism by every Indian citizen. The other view is that secularism is a Western concept that is unsuitable for the Indian context and must be replaced with cultural nationalism. Former view is represented by Mahatma Gandhi and the latter view is represented by the Sangh Parivar.

At the independence in 1947, British India was divided into predominantly Muslim Pakistan and predominantly Hindu India, setting off a massive migration (of Pakistani Hindus and Sikhs to India, and Indian Muslims to Pakistan), and provoking inter-religious riots that resulted in hundreds of thousands of deaths. Aside from its fierce internecine violence, the partition of India had a more general deleterious effect on interreligious interactions in the subcontinent.

The Partition was often quoted as a powerful example and as perpetual grievance against Muslims or as a warning of what could happen if the Christian community grew large enough to demand separate homeland—but also because it continue to shape how Indians think about other religions and about their religion. Perhaps it is for this reason despite the prominence, in public discourse, of the perceived Muslim threat to the integrity of India during and after partition, traditionalist Hindu organisations continue to voice concern about Christian missions work among lower-caste Hindu and tribal peoples during the Constituent Assembly debates of 1946-1950, in the course of which a constitutional ban on conversion was unsuccessfully proposed. Moreover, conversion remained lively issue in the next decades.

The formation of constitutional provisions reflected complex accommodations between secularism and religion. In the Constituent Assembly debates, the proposals of ardent secularist to constitutionally restrict the scope of religion did not win out. After undergoing several presumptions during its passage through various sub-committees of the Constituent Assembly, a broad definition of the right to freedom of religion was adopted, encompassing the right to 'practice' and 'propane' religion as well as to 'profess' religion that extended to all persons, not only citizens.

After extensive debate, the Constituent Assembly eventually

decided that the state could aid educational institutions that imparted religious instruction, a position that was in keeping with the wishes of the religious-minded, including among minority representative. Freedom of religion was, of course, not left untrammelled: constitutional provisions explicitly permitted the state to enact laws for social welfare and reform, and also permitted state interventions in the interest of public order, morality and health; for upholding other fundamental rights provisions; and for the regulation and restriction of any economic, financial, political or secular activity associated with religious practice. Nevertheless, religious personal laws that governed marriage, divorce, inheritance were retained, despite secularists pressing for a uniform civil code.[16]

In earlier chapter we have read about the arguments of M.K. Gandhi (Mahatma) against conversion in his struggle with the British Raj were based on his ideology of the equality of religions, which he promoted in order to embrace different religious communities and create a common identity of India as a nation that shares traditional Indian value. For him religious differences were unimportant and even irrelevant in his search for a common Indian identity because Hinduism was tolerant of a variety of religious beliefs and practices. Gandhi has developed in the concept of 'secular India', which was promoted by Jawaharlal Nehru and other leaders of the nationalist movement at the time of Constitution Assembly and continued to be a guiding principles in Indian politics in the 1950s.

The struggle of Indian Christian community at the time of Independence was to maintain themselves as a part of a wider and at the same time identify themselves as a part of India, whose culture was entwined with Hindu tradition.

The former gave them a sense of belonging and commitment with people worldwide but also laid them open to Hindu accusation of less than full allegiance towards common Indian heritage and furthermore of associating with the people who exercised colonial power over India. They later gave them shared dignity and pride in being Indian but led to a situation in which their religious freedom might be restricted by the majority Hindus. For Hindus, Hindu religious conversion meant changing one's heritage and thus losing one's identity. It went against the tradition of social, moral and religious order, established by *dharma*. While

Christians feared that the majority Hindus would use their social and political power to suppress conversion. Hindus resented the fact that Christians were determined to have their way over the right of conversion, which they saw as a symbol of colonial oppression.

As we will see in the coming chapters, Hindus did take various preventive measures against conversion and these were supported by the leaders of Hindu nationalist movements as they expanded their political influxes in the 1950s and engaged in active promotion of *Hindutva*.

From now on, the issue of fundamental rights and tolerance were to become major themes of the ongoing debate between Hindus and Christians on conversion.[17]

Conclusion

To recapitulate, in Indian constitutional and legislative debate, secularism has been interpreted as a consistent with religion, and laws have frequently embodied ideas compromised between the advocates of secularism and religion.

During the constitution making, many agreed that religion had been kept separate from the state for the sake of political integrity of the country but the violent Partition of India on religious lines was regarded as a direct consequence of mixing religion and politics. A secular state was considered instrumental for national unity in a negative state, in that political unity would be the means for consolidating national unity in a positive sense. The state was to be the agency for welding together diverse and conflicting religious groups into a nation, and it was felt that the state could only fulfil this role if it abstained from identification with any religion. A second kind of relationship between secularism and national unity was constitutive. A few Constitution-makers subscribed to a secular view of the national identity, where Indianness was defined primarily in political term, in terms of membership of a state where religion was irrelevant for purposes of citizenship.

Official secularism in India has largely been respectful of religious belief and practice, although the extent and the grounds of respect for religion have varied over time and among actors, as we shall note in coming chapters.

Notes

1. Brass, Paul R. (1994). *The Politics of India Since Independence,* New Cambridge History of India IV; Cambridge: CUP.
2. NCCR January 1946: 32: NCCR, March, 1947: 103-56-62.
3. Baird, Robert D., (2005). *Religion and Law in Independent India,* Delhi: Manohar Publishers & Distributors.
4. NCCR, January 1947:21.
5. *Indian Social Reformer,* December 28, 1946.
6. Constituent Assembly Debates: Official Report, Volume 9, Lok Sabha, Secretariat, 1949, New Delhi, India.
7. Kashyap, Subhash C., (1995). *History of the Parliament of India,* Vol. II, Delhi: Shipra Publications.
8. *Ibid.*
9. *The Examiner,* September 20, 1947.
10. *Constituent Assembly Debates,* Volume 7: 834-35.
11. Morris-Jones, W.H. (1957). *Parliament in India,* London: Longmans.
12. Kim, S. (2003). *In Search of Identity,* New Delhi: OUP, p. 57.
13. Ghosh, Sanjay (2001). *Unsustainable Laws: The Lawyers Collective,* Tahir Mahmood (2008). *Laws of India on Religion and Religious Affairs,* New Delhi: Universal Law Publishing.
14. Smith, D.E., (1963). *India as a Secular State,* Princeton: Oxford University Press.
15. Masud, Kazi Anwarul (2003). "How fares secularism in India", *The Daily Star,* http://www.thedaily stqr.nert 2003/09/07.
16. Upadhyaya, Prakash Chandra (1992). "The politics of Indian secularism", *Modern Asian Studies,* 26(4), p. 845.
17. Kim, Sebastian, (2003). *In Search of Identity,* OUP, p. 58.

3
Religious Freedom and Laws in India

Introduction

Plurality and freedom of religion have acquired new public attention in India due to Muslim-Hindu Gujarat Riots (2002), violence against Christians in Kandhmal (2008), *Ghar Wapsi* in Agra (2015), and violence by cow vigilant groups against Muslims and *Dalits* (2016). Describing the Constitutional provisions for religious freedom and articulating the distinctive character of Indian secularism, this chapter turns to two major issues of religious freedom in contemporary India—right to choose religion of choice and personal laws. Several Indian states have enacted 'Freedom of Religion' Acts (often referred as anti-conversion laws) and there is a growing demand for a national law of similar kind. The present debate over religious freedom in India has thrown number of questions: What model of religious freedom can be identified in the Constitution of India for a plural landscape of religious co-existence? Who mobilizes them, and towards what ends? How are local practices of religious co-existence being transformed by the introduction of 'anti-conversion' laws? What differences and incommensurabilities may be identified between state-centred notions of religious freedom and forms of religious co-existence practiced by the communities?

Religious conversion has become the subject of passionate debate in contemporary India since 1981 when large number of *Dalits* in Tamil Nadu left Hindu fold and embraced Islam.

This issue has surfaced repeatedly in the political realm, in the media and in the courts. During the last two decades, the dispute has attained a new climax in the plethora of newspapers, journals, and books whose pages have been devoted to the question of *Dharmantaran*—changing religion. Apparently, a large group of Indians considers this an issue of crucial importance to the future of their country.

Before we move on to the constitutional provision for religious freedom, let us have a brief look at the legal situation on freedom of religion in colonial India.

Laws in Colonial India

Anti-conversion laws have arisen from a long history of religious activity in India. These laws were first enacted by the princely states during the British colonial period, although the government did not promulgate any anti-conversion laws.[1]

First anti-conversion law was enacted in 1936 by the Raigarh State. According to the Act, person wishing to change his religion had to submit an application in a prescribed form to a government officer who would give permission or refuse. The Act made liable to punishment any person found guilty of misinterpretation, fraud, intimidation, coercion, or undue influence in the matter of conversion. The law also forbade preaching in order to convert. Soon other princely states followed the suit and the Bolangir Freedom of Religion Act (1938), the Patna Freedom of Religion Act of 1942, the Sarguja State Apostasy Act, 1945 and the Udaipur State Anti-Conversion Act, 1946 came into existence.[2] Similar laws were enacted in Bikaner, Jodhpur, Kalahandi, Kota, and many other princely states. These early anti-conversion laws may have been the foundation and inspiration of post-colonial Indian anti-conversion laws.

Tribal dominated Hindu princely states were first to introduce anti-conversion laws. Between 1880 and 1910, large number of tribals were bereft of their land by the local *Zamindars* (property owners) and the missionaries fought their case in the courts and got their land back. Fearing that after independence the *Rajas* might lose all their lands the princely states started enacting anti-conversion laws. The land reform initiated by the missionaries (getting *adivasis* their land back from the *Zamindars*) in the region of Chotanagpur (now in Jharkhand) played a major role in the enactment of early anti-conversion laws in India.[3] These laws were enacted out of a concern for the maintenance of sovereignty in regions habituated by an intense concentration of tribal communities. These regions were later merged into the post-independence states of Madhya Pradesh, Orissa, and Bihar and enactment of new anti-conversion laws illustrates the continuity of tensions over freedom to choose religion—tensions that ultimately resulted in a pivotal Supreme Court case.[4] The political concern for Hindu sovereignty also formed the basis for the Niyogi Report 1956, which in turn, bolsters contemporary anti-conversion campaigns.

Constitutional Basis for Religious Freedom

The Constitution of India, enacted in 1950 includes Fundamental Rights as well as Directive Principles, which guide state policies and actions. The Constitution was written at the fag end of 1940s—a key period in the global development of human rights, including the crcation of the Atlantic Charter (1941), UN Charter (1946), and the Universal Declaration on Human Rights, 1948. Members of India's Constituent Assembly "were sensitive to these currents, which supported their own faith in the validity of written rights."

Under Article 25 of the Constitution, all persons are equally entitled to freedom of conscience and the right to freely profess, practice, and propagate religion subject to public order, morality, and health. Article 26 gives to every religious denomination a fundamental right to manage its own affairs in matters of religion. This cannot be abrogated in any way. Article 29 gives the absolute and unqualified right to minorities to conserve their distinct language, script, and culture. Article 30 gives the fundamental right to all minorities, whether based on religion or language, to establish and administer educational institutions of their choice, but the religious denominations right to manage its own affairs is restricted to "matters of religion" which are "subject to public order, morality and health." The only rights that are absolute and unfettered are the right to freedom of conscience under Article 25 and the right of minorities to conserve their distinct language, script, and culture under Article 29. In the Constitution, the freedom of religious practice was also modified to ensure that the government could outlaw certain forms of caste discrimination, particularly the practice of barring low castes from temples.[5]

Another section of the Constitution of India, the Directive Principles, also addresses religion—in particular, the future of various religious personal laws that continue to be recognized in Indian courts for certain family law cases. One of these Directive Principles calls for a "Uniform Civil Code for the Citizens", directing that "the State shall endeavour to secure for the citizens a Uniform Civil Code throughout the territory of India."[6]

The Constituent Assembly placed the contentious issue of a uniform civil code in the Directive Principles. They are not enforceable by any court, but "the principles therein laid down are nevertheless fundamental in the governance of the country and it shall be the duty of the State to apply these principles in making laws." Until now, the Indian Government has not unified its civil code.

In 1976, the word 'secular' was added to the preamble to the Constitution of India. The Constitution's opening phrase now begins: "We, the people of India, having solemnly resolved to constitute India into a [sovereign socialist secular democratic republic]." The preamble goes on to commit India to "justice, liberty of thought, expression, belief, faith, and worship [,]... equality [,]... [and] fraternity." The original mention of religious liberty and the later addition of the term secular signal India's commitment to maintaining a government that is autonomous from religious leaders, yet responsive to the concerns of minorities in India's incredible diverse society.[7]

Secularism in India is about symmetry rather than complete separation between the state and religion.[8] India is a secular state, which has no religion of its own. The Constitution of India contains several constitutional provisions pertaining to religious freedom and freedom of conscience as fundamental rights. Part III of the Constitution deals with 'Fundamental Rights'. Amongst the rights which are treated as fundamental are Articles 14 to 18, which deal expressly with the 'Right to Equality', and Articles 25 to 28, which guarantee 'Right to Freedom of Religion', are but is subject to public order, morality and health.[9]

Limits of Religious Freedom

Part III of the Constitution of India dealing with the Fundamental Rights, including those concerning religion, were prompted by concern for the liberty, dignity and well-being of the individual. This distinguishing feature of the Constitution of India also provides for limitation of freedom of religion.

Articles 25 and 26, on the freedom of religion reads as follows:

Article 25. ***Freedom of conscience and free profession, practice and propagation of religion—***

(1) Subject to public order, morality, and health and to the other provisions of this Part, all persons are equally entitled to freedom of conscience and the right freely to profess, practice, and propagate religion.
(2) Nothing in this article shall affect the operation of any existing law or prevent the State from making any law—
    (a) Regulating or restricting any economic, financial, political, or other secular activity, which may be associated with religious practice;
    (b) Providing for social welfare and reform or the throwing open of Hindu religious institutions of a public character to all classes and sections of Hindus.

Article 26. ***Freedom to manage religious affairs—***

Subject to public order, morality and health, every religious denominations or any section thereof shall have the right:

(a) to establish and maintain institutions for religious and charitable purposes;
(b) to manage its own affairs in matters of religion;
(c) to own and acquire movable and immovable property; and
(d) to administer such property in accordance with law.

It may be noticed in the first place that Article 25 and its ancillary Article 26, open with the recitation of the limitations to which the fundamental rights enshrined in these articles are subject.

The Fundamental Right to religious freedom cannot be enjoyed in an unrestricted way. There are limitations within which these rights can be exercised, as also lawful restrictions, which can be imposed by the State on such rights. The State is also empowered to make any law "regulating or restricting any economic, financial, political or other secular activity which may be associated with religious practice" with the object of bringing about a uniformity, an equalization of the rights and obligations of the people thereby minimizing differences in areas which do not interfere with any religion.

The general scheme of the Constitution, followed in all other articles of Part II without exception, is to state the right first, thus giving it a primary place, and to mention the limitations only subsequently. A perusal of the public interest to which the fundamental rights encoded in Article 25 is subjected will reveal the significance in this departure. This includes not only the usual categories of public order, morality, and health but also the unique category, found again in no other article, namely "the other provisions of this Part."

Sub-clause of Clause (2) of Article 25 recognizes the overriding power of the state to regulate and restrict over the entire areas where the secular and the religious are found to commingle. It recognizes and asserts power of the state to regulate any economic, financial, political, or other secular activity without stopping where such activities begin to touch or commingle with religion. State jurisdiction exists as long as this secular element persists, and is not affected by the presence of the element that may be found to be enmeshed with it.[10]

These limitations are not an assault on religious freedom but a deeper defence of its basic principle. Freedom of religion can be secured only to the extent that the public sphere is free from religion, which is the premise of secularism.

It must be always remembered that social justice is the main foundation of the democratic way of life enshrined in the provision of the Constitution of India.

Laws in Independent India

Post-independence, the Indian Parliament took up for consideration a legislative enactment regulating religious conversion known as Indian Conversion (Regulation and Registration) Bill of 1954, and later the Backward Communities (Religious Protection) Bill of 1960 aimed to stop conversion. However, these measures were dropped for lack of majority support. Meanwhile, the ultra-nationalist section, which was influential in central India, managed to manoeuvre Madhya Pradesh government to appoint the Niyogi Committee to investigate conversions in the state.

The Niyogi Commission report included recommendations to restrict conversions; in fact, the committee recommended prohibiting "any attempt or effort (whether successful or not), directly or indirectly to penetrate into the religious conscience of persons (whether of age or underage) of another faith."[11]

Suspicion of conversions and assumptions about the gullibility of poor converts, voiced in this report, paved the way for legal restrictions.

Taking clue from the Niyogi Committee report, the first state to enact the Freedom of Religion Act was Orissa in 1967 during the rule of the then Swatantra Party, which was known for its Right leanings.

The Madhya Pradesh Freedom of Religion Act was enacted in 1968 by the Samyukt Vidhayak Dal Government, headed by a leader of the Congress Party, Govind Narayan Singh, who defected to form his own party and coalition and eventually joined the Jana Sangha, the former *avatar* of rightwing nationalist Bharatiya Janata Party (BJP). Moreover, when Chhattisgarh was carved out of Madhya Pradesh in November 2000, it inherited the anti-conversion law from the latter.

The Madhya Pradesh Dharma Swatantrya Adhiniyam in 1968, stipulated "prohibition of conversion from one religion to another by use of force or allurement, or by fraudulent means, and matters incidental thereto." It also required that a person who converts another person report the conversion to the District Magistrate within a set period, or risk imprisonment (one year) or a fine (up to Rs. 1000), or both—requirements that recently have been made even more stringent.

Many other State legislatures followed the Madhya Pradesh model. India's federal structure, based on Article 246 of the Constitution, defines the power distribution between the Federal or Central Government and the State Governments, as well as some powers that are to be shared concurrently by both. Law and order is a state responsibility and prerogative.

The Madhya Pradesh Law 1968 and a similar 1967 law in the state of Orissa became the subjects of the Supreme Court decision of 1977 upholding such legal restrictions on conversions. This decision of the Supreme Court encouraged other state governments to enact similar laws. In 1978, the Congress government in Arunachal Pradesh passed anti-conversion law.

Similar laws were passed by the state assemblies of Chhattisgarh (2000), Tamil Nadu (2002), Gujarat (2003), Himachal Pradesh (2006), and Rajasthan (2006). The Governor of Rajasthan refused to forward the Bill to the President of India for approval. Therefore, in 2008, the BJP Government in Rajasthan re-introduced the same anti-conversion Bill in the Assembly despite the previous Rajasthan Dharma Swatantraya Bill, 2006, still awaiting the approval of President.[12] The BJP in Madhya Pradesh and Chhattisgarh sought to tighten the existing laws by amending the law in 2006.

The Congress Party government in Himachal Pradesh passed the Freedom of Religion Act for political considerations months before state assembly elections. In 2007, the BJP government in Uttrakhand was all set to introduce anti-conversion Bill but could not do so due to other pressing political concerns. The Tamil Nadu Law (2002) is currently inactive, having been repealed in 2004. Jharkhand state passed anti-conversion law in August 2017 in hurriedly conveyed assembly session.

In light of the introduction of a Freedom of Religion Act in Rajasthan state and the amendments to the laws in Gujarat, Madhya Pradesh and Chhattisgarh, senior religious, legal and secularist spokespersons in India have expressed their concern about the Freedom of Religion Acts in Indian states. In 2015, the Hindu fundamentalist groups have raised demand to enact a national law to restrict freedom to choose religion.

Basic Features of the Acts

Most of Freedom of Religion Acts of independent India is based on colonial time princely states anti-conversion laws. These Acts have identical objective and use certain words such as 'forcible' or 'fraudulent means' or by 'allurement' or 'inducement'. They orchestrate any 'right' to choose religion of choice and are based on doubting motives of conversion from national security perspective rather than spirituality and higher experiences of an individual. All these 'anti-conversion laws ' seems to be governed from hidden agenda of obstructing the 'free choice' of socially oppressed and exploited people who may be aspiring for a different spiritual system. All these Acts are significantly directed against Christians and Muslims, as they do not prohibit 'conversion' to Hinduism. Most of the Acts restricting conversion were aimed at preventing use of force, inducement, or fraudulent means in conversion but, in effect, they restrict the general practice of religious freedom and propagation.

Some of the common features of these Acts are listed below.

Imprecise Definition of Prohibited Activities

Among the most important charges brought against the various anti-conversion laws is the lack of precision and clarity in their definitions of the conditions under which conversions are prohibited.

The chief ostensible objective of these laws, grouped together under the collective heading of 'anti-conversion legislation', is the prevention of conversions carried out by 'forcible' or 'fraudulent' means or by 'allurement' or 'inducement'. While there are no grounds for objection to the prohibition of 'forcible' or 'fraudulent' conversion activity, *per se*, it is the definition given to such terms, which have given grave cause for concern. The terms like 'forcible' or 'fraudulent' and 'allurement' or 'inducement', are not clear in these Acts. This creates the potential for arbitrary interpretation and application of the legislation.

The definitions of the Gujarat law are illustrative of those in other Freedom of Religion Acts in India:

(a) 'allurement' means offer of any temptation in the form of—
 (i) any gift or gratification, in either cash or kind;
 (ii) grant of any material benefit, either monetary or otherwise;
(b) 'convert' means to make one person to renounce one religion and adopt another religion;
(c) 'force' includes a show of force or a threat of injury of any kind including a threat of divine displeasure or social ex-communication;
(d) 'fraudulent' means includes misrepresentation or any other fraudulent contrivance.

Definitions (a), (c), and (d) in particular are open to wide interpretation, which gives rise to the potential for the law to be misused. Under the definition of 'force', for example, the inclusion of 'a show of force' may allow the law to be invoked to prohibit a religious rally. The inclusion of a 'threat of divine displeasure' is both extremely imprecise and contrary to the nature of some religious teaching. Similarly, the definition of 'fraudulent means' as including 'any fraudulent contrivance' is excessively vague to serve with any usefulness as a legal definition.

It is further feared that the clauses prohibiting 'allurement' or 'inducement' to convert, linked to the offer of any material or monetary grants, may be used against charitable activity undertaken by religious groups, which could be portrayed as a form of temptation to convert. Alternatively, this category could be invoked where a convert had expectations of a better education, of support co-religionists or of certain religious benefits, such as absolution from sins.

The rules of the Orissa and Madhya Pradesh law stipulate that a religious priest (or, in the case of the latter law, a participant in a conversion ceremony) must sent an intimation to the District Magistrate about this conversion, though permission need not be sought.

In the Orissa and Arunachal Pradesh laws, the term, 'inducement', is used in the place of 'allurement', though it is defined in almost identical manner.

These considerations are particularly relevant to members of the marginalised section of society in India, among whom many NGOs including Christian organisations undertake charitable and evangelistic activities.

The definition of conversion in these Acts overlooks the fact that conversion is primarily a thought process, which may span several days, weeks, or even years.

Imprecision of Criminalising Clauses

The criminalising clause in Section 3 of the Rajasthan law, which closely follows the equivalent clause in other laws, stipulates that:

> No person shall convert or attempt to convert, directly or otherwise any person from one religion to another either by use of force or by allurement or by fraudulent means, nor shall any person abet any such conversion.

The scope of this clause is extremely wide. Concern has been expressed that a wide range of religious activities, including propagation, could be included under the umbrella of attempts 'to convert, either directly or otherwise'. This clause is, therefore, capable of impeding constitutionally protected religious activities. The lack of clarity in the legislation about the nature of conversion and the absence of clear definitions of religious parties cause serious problems at the field level.

The Rajasthan Freedom of Religion Act defines 'conversion' as 'renouncing one's own religion and adopting another'. This closely follows the text of the Orissa, Madhya Pradesh, and Chhattisgarh laws. The Arunachal Pradesh law defines conversion as specifically 'renouncing an indigenous faith and adopting another faith or religion'. The Gujarat law clarified its definition of conversion by excluding from its purview any conversion between denominations of the same religion. The Gujarat law construed Jainism and Buddhism as 'denominations of the Hindu religion'.

Force

The definition of the term "force" as "threat of divine displeasure" unjustifiably impinges on possible interactions between potential converts and those seeking to propagate their faith. It restricts the latter from informing the former about non-adherence, for example, as that may involve teachings on hell or God's wrath. In addition, without being informed, a potential convert cannot meaningfully exercise his or her freedom to change religion.

Proponents of these laws often quote the Orissa High Court ruling in *Yulitha Hyde* v. *State of Orissa*[13], which held, "Threat of divine displeasure numbs the mental faculty; more so of an undeveloped mind and the actions of such a person thereafter, are not free and according to conscience". The courts in India have also reasoned that threatening anyone with divine displeasure puts great pressure on the threatened person and deprives them of the capacity of exercising their rational judgment. Repeatedly the courts have held that a suggestion of divine displeasure deprives a person of their abilities to make a choice. However, this argument overlooks the fact that inherent in the propagation of a faith or religious belief is the articulation of the effects of failure to comply with the said beliefs.

Fraud

The definition of the word "fraudulent" as "misrepresentation or any other fraudulent contrivance" may seem innocuous on the face of it, but it is not. In spiritual matters, what would constitute misrepresentation?

Could a statement like, "Prayers will heal you", or "God will grant you material blessings", be construed as employing fraudulent means? There is no answer.

Inducement/Allurement

A problem in defining the term "inducement" or "allurement" as "offer of any temptation in the form of any gift or gratification either in cash or kind or grant of any material benefit either monetary or otherwise" was noted by the Orissa High Court in *Yulitha Hyde* v. *State of Orissa*. The Court held that the vague nature and wide scope of the term would impinge on various legitimate methods of proselytizing. While the Supreme Court subsequently overruled the Orissa High Court's decision in *Rev. Stanislaus* v. *Madhya Pradesh*, the Court chose not to comment on definitions provided under the Acts.[14] The vague term "allurement" many say has meaning "to entice by charm or attraction", and one that potentially covers many conversion bases, including the promise of economic or potential gain for marginalised groups. The implications of conversion politics and of allurement in particular, have particular relevance for post-colonial studies, but have received little or no attention in globalised world.

Supreme Court senior advocate Prashant Bhushan commenting on the provision is quoted as saying, "Anything can be called allurement. In many Christian institutions, education for Christians is free, so if somebody changes his or her religion, even education can be defined as allurement."

Disproportionality of Penal Provisions

The seeming disproportionality of punishments under anti-conversion legislation has been illustrated in India by comparison with punishments for various other offences. For example, the punitive provisions of the Rajasthan and Gujarat laws are greater than those stipulated in the Indian Penal Code for rioting or causing death by negligence. The provision for this level of punishment could deter any legitimate attempts to propagate a religion.

A further concern arises from the provision of an equal punishment for any violation of Section 3, which prohibits both converting and attempting to convert others. This is in contravention of the principle of criminal jurisprudence, recognised in the Indian Penal Code, whereby an attempt to commit an offence is less serious than the actual commission of an offence.

The Acts give district authorities wide and sweeping powers to inquire into both the reasons behind a religious conversion and the procedure adopted for the same. This is a gross violation of the right to freedom of association, the right to privacy and the freedom of conscience.

The Acts cast an onerous burden on the part of the convertee and the persons seeking to propagate their faith without providing the required checks and balances to ensure protection against misuse of authority.

For example, Section 4 of the Himachal Pradesh Act makes it obligatory for a person to give a 30-day prior notice to the District Magistrate about his or her intention to convert. As per the Rules, the District Magistrate who then "shall get the matter enquired into by such agency as he may deem fit." No time limit is prescribed for the conduct of such an enquiry nor have its modalities been defined.

The procedure is oppressive as it will deter a person from changing his religion due to unnecessary revelation of an individual's personal choice and belief to the public at large along with the stigma of having a police inquiry in matters relating to one's belief and conscience.

Intimidation of Potential Converts

The prospect of informing a potentially antagonistic authority about a religious conversion may prove a source of serious intimidation, particularly for those unfamiliar with dealing with political authorities.

The provisions of Article 5 in the Gujarat, Madhya Pradesh and Chhattisgarh anti-conversion laws, and clause 5 of the rules of the Orissa law are a source of intimidation and as such constitute an effective obstacle to their freedom of faith.

Article 5 of the Gujarat law stipulates that a religious priest or participant in a ceremony of conversion must seek permission from the District Magistrate for this ceremony, and that the converted person must send intimation to the District Magistrate about their conversion. The proposed amendments to the Madhya Pradesh and Chhattisgarh laws require an intimation to be sent by the priest and prospective converts to the District Magistrate one month before a conversion ceremony may take place. Clause 5 of the rules of the Orissa law requires that a priest send a prior intimation of the conversion ceremony to the District Magistrate, and stipulates that the District Magistrate must inform relevant police authorities, who 'shall ascertain objection, if any, to the proposed conversion by local inquiry and intimate the same to the District Magistrate'.

In creating, an intimidating obstacle to religious conversion, the stipulations of Article 5 in both the Gujarat and Madhya Pradesh/Chhattisgarh laws, and clause 5 in the rules of the Orissa law, is, therefore, discordant with the right to adopt a religion.

It is also feared by Christian representatives in Gujarat that Article 5 could allow for the collection of religious demographic information, which could be used for the monitoring of religious minority communities. This concern has existed since 1998, when Gujarat police undertook to gather religious demographic information in the Dangs district, prior to the violent anti-Christian demonstrations.

Requirement of Notice/Prior Permission

Most Freedom of religion Acts in India require the person converting to give details of his or her conversion to the District Magistrate prior to the conversion ceremony. The Gujarat law states that the person seeking to be converted must take prior permission from the concerned District Magistrate before any conversion ceremony is performed.

The Acts, therefore, greatly impinge on the freedom of conscience of a prospective covert and on their right to privacy. The person is rendered incapable of taking the final decision about his or her faith and instead requires the seal of approval of the local district authority.

This approach is aggravated if such a Freedom of Religion Act awards specific protection to the state government and its officers against prosecution or legal proceedings with regard to 'anything done in good faith or intended to be done under the Act or any rule made thereunder.' Moreover, it seems unclear who may bring an action for, or lodge an appeal against, decisions with regard to the permissibility of a religious conversion.

Exemption of Reconversion

None of the laws includes 're-conversion' under its definition. This category is used by Hindu fundamentalist groups to describe their own proselytism. Because the legislation does not stipulate conditions for re-conversions, it, therefore, inherently tends in favour of Hinduism and against minority religions.

Similarly, the definition of conversion as the renunciation of an indigenous religion and adoption of another, as used in the Arunachal Pradesh law, reflects an inherent prejudice against religions perceived as non-Indic, but also, therefore, restricts the freedom of adherents to 'indigenous religions' to adopt a religion according to choice. Indigenous religions are defined as the religions, beliefs, and practices, which are 'sanctioned, approved [or] performed' by the indigenous communities of Arunachal Pradesh, including Buddhism, Vaishnavism (a principal division of Hinduism) and 'nature worship'.

Social Impact of Legislation

It is important to consider the social impact of the various Freedom of Religion Acts alongside the legal analysis. This provides an important test of the restrictions imposed by such legislation on freedom of faith. The importance of this factor is heightened by the fact that many Christian priests, nuns, pastors and preachers have been harassed under this Freedom of Religion Acts in India.

The assessment of the social impact of anti-conversion legislation requires a caste-based analysis of religious freedom in India. *Dalits* and tribals are the primary victims of religious persecution and discrimination in India, as the agenda of right wing conservative *Hindutva* pertains largely to the preservation of the caste order. Religious freedom is perceived among many

Dalit and tribal groups as an important factor in their emancipation movement, but it is threatened by discrimination and religiously motivated violence.

The factor of caste is, therefore, relevant to the various Freedom of Religion Acts, not only within their provisions but also in terms of their social impact. Orissa, Madhya Pradesh, Chhattisgarh and Gujarat laws stipulate higher penal provisions when an offence is committed in respect of a member of the Scheduled Castes or Scheduled Tribes, and the Rajasthan law uniquely defines a person's religion as that of their ancestors, which, according to some critics, is aimed at containing *Dalits* and tribals within the caste system. However, the experiences of religious minority adherents 13 Penal provisions for the equivalent article in the other anti-conversion laws, applying to adult males who do not belong to the Scheduled Castes or Scheduled Tribes.

Situation in states, which have, enacted anti-conversion legislation indicates that the laws have created a climate in which their religious freedom is further threatened and impeded. An important objection to the various laws relates to the climate of intimidation, which they generate, and the consequent vulnerability of minority religious groups. The rhetoric of 'conversions' carried out by 'force' or 'fraud' is used by right wing extremist groups against Christians in particular; this rhetoric is given credence when enshrined in legislation.[15]

The states in India in which anti-conversion legislation has been enacted, particularly Orissa, Madhya Pradesh, Chhattisgarh, Gujarat, and Rajasthan have continued to see considerable violence against religious minority groups, particularly Christians, through 2000s. The rationale for many attacks is given as opposition to activities undertaken by the victims, allegedly to convert people.

With reference to the promulgation of a Freedom of Religion Act in Rajasthan, this must be viewed in the context of the intensified attacks perpetrated against the Christian minority in the state in mid-2000s. In particular, the widespread attacks on various institutions of Emmanuel Mission International, apparently committed with the complicity of the state administration, provide the backdrop for its introduction.

A two-member team of the National Commission for Minorities in India comprising Harcharan Singh Josh and Lama Chosphel Zotpa, after their visit to the states of Madhya Pradesh and Chhattisgarh between June 13 and 18, 2007 noted that Hindu extremists frequently invoked the anti-conversion law in Madhya Pradesh and Chhattisgarh as a means of inciting mobs against Christians or having them arrested without evidence.[16]

The report stated that:

> "Obviously, the life of Christians has become miserable at the hands of miscreants in connivance with the police,...There are allegations that when atrocities were committed on Christians by the miscreants, police remained mere spectators and in certain cases they did not even register FIRs [First Information Reports]."

The extent of violence and anarchy that came to prevail in India in the name of 'anti conversion laws' is probably unparalleled anywhere else in the world. These laws have tarnished peaceful social fabrics even in the areas where traditionally Hindus and minorities have lived in harmony for many centuries.

The freedom of religion Acts have induced a new parameter in underlying moral premise that conversion itself is an immoral act which seeks to uproot an individual from one religion and transplant him into another, thus devaluing both the religion and the person. It does not take into account the possibility that the conversion can be motivated by *bona fide* intentions and an actual change of heart or acceptance of the belief propagated by that religion.

Critique of the Acts

The various laws are widely considered an affront to religious freedom, and in violation both of India's obligations under international laws and her domestic constitutional protections with regard to the adoption, practice, and propagation of religion. Of particular concern are the loose definitions in the laws, which are seen as creating wide potential for their misuse (Tahmina Arora, 2015). The seemingly disproportionate magnitude of punitive provisions is another cause of concern.

While minority religious commentators in India have been quick to denounce any unscrupulous, coercive, or unethical attempts to convert, which are indeed prohibited in Article 18(2) of the International Covenant on Civil and Political Rights (ICCPR), they have also articulated deep concern about a number of flaws inherent to the legislation, and about its social impact.

The primary critique of the Acts has come from several jurists due to their vague and overtly broad definitions. Asma Jahangir the United Nations Special Rapporteur on Freedom for Religion or Belief has stated in her report[17]:

> "While these laws appear to protect religious adherents only from attempts to induce conversion by improper means, they have been criticized on the ground that the failure to clearly define what makes a conversion improper bestows on the authorities unfettered discretion to accept or reject the legitimacy of religious conversions. All of these laws include in the definition of use of force any 'threat of divine displeasure or social excommunication.' Moreover, the terms inducement or allurement are defined to include the offer of any gift or gratification, either in cash or in kind, as well as the grant of any benefit, either pecuniary or otherwise.
>
> These broad and vague terms might be interpreted to cover the expression of many religious beliefs.
>
> In addition, some provisions are discriminatory in giving preferential treatment to re-conversions, for example by stipulating that returning to the forefathers' original religion or to one's own original religion shall not be construed as conversion."

In March 2007, the National Commission for Minorities noted with concern the enactment of the Himachal Pradesh Freedom of Religion Act and observed that "the terminology used in the [Himachal Pradesh Freedom of Religion] Act and the methodology prescribed for implementing it" and the "attempt of the Act, and reportedly by similar pieces of legislation contemplated in some other States, to interfere with the basic right of freedom of religion that is the birthright of every Indian."[18]

The anti-conversion laws in India say that a person must take prior permission and give advance notice before changing his religion. The United Nations Special Rapporteur on Freedom of Religion or Belief, Asma Jahangir, noted in her report that:

"...The requirement of advance notice or prior permission seems to be unduly onerous for the individual who intends to convert. Any state inquiry into the substantive beliefs and motivation for conversion is highly problematic since it may lead to interference with the internal and private realm of the individual's belief (*forum internum*).

She also said that:

"Any concern raised with regard to certain conversions or how they might be accomplished should primarily be raised by the alleged victim."

The provisions of the Acts fail to provide any safety mechanisms for those on whom they are casting a burden to disclose sensitive information.[19]

Article 18 of the Universal Declaration of Human Rights distinguishes the freedom of thought, conscience, religion or belief from the freedom to manifest religion or belief.

It does not permit any limitations whatsoever on the freedom of thought and conscience or on the freedom to have or adopt a religion or belief of one's choice.[20]

Judicial Review of Anti-Conversion Laws

The Orissa Freedom of Religion Act, 1967 and the Madhya Pradesh Dharma Swatantra Adhiniyam, 1968 went through several levels of judicial scrutiny. Orissa High Court declared the Act passed by the Orissa Assembly *ultra vires* to the Constitution, as it infringed upon the Right guaranteed by Article 25.

The ruling cited Entry 97 of the Union List under the Seventh Schedule to the Constitution and stated that the state legislature had no 'legislative competence' to enact such a law on matters concerning religion. Madhya Pradesh High Court upheld the Madhya Pradesh Freedom of Religion Act.

The Supreme Court, in 1977, heard appeals against these two verdicts in *Rev. Stainislaus* v. *State of Madhya Pradesh and others*. The five member Bench considered the literal meaning of the word 'propagate' and upheld the two Acts. In this case, the Court made a clear distinction between the right to propagate one's religion or faith and the right to convert. The former is guaranteed by Article 25 of Constitution. Conversion enjoys no such protection.[21]

The Court's words are worth noting: "The freedom of religion enshrined in Article 25 is not guaranteed in respect of one religion only but covers all religions alike which can be properly enjoyed by a person if he exercises his right in a manner commensurate with the like freedom of persons following other religion. What is freedom for one is freedom for the other in equal measure and there can, therefore, be no such thing as a fundamental right to convert any person to one's own religion."

Discussion

Today faith base hostilities have increased all-around the world. Although freedom of religion and belief was formally recognized in the Universal Declaration of Human Rights 1948 (UDHR), and the United Nations appointed its first Special Rapporteur on Religious Intolerance and adopted a second declaration on religious intolerance in 1993. There are reports of denial of religious freedom across the globe. There are multiple reasons for this, while the larger consequences of such developments are unknown, what is clear is that religious liberty has become a key site of legal and political struggles to negotiate communal relations across lines of religious difference. The subject of religious freedom is multifaceted, whether seen from the political, philosophical, or legal points of view.

The controversy with regard to the right to propagation of religion has always existed and is a particularly live issue in our country. There were Bills and Acts in relation to religious conversion even before the independence in princely states of India. After independence some states enacted "Freedom of religion Acts" which are popularly referred to as anti-conversion laws. These Acts once again brought the issue of proselytisation and conversion to the centre of debate particularly after violence against Christians in the Dang area of Gujarat in 1998. Debates over the boundaries of religion and "religious activity" occur in legal discussions of whether proselytizing is essential to the practice of certain religions and thus protected by the right to freedom of religion. This question is central to determining the constitutionality of state laws limiting conversion in India, often entitled "Freedom of Religion" laws. Do these laws protect the religious freedom of groups that are "vulnerable" to missionary inducements, or are they restricting the freedom of citizens to propagate their religion to others or to change their own religious identity?

Anti-conversion legislations, euphemistically called Freedom of Religion laws, adopted by several Indian states have been the subject of much scrutiny.

In 1968, the State of Orissa enacted the Orissa Freedom of Religious Act. It said that "no person shall convert or attempt to convert either directly or otherwise any person from one religious faith to another by the use of force or by inducement or by any fraudulent means nor shall any person abet any such conversion." Punishment for contravention of the prohibition was imprisonment of up to one year and/or a fine of up to Rs. 5,000. In the case of a minor, a woman, or a person belonging to a Scheduled Caste or Tribe, the punishment was up to two years of imprisonment and the limit of the fine raised up to Rs. 10,000.

Many Christian denominations protested. They said propagation of the Christian faith was an essential part of Christianity. The High Court in Orissa accepted this but said that Article 25 did not protect conversion by force since this would be contrary to public order.

Nevertheless, the right to convert by inducement was affirmed because "the definition of the term 'inducement' is vague and many proselytizing activities may be converged by the definition." The Act itself was struck down as a whole, however, on the ground that the state legislature did not have the right to legislate matters of religion. At about the same time another state, Madhya Pradesh, enacted the Madhya Pradesh Dharma Swatantra Adhiniyam, 1968, which also sought to restrain conversion by "force, fraud, and allurement." Some Christians said that the provisions violate their fundamental rights under Article 25 challenged the M.P. Act. The Madhya Pradesh High Court rejected their argument. The decision of the two High Courts were challenged before the Supreme Court. The Supreme Court upheld the decision of the Madhya Pradesh High Court and reversed the decision of the Orissa High Court. It was said "What is freedom for one is freedom for the other in equal measure, and there can be, therefore, no such thing as fundamental right to convert any person to one's own religion" and that the state legislatures were competent to enact such laws.

The decision of the Supreme Court was widely criticised and even Justice Ruma Pal (Retd.) Judge of the Supreme Court opined that the judgement ignored the legislative history of Article 25 and that the Supreme Court did not draw a distinction between conversion by force and conversion by persuasion.

Article 25(1) confers freedom of religion—a freedom not limited to the religion in which a person is born. Freedom of conscience harmonizes with this, for its presence in Article 25(1) shows that our Constitution has adopted a "system which allowed free choice of religion" The right to propagate religion gives a meaning to freedom of choice, for choice involves not only knowledge but an act of will. A person cannot choose if he does not know, what choices are open to him. To propagate religion is not only to impart knowledge and to spread it more widely, but to produce intellectual and moral conviction leading to action, namely, the adoption of that religion.[22]

An analysis of the legislations reveals that the language used is often extraordinarily broad and vague, posing serious challenges to religious freedom as guaranteed by the Constitution of India and enshrined in international human rights instruments.[23]

Freedom of Religion Acts does not ban conversion outright as such but are inconsistent with India's secular Constitution, which subscribes to the right of freedom of religion. What they do enact is the illegality of conversions by force, fraud, or allurement. As the South Asian Human Rights Documentation Centre (SAHRDC) has pointed out, definitions of force, fraud and allurement are often vague, imprecise, and the, "danger of discriminatory abuse in their application" is very real (2008). Instead, the "terminology used by these legislations transforms them from their purported role as protectors of constitutional rights into violators of these very guarantees". Furthermore, as the SAHRDC points out, what these Acts do is legitimize violence against Christian and other minorities' religious identities, which are deemed non-indigenous to India. These laws in various states provide the governments and other anti-Christian's fundamentalist individuals and communities the 'legitimacy' to harass the minority communities particularly Christians to suit their political opportunism (Kanjamala, 2014).

Two major concerns have arisen from the penal provisions stipulated in the various laws: the seemingly disproportionate magnitude of the punishments, and the fact that more severe punishments may be exacted where the law is contravened with respect to a woman, a minor, or a member of the Scheduled Castes or Scheduled Tribes. In Orissa, Madhya Pradesh, Chhattisgarh and Gujarat state laws, the punitive provisions (including both prison terms and fines) are extended for any person found guilty of attempting to convert a person belonging to these categories.[24]

Dalit rights groups in India have, therefore, suggested that the chief aim of anti-conversion legislation is the prevention of *Dalits* and tribals from embracing a new faith. This alleged goal would closely reflect the agenda of the Hindu fundamentalist 'Sangh Parivar' groups, including the Rashtriya Swayamsevak Sangh (RSS) and its affiliate organisation, the Vishwa Hindu Parishad (VHP). Sangh Parivar groups have long been implicated in widespread violence against Christians, particularly those of *Dalit* background, throughout India. The RSS 'controls' the Hindu nationalist Bharatiya Janata Party (BJP), which has recently been responsible for introducing the Rajasthan and Gujarat law, and which promised to introduce a nationwide anti-conversion law, before losing power in the 2004 General Election.

The anti-conversion laws have been enacted on the basis that conversions by force, fraud, or inducement disrupt public order. However, the Indian Penal Code carries enough provisions to deal with it, such as Section 153A, which prohibits: promoting by words or symbols "feelings of enmity, hatred or ill-will" against religious groups, committing acts prejudicial to the harmony of religious groups, or organizing activities with the intent that participants train to use force or actually use force against religious groups. The punishment for these offenses is increased if they occur in a place of worship or at a religious ceremony.

According to Dr. John Dayal, long time campaigner for minority rights and Secretary-General of the All India Christian Council many states, particularly in northern India, want to enact anti-conversion laws to appease local rightwing groups affiliated to the RSS, and the Bharatiya Janata Party. The BJP has made it known it will bring about a national legislation to curb the activities of what it calls "missionaries", and to bring proselytizing to an end.

The bane of the Christian community has been anti-conversion laws, ironically called Freedom of Religion Acts, which brought officialdom firmly into a process that was otherwise between a person and his conscience. Six states have these laws; another has enacted but not implemented them. The BJP said in its election campaign it intends to make this a national law. Governmental permission and severe penalties are the cutting edge of these laws. Political parties, barring perhaps the Marxists and even the Supreme Court of India tend to agree to the need of the anti-conversion laws. The UN Human Rights Council, European Union, and international freedom of faith organizations have called them a grave violation of the UN Universal Declaration of Human Rights.

The so-called "Freedom of Religion Acts" smack of religious nationalism and religious racism. These acts on 'Freedom of Religion' can be equated with the South African Apartheid Law of 1948. India's civil society, judiciary, legislature and executive, as well as the international community, need to work towards the repealing or striking down of these laws as they threaten not only the Indian ethos of tolerance and communal harmony but also set a dangerous precedence for other nations in the area of religious freedom.

In globalizing future religious liberty has emerged as a major challenge in the twenty-first century. The creation and proliferation of new technologies and modes of communications manifest encomiums to the liberating powers of technology and communications, a less acknowledged but more pernicious fact may be how those technologies can be used to constrict liberty, particularly religious freedom.

Advances in the quality, efficiency, and especially accessibility of Internet based communication technologies including video production, online networking, and mobile device delivery are being used by religious militants to promote their perverse agendas of violence and religious intolerance. The use of globalization's new technologies for oppressions not confined to governments security services but organization promoting communal hatred and intolerance who have proven remarkably adept at adapting new communication and media technologies for their own purposes of fomenting religious intolerance. Internet forums, interactive websites, television, and especially propaganda videos produced rapidly and disseminated *via* mobile phone and the Internet have all become indispensable elements in the national conservative forces arsenal to publicise its views, agenda, campaign' counter criticism and stigmatize and even incite violence against other religious groups or the perceived enemies (most often minorities). All of these actions are deeply inimical to the culture of pluralism and religious liberty.

Conclusion

A detailed analysis of India's 'Freedom of Religion Acts' reveals that, far from promoting or protecting religious freedom, they have served to undermine the religious freedom guarantees under the Constitution of India and international laws and the Covenants to which India is a signatory. These anti-conversion laws have also been emulated by other countries in South Asia particularly Nepal, Bhutan, and Sri Lanka. The introduction of similar provisions in the other South Asian legal systems is a disturbing trend and requires the attention of the international community, as they stand in direct contrast to the rights and liberties guaranteed under many international laws and UN conventions.

The UN Rapporteur recommended that laws and Bills on religious conversion in several Indian states should be reconsidered since they raise serious human rights concerns. Yet, the laws are still in place. And there is every likelihood that these 'freedom of religion' laws will remain on statue books of India as there is no political party which can now dare to repeal them. These laws are like Albatross around the neck of Indian secularism.

In sum, the prevalence of anti-conversion laws constitutes a decisive shift in the language of legitimacy regarding the freedom of religion.

Notes

1. Pandey, Ravi Bhushan (2005). *Christianity, and Tribes in India,* Delhi: Academic Excellent.
2. Boulanger State at that time was part of Bihar State but later merged with the state of Orissa in 1956.
3. Bandyopadhyay, Madhumita (2006). *Contesting for Space: A Study of Consequences of Non-Tribal Migration into Tribal Homeland,* Chota Nagpur: Rajat Publications.
4. Ghosh, Sanjoy (2001). *Unsustainable Laws,* The Lawyers Collective.
5. Premawardhana, Shanta (2015). *Religious Conversions: Religion Scholars Thinking Together,* UK: John Wiley & Sons.

6. Paylee, M.V. (2000). *Our Constitution, Government, and Politics*, Delhi: Universal Law Publishing.
7. Bakshi, P.M. and Subash C. Kashyap (2012). *The Constitution of India*, Delhi: Universal Law Publishing.
8. Sen, Amartya (2005). *The Argumentative Indian: Writings on Indian History, Culture, and Identity*, UK: Penguin.
9. *Ibid*.
10. Sharma, G. (2014). "Freedom of religion's comparative study between India and the United States", *International Research Journal of Commerce, Arts and Science*.
11. Niyogi Committee Report 1956, Government of Madhya Pradesh.
12. Arora, Tahmina, *India's Defiance of Religious Freedom: A Briefing on Anti Conversion Laws*, IIRF, BONN.
13. AIR 1973 Ori. 116.
14. 1977 (1) Supreme Court Cases 677.
15. Suleman, Saadiya (2010). "Freedom of Religion and Anti-Conversion Laws in India: An Overview", (February 1, 2010). Indian Law Institute, *Law Review*, Vol. 1, No. 1.
16. *State in India Tightens Controls on Conversions*, Compass News Direct, July 25, 2006.
17. A/HRC/10/8/Add.3, p. 17.
18. The full press release is available at the National Commission for Minorities website at http://ncm.nic.in/The-Himachal-Pradesh-Freedom-of-Religion-Act.html (last accessed on November 11, 2011).
19. Human Rights Committee, General Comment 22, Article 18 (Forty-eighth session, 1993). Compilation of General Comments and General Recommendations Adopted by Human Rights Treaty Bodies, U.N. Doc. HRI/GEN/1/Rev.1 at 35.
20. Shourie, Arun (2000). *Harvesting Our Souls*, New Delhi: ASA Publications.
21. Larson, Gerald James (2001). *Religion and Personal Law in Secular India: A Call to Judgment*, Indiana University Press.
22. Sreevai, H.M. (1978). *Constitutional Law of India*, Bombay: N.M. Tripathi Publication.
23. Chin, Peter Dan, Winifred F. Sullivan, Saba Mahmood, and Elizabeth S. Hurd (2014). "Politics of Religious Freedom: Case studies", 29 *Md. J. Int'l L.* 293.
24. Onnudottir, Helena and Adam Possamai (2016). *Religious Change and Indigenous Peoples: The Making of Religious Identities*, Routledge.

PART II
SPRINGS UNCOILED

We should be alert to the fact that missionaries have but one goal—that of harvesting us or the Church, and they have developed a very well-knit, powerful, extremely well empowered organizational Network for attaining that singular goal. Their 'spiritual quest' for power and control, their commercial interests are well intertwined with they are in fact dependent on that one goal—converse.

—*Arun Shourie, Harvesting Our Souls* (1994)

Denying the pluralistic cultural heritage and the right of the poor to developmental resources, these forces strike out against anyone who disturbs *status quo*. The Church and the Christian community is a special target because of its long-standing work in empowerment of the poor, the marginalised, the *Dalits*, women, and tribals.

—*Archbishop Alan de Lastic* and *K Rajaaratnam*

Joint statement of Catholic Church and various Protestant denominations on February 2, 1999.

4

Under the Shadow of the Empire

Setting the Agenda 1950s-1960s

Introduction

After the Independence, many rightwing religious groups demanded a series of discontinuation between pre- and post-Independence era. There was discussion about, those who were loyal to Indian tradition and those Westernised; between Indian-ness and foreign-ness, all of which hinged on Hindu *dharma.* Missionary work was regarded not only intrusion undermining confidence in Hindu groups' ideology but also a political scandal because it allowed the continuation of foreign influence and dominance even after the Independence.

Although the idea of secular India was widely shared by the political leaders, particularly where the relationship between then state and religious communities was concerned and the Constitution of India also guaranteed, "the right to freedom of religion", which it defines to include "freedom of conscience and the right freely to profess, practice and propagate religion", its actual implementation has not always between without tension and struggle. India recognized Vatican as a state and accepted its religious representative both as an ambassador of Vatican and head of spiritual leader of organized Catholic Church in India in 1952. This caused severe heartburn among conservative nationalist leaders as they saw this as 'divided loyalty problem'.

In the run up to and aftermath of Partition, the RSS greatly expanded its reach and influence in northern India. The communal riots had deeply polarised community and public opinion, as had Pakistan's invasion of Kashmir. A campaign top target the enemy within and the enemy without attracted considerable support in an atmosphere of tension and suffering. In the 1950s and 1960s as tempers cooled in northern India, Golwalkar and the RSS worked to make their presence felt in the southern parts of the country. Golwalkar identified Muslims as unreliable fifth column who threatened the unity and strength of the Hindu nation. He counted them as the chief among three enemies—the others as noted, being Christians and Communists (Guha, 2011). He was particularly bitter about Muslims. The Niyogi Report and the visit of Pope Paul VI to India in 1964 raised alarm in the RSS circle and demand for anti-conversion law grew in India. Ultimately, first such law was introduced in 1967. These laws were challenge to the Constitutional provisions on freedom of religion in India.

Secularism in Independent India

Hinduism, in the sense of Hindu identity, played an ambiguous role in politics after Independence. Jawaharlal Nehru (1889-1964), the first Prime Minister of India from 1947 until his death in 1964 was an ardent advocate of secular identity that favoured secular socialist policies to develop an India within which people could worship as they wished. Nehru's understanding of secularism was reflected in the Hindi word he used *dharmnirpeksh* for it. This gives a sense of 'not being aligned with any religion'. This was quite different from the term coined by Gandhi in 1932 for secularism, which was *sarva dharma sambhava,* which means holding similar sentiments for all religions. It is also notable that the BJP later rejected Nehru's Hindi word for secularism and adopted Gandhi's point of view to some decree. Nehru's position was reminiscent of that of Ashok, India's legendary emperor, as his state fostered the growth of all religions in India, and in particular the Indic religions of Hinduism, Buddhism, and Jainism.

The Congress, which was the dominant party, tried to follow strictly the concept of unity in diversity envisioned by the Founding Fathers as the only way to strengthen an integrated and untied India. However, India in January 1966 was in a worse shape than it had ever been under either Nehru or Shastri. Severe droughts had led to food shortages and famine conditions in large parts of the country. This generated unrest, especially in Kerala where there were 'rice riots'. The economy was flagging with rampant inflation and a shortage of foreign exchange. There was agitation in the Punjab for a separate Punjabi speaking state. The Naga people of the North-East were threatening secession. Kashmir was also on the boil.

There were further troubles. In November 1966, a mob of thousands of *trishul* (trident) bearing, naked *sadhus* (holy men) staged a demonstration in front of Parliament calling for ban on cow slaughter. The religion was casting its shadow on secular India. The Congress Party under Indira Gandhi won 1967 federal level general elections but in eight states, Samyukta Vidhayak Dal (SVD) governments were formed.

During the early years of Independence, the presence of foreign missionaries involved in the medical and social work was generally accepted and appreciated by the majority of Hindus in India and other religious minorities. Conversion was seen as going out and getting rid of 'undesirable elements away from Hindu fold for good'.

It was the time when UN discussion and debates were full of talk of religious freedom and right to convert to any faith a person wanted to. It is due to this globally prevailing environment that immediately after Independence, India allowed foreign missionaries from philanthropic point of view. However, the fact that the number of foreign missionaries were increasing and that the conversion of tribal communities in North East Frontier (which is linked to Naga militancy), *adivasis* of central India and 'backward classes' made the government anxious about the foreign missionaries and their activities.

It was also the time when *adivasi* leader Jaipal Singh raised demand for homeland for tribals was increasing sent chill to the government that another militant struggle on the pattern of Nagaland might develop in Chotanagpur (now in Jharkhand area). This fear among the Government circle lead to severe restriction on giving Visa to foreign missionaries in 1960s. The Ministry of Home Affairs announced the intention to restrict the entry of foreign missionaries henceforth.

I. Niyogi Committee Report (1954-1956)

In April 1953 Kailash Nath Katju, the Home Minister, commented in the Lok Sabha that, although foreign missionaries were welcome, it would be undesirable if any of them is found indulged in 'proselytization'. He also stated that he had received several allegations that foreign missionaries were engaged in *dharma parivartan* (proselytizing) activities in the Surguja and Raigarh districts of Madhya Pradesh, and that an enquiry was desirable.

Eventually, on April 16, 1954, the Madhya Pradesh government announced the launch of an enquiry into missionary activities. The Government press release stated that the government had often received complaints against illegitimate means of converting people and that, on the other hand, missionaries also alleged harassment by non-Christians: hence, an enquiry headed by Bhawani Shankar Niyogi, retired Chief Justice of Nagpur High Court, and all members were Hindus except S.K. George, a Syrian Christian to which other Christians objected.

The Niyogi Committee was appointed to enquiry into any 'political and extra religious objectives' in missionary work by examining missionary activities in the light of 'a thorough review of the question from the historical and other points of view' and to make recommendations to the government for necessary action.

The fact that the enquiry into missionary activities was launched in Madhya Pradesh was not only because of the missionaries in the area but also, more significantly, due to the state's particular socio-political background. The inauguration of the Constitution in January 1950 and the amalgamation of certain princely areas into Madhya Pradesh meant that the 'anti-conversion' laws of these states were no longer 'valid'. After Independence, the Christian missionaries started to enter these areas, and began to work among the tribals. However, the authorities of the former princely states regarded the entrance of missionaries as intrusion on the autonomy that they had maintained even during the British Raj. The Christian leadership challenged these by appealing openly to enter these states for missionaries work, as they believed the local authorities were violating the constitutional rights of the Christians.

As the committee set to work with the full support of the state government, they faced furious opposition from Christians, especially the Catholic community. When the Madhya Pradesh government first announced its enquiry committee, the Catholic Regional conference immediately responded by questioning the legitimacy of such a committee. From then onwards, the relationship between the enquiry committee and the Catholic community gradually grew worse. The Catholic Bishops' Conference of India expressed its 'deep concern' over the situation in Madhya Pradesh and made a strong objection to the committee; they insisted that the propagation of faith by missionaries was guaranteed in the Constitution.

The Catholic Church's main objection were: First, the *adivasis* and other lower caste people were not free to testify to the enquiry committee for fear of retaliation from Hindus unless some protection was given. Second, since Hindu organisations and other denominations were involved in conversion activities, it was not fair for the government to take up an enquiry into Christian missionaries activities only. Moreover, the government must have given chance to the missionaries to explain their point of view. Third, the composition of the enquiry committee was five Hindus and only one Syrian Christian, who the Catholic Church argued had no *locus standi* to represent Christians (St. Thomas or Syrian Christians in Kerala existed in India before the arrival of Portuguese and were not under Pope). Fourth, on some occasions during the enquiry, speeches were allowed and in some cases, Hindus made accusations against Christians and commented provocatively on the missionaries.[1]

One strong critic came from Eugene D'Souza, the Archbishop of Nagpur (who later was shifted to Bhopal). This writer met him on three times and he commented *Dharmantaran ki jagah hridaya parivartan shabd use hona chahiya*). Speaking on behalf of the Catholic Community of Madhya Pradesh, he expressed his regret that it appeared that the 'whole community is on trial' and that the fundamental rights stated in the Constitution were questioned, and declared that the Catholic community would not cooperate with the enquiry committee any longer.

In spite of the opposition and non-cooperation of the Catholics, the committee continued to conduct the questionnaire as well as tour of different regions to cross-examine the written response. The Committee eventually submitted the first volume of its report to the government on April 18, 1956. It was published later the same year, which made a 939-page document in all.[2]

The Making of Niyogi Report

The Committee examined published books, pamphlets and periodicals, utilized the results extensive interviews, questioning, and cross-examinations and exhibited remarkable knowledge of Christian documents on missionary activities. The committee also thoroughly examined Christian critiques of missionary activity, Hindu rereading of history, and documents produced by Christian conferences. The committee used Christian writer's opinions extensively. Roland Allen's criticism of the attitude of Western missionaries towards the people of the mission fields, the dependency of the national Christians on the missionaries, and the 'professionalism' of the missionaries were frequently referred to by the Committee. Another report extensively used by the Committee was William Laymen's Enquiry, which particularly questioned the exclusive claim of Christianity in spite of the existence of other religious traditions and the use of social and educational means for conversion.

Taking a leaf from K.M. Panikkar's *Asia and Western Dominance* (Panikkar, 1953), the Committee also stressed that contemporary missionary activities were continuation of Western imperialism. The Niyogi Report at several places emphasised and tried to point out that the various missionary activities were aimed not only at the conversion of the Indian people. Nevertheless, were also art of a Western Christian agenda to further their influence in India. A brief summary of the report is needed in order to understand the debates that followed thereafter.

Main Findings

Going through the Report one gets the impression that the Niyogi Report first tried to establish that religious liberty under the Constitution of India is not without conditions. It argued that, since the preamble to the Constitution begins with 'We, the people of India...' the fundamental rights are meant for its citizens primarily and that the rights of citizens and foreigners ought to be different—as their duties. On the issue of secular state, the committee insisted that, in India, secularism keeps 'equal regard for all religions and no discrimination in favour of any other' and the Constitution guarantees 'equality to all religions', but at the same time it warned that if the followers of any religion deny this equal right, it is the 'duty of the state' to keep public orders and solidarity."[3]

Most significant conclusion of the Niyogi Report was that:

> "Freedom to propagate religions confers a right not only on the preacher, but also corresponding personal right on the listener to accept any religion he deems fit or right."[4]

Examining the source of finance the Committee found that most Christian work depends on overseas donations received by the various mission organizations and churches from the West, and it was with this considerable financial assistance that the mission organizations were "carrying on proselytization amongst backward tribes, especially in areas freshly opened". The Niyogi Report also gave detail of foreign funds received by the missionaries in India between 1950 and 1954.

The report pointed out that the money brought into India was not merely for educational or medical work: a large share went to "professional proselytizers, foreign and indigenous". The Committee found that almost all the missions employed national *pracharaks* (preacher or catechists) whose main role was securing converts. Their entire livelihood depended on the mission from which they received a salary.

Commenting on the intention of running various social services and educational and medical services, the Committee argued that the missionaries' intention was conversion through evangelism using the various means of hospitals, schools, and orphanages. They examined number of patients who were converted in various Christian hospitals and orphanages and concluded that most conversions were brought about in "expectation of social service benefits and other material considerations". Money-lending practices carried by some Catholic missions were strongly attacked in the report. However, the main problem of the methods of propagating Christianity was the abuse of Hindu deities by the missionaries and the *pracharaks* as they tried to convince the people of the truth of Christianity. Furthermore, it appeared to the Committee that attacks on the Hindu religion and its deities were not occasional but 'an important and integral plank of Christian propaganda' and that they, therefore, provoked the Hindu violence against them.

The Committee insisted that, "the only motive that brings Christian Missionaries away from their homes... is the urge to carry out Christ's command [to convert others]". They acknowledged the Christian claim that conversion was an act of God, and that religion should be an individual matter of the free choice, but objected to it on the grounds that they had discovered the large majority had not converted in 'the real sense of the term' but from ulterior motives. This was underlined in their assessment of the motives of conversion:

> "It is true that material inducements are not offered in all cases directly but by way systematic parading of their wealth and power, grants of liberal loans, preferential treatment to Christians in hospitals and schools and various other methods of propaganda, a general impression is created in the minds of simple aboriginal [*sic*] that the only way to escape from material poverty is... embrace Christianity."

Recommendations and Reactions

Of the principal recommendations made in the Niyogi report, the first point is, "that missionary whose primary object is proselytization should be asked to withdraw. The large influx of foreign missionaries is undesirable and should be checked." A related recommendation calls for an amendment to the Constitution specifying that the right to propagate religion apply only to citizens of India.

Another recommendation is that law very similar to one enforce in Greece be enacted. The effect of such legislation would be to eliminate the propaganda of religion. The report states that "any attempt or effort (whether successful or not), directly or indirectly to penetrate into the religious conscious of persons (whether of age or underage) of another faith, for the purpose of consciously alerting their religious conscience or faith, so as to agree with the ideas or convictions of the proselytizing party should be absolutely prohibited."[5] The Report makes no mention of a constitutional amendment at this point, but it is quite clear that the Article 25 would have to undergo vital changes if such legislation were to be enacted.

Another recommendation urges a piece of advice on the Indian Christians: "The best course for the Indian churches to follow is to establish a United Independent Christian Church in India without being dependent on foreign support."

The Report recommends the creation of a department of cultural and religious affairs in the state government, with powers of censorship. "Circulation of literature meant for religious propaganda without approval of the state government should be prohibited." An Indian writer saw in these proposals the end of the cherished ideal of the secular state. According to M.M. Thomas, such steps would initiate the process of making the state "the final arbiter of the religious and cultural life of the citizens".

Other recommendations are that the state government be solely responsible for maintaining orphanages and for providing education, health and other services for members of the SCs and STs. It is also specified that unofficial organizations should not be permitted to operate intuitions only for members of same faith, if at all—only with the prior approval of the state. In view of the fact that there are constant requests from the public to enlarge the services of these institutions, "we can easily imagine the reaction that a policy of exclusive would evoke among the people in general."[6]

In summary, the report recommended that: (1) missionaries whose main object is conversion 'should be asked to withdraw' and their entry to the country should be monitored, (2) use of any professional services as a means of making converts should be prohibited by law; (3) an amendment of Article 25 of the Constitution was needed to limit the fundamental rights to Indian citizens only, and clarify that it does not include conversion brought about by undue means; (4) suitable controls should be implemented on conversions brought about through illegal means, and if necessary legislative measures should be enacted; (5) distribution of literature for propaganda without the approval of the state government should be prohibited.

The report demonstrated the thoroughness of the Committee's research and their clear objection to Christian mission in general and to Christian conversion in particular. However, the report's serious shortcomings—such as unclear objectives and terms of references, its partisan approach to the subjects, a lack of fair treatment of the material and questionnaire, and the uncritical use of witness—led to furious criticism from Christians, especially from Catholics.

Nine distinguished non-Christian leaders issued a statement in November 1956, which paid tribute "to the high standards of integrity and public service generally maintained by Christian missionaries in their work."

Dr. A. Krishnaswami, a Member of Parliament, was among the nine non-Christian signatories to a statement, which took note of the "indiscriminate and extravagant attacks on missionaries" although it did not mention the Niyogi Report by name.

In considering these recommendations—banning of conversion, rigid control of religious literature by a department of cultural and religious affairs, the total absorption of social services by the state—M.M. Thomas asserted that the implications of the Niyogi report go far beyond the question of foreign missionaries or the Indian Christian community." The philosophy of state and its relation to religion, culture, and society underlying the report and advocated by it is unshamelessly totalitarian and.... At that time as young activist, I pinioned that the political ideas the report represents and its effect on the future of the state in India will go long way in shaping future opposition to conversion. Christianity is an anvil that has survived many hammers. It will outlive one more. However, the infant democratic state of India was imperilled by totalitarian ideas finding their place in government committees. The clear trend of the committee's thinking was that the state is everything and should bring virtually every aspect of society under its detailed regulation.[7]

Christian Response to the Niyogi Report

Several books and compilations of articles appeared in response to the Niyogi Report. Dr. Oscar Sevrin, the Bishop of Raigarh-Ambikapur, in his *Annotations on the Niyogi Report Relating to Raigarh and Surguja* gave a paragraph-by-paragraph rebuttal of the report. In addition to the charge of using concocted evidence, he accused the Committee of deliberate mistranslation of books written on Christianity. Bombay Governor Hare Krishna Mahtab was among the prominent Hindus who repudiated the report. Expressing sorrow over the controversy, he stated that it was caste Hindus and not Christians who had exploited the tribal people.

When the Report was made available to the public, the Catholic community responded vigorously. The deep resentment of the Catholic community over the report was articulated in several books the following year. Oscar Severin, the Bishop of Raigarh and Ambikapur, disputed the information collected by the Committee which he regarded as either false or distorted—at least in Raigarh and Surguja districts—to suit the purpose of the Committee to criticise Christian community. Again the assertion of the report that conversion must be an act of individual, internal convictional and must be based on purely spiritual motives, he argued that there were undeniably complex motives in conversions, including temporal advantages such as freedom from caste oppression, education of children, a lift in the social scale, deliverance from the tyranny of feudal system and the Christians need make no apology for the conversion in such circumstances. He highlighted the dangers of government imposing its power on personal and religious matters: "Who has a right to ask whether another man's motives are pure?"[8]

Another Catholic Christian leader A. Soares, Vice-President of the Catholic Association of Bombay, insisted that the purpose of Christian mission was evangelizing—"A presentation of life and teaching of Jesus Christ" which may not be necessarily lead into conversion. He also argued that unlike Hinduism, Christianity is a social religion that concerns the whole person and that the social activity of the church is of the 'very essence of our faith' as it is the 'radiation of living faith.'

Severin and Soares' argument represent the two main contemporary Christian justifications for conversion. Severin's argument was, that whereas there may be motives for conversion, not all of which can be described as 'spiritual', conversion is undeniably an act of faith because, contrary to the Hindu expectation of a purely spiritual and individualistic conversion, he understood Christianity to embrace material and community aspics of life as well. For Soares, conversion is inevitable were truth is encountered and in Christianity, truth has social ramification.

M.M. Thomas, the Christian leader who started ecumenical movement in India, criticised the Report for the "... political idea it represents and its effect on the future of the state in India". He wrote that the "infant secular democratic state of India has yet to find roots in the indigenous cultural soil and is imperilled by totalitarian ideas finding their place in government committee."

Though they had been less outspoken during the enquiry, faced with its outcome, Protestant leaders too responded. The editor of NCCR pointed out that the Committee used historical material out of context, that it had not followed any accepted juridical procedure, and that it was far from impartial. He argued that the report without acceptable evidence, undermined the entire missionary contribution as a political one, and furthermore, its recommendation to limit the freedom of people would "pave way for the end of democracy in India".[9] At the triennial meeting of the NCCI in November 1956, the participants called for Christians to stand up and protest not only because of the absolute Christian obligation to preach the Gospel but because of 'the fundamental rights of every man'. They denounce unfair methods of evangelism but further asserted that 'evangelism is the very heart of the Gospelca',and the calling for conversion is "the affirmation and not the denial of human integrity".[10] While the response of the Catholic community was to protest strongly against the enquiry during its course, and to directly oppose almost all the charges of the report, Protestants, who were a disparate group and not the main target of the report's criticism, responded overall more cautiously. Whereas Catholics argued from theological first principles, Protestants took the pragmatic view that the real problems were the involvement of foreign missionaries in the process of conversion and the alien identity of Indian converts in relation to Indian culture and tradition created by a radical understanding of conversion.

Therefore, Protestant, especially as reflected in a Protestant symposium in the following year, took the report as a challenge to develop new patterns of mission compatible with Indian traditions and cultures. As will become apparent in the coming pages this Protestant understanding of the issue was also influenced by theological changes taking place in the wider Christian churches and the view that Hindu objections to Christian conversion were on a socio-cultural and political level.

II. Debate over 'Freedom of Religion' Legislation, 1967-1968

The Niyogi Report's recommendations were implemented in the

Freedom of religious act in Orissa (1967), and Madhya Pradesh (1968). Nevertheless, before that several changes were made in Hindu personal laws in the mid-1950s that were applicable only to Hindus. Though generally progressive as far as democratization and the status of women were concerned, they had serious negative implications for conversion including loss of identity in Hindu society and a loss of certain marital parental and inheritance rights of converts and their children.

The Hindu Marriage Act (1955) states that a partner ceasing to be family by converting to another religion gives legitimate ground for divorce. The Hindu Succession Act, 1956 lays down that although a convent retains the right to inheritance, the children born to that person after conversion and their descendants are disqualified from inheriting the property of their Hindu relatives unless the children remain or become Hındu. The Hindu Minority and Guardianship Act, 1956 disqualify a convert from being the guardians of his own child and from being the natural guardian of his wife if she is a minor. The Hindu Adoptions and Maintenance Act, 1956 states that convert does not have any say over his/her partner adopting a child; one parent can give his/her child in adoption without the consent of the partner if she/he has converted; and no one can claim maintenance if he/she has converted to another religion.

It is important to note that in these Acts, in legal terms, a Hindu was defined as 'a Hindu by religion in any of its forms of developments' which included Buddhist, Jain, or Sikh by religion and also included any person who is a 'convert or reconvert' to the Hindu, Buddhist, Jain or Sikh religion, but excluding Muslim, Christian, Parsi or Jews by religion. There is no doubt that this legislation made it extremely difficult for caste Hindus to change their religion.

Furthermore, as far as converts with a Scheduled Caste background were concerned, the President's Constitution (Scheduled Caste) Order issued on August 10, 1950 stated that 'no person who professes religion different from Hindu shall be deemed to be a Scheduled Caste, which means that converts from these castes were outside the scope of state aid applicable to members. The special rights and privileges of the Scheduled Caste included political representation, educational opportunities, and economic aid, and exclusion from them generated considerable tension and economic hardship.

Freedom of Religion Act—Orissa (1967) and Madhya Pradesh (1968)

After independence from the British rule, although Parliament has never enacted any law on this subject, but the Niyogi Committee Report 1956 in Madhya Pradesh paved the way for introducing local laws imposing restrictions on religious activities. There were several attempts to implement the recommendations of the report in Madhya Pradesh but it was only in 1967 that the government of the neighbouring state Orissa passed the Freedom of Religion Act, the government of Madhya Pradesh also introduced Dharma Swatantra Adhiniyam (Freedom of Religion Act) in 1968. The Orissa Act said, "No person shall convert or attempt to convert, either directly or otherwise, any person from one religious faith to another by the use of force or by inducement or by any fraudulent means."

The Madhya Pradesh also stated that conversion by "force or allurement or by fraudulent means" were punishable and any conversion require registration with the local state authorities.

The Orissa Act followed the Niyogi Committee:

> Conversion in its very process involves an act of undermining another faith.
> It becomes all the more objectionable when this is brought about by recourses to methods like force, fraud, material, inducement exploitation of one's poverty, simplicity and ignorance. Conversion or attempts to conversion in the above manner besides creating various maladjustments in social life, also give rise to problem of law and order. It is, therefore, of importance to provide for measures to check such activities, which also indirectly impinge on the freedom of religion. The Bill seeks to achieve the above objectives." (Niyogi Committee Report)

Christians strongly criticized these states for passing these Acts. The editor of the NCCR responded to the concept of conversion raised in the Acts by stating that conversion is wide than the issue of changing one's religion: it is about freedom of individual choice, which is fundamental to human nature and closely related to the 'right for the search for Truth' (NCCR, March

1968: 20-22). Eugene D'Souza, the Catholic Archbishop of Bhopal, wrote a strong letter against the Act to the Chief Minister of Madhya Pradesh, in which he described it as a direct attack on the constitutional fundamental rights and something that had certainly 'shaken the confidence of the Christian community'.[11]

Christians in various parts of the country protested against the Acts, concentrating on the following issues—First, although, it was clear in the Orissa Act that conversion itself was regarded objectionable since it was said to undermine another's faith. Therefore, it appeared that, in spite of the Hindu claim of there not being any objection to genuine contended to regulate the limit of only conversion done by undesirable means but also conversion in general. Second, the fact that they regarded as a personal matter would be under the scrutiny of government officials without sufficient safeguards against the abuse.

Probably, the strongest case against the Acts from the Christians point of view was that, as Nehru wanted the Acts could create more problems than they solve. As the texts of the Acts show, especially in the case of Madhya Pradesh, they were aimed to regulate the activity of the instigator of conversion rather than the one who he/she convert to another religion. Therefore, when Christian insisted that the Acts were *ultra vires* the Constitution, they had to establish that the fundamental rights 'to propagate' mean a fundamental right to seek the conversion of others. This was the key point in the debate.

Redefining Identities—Vatican Council II (1962-65): New Approach

After Second World War, many colonies gained independence in Asia and Africa. The nationalist forces in these continents equated Christianity with "Whiteman's religion" and thus closely linked to it to the colonial powers. At the same time growing influence of Communism was seen as a challenge to religions particularly Christianity. The Communist vision was largely secular, remaking all of society as an egalitarian, strict, and austere state. This threatened the established social and political powers globally and posed new challenges before the Churches, both Catholics and Protestant, because of commitment to conversion and because of their emphasis on the *Bible*. Thus, once again religious freedom emerged one of the key international concerns in 1960s.[12]

By the early 1950s, the teachings of the Catholic Church had developed considerably in its explicit affirmation of the place of 'indigenous' cultures in relation to missionary activities and Christian living. The Catholic Church in particular in the period following the Second World War, officially recognized the needs to which missionaries had been pointing for many decades. Paradoxically in the period after the War, the rise of Communism in China and Eastern Europe and secularization in the West, led to these developments in Catholic teachings. It is upon these teachings, the later decrees and instructions of Vatican II are built.

Pope John Paul XXIII announced commencement of Vatican Council II on January 25, 1959, until its conclusion on December 8, 1965 by Pope John Paul VI. The first met under the pontificate of Pope John Paul XXIII and the last three under his successor, Pope John Paul VI and some 2200 bishops participated in the deliberations. Because of Vatican II, the Catholic Church opened its windows. The Second Vatican Council, more popularly known as Vatican II, was designed to assess the church's role in a rapidly changing world. The Vatican II called all Catholics play a role in evangelizing through their lives. At Vatican II, the church adopted a spirit of respect and dialogue towards non-Christian religions. Church relationship with other Christians and the non-Christian world were also discussed.[13]

By mid-1960s, the topic of conversion rose to prominence in Indian Christian Theology particularly during the second half of the 1960s as the strength of Hindu opposition to it became evident in the findings of the Niyogi Report and the various attempts to regulate conversion in Central Government and local states. Attempts to restrict religious conversion provoked strong reactions from Christian groups citing fundamental rights guaranteed in the Constitution and that conversion is at the heart of Christian belief and practice. However, this opposition to conversion also forced Christian theologians rethink the meaning and practice of conversion, and it resulted in intra-Christian debates. In 1960s, Religious theologies became one of the most important disciplines in mission studies and, along with secular humanism, it became a major challenge for Christian theology. Therefore, the debate in India cannot be seen in isolation but as part of a theological debate in the wider Christian world. In India, the question of conversion was examined in the light of some Hindu nationalists who accused missionaries of forced conversion.

Who Can Go to Heaven?—Conversion Debate 1966-1968

Conversion is not an issue limited to the Indian context since it touches on the wider theological questions of the Christian approach to other religions and of the secularization of the gospel. In the 1960s, many Western theologians regarded secularization as inevitable and believed that the proper Christian response was to express the gospel in secular terms. 'Secular Theology' or 'Secular Christianity' was expressed, for example, in Paul van Burner's *The Secular Meaning of the Gospel* (1963), John Robinson's *Honest to God* (1963) and especially Harvey Cox's *The Secular City* (1965), which led to a theology of building 'the new humanity, the new secular city of humankind'. In this reference to India, Cox urged that Indian Christians should not only accept secularization but also actively support it in the context of possible Hindu secularization of India (1965).

While the debate on the secularization of Christianity was dominated by Western theologians, some non-Western theologians also contributed, most notably M.M. Thomas, who became a leading figure in WCC, attempts to supply the theology and principles of secular theology to the solution of the problem of the Christian response to the other religions. In its opening address at the meeting of the Commission on World Mission and Evangelism of the WCC at Mexico City. In 1964, he developed P.D. Devanandan's idea of a 'creative fellowship'. Thomas forcefully presented the challenge of both the religious and secular quests for humanization and argued that the role of Christian mission was to find 'a new pattern of human society' and search for 'an adequate spiritual dynamic' for this pattern by participating in common human struggles.[14]

The debate on secularization continued beyond Mexico City. In 1965, Paul Loffler, Secretary in the Division of World Mission and Evangelism of the WCC, arranged a debate between Thomas and G. Hendrikus Berkhof, Professor of Systematic Theology at the University of Leiden, Netherlands, on question of the form and content of the salvation, which Christ offers to people in the secular world and the form and content of the conversion with which they respond in the context of the secular age. Dealing with the question of conversion, Thomas argued that the meaning of the gospel for a contemporary person comes alive at the cutting edge between the Gospel and the quest of modern man for commitment to the Christ-event, which is unique, but in order for it to be universal, it must be understood and lived out in the present historical situation; thus the church must adapt a 'new pattern' for the conversion of secular Hindus. However, this search for a new pattern outside the church faced considerable opposition. Even though the section report of the Mexico City meeting recognized that there were 'secret believers' and those who are influenced by Christian truth sometimes do not commit themselves, it made it clear that "to be a Christian necessarily involves being brought by Christ into the visible, witnessing community of faith."

In 1967, in the run up to the WCC Uppsala Assembly, the Ecumenical Review took up conversion as a theme as a part of its response to the contemporary debate on secularization. In his introduction, Loffler argued that conversion belongs to the very nature of the Christian faith since it calls for 'response to god's presence in history, for personal commitment and human participation' and it is a force of renewal in both the church and society. Therefore, in view of the theme of the Assembly, 'Behold make all things new', renewal of the theme of the church cannot be understood without individual conversion. In his closely argued article, he insisted that conversion refers both personal experience and entry into new fellowship with other Christians and these cannot be regarded as alternatives. Starting from Biblical principles, Loffler considered conversion as primarily an individual and personal decision, regarded the church as representative to God for all, and saw personal commitment and social responsibility as in 'tension'. However, this did not seem to answer the questions that the Indian theologians were asking questions relating to the communal nature of conversion in India, the relationship of Christians and Hindus, and of the Church and Hinduism.[15]

In the theological discussion of secularization, many evangelicals felt that the emphasis of mission had shifted from 'salvation through conversion' to 'humanization' by means of social service. The evangelicals, particularly collective evangelical response to what they saw as the weakening of conversion in the consular ecumenical movements was first clearly articulated from North America at "The Congress on the Church's Worldwide Mission' held at Wheaton, Illinois, in April 1966. The Wheaton Declaration introduced a section on 'Mission and Proselytism'.

While repudiating 'forced conversion' and the use of, 'unethical' means' to achieve conversion, it declared that 'all followers of Christ must disciple their fellowmen', and [w]e seek the conversion of unregenerate men, even though they may be attached to some church or other religion, we are fulfilling our biblical mandate'. This was because of the belief that 'if men are not born again they will be subject to eternal separation from a religious, holy God.'[16]

Anticipating a preoccupation with social issues at the forthcoming WCC Assembly at Uppsala 1968, rather than a concern for 'that great number of men, at least two billion, who have either never heard of Jesus Christ or have no real chance to believe in Him as Lord and Saviour. Donald McGavarn published an article in which he charged that the WCC would 'betray' the unevangelized. McGavarn believed that the drive for conversion had all but evaporated from the ecumenical movement. For many evangelicals' subsequent events at Uppsala justified McGavarn's views. The Assembly, while incorporating some of the critique, consistently played down 'world evangelization' in favour of 'humanization'. Declaring the 'church in mission is the church for others', Uppsala asserted the solidarity of the church with all who 'wait for the new humanity', whether Christian or not. The difficulties of this position were felt in Christianity by participants and the debate on salvation and humanization in Christian mission proved to be one of the most controversial topics of the Assembly. Despite the opposition, the debate at Uppsala gave room for Indian theologians to explore a 'point of contact' for Christians and Hindus.

III. Hindu Tolerance, Law, and Conversion

The debates on conversion in the 1950s and 1960s were focused on the legal implications of conversion in the struggle between fundamental rights and religious tolerance, between majority Hindus and minorities (Muslims and Christians), between law and religion. Even after the Constitution was introduced in 1952, Parliament took up for consideration in 1954 the Indian Conversion (Regulation and Registration) Bill and later in 1960 the Backward Communities (Religious Protection) Bill, both of which had to be dropped for lack of support.

As early as 1967, it became evident that the concern was not just with forced conversion, but also with conversion to any religion other than Hinduism and especially Christianity and Islam.[17] These may be seen as further reinforcing the several statutory penalties for ceasing to be a Hindu such as the 1955-56 Hindu Law enactments, namely Hindu Minority and Guardianship Act, 1956 (Section 6), Hindu Adoption and Maintenance Act, 1956 (Sections 7, 8, 9, 11, 18-24), Hindu Marriage Act, 1955 [Sections 13(ii), 13A] and the Hindu Succession Act (Section 26). The picture is complete if we account for the fact that most of these laws are aimed to keep the low caste Hindus within the fold of Hinduism. Therefore, while law prohibits conversion, 'reconversion' of low caste Hindus is permissible. If a low caste Hindu who had converted to another faith or any of his descendants reconverts to Hinduism, he might get back his original caste [*Kailash Sonkar* (1984) 2 SCC 91; *S. Raja Gopal* AIR 1969 SC 101].

In a way, these laws meant that converts were not treated as a part of the Indian community but as 'outsiders' if they continued to uphold their identity as Christians or minorities. Christians felt that Hindus were alienating the Christian communities and its members from Indian society through the powerful means of legislation. They insisted that conversion was personal and private decision in nature but the legal debates in the courts resulted in it becoming a public matter, especially in Orissa, Madhya Pradesh and Arunachal Pradesh, so that Christians in these states had to abide by the 'Freedom of Religion' Acts.

Despite the Hindu claim that the laws were intended to regulate undesirable Conversions only, the potential misuse of the law was great and Christians were not convinced. As the debate, continued, Christian arguments increasingly shifted their basis from the Fundamental Right in the Constitution of India of all persons to propagate their faith to the human rights in the Universal Declaration of Human Rights to orifice their faith as a minority religious community.

In the period immediately after the Independence, there was strong move to restrict Indian-ness as essentially Hindu and accuse the Christians as following *'firangi'* tradition and of being a prolongation of the Western cultural colonialism.

The Hindu groups raised the issue of the national heritage, which they said is a country's framework of traditions that it deems crucial for its social cultural cohesion and political autonomy. The national heritage is a country's icon of the world, comprising products of thoughts, morality, and art. It is not so much a showcase; it rather reflects the ethos or lifestyle of a people according to which they practice, protect, and pass on their national-traditions with keen interest to subsequent generations. The Nationalist rightwing Hindus accused Muslims and Christians of not sharing national heritage and thus term them alien.[18]

The arguments of the Hindu nationalist movements against conversion were focused on presenting the supremacy of the Hindu philosophy of tolerance and persuading Christians of the 'openness' Hindu thought. This was expressed particularly vividly in the articles in the *Vivekananda Kendra Patrika* where the fundamental difference between Hinduism and Christianity was seen in the assertion that there is freedom of thought within Hinduism whereas Christianity has no freedom within it but confirms to its members to particular doctrines. In other words, as Savyaksh argued, Hinduism 'tolerates' other beliefs, modes of worship or codes of behaviour since it teaches that divine revelation must be understood in pluralistic terms.

Therefore, Hindus argued that Hinduism having this ideology of the plurality of truth, embodied a 'philosophy of toleration' which exhibits is an immature understanding of God and nature as against the exclusive claims to the truth by Christians. In Hindu understanding, then, it is not necessary to convert to Christianity to find truth since within Hinduism there is a built-in provision and scope for finding the truth in various religious forms and ways. Conversion confines the convert to one particular side of the truth, hindering his/her search for the whole truth.

A section of Indian policy-makers feared that the large-scale conversion in certain pocket areas could lead to political crisis as it happened in Kerala in 1950s. Catholic bishops had issued circulars at the time of the Andhra elections of 1955 and the crucial Kerala elections of 1959, warning that Catholics who supported the Communist party faced excommunication. In early 1960s, the Roman Catholic bishop of Trivandrum, Kerala, ordered the excommunication of all Catholics who were members of the Communist or Revolutionary Socialist parties. In a pastoral letter to churches in his diocese, the bishop directed priests to deny sacraments to anyone who support or have voted for candidates of these parties in the state elections.[19]

It will not be out of context at this point to mention the unsuccessful attempt to restrict church control on political freedom of the faithful. In 1960, both houses of Parliament rejected Communist sponsored bills seeking to restrict "the use of the Catholic Church for political purposes and the participation of ecclesiastical personnel of the Catholic Church in political activity."

The enactment of Hindu laws, the state benefits for the Scheduled Castes, and the legislation against conversion made clear distinction between Hindu and non-Hindus and Hinduism and other religions. It is important to note that these distinctions drew definite boundaries for Hindu religious affiliation, belief, and practice. Both caste and non-caste Hindus were required to remain in their own fold, for there were now penalties for those who deliberately moved out through conversion to another religion. However, these boundaries were not completely closed from the other side for those who were willing to assimilate into the wider Hindu family. For non-Hindus, to be associated with Hindus became an attractive option, as it is suggested by the inclusion of various 'indigenous faiths' in the Arunachal Pradesh Act.

More significantly, the interpretation of Christian conversion was no longer confined to the Christian community but open to the scrutiny of the law, and it had to be approved by the majority Hindus. Although both Hindus and Christians called for tolerance in their debate on the legislation of conversion. Because, they were operating in an overwhelming Hindu context, and the Christians were under pressure to make adjustments with Hinduism. Therefore, during the beginning of the 1970s, while Western theologians were more interested in religious pluralism and the question of the uniqueness of Christ, Indian theologians were most concerned with conversion.[20]

This eventually led to the debates among Christians of which that between M.M. Thomas and Lessie Newbigin in 1971 is the outstanding example. Nevertheless, these debates were limited by the awareness that the Hindu majority was determined to see that the boundaries should allow passage in one direction only and that the Christian reinterpretation of the meaning of conversion would have to fit into Hindu religious 'compartment' if it was not to be rejected by the majority.

IV. Conclusion

After Independence, the RSS imposed itself as the major movement favouring (re)conversion to Hinduism. The opposition by its three affiliates, the Vishva Hindu Parishad (VHP), the Vanvashi Kalyan Ashram (VKA), and the Bharatiya Jana Sangh (BJS). The creation of Nagaland in 1963 provided increasing legitimacy to the Niyogi Report, as four fifths of the Naga tribes were Christians who demanded creation of a separate state. With such a fear, a number of states introduced the anti-conversion legation ironically known as the Freedom of Religions Act.[21] The RSS established the VHP in 1964 with an object of saving Hindus from the conversion to either Islam or Christianity or turning Communists. The focus of the RSS during this period was to establish a network of dedicated people for propagating dynamic Hinduism representing the fundamental values of life. During 1960s, the RSS concentrated on establishing orphanages, schools, student hostels and dispensaries to compete with those developed by the Christian missions, in particular among the tribes in order to reclaim persons who had left Hinduism for Christianity.

Parallel to this effort to rival the Christian missions by initiate their techniques, the Hindu nationalists, through their party, strove to have law passed which would place restrictions on conversions. In Madhya Pradesh, Jana Sangh, when it came to power by means of a shortlived coalition in 1967-69, had a law passed called Dharam Swatantra Adhiniyam which foresaw a punishment for two years imprisonment for persons involved in conversion. Leaving aside the obviously large and complex question of whether missionaries were in fact using coercion or other illicit means to convert people, it is important to point out here that the recommendations in the Niyogi Report became the basis for various freedoms of religion Bills, also known as anti-conversion laws in India.

During the 1950s and 1960s, the Hindu Mahasabha and the RSS had only a shadowy presence, outside the mainstream of Indian political life. However, the continuing conflicts with Pakistan and the hostility to India's own Muslims it helped generate, combined with the growing disillusionment with both the Congress and the parties of the left, gave the Hindu right by the 1970s an opportunity to increase its strength.

Notes

1. Kim, Sebastian C.H., *In Search of Identity: Debates on Religious Conversion in India,* Oxford: Oxford University Press.
2. Report of the Christian Missionaries Activity Inquiry Committee, known as Niyogi Report, Madhya Pradesh Government, 1956.
3. Niyogi Report, I: 134, 160.
4. Niyogi Report, IIB: 6.
5. Niyogi Committee Report, Vol. I, p. 163.
6. Soares, A. (1957), *Truth Shall Prevail: Reply to Niyogi Committee,* Catholic Association of Bombay.
7. Niyogi Committee Report, Vol. I, p. 164.
8. Oscar, Sevrin, (1957). *Annotations on Niyogi Report Relating to Raigarh and Surguja,* Nagpur: Pushpa Publication.
9. NCCR September, 1956: 318-21.
10. NCCR December, 1956: 484-89.
11. *The Examiner,* October 12, 1968: 651.
12. Lamb, Matthew L. and Matthew Levering (2008). *Vatican II: Renewal within Tradition,* Oxford University Press.
13. Martin, David (2011). *Vatican II: A Historic Turning Point: The Dawning of a New Epoch,* Author House.
14. Collins, Paul M. (2016). *Christian Inculturation in India,* Routledge.
15. Kim, Sebastian C.H., *In Search of Identity: Debates on Religious Conversion in India,* Oxford: Oxford University Press.
16. Harod, Lindsell (1966). *The Church Worldwide Mission,* Waco Taxas: Wood Books.
17. Laing, Mark T.B. (2005). *Nationalism and Hindutva: A Christian Response,* Papers from the 10th CMS Consultation, New Delhi: ISPCK.
18. Tripathi, R.C., and Purnima Singh (2015). *Perspectives on Violence and Othering in India,* Springer.
19. Smith, Donald Eugene (2015). *India is a Secular State,* Princeton University Press, p. 224.
20. Dou, Ian H. and John Carman (1966). *The Post Colonial Crisis in Mission: Comments,* IRMLV/220, October, p. 483.
21. Kalu, Ogbu, Alaine Low (2008). *Interpreting Contemporary Christianity: Global Processes and Local Identities,* Wm. B. Eerdmans Publishing.

5

From Sermon to Mantras

Conversion Debates in 1970s

Introduction

The 1970s was turbulent decade for India. This was an era of *'garibi hatao'* campaign after Indira Gandhi's successful won 1971 Indo-Pakistan war. However, the Emergency was declared in 1974 during which civil rights were suspended. During popular upsurge against the Indira Regime led by the late Jaya Prakash Narayan in 1970s, the RSS made a major entry into the popular arena. This accorded the RSS much needed legitimacy in the minds of the people. The religious conversion issue was also the subject of major news headlines and controversies due to the Supreme Court decision on Madhya Pradesh Freedom of Religion Bill in 1977, and then from in 1978, first with 'The Arunachal Pradesh Freedom of Indigenous Faith Bill' and later with the 'Freedom of Religion Bill' in the Parliament in 1979. The RSS spearheaded rightwing militancy, and one of the main objectives of the Vishwa Hindu Parishad became the conversion of all non-Hindus to Hinduism, discursively presented as a home-coming or *'ghar-wapsi'*. The demand for an all-India anti-conversion Bill grew louder and louder in the Hindi language newspapers which are in opinion forming role in the North India. The churches in India could not find suitable means to counter this surge in opposition to Christianity. More and more movements were launched with slogans *"videshi dharam bharat chhodo"* (foreign religions quit India). The church did initiate *ashram* style of living by some priests and nuns but it did not cut much ice as Hindus felt it was another trap. Thus, since the beginning of 1970s, nationalist movement based on the assertion that only one majority ethnic or religious group defines a nation gained new ground.

I. Long Shadow of Religion

The beginning of the 1970s saw religious controversies in new light. This was also time when many Indian *yogis* often motivated by nationalism, saw *yoga* as a tool for "reforming the physical body" in the battle to reclaim India from 'foreign influence' through popularization of *yoga* as a health and fitness practice, especially in the United States and Europe. This resulted in influencing UK's legendary Beatles Band by Maharishi Mahesh Yogi, which had helped inspire worldwide interest in the TM. Christian evangelical groups were baffled by this phenomenon. While in India, the ultra rightwing Hindu groups were raising the question whether the salvation is only in the Christianity, globally the teachings of Vatican II appeared making headings. Moreover, the Christian theologians were coming to terms with the new realities of social, cultural, and political power in India. Among Catholics and Protestants alike, the theological movement for indigenization in Africa and Asia accelerated. By the 1970s, the terms contextualization or enculturation were being used to describe efforts to appropriate for theological rethinking.

The politics in independent India until around mid-1960s was almost secular. While the communal strife and occasional violence did occur in the earlier times, India in the first 15 years of independence experienced rather peaceful communal existence but by early 1970s scenario began changing due to increase of power hungry politicians who were politicizing religion. Separatist movement in Kashmir, Punjab, and Nagaland brought issues of national security and religion in the public discourse. From the beginning of 1970s, *dharma parivartan* (religious conversion) once again aroused public emotions.

The emergency rule imposed by the Prime Minister Indira Gandhi from 1975 to 1977 weakened the democratic institutions. In the post-Emergency election in 1977, the Jana Sangh became a constituent of new coalition Janata Party that formed the Central Government under Prime Minister Morarji Desai, a Gandhian and two Janasanghis Atal Bihari Vajpayee and Lal Krishna Advani became ministers at the Centre. The inner relations of erstwhile Janasanghis and the RSS came into focus as other Janata Party leaders who did not come from the Jana Sangh background objected to dual loyalty: the party and the RSS. The dual membership controversy ultimately caused the downfall of Janata Party in 1979; the Jana Sangh members of the Janata Party walked out of the government, and the Jana Sangh was incarnated with the new name BJP in 1980 under the leadership of Atal Bihari Vajpayee reasserting the traditional Hindu fundamentalist political ideology.

The decline of Congress hegemony has been met by two important political developments: the rise of the Bharatiya Janata Party (BJP), especially in India's Hindi speaking 'heartland' that comprises states in north-central and western India; and the growing significance of neo-regional parties and caste based politics. Indira Gandhi came back to power in 1980, abandoned her nationalising socialism, and buried the land ceiling programme. A new phase of importance of religion in Indian politics grew with the rise of Khalistan movement in Punjab.[1]

Following the Niyogi Report, the Hindus considered imitating a movement called Missionaries '*Bharat Chhodo*' (missionaries quit India). In 1967 for the first time Non-Congress governments were formed in six states including Orissa and Madhya Pradesh. Orissa was the first state to bring such law named as Orissa Freedom of Religion Act, 1967, followed by Madhya Pradesh in 1968 and Arunachal Pradesh in 1978. The Niyogi Report corniced the status of missionaries and raised the issue of conversion and many missionaries subsequently left India, beginning the process of handing over church leadership to Indians. In 1970, the Government of India began restricting visa to missionaries and in 1972, the Parliament of India passed the Foreign Exchange Act to regulate and control purchase, holding, sale of or purchase of property by foreigners in India.[2]

The topic of freedom of religion and conversion rose to prominence in Indian Christian Theology as the strength of Hindu opposition to it became evident in the finding of the Niyogi Report and the various attempts to regulate conversion in Central Government and local states. Attempts to restrict religious conversion provoked strong reactions from Christian groups citing fundamental rights guaranteed in the Constitution and that conversion is at the heart of Christian belief and practice. While, this opposition to conversion forced Christian theologians rethink the meaning and practice of conversion, and reinterpret Kingdom of God, Christian community was baffled not knowing how to react when middle class Hindus educated in Christian schools too supported anti-conversion move. Therefore, the debate in India cannot be seen in isolation but as part of a theological debate in the wider Christian world and political development in India.

II. Supreme Court on the 'Freedom of Religion' Legislation, 1972-1977

The laws enacted in the name of "freedom of religion" were challenged in different High Courts. Because of the enactment of the anti-conversion laws in Orissa, the authorities arrested some Christians, which resulted in others engaging in legal action against the Acts. The Catholics Union of India filed a case against the Orissa Freedom of Religion Act because the Act violated the fundamental rights guaranteed in the Constitution, and that it was beyond the competence of the state legislature. In their decision on October 24, 1972, the Orissa High Court acknowledged, based on the petitions' argument, that "it is the religious duty of every Christian to propagate his religion as far as the scope of Article 25(1) of the Constitution was concerned" (AIR 1973 Orissa 120).

In Madhya Pradesh, a Catholic priest alleged that the state did not have authority to make such a law. In the case of Madhya Pradesh, the High Court upheld the Act (April 23, 1974) and the judges concluded that the disputed sections of the Act, far from violating the Constitution, actually establish the equality of religious freedom for all citizens by prohibiting conversion by objectionable activities such as coercion by force, fraud and by allurement...[T]he provision relating to conversion by allurement cannot be challenged either on the ground of legislative contempt or on the ground of violation of Article 25(1) of the Constitution. (AIR 1975 MP 163)

The difference in the verdicts of the Orissa High Court and the Madhya Pradesh High Court inevitably led the case being brought before the Supreme Court, which gave its final verdict on January 17, 1978. The Supreme Court, in case of Madhya Pradesh, however, affirmed the right of the State Government to pass the

Acts for the overriding purpose of maintaining "public order", and in case of Orissa found that Article 25 was not infringed (*Rev. Stanislaus* v. *State of M.P.*, AIR 1977 SC 908).

Since the Supreme Court is the final interpreter of the Constitution, the decision was of crucial importance to the Christian community. It not only authenticated the Orissa and Madhya Pradesh Acts but it also paved the way for other states to enact such legislation if they so desired.

The decision of the Supreme Court was based on the questionable assumption that in the process of conversion, the one who is converted is merely passive and the one who propagate the faith is the active party.

While the verdict guaranteed freedom of conscience not to change one's religion, in practice, it severely limits freedom of conscience to change one's religion by denying the other's right to propagate.

The Supreme Court decision clarified the meaning of the word 'propagate'. However, it was unjust in that, by endorsing the 'freedom of religion' Acts. It opened the way for political abuse of the legislation to intimidate people involved in conversions. Therefore, in the final analysis, not only did the verdict fall on only one side of the meaning of religious freedom, the Hindu interpretation, but more significantly, it limited freedom of choice and therefore, had wider inflictions for choice in other areas of life.[3]

Debate Over the Arunachal Pradesh Freedom of Indigenous Faith Act, 1978

Christians fear that the verdict of the Supreme Court would trigger adoption of similar Acts by other State Governments were affirmed when the Government of Arunachal Pradesh passed the Freedom of Indigenous Faith Act on May 19, 1978. The Arunachal Pradesh Freedom of Religion Act, 1978 was on the similar lines that of Orissa and Madhya Pradesh, and was enacted to provide for prohibition of conversion from one religious faith to any other by use of force or inducement or by fraudulent means and for matters connected therewith.

The Freedom of Religion Act, 1978 was tabled in the Legislative Assembly on 19th May, 1978 and, the copy of the said Bill was made available to the members only a day before debate. It seems that the Bill was poorly debated and passed hastily in the Assembly on May 19, 1978. The Bill finally received the assent of the President of India on 25th October, 1978 and became operational (Act) in Arunachal Pradesh as law of the land.

The Act provides among others in Chapter III "that no person shall convert or attempt to convert, either directly or otherwise, any person from one religious faith to any other religious faith by the use of force or by inducement or by any fraudulent means nor shall any person abet any such conversion." Chapter IV says, "any person contravening the provisions contained in Section 3, shall without prejudice to any civil liability, be punishable with imprisonment to the extent of two years and fine up to ten thousand rupees". Similarly Section 6 says that, "an offence under this Act shall be cognizable and shall not be investigated by an officer below the rank of an inspector of police."[4]

It is important to notice that although the Arunachal Pradesh Act is similar to the Madhya Pradesh Act, it specifies 'indigenous faith' as 'religions belief and practices' which have been 'sanctioned, adopted, performed by indigenous communities, and this in their view, include certain forms of Buddhism, Vaishnavaism and 'Nature worship'. In this way, many of the indigenous communities of the state were included under the umbrella of Hinduism.

While participating in a seminar the subject in 1978 at Delhi Dr. Rahmutulla Khan of JNU (Jawaharlal Nehru University) argued that the title of the Act was misleading and an ordinary police official has been vested with extraordinary power. In the RSS weekly newspaper *Organiser*, Savyaksh argued that Christianity is not an indigenous faith because it did not fit into any of the versions of what indigenous faith meant. These were that it must rise from within the people, it must not be dependent on external financial, ideological, or political support; and it should not oppose the prevailing 'cultural norms' which have been practised by the majority. He put forward the view that Indian traditions uphold the principle of freedom of thought in religion and respect for the religious beliefs of others, which is based on 'Vedic Truth' and is vital to Indian identity to the extent that the destruction of it would be the destruction of India.

All India Freedom of Religion Bill, 1979

In 1978, Hindus tried to solve the problem of conversion by arguing the supremacy of the Hindu philosophy of tolerance as preached by Vivekananda and accused Christianity of being intolerant. On December 1978, a Janata Party member (belonging to Jana Sangh camp) O.P. Tyagi presented a private Bill called—All India Freedom of Religion Bill, 1978. It caused great anxiety among Christians and intensified the Hindu-Christian debate. The Bill was almost identical to the Orissa Freedom of Religion Act, except that Tyagi justified it by stating that, although conversion by 'free consent and will' cannot be questioned, 'state protection' is required in the case of conversion by undesirable methods and for the people of Scheduled Caste and Scheduled Tribe.

As the Lok Sabha session for discussing the new Bill drew near, the debates intensified, for action, especially during the months of May and June 1979, but for this was rather abruptly called off and the Bill was never discussed due to the fall of Government in July 1979.

The Catholic response to the Bill is to illustrate by the response of the editor of '*The Examiner*' who wrote, that [t]he worst fears of the Christian communities in India have alas now been confirmed, and that it would not only make even genuine conversions illegal and prevent each and every conversion, it would also lead to a totalitarian state. He alleged that this was a systematic challenge by the Hindu majority to Christian minority backed by the Central Government and therefore, urged Christians to 'rise up as one man in protest against the glaring injustices' (*The Examiner*, January 20, 1979). The Catholic bishops of the western region of India issued a statement on the Bill, which they described as a 'subtle and deceptive move to stop all conversions 'to the Christian faith', and as giving the state advantage to 'encroach in the sacred realm of conscience of the human person'. They insisted that, contrary to the Supreme Court decision, the freedom to propagate guaranteed in the Constitution includes "the freedom to persuade others to join that religion... to be converted and that preventing people from 'converting others' would be against the fundamental rights."[5]

As the debate went on, Hindus supported the legislation and attacked the arguments of the Christians.

The Vivekananda Kendra Patrika devoted its August 1979 issue to "Christianity in India: A Critical Study", dealing mainly with the problem of conversion caused by Christian missionary activities. The VKP identified 'fundamental' differences between Hinduism and Christianity, the former embodying for him a philosophy of toleration and the later a fervent desire to seek converts. The editor wrote that the encounter of these two ideas was bound to create tension. However, in his conclusion, he called for mutual understanding on conversion from both Hindu and Christian point of view.

Articles in the VKP represented various Hindu approaches to conversion. First, some articles attempted to address the Indian 'connection' of Jesus, suggesting that Jesus lived and died in India and there are many similarities in the teaching of Christ and Krishna. They argued that conversion is not necessary since there is common gourd between Christianity and Hinduism and both need to see commonality rather than differences. Second, many argued that the problem of conversion is an historical one of missionary expansion in connection with the imperialism of the West, with examples of 'forceful conversion' in the past. Therefore, conversion is 'subversion' and India must reject it. Third, some saw the problem of conversion as lying in some Western Christians and missionaries who took certain passages literal. Therefore, Indian Christians should be free from the influence of Western missionaries and their teaching, which is irrelevant to an Indian understanding of faith. Fourth, a number of articles strongly supported the Freedom of Religion Bill as a way to prevent communal problems caused by the conversion activities of Christian missionaries.[6]

III. In Search of Identity—Indianization or Hinduization

The topic of conversion rose to prominence among Indian Christian theologians particularly in early 1970s. Theology of conversion is a key issue for both Christian and Hindu communities, along with *Dalit* theology, which is part of the socio-economic liberation movement, and the theology of inculturation, which emphasises the interaction of Christian theology with Hindu religions and philosophy.

After Vatican II the 'Inculturation' became the dominant

concept of Catholic Mission Theology, and the precise meaning of the term and its applications could range from adopting the gospel to local culture to encouraging 'theology from below', or 'local theologies', as a way forward in Christian mission.[7]

Inculturation encompasses many elements: liturgy, language, music, dance, clothing, architecture, and interior ornamentation. I have used the term inculturation and applied it to both Catholic and Protestant churches in India. Although the term and practices of inculturation originated in the Catholic Church, they were adopted later by Protestant churches, which sometimes prefer to call this phenomenon "contextualization". Here, I do not differentiate between the two terms since their essence is very much alike.

Among the Indian theologians, M.M. Thomas was prominent figure who worked on the enculturation theology. He believed in Gandhi a political philosophy with a strong socialist agenda. He was involved in various worldwide ecumenical movements chairing committees, and speaking both in the church and in public. Later he took up direct involvement in politics as Governor of the state of Nagaland for two years. Throughout, his main concern was the relationship between Christian community and wider Hindu society in India. Thomas strongly criticised the 'minority consciousnesses' of the Indian Christian community and urged Christians to overcome their isolation from the national mainstream and live for the larger community. The goal of Christian mission, he argued, should not be to create an exclusive 'Christian' culture but an 'open' culture.[8]

Thomas developed his thoughts on conversion and raised the question of the 'form of the Christian community within the human community.' He introduced the concept of the 'Christ centred secular fellowship' a *koinonia* that was the 'manifestation of the new reality of the Kingdom at work in the world of men in world history'. For Thomas, 'secular fellowship' does not mean making the gospel secular. What he intended was not for Christians to lose the religious or spiritual aspect of the gospel, nor for Christian to be absorbed into Hindu religion but for the secularisation of the Christian community in order to bridge the gap with the wider Hindu community and identify with Hindus. Secular for him meant the Christian community becoming truly 'religious' without being 'communal'. He insisted that the 'secular fellowship' was the 'point of contact' and could be in 'partnership in the struggle' and he called on the church to break the communal structure and build up a new partnership of Christians and non-Christians—the human *koinonia*.[9]

Conversely, M.M. Thomas challenged the wider Hindu community to expand their public space to include the Christian community for a healthy and frank discussion for the common good. Thomas wanted to overcome the problem of the Christian community becoming more and more isolated from the main community, especially because of the insistence on a radical discontinuity between the gospel and Hindu religion through the means of conversion. It was this, he believed, which led to the exclusion of Christians by the Hindu majority as 'outcastes', which resolved in the fact that the Christian community was no longer able to make an impact on Hindu society. Thomas' suggestion of 'human *Koinonia*' was intended to facilitate open discussion between the Hindu and Christian communities.

Thomas' secular fellowship could provide a mutual space between Christians and Hindus. However, the permeation of Christian principles and values, the Church could be more effective in engaging in wider society. Integral to this thesis is the close relationship between salvation and humanization; that the Christian community should be an 'open community' in order to achieve this permeation that the meeting point would be the mutually inclusive space of human *Koinonia* or secular fellowship; and that Christians would achieve this through permeation of gospel values and principles.[10]

While Protestant attempts to solve the problem of conversion involved finding a 'meeting point' with Hindu society, such as that expressed by M.M. Thomas in his 'Christ-centred fellowship', Catholics in India initially found it hard to share this theological premise because of the traditional Roman Catholic emphasis on the doctrine of *extra ecclesiam null salus* (no salvation outside the church). As Robert Schreiter explains, traditional Catholic Church (*plantation ecclesiae*), and these methods of mission were supported by God's 'universal salvific will' and the 'church as the concrete manifestation of that will'.

In the first half of the twentieth century, the idea of inculturation was led by the Protestant theologians. The Catholic Church in India entered in this area only after the Vatican II. The impact of Vatican II on the life and mission of the Catholic Church was immense and nowhere more as visible as on its ecclesiology. In its wake, Catholics developed new and more sympathetic approaches to other faiths and challenged the authority of the church hierarchy through various liberation theologies. I shall look at the effect of these charges in the Indian context below.

In the 1970s, the development of Indian Catholic thinking on conversion was greatly influenced by two competing approaches to contextualizing the gospel, the enculturation model, and the liberation model. Representing the double confrontation of contemporary Christianity with the great world religions on the one hand and with the non-Christian 'secular' humanism on the other. In Asia, these were responses to the dominant realities of the context: religiousness and poverty. The tension between these two loose movements in the 1980s was due to a number of factors, chief among which was the fact that inculturationists tended to relate to the upper caste and "Brahmanical" religion, whereas liberationists were victims of caste Hinduism. Liberationists thus accused inculturationists of indifference to matters of social justice and even of complicity with high caste oppression, whereas inculturationists saw liberationists as insensitive to Hindu religion and as a threat to communal harmony.

The Catholics took the lead in the debates with Hindus in this period, and there were debates between those who held each position within the Catholic Church. It is important to notice that, as in the case of Protestants, the conservative Catholic understanding of conversion also persisted alongside the inculturation and liberation model, and that there were many who sought to combine both models, so within the Catholic Church there was great diversity of views on the issue.[11]

The CBCI issued 12 points about the inculturation in India, which included instruction on posture during the mass, bowing head, and joining hands in Indian style (*anjali hasta*), *aarti*, use of oil lamps instead of candles etc. Soon these 12 points met with controversy and in 1975, Vatican halted these experiments. In fact, all liturgical renewal came to a standstill. Catholic priest Fr. Amlorpavadass, who was leading the inculturation at that time was quietly sidelined by the CBCI. The local community was neglected in the process of enculturation. It was an academic endeavour rather than a spiritual journey. This writer visited several Christian *ashrams* but the 'aura' of Hindu *ashrams* was missing. This in fact reflects the state of confusion particularly in the Catholic Church. Most importantly, the lay people were never made part of this *ashram* movement. Hindus were sceptical of this move by the churches in India.

IV. Changes After Vatican II

At the time of Second Vatican Council, Karl Rahner's theology had a great impact on the Catholic approach to the salvation of the people of other religion. Rahner emphasised the universality of God's grace such that every individual, regardless of religious background would have an opportunity of partaking in a genuine saving relationship with God (1966). He further argued that the non-Christian religions are 'a positive means of gaining the right relationship to God and thus for attaining salvation which is, therefore, positively included in God's plan of salvation. He posited a 'Christianity of an anonymous kind', of which the members may be called 'anonymous Christians'.

Rahner's theology of 'anonymous Christianity' had many followers, but at the same time, it faced serious criticism. However, it did allow the possibility of the salvation of individuals outside the Catholic Church within the traditional Catholic theological framework and therefore, broke new ground in Catholic theology of religions.

Though Vatican II marked a significant change in Catholic ecclesiology when the church was defined as the people of God, the doctrine of the church in relation to people of other faiths and their salvation was ambiguous. Regarding the conversion of people of other faiths, the Council affirmed that 'it is through Christ's Catholic Church alone, that the fullness of the means of salvation can be obtained', therefore, everyone ought to be converted to Christianity. At the same time, it opened up the possibility that those outside the church, who do not receive the gospel 'may achieve eternal salvation'. Therefore, it appears that the statements of the Council represent both traditional and new thinking on conversion. Although, as Miikka Ruokanen rightly argues, the documents do not explicitly endorse the non-Christians religions as means of salvation, the affirmation of possibilities for salvation—at least for individuals—without conversion to Christian faith and the positive attitude towards other religion were a highly significant step.

In the open climate fostered by the Council, an attempt to deal with the problem of the relationship between Christianity and Hinduism was presented in the shape of Raymon Panikkar's well-known work, *The Unknown Christ of Hinduism* (1964). Panikkar was convinced that there must be a 'meeting place' between Christianity and Hinduism in the religious sphere. He then argued that this place must be Christ, because Christ is the 'ontological meeting point of any religion' and the 'only one' mediator between God and the rest. He insisted that 'Christ' is already there in Hinduism, and the Christian mission was to unveil the 'unknown Christ' in Hinduism.

Hence, conversion does not mean speaking from a Christian point of view, a changing over to another culture, tradition or even another religion but a changing into a new life, a new existence, a new creation, which is precisely the old one—and not another—but transformed, lifted up, risen again.

As the outcome of his careful study of the relationship between Hinduism and Christianity from philosophical and theological perspective he concluded:

> God is at work in the 'pagan' religions. The Christian proclamation, does not preach a new God but just the mirabilia of God of which the mystery of Christ hidden in God is the first and last one.

Although the work of Panikkar was in many ways in line with the new thinking of Vatican II and with Rahner's theology, there was a significant difference in that Panikkar affirmed Hinduism itself as a way of salvation, which neither the Vatican document nor Rahner did. Both Rahner and Panikkar attempted to bring Christianity and Hinduism together in a normative salvation, though in different ways. For Rahner, salvation was through God's grace and for Panikkar; it was by acknowledging the *'Unknown Christ within Hinduism'*.

In Rahner's theology of religions, the non-Christian religions were not really the focus of discussion was on individuals of other faiths, that led to Hans Kung's criticism that Rahner was reaffirming the doctrine of extra ecclesiasm *nulla salus* through the 'back door', Panikkar on the other hand, believed that Hinduism can be and should be a vehicle for salvation because of the presence of the 'unknown Christ' within it, and it rendered conversion unnecessary.

Christianity and the church were not his concern since it is Christ who mediates and brings salvation. However, although he may have appeared to solve the problem of conversion of Hindus, his approach was still based on the concept of Christ and relied on the acceptance by Hindus of the need for one mediator. Although Panikkar's combination of Thomastic and Vedantic terminology very much impressed Boyd and others, many critics saw him as still holding the superiority of Christianity over Hinduism, which pleased neither those theologians who wanted to acknowledge the legitimacy of Hinduism on a par with Christianity, nor Hindus, who felt insulted. Nevertheless, Panikkar's acceptance of Hinduism as a legitimate way of salvation laid the groundwork for Catholic theologians in India to move from 'Indian Christianity' to 'Hindu Christianity'.

V. Hindu-Catholic Approach to Conversion

It was Hans Staffner, an Austrian Jesuit and Bede Griffiths, an English Benedictine, who applied the inculturation approach to the problem of conversion in India by attempting a synthesis of the two religions. Staffner, following Uppadhyay's Hind-Catholic approach looked for complementariness in the two faiths, that do not conflict with the vital belief and practice of either, Staffner's theological synthesis clearly originated in the struggle of Indian Christians over conversion. It was his conviction that conversion was a 'purely spiritual event' and therefore, changing one's community should not be any part of it. He argued that, since Hinduism is the religion of the Hindus and is defined by race or geography, membership of the Hindu community, it is not based on defined creeds or belief.

Echoing Uppadhyay, he regarded religion as having two dimensions *Samaj dharma* (social custom, ritual purity, diet etc.) and *Sadhana dharma* (the way of salvation). Hinduism, he believed, falls primarily into the former category but since the essence of Catholic Christianity is doctrine, faith in God and it is quite accommodating of social customs, and culture, Christianity is primarily *sadhana dharma*.[12]

Therefore, Christianity and Hinduism complement each other and can be synthesized. Conversion is then no longer necessary, since adherents of each can 'embrace' rather than 'renounce' the essence of the other religious tradition while remaining in their own community. Hindu-Catholic theology was very influential among Indian Catholic theologians in the 1970s stimulated inter-religious dialogue initiated mainly by the Catholics.

Ashram Paddhati

Although there had been some Protestant *ashrams*, the leading proponents of *ashram* after Vatican II were Catholics, led by Fr. Jules Monchanin and Swami Abhishakananda, who were both French Benedictine.[13]

The inspiration of the early Christian Ashram movement can be traced to the 'Brahmo Samaj' as well as to the Gandhian traditions, which drew inspiration from the Vedas. The practice of Christian *ashram* nonetheless the origin and practice predates the initiatives of the 1960s. It should not be forgotten that *ashram* movement also has its roots in the practice of Roberto de Nobili and those who came after him, who lived as monks, *sannyasi* until the Vatican withdrew its support from the experiment and indeed forbade continuing. The work of these *ashrams* is the subject of the Helen Ralston's volume *Christian ashrams: A New Religious Movement in Contemporary India.*

The calling of four European men in the 1950s is also important for the development of Christian *ashrams* in South India. Jules Monchanin (1895-1957), a Frenchman came to India in 1939. Monchanin embraced the *Sannyasi* ideal and in 1950 together with another Frenchman Henri Le Saux founded the *Sachidananda Ashram* at Shantivanam near Kulittalai on the banks of the Kavery River in Tamil Nadu. The second figure Hemi Le Saux (1910-1973) is also known as Abhishiktananda. The third figure is Bede Griffiths (1906-1973) who developed the work of Shantivanam taking the role of the *guru* there in 1968. The fourth is Francis Mahileyu (1912-2002), a Belgian priest and mind who with Bede Griffiths founded an *Ashram* in Kerala in 1958.

In the 1970s, Griffiths became a leading figure in the Catholic *ashram* movement and engaged in debate with Hindus. The theological understanding of Griffiths is clearly expressed in his book *Christ in India* (1966) collection of his papers. Like Panikkar, he believed that the meeting place between Christianity and Hinduism must be in Christ, insisting that Christ is 'reality', whereas Christianity and Hinduism are religions, which are manifestations of the reality and not reality itself. He sought to present Christ by adopting the *Sarvodaya* or 'service of all' movement popularized by Gandhi's disciple Vinoba Bhave. It is based on the Hindu philosophy of self-realisation, that is, Christ is found by entering into deeper realm of spiritual reality and conversion into Christianity is not required. While, in his interpretation of Hinduism, he exhibited a great sense of respect and appreciation of Hindu culture, in his theological thinking, like Staffner, he held a 'fulfilment' approach to Hinduism, separating religion from Hindu culture. He wrote:

> Christ did not come to destroy the religion; he came to correct, complete, and fulfil them. It can even be asserted that these other religions are a providential preparation for Christianity, by which the people of the East have been led through the course of their history towards their fulfilment in Christ. Thus, Buddha can be viewed as a forerunner of Christ, Krishna as a type of Christ.

He concluded that the church's mission is to identify the 'true place of Christ in India' for the purpose of 'saving' anything good and true in Hinduism and purifying anything erroneous or corrupt so that Hindus could learn to discover Christ as the true fulfilment.

Protestant Debate—1970s

Both the Nairobi Assembly of the WCC in 1975 and the Willowbank Report 1978 emphasized on the promotion of dialogue with people of other faiths and felt the need to redefine 'conversion'. This non-confrontational approach necessitated a reinterpretation of the meaning of conversion within the consular ecumenical movement.

This redefinition was necessitated due to growing opposition to conversion and both Orthodox and Catholic churches were under pressure to separate conversion from proselytism. The later was defined as a "corruption of Christian witness" in which "cajolery, bribery, undue pressure, or intimidation is used—subtly or openly—to bring about seeming conversion."[14]

In a Protestant consultation held in 1977 on 'Re-Reading Mass Movements in India' considered different motives and modes of conversion, and suggested to the Indian Church the adoption of methods more sympathetic to the cultural context.

'Inculturation' became the dominant concept of Catholic Mission Theology soon after the term was introduced in the second half of the century, but the precise meaning of the term and its applications could range from adopting the gospel to local culture to encouraging 'theology from below', or 'local theologies', as a way forward in Christian mission.

Any form of proselytism was renounced in Christian mission, and even condemned as a scandal and counter witnesses. As the century wore on, the earlier disapproval of proselytism for its unethical methods both towards Christians on other traditions and towards people of other religions developed into renunciation of any attempt to convert those of other confessions or faiths.

The condemnation of proselytism encouraged the application of the term 'conversion' to Christians themselves rather than to people of other faiths. There was a move to justify secular Christianity in which conversion was of Christians 'to the world'. This was accompanied by a widening of the understanding of mission.

Inter-Religious Dialogue

In 1960s, the churches in India tried their hand on *Ashram paddhati* (*ashram* style). Dialogue with Hindus was in vogue in the 1970s. Before the Second Vatican Council, the spirit of most Catholic missionaries was that of "active hostility or grudging tolerance towards the practices and beliefs of non-Christians."

However, much before Vatican II in December 1956 at Madras a "Study Week on Indian Culture and Fullness of Christ" was organised whose conclusions stressed the need to recognize the positive values in Indian thought and to use Indian philosophy to express them with Christian wisdom. In 1958, a seminar held in Bangalore discussed Christianity and Hinduism. In these decrees and seminars, the initiatives in formulating an increasingly positive attitude towards Hinduism most often seem to come from non-Indian sources (from foreign born theologians and missionaries and non-Indian theologies).

The Christian-Hindu dialogue now advocated in India is not a direct development of the relationships that existed during the first six decades of this century and earlier. In the 1960s, the

Protestants initiatives appeared to have been more significant than the Catholics. One organisation closely involved in dialogue at both theatrical and practical levels had been Christian Institute for the Study of Religion and Society (CISRS) founded in Bangalore in 1957 with aim to facilitate Christian participation in nation-building and to promote inter-religious dialogue. The CISRS called for building a common secular society in India "based on consideration of social justice, personal values and human rights." The CISRS also came out with a pamphlets and monographs on inter-religious dialogues. One major figure in this movement was the lay theologian M.M. Thomas (1916-1996) who was Director of CISRS from 1962-1975. During 1960s not only did CISRS continue to sponsor meetings to discuss inter-religious relationships but other Protestant bodies were also willing to take or to be associated with such initiatives.

In the Indian Catholic Church, a small ecumenical group committed to dialogue emerged as 'the Circle' in the early 1960s under the leadership of Jacques Albert Cuttat, Murray Rogers, and Swami Abhishiktananda (a Catholic priest) in order to discuss Christian and Hindu spirituality. This was non-Indian initiative. These efforts suggest a steady shift towards a more liberal attitude towards other religions during the 1960s and 1970s. A conference was held in Bombay in 1964, which became reference for dialogues with other religions. With the formation of the Secretaries for Non-Christian Religions at the Vatican in 1964 new approaches were consolidated by the Second Vatican Council.

By 1966, the word "dialogue" was firmly established in CBCI deliberations and statements and in the title of the CBCI Dialogue Commission, which began in 1966 as a 'Commission for Ecumenism, and Dialogue'. It later became the separate Commission for Dialogue and Relations with Non-Christian Religions and Others. The Commission "promotes the spirit and practice of dialogue in the Church in India; it offers inspiration, direction and help where necessary, and is a centre for coordination and information about the practice of dialogue by the Church."

However, despite wide ranging statements of its Commission of Dialogue, a search of the minutes of its meeting reveals that the CBCI itself gave little and often no attention to inter-faith relationship. In 1970, the Vatican II spirit did push the CBCI to look into pluralism in a realistic way.[15]

The dialogue became part of the CBCI but its future role seems less clear with the absorption of the Commission into the larger "Commission for Proclamation, Ecumenism and Dialogue" (from 1982) although from April 1986 it became the "Commission for Ecumenism and Dialogue".

Another rich source of information about attitudes to dialogue is found in statements from four meetings held during a six-year period of considerable reflection on dialogue and related themes. They are:

- The Declaration of the All India Seminar on the Church in India Today held in Bangalore, 1969.
- The Declaration of International Theological Conference on Evangelization and Dialogue in India Nagpur, 1971.
- The Declaration of the All India Consultation on Evangelization, Patna, 1973.
- The Communication of the CBCI to the Roman Synod in 1974.

Of the many subjects discussed in these statements what seems to have contributed significantly to interest in dialogue is the need for the church in India to become more deeply Indian in its whole life. All these led to realize among Christian theologians that a dialogue with Hindus is important in a pluralistic country like India. However, did Hindus consider inter-religious dialogue of any use? What was their reaction to inter-religious dialogue after Ecclesia Asia issued in 1999 by the Pope in India. More on this in the coming chapters.

Christian advocates of dialogue have often faced difficulty in the perceived lack of interest or response by potential Hindu partner in dialogue. Almost all imitatives for dialogue seem to come from the Christian side.

VI. Conversion, Secularization, and Community

The Protestant debate on conversion in the 1970s and early 1980s was a part of the wider Christian discussion in the face of the political and social revolution—taking place in many parts of the world and urgent calls for the church to take parts in the struggle of humanization. There was a conscious shift of emphasis in mission from evangelism (leading to conversion) towards social involvement. In India, Christian theologians faced increasing challenges from the Hindu nationalist movement, especially as it started to gain support from certain states and pressured the Central Government for the rights of Hindus over other minority communities.

As discussed above, some Indian Protestant theologians searching for a solution suggested that the Christian community in India should be part of the wider Hindu community in apparently rapidly secularizing India, for they believed that not only was secularization an inevitable process of modernity but also that it would gradually overcome communal tensions. They insisted that a 'point of contact' between the Christian community and the Hindu community must be established so that Hindus would not need to convert to the Christian community. This point of contract must be located inside the wider Hindu community since the Christian community was either an obstacle in this process, or an entity that naturally transcended religious divides to produce a secular fellowship.

One of the key points in the debates among the Protestant theologians was the question of whether the Church is a legitimate 'point of contact' for Christians and Hindus. Thomas and Baggo rejected the church and found the 'point of contact' outside the church. In contrast to Catholic theologians, many Protestants were ready to discard the church as non-essential part of the gospel.

The problem of the association of the church with the colonial authority and, even after the independence, the continued dependency of Indian churches on Western churches, particularly in the area of leadership and finance made it difficult for Thomas and others to treat the church as non-essential part of the gospel.

However, though it was a sincere search for a solution to the problem of conversion in India, Thomas' work has serious shortcomings, the most obvious of which was that he assumed that secularization would prevail in India and that the 'secular fellowship' would not only be possible but also be the only possible means of Christian witness in secular society. His optimistic predictions of the disappearance of differences between religious communities, the demise of religious fanaticism, and the placing of greater value on humanization over religious matters did not materialize.

Instead, despite modernization, religious values, religious communities, and fundamentalist groups were to play important role in the daily socio-political lives of the Hindus. In fact, this tendency was quite evident in the 1960s, as shown by the Niyogi Report and the emergence of various Hindu nationalist movements into the mainstream of political power in India. Thomas failed to read the driving intention of the Hindu objections to Christianity, particularly Christian conversion. Along with many other contemporary Indian Protestant theologians, he thought that the main Hindu objections were the foreignness of the Indian church, the communal aspect of Christian experience, and the exclusive interpretation of the Christian gospel. He did not foresee that the Hindu nationalist movement would grow and exhibit strong opposition towards anything that did not fit into Hindu socio-cultural and religious compartments.

Furthermore, the attempts of Thomas and others at creating a 'secular fellowship' within the Hindu community led to an identity crisis for caste Hindu converts who found themselves neither fully belonging to the Hindu community nor to the Christians. The dilemma was even more acute for Christians from *dalit* background, which made up the vast majority of the Indian churches. For them, conversion to Christianity was part of a struggle for religious and social identity that they had previously lacked and now they were being expected to deny this identity. The problem of Thomas' approach was that Indian Christians would become individuals who follow Christ but no ground for their social and religious interaction with their fellow believers. In the midst of communal tension and rising Hindu nationalist movements, Christian converts would find themselves rootless individuals feeling that any support of the Christian community would be understood as communal and therefore, unethical.[16]

There was a tendency to think that anything particular to Christianity and against the interest of the larger Hindu community was incompatible with the search for a 'common humanity' and must, therefore, be rejected, not on the grounds of whether it was right or wrong but on the grounds that it contributed to communal tension. Religious conversion was certainly viewed in this category: among all the Christian teachings and practices, it was regarded as most destructive for Indian society in general and for communal relations between Hindus and Christians in particular.

The decade of 1970s was an era of confusion among churches in India. The role of Christian's *ashrams* is unclear. Many of them started under Protestant leadership have often faltered under their second generation leaders. Stanley Samarth, in an article published in 1980 comments that the *ashram* movement "has almost dried up." The prevalent view among Hindus is that Christian *ashrams* are mainly for 'foreigners' and some recent conservative Hindus' comment were extremely negative. They (Hindus) are apprehensive of Christians' real intentions behind dialogue. They feel that it is a means to 'convince' them that conversion is not wrong. Hindus feel that these dialogues are a 'trap' for acceptability and not for serious search for Indianness or to understand India.

The WCC and the Vatican took initiative to invite Hindus for inter-religious dialogue but there is not a single example of Hindu *sadhus, Akharas* of Haridwar or Ayodhya or Varanasi inviting any Christian representative from Vatican or WCC. Why? It indicates who is in need of inter-religious dialogue and for what reasons. The experience of the inter-religious dialogue indicates that Hindus rejected any exclusive claim to possession of religious truth by either Islam or Christianity.[17]

One major weakness is that majority of Indian Christians are not clear about the purpose of inter-religious dialogue and think it unnecessary or unwise. One reason for this may be that generally ordinary Christians are closer to the Hindu community in their daily life than religious living in ivory towers of Bishop's houses or pastoral centres.

In summary, in spite of their honest search for an answer to the communal problems supposedly caused by conversion, Indian Protestant theologians appear, by limiting the implications of conversion to the individual and spiritual realm of life, to have caused a weakening of the 'character and energy' of the Christian community. Any theology that encouraged Indian Christians to conform to Hindu society left them in the dilemma that they were neither accepted as Hindus nor able to identify themselves with a Christian community.

Conclusion

The 1950s and 1960s appeared to be decades of relative cooperation and consensus but that apparent religious conflict re-emerged from the alter 1970s. In the 1970s new economic pressures, serious drop in crop production, disrupting in public distribution system in the shape of a global economic crisis and new political—the loss of Congress power after the Emergency—altered context of ethnic and religious mobilisation. The Congress government under Indira stressed on the affirmative action is based on caste that threatened the power structure in the rural areas most. The RSS subscribed to the idea of reservations to have an economic basis. The Christian leaders sided with the *Dalits*. From the early 1970s, spearheaded by the militant *Dalit* Panthers of Maharashtra, new social movements emerged on the Indian political arena challenging the system.

India experienced other social transformations, including the rise of new intermediate peasant classes, and by the end of that decade, the dominance of the Congress regime faced some of its first serious challenges. The RSS through Jana Sangh had first taste of power at the centre in 1977 in the aftermath of the Emergency, with the formation of the Janata Government under the leadership of Morarji Desai. The Janata Government of 1977-1980 was composed of a somewhat uneasy alliance of Bharatiya Lok Dal (led by Choudhry Charan Singh), the Congress (O), the Jana Sangh led by Atal Bihari Vajpayee, the Swatantra Party and the Socialists. The widespread conflict over reservations that erupted regularly in northern and western India from the 1970s through the 1980s changed the public discourse on religious freedom.

In the 1970s, Indian political system faced a many challenges: the ethno-linguistic plurality of the country, autonomist and/or communal conflicts, affirmative action tension and so on. Nevertheless, overall India controlled disintegrative tendencies and Rajni Kothari, the eminent analyst of Indian political development, attributed this success to India's adherence to secularism as a state policy and the development of the institutions of participate democracy as a 'mechanism' for the change.

From legal point of view, some drastic changes came into existence relating to the religious freedom during the 1970s. In 1976, the 42 Amendment was enacted by Prime Minister Indira Gandhi, which formally added the word 'secular' before the words Democratic Republic in the Constitution of India. The next year in 1977, Article 25 was amended in Supreme Court ruling that the right to propagate religion, after all, did not extend to the right to convert. Thus, even as India was increasingly being defined as a secular state, limits were being placed on the practice of prosetelizing religions—specially Islam and Christianity.

Notes

1. Kohli, Atul and Prerna Singh (2013). *Routledge Handbook of Indian Politics,* Routledge.
2. Somerville, Barbara A. (2007). *Indira Gandhi: Political Leader in India,* Capstone.
3. John, Aruthuckal Varughese, Atola Longkumer and Nigel Ajay Kumar (2017). *Religious Freedom and Conversion in India,* Papers from 4th SAIACS Academic Consultation, SAIACS Press.
4. South Asia Human Rights Documentation Centre (2007). *Anti-Conversion Laws in India,* Human Rights Features, HER/157/07.
5. *The Examiner,* February 10, 1979.
6. World Council of Churches (2006). "Report from Inter-religious Consultation on Conversion: Assessing the Reality", *Current Dialogue,* Issue 47, June.
7. Kuttiyanikkal, Ciril J. (2014). "Khrist Bhakta Movement: A Model for an Indian Church? *Inculturation in the Area of Community Building,* LIT Verlag Münster, p. 82.
8. Robinson, Bob (2004). *Christians Meeting Hindus: An Analysis and Theological Critique of the Hindu-Christian Encounter in India,* OCMS.
9. Thomas, M.M. (1971), *Salvation, and Humanisation: Some Critical issues of the Theology of Masson in Contemporary India.* Madras: CLS, pp. 4-12.
10. Ninan, M.M. (2009), *Life, Legacy and Theology of M.M. Thomas: An Anthology, Create Space,* Independent Publishing Platform.
11. Swamy, Muthuraj (2016), *The Problem with Interreligious Dialogue: Plurality, Conflict and Elitism in Hindu-Christian-Muslim Relations,* Bloomsbury Publishing.
12. Robinson, Bob (2004), *Christians Meeting Hindus: An Analysis and Theological Critique of the Hindu-Christian Encounter in India,* OCMS.
13. Monchanin, also known as Swami Param Arubi Ananda, started Sacchidananda *Ashram* at Tiruchirapalli in South Tamil Nadu in 1950. Abhisekhananda, formerly Dom Henri Le Sauzx, worked with him there and later lived the life of a *sannyasi.*
14. "Towards Common Witness—A call to Adopt Responsible Relationships in Mission and to Renounce Proselytism", *IRM,* October 1997: 463-73.

15. Merrigan, Terrence and John Friday, (2017). *The Past, Present, and Future of Theologies of Interreligious Dialogue,* Oxford University Press.
16. Buckser, Andrew and Stephen D. Glazier (2003). *The Anthropology of Religious Conversion,* Rowman & Littlefield.
17. Latinovic, Vladimir, Gerard Mannion and Peter C. Phan (2016). *Pathways for Inter-Religious Dialogue in the Twenty-First Century,* Springer.

6
Fire in the Dump
Religious Freedom Debates in 1980s

Introduction

During the 1980s, a strong current of Hindu revivalism became apparent in India. While nation's tension between tradition and change were broadly shared with other societies, including Western Europe and the US, the specifics remained distinctive. Starting in the mid-1980s, a series of economic reforms, implemented under the banners of 'liberalization' and subsequently, 'globalization' had brought a movement towards new, externally oriented, consumption-led path to national prosperity. It was also era of the rise of mass consumerism in India, as an explicit challenge to the developmentlists dispensation of the post-independence years. It created the crisis of value.

It was time when highly articulated rightwing spokespersons of Indian society argued that Hinduization of India would be good not just for the Hindu majority but for the entire nation. We cannot explain the sudden impact and diffusion of *Hindutva* but a number of incidents in the national arena in the early 1980s caused the RSS, and the affiliated organisation like VHP to develop strategies for making Ayodhya focus of Hindu-Muslim tension. These incidences include the conversion of *Dalit* Hindus to Islam in Meenakashipuram in South India in 1981; the violent reactions of Muslims in India at the killings of more than one thousand Muslims by 'tribals' at Nellie in Assam in 1984; the agitation of Muslims against the ruling of Supreme Court in 1985 on the *Shah Bano* case which they perceived as a secular threat to the *Sharia* in matters of personal law; and Muslim agitation in 1988 demanding that Rushdie's book *The Satanic Verses* be banned as blasphemous of Islam and government's refusal to ban book which rightwing leaders considered blasphemous to Hinduism.[1]

In the 1980s, three campaigns were launched: one of them—and by far most successful—was the *Ramjanmabhumi* campaign to awaken and unite Hindus; second, legal restrains on conversions of Hindus to other religions particularly Islam or Christianity and, the third was common civil code. This era saw renewed efforts for creation of dynamic Hinduism, which encompasses Sikhs, Buddhists, and Jains as Hindus. The *Ramjanmabhumi* campaign was represented as a protest against symbols of rule over India.

Meanwhile, a new dimension of liberation theology was brought into freedom of religion debates by the Christians particularly by the Roman Catholics. The debate on conversion between the Hindu-Catholic approach in this period was influenced by theological changes fostered by the Latin American liberation theology. The debate over Hindu *Dalits'* mass conversion to Islam in the 1980s apparently for socio-economic and caste reasons made Catholic theologians to systematically interpret liberation theology in India.

Fire in the Dump

The reaction to Meenakashipuram conversion in 1981 gave impetus to a new hegemony: the Bharatiya Janata Party (BJP), a party ideologically motivated by *Hindutva* ('Hindu-ness'), an amalgam of nationalist and religious concerns. During this time, religious parties and tensions arose for a mix of political, psychological, socio-economic, and cultural reasons, in the overall context of swift modernisation. It is important to note that they are not mutually exclusive—and none can claim to be exclusively 'correct'—but taken together they may explain reasonably well the rather unexpected resurgence of religious tensions in politics in India in recent years.

During the 1908s, the BJP adopted Hindu profile and has since progressively raised it. At the same time, the polarization of Hindus and Muslims became more accentuated. During the 1980s, there was a steep rise in militant confrontations between the two communities. In the process of growing Hindu resurgence and reinforced polarization between Hindus and Muslims, religion played a focal and multidimensional role. In 1984, the idea of liberating what was called the *Ramjanmabhumi* was introduced by the Vishwa Hindu Parishad.

More fuel to the fire was added in 1985 by Muslim agitation against the ruling of the Supreme Court in the *Shah Bano* case that proved to be a watershed in Hindu-Muslim relations, in that it exposed the inconsistent secularism of the ruling Congress Party. Hindus began to perceive it in terms of demands being made on them to accept reforms of their religious customs in accordance with the secularism of the state, and allowing the Muslims to continue to be governed by the *Sharia* laws immune from similar secular reforms, for fear of losing the Muslim bloc vote in elections. This became especially apparent when in 1986 Rajiv Gandhi forced the Muslim Women (Protection of Rights on Divorce) Act through Parliament to overrule the decision of Supreme Court in the *Shah Bano* case.

The importance of religion in this period was also highlighted by the conflict between Indira Gandhi and Sikh sentiments in support of the Punjab becoming a separate state to be called 'Khalistan'. In the late 1981 and 1982, Punjab burned and several Hindus were killed by the Khalistan commandos. The fear and terror let loose in Punjab helped to contribute to the growth of a militant movement for a separate Punjab, which culminated in the occupation of the Golden Temple in Amritsar by the militant leader Jarnail Singh Bhindrawale and his armed supporters. In an effort to end this situation, Indira Gandhi ordered the military to storm the temple in June 1984, which led to the death of Bhindrawale and many of his followers. This led to a cycle of violence when Indira Gandhi's Sikh security guards assassinated her in October 1984, which itself then led to widespread anti-Sikh rioting in which a very large number of people lost their lives.[2]

In 1981, large number of Scheduled Caste families converted to Islam in Meenakshipuran and several villages in South Tamil Nadu brought about unprecedented public controversy. This collective conversion was only the first in a series in the course of the next seven months during which some 3,000 Untouchables went over to Islam.

In 1982, session of Parliament opened with the announcement that in the past two years 900 *Dalits* had been killed in the country. The communal situation was further exacerbated by way of lower castes conversions to Islam or Christianity—the only way an 'untouchable' could escape his fate of caste. The mass conversion of lower castes sparked off yet more atrocities against them. Hindu organisations demanded that the government should ban conversions. Indira did not yield, insisting that India was a secular state and that banning conversion was 'incompatible' with the religious freedom guaranteed by the Constitution. Nevertheless, Indira Gandhi advised them to create a peaceful atmosphere to facilitate the task of the government. The erstwhile Maharaja of Kashmir, Karan Singh, a Congress leader and a former central minister, established Virat Hindu Samaj in September 1981, to protect Hinduism with the cooperation of RSS and BJP leaders who later hijacked the movement.[3]

The Meenakshipuram conversion to Islam resulted in the so-called "Hindu backlash"—a term coined during the 1984 elections. Nevertheless, due to brutal assassination of Indira Gandhi by her two Sikh bodyguards in October 1984, the Congress Party won the Lok Sabha elections due to sympathy wave and Rajiv Gandhi became the Prime Minister of India.

During 1980s when Indira Gandhi's son Rajiv Gandhi became Prime Minister, the Hindu identity politics became more visible and aggressive in India. A number of factors contributed to this including underlying dissatisfaction with dynastic Congress policies. However, two other factors were vitally important: the growth of mass media (Television) and growing influence of ultra rightwing Hindu political groups. The spread of television after 1984 outside the metro cities a new mass audience of Hindus and other vernacular languages became more important. This created a split public with liberal secular views more associated with the older English language media, and more radical Hindu identity characterizing the Hindi and vernacular channels. Within this, a major contribution was made by nationally serialised TV version of the Indian epics the *Ramayana* and the *Mahabharata*. Ramanand Sagar's 78-episode serialisation of the *Ramayana,* directed by Ravi Chopra, broadcast from 1988 to 1990 was a new focus for community viewing and became way in which new understanding of what it meant to be Hindu came into existence based on the values of the epics.

Around this time, the BJP under the leadership of A.B. Vajpayee and L.K. Advani joined a major campaign of public agitation to construct temple in Ayodhya at the reputed site of the birth of Ram, the hero of the *Ramayana* and an incarnation of God Vishnu. However, the location was in dispute and had been the site of mosque since 1572 when the Mughal emperor had a mosque built there called the Babri Masjid.

In May 1989 at the Hindu festival of the *Kumbh Mela* at Allahabad, which was attended by around twenty nine million people, Hindu groups led by VHP encouraged volunteers (*karsevaks*) to converge on the Babri Masjid site bringing with them bricks from every one of the 6,00,000 villages in India. Advani was very prominent in this campaign. To encourage the *karsevaks* he rode in a truck converted to a replica of an ancient chariot and staged a Ram Rathyatra from Gujarat to Ayodhya in September and October 1990. His followers were prevented by the Uttar Pradesh state government under Mulayam Singh Yadav from actually reaching Ayodhya and Advani himself was arrested in Bihar at the orders of Chief Minister Lalu Prasad Yadav.

This was difficult period for minorities such as Muslims and Christians. Religious conversion came under fire for various reasons. Muslims were criticised for their population growth and the Christian activities were targeted due to Mrs. Sonia Gandhi (an Italian Catholic married to Rajiv Gandhi) becoming powerful leader of the Congress Party. Missionary social work and philanthropic activities were particularly targeted. Propaganda was carried by the rightwing Hindu forces that there is 'conspiracy' to make India a Christian country.

Ramjanmabhumi Movement, 1984

Between 1984 and 1992, the VHP and BJP planned and executed three nationwide politico-religious manifestations with Ayodhya as their focus. The aim was to mobilise the Hindu community in order to liberate Lord Rama from his imprisonment in the Babri Masjid, to demolish the mosque, to regain Ramjanmabhumi, to built a temple on it for him, to gain electoral victories for the BJP; to reduce the Muslims to their proper place, and so promote the Hinduism of *Hindutva,* i.e. of India as a nation of Hindus.

The VHP organised first *dharmasansad* (religious meet) in New Delhi from 7 to April 9, 1984 that was attended by 558 delegates from 76 different Hindu religious groups. One of the items discussed was the Ramjanmabhumi controversy. The basis for the participation of Hindu religious leaders of very different hue in the Ram Rathyatra Yagna campaign of late 1984 was laid at this meeting.

The foundation of these campaigns was laid by the success of the month long *katmata yagna* from November 16 to December 16, 1883. In October 1984, a petition *yatra* was organised from Ayodhya to Lucknow but it lost its thrust due to the assassination of Indira Gandhi on 31st October by her Sikh bodyguards. The BJP lost the elections heavily. It retained only two of its sixteen seats in Parliament.

Although the first results of the Ramjanmabhumi movement were very disappointing for the VHP, a major success followed in early 1986. The VHP resumed the *yatra* from 25 places in Uttar Pradesh and Bihar on October 23, 1985, organizing six processions through the states. In early 1986, one young lawyer obtained a court order from the Farrukhabad judge for the gates of the fence around the Babri mosque to be opened. The court order sparked serious communal violence in the North Indian cities. In 1989 elections, the VHP launched its second nationwide campaign to liberate Sri Rama from 'jail'. A brick campaign donation from every village was also launched. The *yatra* passed through Muslim districts and villages led to bloody riots, particularly Bhagalpur in Bihar, with hundreds being killed on both sides. The *shilanyas* ceremony took place some sixty metre from the gate of the Babri mosque. In 1989 elections, the BJP went from two to 85 seats in the national parliament. In September 1990, the third nationwide mobilising campaign was launched for Rama temple. What happened in 1992 is now history but more on this in the next chapter.

During Rajiv Gandhi rule, famous *Shah Bano* issue made "Muslim appeasement" word summed up Hindus objection to reversing the Supreme Court judgement.

In a landmark judgement delivered in April 1985, India's Supreme Court granted a small maintenance allowance to Shah Bano, seventy three year old Muslim divorcee, to be paid by her husband under the Indian Criminal Code. Shah Bano had been married to Mohd. Ahmed Khan since 1932. Ahmed Khan married again in 1946 and in 1978. Because of property, related disputes between the two wives, Shah Bano, and her children moved out from their family home; in 1978, she filed a maintenance suit against her husband in the Judicial Magistrate's Court in Indore and pleaded for Rs. 500 as monthly maintenance. To avoid maintenance under Section 125 of Criminal Procedure Code. Khan divorced Shah Bano by irrevocable triple *talak*. The case went to High Court, which upheld the previous order. In an appeal to the Supreme Court Ahmed Khan argued that since he had fulfilled his obligations under religious personal laws, Islamic law placed no further maintenance liability upon him; rather Section 125 conflicted with his rights under personal laws. The Supreme Court confirmed the judgement of the Madhya Pradesh High Court. The Court ruled that Section 125, as part of criminal rather than civil law, override all personal laws and is uniformly applicable to all women, including Muslim women.

The judgement sparked off a major political uproar. Outraged by the judgement, the religious leadership, including the Jamat-e-Islami, the Jamait-al-Ulema and the All India Muslim Personal Law Board spearheaded an agitation to repeal it.

To offset the Supreme Court's decision, the Rajiv Gandhi government enacted Muslim Women's Act (MWA) of 1986. Prime Minister Rajiv Gandhi sought to placate the disquiet of the religious leadership and their perception of threat to Muslim identity by enacting the MWA to override the judgement and unequivocally exclude Muslim women from the purview of the Criminal Code, to which all citizens otherwise had recourse. The Act shows that the Indian state has tacitly accepted that it cannot intervene and initiate change in religious personal laws namely, the private spheres of Muslims. This raised two questions here. One is relationship of Muslim person with the state. The second and more complicated question is whether the Indian state, through its courts and parliament can initiate social reform for other religions in the same way as these institutions had intervened to change Hindu family laws. *The Shah Bano* case speeded up the assertion of Hindu identity due to renewed emphasis on Muslim identity by fundamentalist Muslims. This gave impetus to new Hindu nationalism.

Governmental policy in the *Shah Bano* case played right into the hands of powerful religious leaders who do not consult women. It bolstered the existence in the power structure of the community, accepted the clergy as the sole spokespersons, and allowed them to define any potential change in the Muslim community's practices as a distortion of religiously sanctioned practices.

This step of Rajiv Gandhi created an impression among Hindu groups that the government is following minority (Muslim) appeasement policy.

Moving Closer to Majoritarianism

Whether to call it co-incidence or some well thought out plan that, the gates of Babri Masjid site were thrown open to Hindus on February 1, 1986, the same day when His Holiness Pope John Paul II landed in India. Some organisations like RSS and Vishwa Hindu Parishad, which are related to the BJP, opposed Pope's visit to India accusing that Prime Minister Rajiv Gandhi's Italian Catholic wife Sonia of Instrument behind Pope's visit.

On February 1, 1986, in the midst of increasing heated suits and counter-suits that registered competing to the site of the Mosque, the District Magistrate of Faizabad, K.M. Pandey, ordered that the barred gates of the site be thrown open to Hindu *bhajan* and *puja*, and further ordered the State of Uttar Pradesh not obstruct the performance of these rituals in any manner, the five hundred year old Masjid had after all long ago fallen into despair and for several years before the appearance of the statue of Rama, not even been used as house of worship.

In November 1989, Rajiv Gandhi's centre-right Congress government allowed the foundation stone for a temple to be laid at the site of the Babri Masjid and as Dubasi tells us, this was also the time in which the rank and file of the Hindu right became increasingly agitated in their claims for a Ram Temple to be actually built at the site of the mosque. The BJP passed Ayodhya Resolution in 1989.

Before beginning to draft the Ayodhya Resolution in June 1989, the BJPs National Executive Committee had insisted unanimously on one thing: the proposed temple in honour of Sri Ram was first a political issue, and it must be presented to the community at large as in fact the very cornerstone of *Hindutva* politics. At the same time, the Resolution stubbornly proclaimed that the solution to the problem, and indeed the problem itself is outside the bound of law.

Battle of 1989 general election was fought between Rajiv Gandhi and V.P. Singh of National Front. Bofors issue got prominence in this election. The 'National Front' led by Janata Dal won the 1989 general elections, supported by the 'left wing' and the 'right wing' parties. The JD coalition took over, bringing the 'One-Party' dominance of Congress to end. This was the first time that General Elections in India failed to produce a majority for any party. One of the most surprising aspects of the Ninth Lok Sabha Election in 1989 was spectacular performance of the Bharatiya Janata Party, which improved its position from a mere two seats in 1984 General Elections to 85 seats in 1989.

L.K. Advani was at the helm of party affairs at this time. It was a trial and for sweet surprise of BJP, the Ramjanmabhumi issue paid handsome dividends in the very first year of its inception. The BJP leaders have now discovered an emotional formula to go ahead that will bring them to power to rule the North Block in future. While Bofors was the main story of 1989 general election, Ayodhya was also running as side story. In the election of 1991, Ayodhya became the theme in major parts of India.

Debate Over Mass Conversion in Meenakshipuram

The Indian public opinion against religious conversion reached its peak after hundreds of Scheduled Caste families in Meenakshipuram in Tirunelveli district had converted to Islam in February 1981, when the late M.G. Ramachandran was the Chief Minister of Tamil Nadu. This sent Shock Waves across the nation. However, more conversions took place in Madurai, and Remand in southern Tamil Nadu. These mass conversions were seen as evidence of force, fraud, or monetary inducements, and it was propagated that the bounty of Arab petro-dollars had funded a 'political invasion' and entrapped *Dalits*. Hindu groups blamed on the 'lure of the petro-dollar' and the government was urged to ban conversion.

Other events that led to stir latent passions were *Shah Bano* case (1985), Khalisthan movement, Hindus (Kashmiri Pandits) being driven out of the Kashmir Valley by extremists, and several cases of conversion in Assam, Tripura and tribal belts of central India. Alarmed with large number of conversion by tribals and *dalits*, the RSS launched programmes to "reclaim" the lot back to Hindu fold. The belief within the RSS, and thus the VHP, was that the number of Hindus were dwindling because they are being "lured" by minority religions, and if this is allowed unchecked it would result in the loss of political power to the 'other'. According to the leadership of the VHP, Christianity and Islam had plans "to make Hindus a minority in India in the next 30 years; and, that they want to establish their rule in India and completely destroy Hindu culture." The Sangh Parivar also vigorously labelled Islam and Christianity as "foreign religions" and, therefore, to be opposed.

In response to growing opposition, the minorities, particularly Catholic Church was keen to come up with a solid reasons why people wish to convert. The Jesuit priests emphasized on the "liberation theology" as an answer.

Christian Response to Mass Conversion

The liberation model of enculturation in India emerged from a critical analysis of development projects in which many Catholic workers were involved and the oppression of *Dalits* and tribals was analysed in the light of contemporary liberation theology, focusing on issues of human dignity and identity as well as economic condition. The emergence of liberation theology in Latin America has led to a major reinterpretation of conversion in the Catholic Church. The document produced by the Latin American Bishop's meeting at Medellin, Colombia in 1968 stated that the church should follow the example of Christ who demonstrated the 'preference to the poor' and called for a 'sincere conversion for the common welfare' of others. Furthermore, the Bishops affirmed 'the value and legitimate anatomy of temporal tasks', which means what was regarded as outside the scope of 'spiritual salvation' was no longer treated as secondary or inferior.[4] Thus, the focus of conversion to God became 'conversion to the neighbour' a vast part of any 'spiritual liberation'. In his classic book, *A Theology of Liberation,* writer Gustavo Gutierrez claimed:

> "Conversion means a radical transformation of us; it means thinking, feeling and living for Christ—present in exploited and alienated persons. To be converted is to commit oneself to the process of the liberation of the poor and oppressed...".

For liberation theologians, redemption relates to liberation in the context of present historical reality but the exact relationship between the two is unclear, and in practice, liberation theology tends to treat social liberation as a visible manifestation of redemption.

The liberation understanding of conversion appeared to be

an answer for the problem of mass conversion of depressed classes in India in that the motivation in their conversion was put down to their search for social justice or a social protest against caste-dominated Hindu society. In this view, the conversion of *Dalits* were due neither to the proselytizing activities of 'outsiders' ; nor to the depressed classes being swayed by 'ulterior motives', but rather to their own search for a liberation that involved social equality. Because their conversion was a move towards liberation from caste bondage, the church, which proclaims liberation, must not only accept this movement but the church itself must also 'convert' towards some people who are in need of solidarity. This idea of accepting the motives of converts as the legitimate ones in Christians conversion was not new, as the arguments of V.S. Azariah and Oscar Savrin also pleaded the same, but the liberation view on conversion tended to see conversion as entirely due to social problems of Indian society and set aside any religious convictions of converts, this understanding of conversion was seen what were described as 'mass conversion' that took place in southern Tamil Nadu.

Hindu Response to Mass Conversion in Tamil Nadu, 1981

In 1981, the conversion that took place in several villages in south Tamil Nadu caused unprecedented public controversy. The first mass conversion took place in Meenakashipuram on 19 February when about 200 families of the Pallan community converted to Islam.[5] This became nationwide issue as 27 more families from the same village converted to Islam on May 23, and the movement spread to other villages in Tamil Nadu. There was also a threat of conversion from various *Dalit* communities in the north.[6] What seemed to be a major movement for *Dalit* communities in their struggle against injustice, drew the attention of politicians, scholars of sociology and Hindu, Muslim and Christian leaders.

This was widely discussed in the media and, although there were various interpretations, most agreed that the main cause of this conversion was the social inequality and discrimination experienced by the *dalit* community. This view was shared by Muslim scholars such as Mumtaz Ali Khan, whose detailed research led him to conclude that the conversion was the result neither the alleged outside interference, nor of inducement, but of deep resentment on the part of *dalit* community, and the decision was made after 'careful consideration'(1984). Imtiaz Ahmad also found that conversion was due to 'status anxiety' in the villages, but he also suggested that the efforts of local Muslim missionaries and the simplicity of their religious practice, and their status of the Muslim community as economically strong and stable were also the reasons. He believed that the political strategy of the threat of conversion had 'limited utility' but that *dalit* were the 'principal gainer' because of conversion episode. Muslim writers saw *Dalits'* conversion to Islam due to their search for respect and dignity, and accepted that the choice of Islam was not necessarily a spiritual one.

The initial Hindu interpretation of the conversion of the *Dalits* to Islam was also to recognize the movement as a 'protest against caste discrimination after long years of harassment, humiliation and civil disability or social inequality and persecution by the caste Hindus and to see it as a challenge to the caste problems of Hindu society. Hindu reformers were sympathetic towards this movement of deprived section of society and saw this as an opportunity for a 'new awakening' and 'new sense of camaraderie' for caste-Hindus or a 'new revolution' among *dalits* (*Indian Express*, July 15, 1981). Therefore, the Hindu response was to campaign against untouchable among Hindu and urged the government to raise more aid for *Dalits*.

However, as the mass conversion spread to other villages in south India and some *Dalit* communities in North India threatened local government with conversion unless their conditions were improved, it appeared to Hindus that there was a clear 'politicization of conversion' on behalf of *Dalits* with Muslim aid, and believed it was a Muslim attempt to 'attack' or 'ruin' society. Some Hindu organizations claimed that various Islamic organizations were involved in converting Hindus. For example, Motmar Al-Alam-Al-Islami, which set the target of converting 50,000 *Harijans* in that year 1981 and 2,00,000 by the end of the next year. Hindu groups such as Arya Samaj alleged the conversion were due to undue influence, bribery, power of foreign money and drew conclusion about the outside interference of a pan Islamic movement to destabilize Indian society. Therefore, the three-fold response of the Hindu leadership was to call for legation to ban conversion; to withhold the compensation available to *Dalits* from those who deliberately abandoned Hindu community; and to try to reconvert *Dalits* to Hinduism through *Shuddhi.*

Following the conversions in the South, the VHP launched a campaign to preserve the faith by a return to its version of its original ideals. After Meenakashipuram, the VHP had asked the caste Hindus in the villages where the conversions took place to treat the Scheduled Castes as equals so that converts would return to the Hindu fold. The caste Hindus said nothing when the VHP led the Scheduled Castes into the temple. However, as soon as the representatives left the low caste Hindus were again debarred from temple entry.

The VHP also set up mobile vans containing Hindu deities, which visited the areas where the conversions had taken place. The first time this allowed Scheduled Castes to worship freely as they were barred from temples. Another Hindu organization, the All India Sanatan Dharma Prathinidhi Sabha announced in August 1981 that *Dalits* would be allowed to participate in special prayers at the main temple in New Delhi. After some *Dalits* converted to Islam in Rohtak, Haryana in August 1981; a Hindu religious organization began launching a campaign to counter the conversion. *Darshan,* or the view the deity, was performed in the villages and the sacred thread traditionally only worn by caste Hindus, was offered to every Muslim convert.

This soon started an active campaign against conversions. It held huge rallies in both New Delhi and Ahmedabad in December 1981. The organization appealed for funds 'for saving Hindu culture'. Some leaflets were distributed quoting the Hindu reformer Vivekananda to the effect that 'a person quitting the Hinduism fold is not merely a loss of one Hindu but adding one more to the enemies of Hinduism'. This statement explains the historically unprecedented concessions which Hindu organizations seemed prepared to make.

Hindus complained that the *Dalits* who chose to change their religions exhibited no sign of any spiritual motive. Their conversion appeared to Hindus neither to be motivated by appropriate spiritual concerns not to show courage to take the moral consequences ; it was said, "they want to have benefit of change without experiencing change".[7] This objection to the alleged politicization of conversion was strongly voiced in the Hindu press and later published as *Politics of Conversion* (Ram

Swarup, 1986). The editor Devendra Swarup argued that the mass conversion in south Tamil Nadu was not the result of individual 'inner faith and spiritual quest' on the part of *Dalits,* but rather due to the 'organized efforts of some external agency':

> [T]hey *dalits*] are allured into conversion not through an appeal to their religious consciousness, but to their social and economic needs... religion seems to have lost its grip over the self-appointed leaders of these backward sections and for them the so-called religious conversion means, perhaps, nothing more than a change of clothes.[8]

In a leading article, Dev Dutt, separating *dharmic* (spiritual) and *de-dharmic* (secular) views, accused *Dalits* of lacking a spiritual dimension in their approach to conversion because they were using conversion as a 'powerful weapon' to achieve their political means. He described it as meagrely 'a secular approach to achieve a very secular objective and he saw the recent conversions as:

> Part of this process of *de-dharmification* of the Indian psyche. The way common people were promoted to change their faiths, the facility with which the changes took place and the petty uses to which the conversion process were put to, indicates that the hold of dramatic worldview as a regulation of life is being relegated to the background ...the sense of awe and reverence, the sense of the sacred and the sublime which is a characteristic of the *dharmic* attitude of mind is vanishing among the common people.[9]
>
> Convert her to the poor rather than aiming to convert the poor to her fold. Conversion of the Church to the poor is the concrete sign today of her fidelity to the gospel...To the degree of her conversion to God's poor, she proportionately becomes an environment for conversion to God's Kingdom which is different from being just an institution or agent.[10]

Walter Fernandez, a Catholic priest and briiliant sociologist stated that conversion in India has to be understood as a caste struggle of the *Dalits* against their inhuman treatment and that, although conversion involves both spiritual experience and social change it is the alternative that primarily motivates them. Therefore, he discarded some Christian insistence on conversion being spiritual and the Hindu assertion of its being material, insisting that conversion in India was a social movement in the process of "awakening [*dalits*] to the reality of their oppression in the social context of caste mobility". Another writer Wilfred also criticised the Catholic church for giving positive value to the caste system in order to bring about conversion and, in so doing, allowing the unjust system of caste in the church. Since salvation had to be 'real' to *Dalits* in their sub-human condition, in his view, conversion was a by-product of the movement among *Dalits* for their uplift that took a 'religious form'. He saw it as the church's duty to be part of a movement to liberate people who are oppressed and believed this was the true meaning of conversion in India.

For both Wilfred and Fernandez, conversion was regarded as a means to achieve the social end of socio-economic justice of the *Dalits* and the poor in Indian society. The realization by Christians that the injustice of the caste system were also practised by Christian encouraged both Wilfred and Fernandez to call for the church to 'convert' to the world, to their neighbours, to the *Dalit* themselves, to identify with them and bear their burdens. They criticised the church's preoccupation with salvation as redemption through a spiritual experience of conversion that was confirmed by baptism and saw liberation through breaking away from the oppression as the vital part of God's salvation.

The shift in the definition of conversion in the Indian context to mean a protest against social injustice or the church's turning to the world to be part of the people's struggle was evident in the writings of these and other Catholic theologians. Perhaps George Mathew best summed up the new Catholic understanding of conversion as the "politicization of religion (understood in the sense of 'using religion as an instrument for changing the power balance') describing conversion in India as 'part of the proliferation of an ideology which question the *status quo* and as a structural question.

Conversion as Liberation: Struggle for Social Justice for the Poor

One of the most important and controversial development in

contemporary theology is the Liberation Theology movement, which began in Latin America in the late 1960s. This movement is associated with—some would say indebted to—Paulo Freire and other educators working in Latin America. It emerged as a response to massive poverty in South and Central America, the oppression of indigenous populations during colonial period, and the socio-economic repression of poor and marginalised people in modern times. Liberation Theology professes a "preferential option for the poor" and it addresses social issues that affect the poor within a Christian vision of reality, particularly the Roman Catholic tradition of social justice as promulgated in Vatican documents and the general Conferences of Latin-American Bishops from Medellin Columbia in 1968 to Santo Domingo, Dominican Republican 1992 as well as Biblical imperatives of the prophets. In this approach, future is visualised that is accessible to the marginalised who have been denied their birthright of freedom and hope.

Hindus perceive the church as a powerful institution with international links that in the past benefited from colonial rule. Today, with the power of its institution and money, the church is perceived as involved in the work of conversion. They see its way of life and worship as something alien to the culture of the people. The work of mission and conversion as practiced by Christianity is seen as containing explicitly or implicitly a negative judgement about what is most precious to Hindus their religious and cultural heritage. According to Wilfred, Hindus today critically question the meaning of proclaiming the Good News while the traditionally Christian countries of the West are engaged in the destruction of life, the plundering of wealth and the selling of lethal arms to poor countries.

Wilfred's reflections are in line with the deepened understanding of mission that followed the spirit and teachings of the Second Vatican Council. Thus, Indian theology today tries to understand mission in relation to the eschatological fulfilment of God's plan towards which all people move animated, sustained, and guided by the Spirit present among them in their history. The non-Christians, therefore, are not simply objects of mission on the part of the Christian community; they themselves are moving towards the goal of the kingdom and the ultimate eschatological unity of humankind towards which mission itself is directed.

Indian missiological theology today is also linked to solidarity with the poor, participation in their experience and involvement in their struggles for liberation. Because of the domination in India today by the higher castes and classes of the social, political, cultural, and economic fields and the marginalization of the lower classes and castes, Indian liberation theology is today centring its attention on the liberation of *Dalits*, the most oppressed group of people. Indian theology today is drawing inspiration from the movement for liberation by the *Dalits* and so attempting to make its own contribution to the *Dalit* struggle for liberation. Attempts have been made to read the Old Testament and the New Testament from the perspective of the *Dalits*. Since a major concern of the *Dalit*, movement for liberation has been to reinterpret history and to create a counterculture; Christian theology has been trying to resonate with these concerns.

The context of India calls for a rethinking of mission in relation to religious pluralism, massive poverty, oppression, and injustice. These issues were very much to the fore at various national symposiums and show that Indian missiological theology is indeed breaking new ground in preaching the good news.

Because of their work on behalf of the poor and actions to reduce the power of the landowning elite, Catholic priests, nuns, and church workers suffered violent attack and persecution from the militant societies of 1970s and 1980s. In 1980, Archbishop Oscar Romeo, an advocate of the poor, was gunned down while celebrating Mass in the cathedral. In the midst of increasing violence, Archbishop Romero sent his fourth pastoral letter in which he on the one hand condemned structural violence and the arbitrary and repressive violence of the State and on the other hand endorsed 'violence of legitimate defence' against unjust aggression. He made his position clear, the 'church is peaceful, but not passive'. He interpreted the true meaning of conversion as converting oneself towards the poor and argued that 'the face of the Christ is in the poor who ask the church for their voice to be heard' and the church is persecuted as it tried to 'incarnate itself in the interest of the poor'.

Many theologians of India mentioned above represent how theology can be addressed to struggle against exploitation, oppression, and for social struggle and economic injustice.

Problem of Socio-Political Interpretation of Conversion

The redefinition of conversion involving 'structural question' fails to reflect the complex nature of Indian society and the fact that *Dalits,* like other human beings have mixed motives that may have to do with more than just the socio-economic problems of their present life. In emphasising the liberation motive so strongly, conversion almost lost any spiritual meaning to the people under oppression. In other words, any religion or ideology which is willing to be part of the *Dalit* struggle regardless of its 'spiritual dimension', could be chosen. It is striking that both Muslim and Christian commentators found only sociological reasons and no spiritual motives behind the conversion in Tamil Nadu. It is entirely possible that this interpretation may not reflect the full picture of what was going on in the hearts and minds of the *Dalits,* and that it may have been due to the particular methodological framework used by scholars to deal with social issues, or to the desire to play down religious difference for political reasons.[11]

Deryck Schreuder and Geoffrey Odie have shown that studies of conversion in India during 1980s tended to focus on socio-economic factors rather than religious ideas and conversion. This was because the methodological difficulties of discussing motives which left little room for any spiritual analysis in the conversion process. Socio-economic theories of conversion by definition, can give only limited recognition of the missionary message. Moreover, in a political context of increasing opposition from Hindus, conversion appeared as disrespectful to Hinduism, so Christians were under pressure to find a different justification for it. The argument that it was a manifestation of the common struggle against the social injustices of Indian society avoided the religious issue since caste could be argued to be a social and not a religious problem.

Dhirendra Vajpayi's study of Muslim Fundamentalism in India shows how social and religious motives went hand-in-hand in the conversion movement. Towards the end of the 1970s, increasing number of Indians found employment in Arab countries, among them predictably higher proportions of Indian Muslims than Hindus did. They brought back home more than financial wealth. Vajpayi makes an important observation:

> Being away from home and family, religion brought them close. Their leisure was spent in discussing the commonality of Islamic heritage. When they returned to India they not only brought money, watches and expensive transistors radios, they also came back with new awareness and assertive spirit, the spirit of *din-e-elemi* [the religion of light]. The new money gave them confidence, new mosques, and new *madrasas* for religious education for children, which were deemed necessary to thank *Allah* for their prosperity.[12]

This new consciousness of their religious heritage and confidence in the Islamic faith undoubtedly brought a new zeal to spread their religion. Imtiaz Ahmad attributed the rise of the Islamic missionary movement in the 1970s in South Tamil Nadu to this new enthusiasm. It would be an oversimplification to say that these Islamic missionary groups were presenting only the egalitarian principles of the Muslim community and not Islam as a religion, and it is evident that the conversion to Islam had at last been exposed to—and plausibly also embarked—both Islam as social organization and Islam as a faith.

The sociological interpretation of the conversion of *Dalits* is problematic for Christians in two respects. First, it provides validity to Hindu accusation that conversion of *Dalits* is political rather than religious. Hindus can argue that conversion, especially mass conversion lacks spiritual motives, it is merely means to escape injustice or a social protest. Hindu resentment is not that *Dalit* and *Adivasis* are protesting against socio-economic injustice, nor do they deny the existence of social problems within the Hindu community: what they object to is the fact that the converts choose to abandon Hinduism. Moreover, Christianity or Islam has been shown not to be free of caste and class inequality either, therefore, many Hindu organisations view conversion as a tool to increase Church's political influence. This is confirmed when they find that 'spiritual' motives are lacking in Christian interpretations of conversion and that this worldly approach is supported by Christian theology. Secondly, and more seriously still that in their sociological interpretations Christians and Muslims just like caste-Hindus give the impression that *Dalits* are motivated only by desire for their own material betterment or social uplift. The obvious inference is that *Dalits* lack spirituality; hence, conversion itself is seen negatively as opportunism and not as the outcome of an active and considered search by a community for an answer to a spiritual quest. When theologians themselves argue that *Dalit* conversion must be understood sociologically, *Dalits* are in danger of being deprived again, this time of a fully rounded conversion, which has both sociological and spiritual, both temporal and eschatological dimensions.

Hindu Response

The Hindu response to the Christian *ashram* movement was initially either to ignore it or to tolerate. However, in the mid-1980s, Hindus started to raise objections and this led to vigorous debates between Griffiths and three Hindus, Swami Debanand, Ram Swarup and Sita Ram Goel. Debate was triggered by an article in *Hinduism Today* (November /December 1987) which criticised the Christian *ashram* movement, and several articles in response to an article in *Indian Express* (March 18, 1987) that quoted W. Robert Teasdale's praise for the work of Griffiths. These articles elicited mixed responses from both Catholics and Hindus, and soon Swami Debanand and Griffiths were engaged in a rather heated debate. Debanand objected to Griffiths' appropriation of the term *'sannyasin'* which he argued could be applied only to Hindus and the use of the *Paranava* symbol on the top of the cross, which he regarded as a 'perversion' which 'impugned Hinduism'. He felt that, far from bringing Hindus and Christians together, Griffiths only hurt Hindu religious sentiments with his 'original iconography'. He was particularly uneasy, not only about Griffith's insistence that the true reality was in Christ, but also about his claim to know what most Hindus believe about the truth. He expressed his resentment, "We do not need Christian priests to interpret and teach us our *dharma*", and accused Griffiths of promoting Christian arrogance.

In response to Griffiths' argument that religion and culture need to be distinguished, Debanand insisted that Indian culture cannot be divided from Hindu religion, but in fact any such distinction between culture and religion is false, and furthermore that there can be no unity of religion since each is a 'distinct entity'. He dismissed the motive and means of Catholic attempt to synthesis Hinduism with Christianity as merely another approach to convert Hindus.[13]

Ram Swarup, a noted Hindu writer, was very sceptical of the Christians' approach of 'fulfilment', that is, of Christianity as 'revealed' religion and Hinduism as 'preparatory to Christianity.' He saw the appreciation of Hinduism in the *ashram* movement as merely 'a pointer to her conversion to Christianity'. He argued, that this approach still held to the superiority of Christianity, only "conceding spiritual appreciation of Hinduism was not spontaneous or genuine", it simply meant that, as he put it cynically:

> You [Hindus] too good to remain what you are. Your destiny is to become Christian. We see in your country spiritual things deep and uncommon. However, God could not have planned these things amongst you in vain. He must have been preparing you for Christianity, for blessing you with the truth he blessed us with ; in short, he must have been aiming to make you as good as we are.[14]

He regarded Christian *ashram* approach as the outcome of a 'mind prejudiced, self-centred and self-righteous', and not as evident of the spirituality, of respect and genuineness Christians claimed to have. In his book, "The Myth of Christian Uniqueness", Swarup welcomed the Christian attempt at accepting the plurality of religions but asked whether the majority of Christians still hold the attitude of converting others—an attitude he saw as an inbuilt problem of Christianity. A true pluralist would demand that Christianity liquidates its missionary apparatus. What does it matter what theory is pronounced, as long as this apparatus is intact. How Christianity could live without pluralism for the last 2,000 years? Is it an accidental lapse or does it rises from a serious defect in its fundamental spiritual vision, from an inadequate view of man and deity, Ram Swaroop asked.[15]

Sita Ram Goel, a Hindu writer, and publisher, in his analysis of the above debate and his examination of Christian inculturation, alleged that Catholic *ashrams* were yet another 'assault' on Hinduism, and that the attempt to exclude any religious dimension from Hindu culture was a 'deliberate and calculated design' to affect the Christian meaning of Christ into Hindu culture. He pointed out that in the planning process, what happens to the Hindu religion is not the missionary's concern. He insisted Hindu culture grew out of Hindu religion and thus any attempt at separating religion and culture is damaging to both, and he questioned whether any Hindu practices, so deeply rooted in Hindu theology concepts, could be adopted by Christianity without hypocrisy. He claimed that Christian use of Sanskrit terminology implies a close relationship of Hindu theology to Catholic theology, a relationship that does not really exist. Further, he claimed that:

> Such missionaries speak authoritatively on Hindu scriptures and argue that their [Christian] teachings are constant with everything Hindu, but added a final change, 'fullness' to the traditional faith... Hindu spiritual leaders and intellectuals are open to the dialogue Catholics seek but not if cooperation and brotherliness opens Hindu families to unethical conversion strategies.

The above criticism makes it clear that the Hindu-Catholic approach, as an effort to solve the problem of conversion, faced serious objections from Hindus. The main objection made by Hindus in the debate was to the Christian insistence that Hinduism is primarily a cultural and social concept and not a 'religion'. The radical separation between spiritual and socio-cultural elements and the attempt to create a religious synthesis was unrealistic in the context of the caste and Hindu worship of many deities, and Hindu monism, as Stiffner himself admitted. These aspects of Hinduism clearly contradict Christian principles, and they are not only socio-cultural phenomena but are entrenched Hindu beliefs.[16] Behind this there also seemed to be an assumption that the Catholic faith could be a truly world faith by adopting its content to different cultural forms, whereas Hinduism had cultural forms but needed the content which Christianity could provide, and, therefore, would remain a territorial delight.

The inculturation theologians' synthesis of Christian faith and Hindu culture had a theological basis in the concept of fulfilment, but it was supported by Catholic anthropologists gospel and culture as meaning and form respectively, and argued that the former transcendent the latter. Therefore, conversion in the sense of a radical change of religious or 'cultural pattern' was undesirable, instead Luzbeck advocated 'dialect' inculturalism, that is integration by the 'blending' of the Gospel message with the rest of culture by insiders. However, this Catholic 'blending' was questioned on the anthropological grounds by David Moses in his study of Catholic-Hindu synthesis in a village in Tamil Nadu. Moses observed that the local Jesuits attempt—dating back to de Nobili—to accommodate Hindu culture on the basis of the superiority and universality of the Christian religion, had led in practice to a larger measures of retention of Hindu religious beliefs which were embodied in and not separate from cultural forms.[17] That was particularly so in the case of caste system. The net result, Moses suggests, was that both the Catholic missionaries and the caste leaders 'accommodated' each other in order to sustain their own political influence in the village and therefore, *Dalit* theology is strongly critical of forms of inculturation, which draw on high-caste or Brahmanical traditions, and would probably be Christian from high-caste Hindu hegemony.

Among other things, this intra-Catholic debate between those who seek to obviate the need for conversion through accommodation to Hindu philosophy and those who affirm conversion as a legitimate means of protest and affirmation of identity by outcastes from the Hindu community still continue.

Conclusion

The 1980s fundamentally altered India's political landscape and also planted the seeds of an economic revolution. But, a more significant development was the attempted religious simplification of India's multidimensional self. A religious construction of Indian identity was vigorously promoted in politics and an effort was made to subsume all other identities, which Indians traditionally had, under an all-consuming religious framing of politics. With this massive simplification arose terror as a mode of quotidian politics. Concurrently, solid conditions for the rise of Hindu nationalism were also created.

Notes

1. Seshadri, H.V. (1981). *Warning of Meenakshipuram,* Jagarana Prakashana.
2. Mitra, Subrata K. (2007). *The Puzzle of India's Governance: Culture, Context and Comparative Theory,* Routledge.
3. Frank, Katherine (2001). *The Life of Indira Nehru Gandhi,* London: Harper Colins Publishers, pp. 456-57.
4. Medellin Document on Poverty in Maryknoll Documentation, *Between Honesty and Hope,* New York: Maryknoll Documentation Publications.
5. *Times of India,* March 21, 1981.
6. *The Hindu,* August 15, 1981 reported that a community in Kanpur UP threatened to embrace Islam.
7. *Express Magazine,* September 13, 1981.
8. Swarup, Devendra, (1986). *Politics of Conversion,* New Delhi: Deendayal Research Institute.
9. *Ibid.,* pp. 35-45.
10. Wilfred, Felix (1992). *Leave the Temple: Indian Paths to Human Liberation,* New York: Maryknoll.
11. I visited the place in 2001 to find out the process.
12. Dhirendra, Vajpayi (1989). "Muslim fundamentalism in India: A crisis of identity in secular state", In: Vajpayi and Yogendra K. Malik (eds.) *Religious and Ethnic Minority Politics in South Asia,* New Delhi: Manohar.
13. Goel, Sitaram (1995). *Jesus Christ: Artifice for Aggression,* New Delhi: Voice of India.
14. Swarup, Ram (1994). "Liberal Christianity" In: Sita Ram Goel, *Catholic Ashrams: Sannyasins or Swindlers?* New Delhi: Voice of India.
15. *Ibid.*
16. Stiffener, Hans (1988). *Jesus Christ and the Hindu Community: Is a Synthesis of Hinduism and Christianity Possible?* Anand: Gujarat Sahitya Parishad.
17. Moses, C.F.D. (1994). "The Politics of religious synthesis: Roman Catholicism and Hindu village society in Tamil Nadu, India", In: Charles Stewart and Roland Shaw (eds.), *Syncretism/Anti-Syncretism: The Politics of Religious Symbols,* London: Routledge.

7

Cockpit of Orthodoxy

Emerging Challenges to Religious Freedom in 1990s

Introduction

The decade of 1990 was a turning point in India's political situation as it redefined the minorities and majority communities' future relations. During the 1990s, the rise of Hindu nationalism was one of the most important political developments in India; although equally significant in many regions were the growing power of the Other Background Classes (OBCs), and the *Dalits*. These political changes were accompanied by economic liberalization, especially since 1991, when the Government of India embarked on a wholesale policy of economic reforms that particularly led to a sizeable increase in urban, middle class affluence and consumerism. The BJP eclipsed, the once hegemonic Congress Party, and after the 1996 general election became the largest single party. Further, after 1998 elections and more decisively in 1999, the BJP became leading party in the coalition ruling India. This period is also marked by a steady growth in violence as a feature of everyday life.[1]

In this period, freedom of religion became a major socio-religious political issue and was debated in the national press. India witnessed a resurgence of Hindu nationalism, this time involving the promotion of *Hindutva*. This chapter focuses on the Ramjanmabhumi-Babri Masjid controversy, Christian campaigns for world evangelization, the fierce Hindu-Christian debate provoked by Arun Shourie in 1994-95, and attacks on tribal Christians from Gujarat to Orissa. During this period, the rightwing forces raised demand for a total ban on religious conversion in India.

Political Scenario

The 1990s, witnessed the gradual decline of the Congress Party, end of one party dominance, fragmentation of national parties, growth of regional parties, rise of the Hindu nationalist BJP, and the emergence of multiparty coalition politics.

By the late 1990s, however, the repeated failure of the fragmented opposition to reconstruct an effective and stable government brought a halt to third force politics. While the idea of forming a third force coalition remained a possibility, it became increasingly unlikely. By the late 1990s, third force politics was supplanted by the rise of the Hindu nationalist BJP and the gradual emergence of a "bi-nodal" party system built around dominant party coalitions led by the BJP and the Congress.[2]

In 1989, the Janata Dal government was formed and V.P. Singh took over the Prime Minister of India. This was result of the efforts by India's fragmented, centrist, opposition to forge a new national alternative to the Congress. This government was supported by the BJP and JP on one side and the Left on the other. In an effort to attract other backwards classes, the Janta Dal, the main plank of the United Front, committed itself to the implementation of the recommendations of the Mandal Commission Report, the government commission that had recommended that 27 per cent of the government jobs be reserved for OBCs as part of the programme of affirmative action.

In an effort to gain popular support, and strengthen his position, and undercut Devi Lal, the Jat leader, V.P. Singh suddenly announced in August 1990 that he had decided to move on his party's pledge to implement the Mandal Commission Report and reserve 27 per cent of all Central Government jobs for the OBCs. V.P. Singh's announcement resulted in a firestorm of criticism from the press, the public, and the opposition parties. High caste students engaged in numerous acts of self-immolating, and V.P. Singh was accused of having bias for OBCs and starting a caste war.

The BJP was especially incensed by Singh's announcement and accused him of failing to consult his coalition supporters. As an answer to the Mandal politics of V.P. Singh, the BJP in November 1990 planned a *rath yatra* led by L.K. Advani for building Ram Mandir at Ayodhya. Advani was arrested and the BJP finally decided to withdraw its support for the V.P. Singh government.

On November 9, 1990, with only the backing of the left front and what was left of the national front. V.P. Singh lost a vote of confidence in the Lok Sabha and submitted his resignation. Prior to the vote Chandra Shekhar and Devilal had engineered a split in the Janta Dal and formed Janta Dal (Socialist), a new party subsequently renamed the Samajvadi Janata Party. Although the President of India asked, the Congress and the BJP to form the government but both declined. The President then turned to Chandra Shekhar when the Congtress indicated that it would support him from outside. Chandra Shekhar's Government was able to survive only four months before it was forced to resign in March 1991. India's second major effort to build a centrist alternative to the Congress (I) party thus ended in failure.

The Janta Dal coalition partners fought the 1991 Lok Sabha elections separately. The BJP, hopeful of winning more seats could not do better. Rajiv Gandhi was assassinated during the election in May 1991. Riding on the sympathy wave the Congress (I) emerged as largest single party and P.V. Narsimha Rao became the Prime Minister and his minority government lasted full term.

In 1996 Lok Sabha elections, the BJP emerged as the largest party, and the President of India called upon the party to form a government. The BJP, however, faced a solid block of secular opposition parties determined to prevent the formation of a Hindu nationalist government. Because of this solid opposition, the BJP government of Vajpayee lasted only 13 days and was forced to resign.

The opposition parties formed United Front and approached V.P. Singh and Jyoti Basu to head it, both declined. Luck then smiled on Deve Gowda. He became first low caste Prime Minister of India since Independence belonging to Vokkaling community of Karnataka. The UF government lasted only a little over 18 months. Initially, the close rapport between H.D. Deve Gowda and Congress President P.V. Narsimha Rao enabled the coalition to function effectively. However, with the demise of Narsimha Rao and the rise of his successor Sitaram Kesri friction began to develop between the United Front and the Congress I. And the Congress withdrew the support. However, it has to settle to comprise when I.K. Gujaral was brought in place of Gowda. The collapse of UF came when the Jain Commission accusing the one key constituent submitted the report. On November 28, 1997, the United Front government collapsed.

In the new parliament, elections held in 1998 March, the BJP formed the government with the help of other smaller parties and Vajpayee became the Prime Minister. The fragile, inexperienced, and divided BJP led coalition government that came to power in March 1998 was confronted by an economy in turmoil.[3] The economic problems facing the new government included the Asian financial crisis of 1997-98, large fiscal defences, inadequate infrastructure, slow economic growth, high unemployment and stalled process of economic reform. These problems became further compounded by the movement decisions to conduct a series of nuclear tests in May 1998. The Vajpayee government failed to secure the confidence of the House in April 1999 and had to resign. In the Lok Sabha, elections held in May 1999, the BJP emerged as largest single party and was able to form the government with the help of smaller regional parties. This time the government lasted a full term of five years.

Rama Temple

The Ram Janmabhoomi movement, spearheaded in 1984 by the VHP as an expression of pan-Hindu nationalism, demanded to build Ram Temple at the site of an existing Muslim structure, the Babri Masjid, and proposed relocating the masjid to a site in the nearby town of Fakirabad (Andersen and Damle, 2018). A Dharam Sansad (Parliament of Hindu religious leaders) in 1984 (the year Indira Gandhi was killed and the Congress rode to power on a sympathy wave) identified 3,000 sites of potential conflict between Hindus and Muslims that could mobilize the sentiments of Hindus and polarise the nation. The top three sites chosen were at Ayodhya, Kashi, and Mathura. The Dharam Sansad decided to start with the Rama temple in Ayodhya.

The movement to construct the Rama Temple reached its height in the late 1980s and early 1990s. The major effort to prepare the way for a Rama Temple was a botched move by Prime Minister Rajiv Gandhi to play a Hindu card in response to charges of pro-Muslims bias by facilitating the opening of the locked Ram Janmabhoomi premises in 1986 to allow Hindu pilgrims to worship within the disputed structure. The issue of Rama Temple became important during subsequent elections.

In June 1991, the BJP took control of the UP government and it provided a plot to the VHP next to Rama Janmabhoomi site so that it could start the construction process. The issue reached to its emotion height when on December 6, 1992 with the BJP in power in UP, and a strangely acquiescent Narsimha Rao led Congress government at the Centre, the 'Karsevaks' finally succeeded in demolishing the Babri Masjid. This led to short-term ban on the RSS and the VHP, the removal of the BJP from power in the state and, following Central rule, its loss of the state elections in Uttar Pradesh in 1993 and its tactics within the Sangh Parivar.

Following the demolition of the Babri Masjid there were communal riots throughout northern India in which at least 2,000 people were killed. In March 1993, bomb blasts in Mumbai organised by Muslim members of the mafia killed over 300 people. The chain reaction set into motion since those days has still to abate.

Since then, a drawn out legal process eventually reaching India's Supreme Court has delayed any action on the conflicting claims by Muslim and Hindu groups over the rightful possession of the site. Meanwhile, from time to time, the topic of Ram Temple erupts in public discourse as and when some people think it appropriate.

"Abhi hamaari Shakti nahin hai, Jab hogi to mandir banega" (right now we do not have the strength, when we do, the temple will be built) the BJP President Kusabau Thakre told a group of journalists in 1999. Indeed the whole of 1990 decade the right wing party was busy in garnering more and more political support and capture power at the federal level so that it can implement its 'real' agenda.

The issue is still very emotional to majority of Hindus particularly in the northern cow belt.

The Shift: Fear of Small Numbers

The Hindu nationalists discourse changed in the mid-1990s with Muslims ceasing to be the principal threat to the *Hindu rashtra* concept and ceding their place to Christians. Regardless of the precise nature of this shift, in 1992 edition of his book *People of India: Introduction,* Kumar Suresh Singh, Director General of the Anthropology, Survey of India, wrote that Christians form 7.3 per cent of Indian communities.[4]

The Census of 1991 indicated that number of Christians in tribal areas has increased.

The Hindu nationalists argued that the proportion of Indian Religionist in the population of India declined by 4.96 points, from 73.81 in 1951 to 68.72 in 1991.

In Assam IR declined from 70.53 in 1981 to 68.25 in 1991 whereas Muslims grew from 26.52 per cent to 28.43 and Christians from 2.95 to 3.32 per cent.

The share of Christian population in the north-eastern areas rose from 33.0 in 1981 to 39.0 in 1991. In Arunachal Pradesh from 4.32 in 1971 to 10.29 in 1991.

Table 7.1: Progress of Christianity in North-East

Year	*1981*	*1991*	*2001*
Arunachal Pradesh	4.32	10.29	18.72
Nagaland	80.22	87.47	89.97
Manipur	29.68	34.12	37.31
Mizoram	83.81	85.73	86.97
Meghalaya	52.61	64.58	70.25

Source: Census of India.

Based on the figures, the VHP decided to concentrate in the tribal areas to checkmate Christian missionaries. Experts say that the attention of the Hindu rightwing groups towards *adivasi* Christians has been driven not only by the threat of conversion that has been newly fuelled by the RSS but the more practical concerns of electoral representation and the need to move beyond traditional bases of support. In mid-1990s, the BJP adopted policy of courting marginal groups and in 1996 with regional parties with a strong base among the low and intermediate castes, rather than directly promoting such people within its own party.

It was partly in response to this potential that, in 1990s, the Hindu nationalist agenda for *adivasi* communities came to revolve around a twofold strategy: to bring *adivasis* into the Hindu mainstream by revealing to them their 'true' identity as 'Hindus'; and to counteract minority Christian cultures that have taken *adivasis* away from the Hindu fold. To advance their aims, the RSS mounted a number of educational and cultural campaigns in rural *adivasi* villages across India.

Taking clue from 1989 elections, the BJP also decided to expand political base in the tribal areas, which had two advantages: one increasing inclusion in Hindu fold and to checkmating Christian missionaries. This shift could also be related to Sangh Parivar's wider discomfort with aspects of globalisation and liberalization processes that unfold rapidly under the BJP government. In a cultural and political context that is rooted in nationalist, indigenous values Christianity's foreign origin provided a convenient 'surrogate'—in place of multinational companies—against which Hindu nationalism can reconfirm their nationalist agenda.

Campaign for Kingdom of Heaven

In the 1990s, there was a growing tendency to make AD 2000 a milestone for world evangelization. To reach the Gospel to the 'unreached' before the end of the millennium became an urgent goal of the churches. The AD 2000 and Beyond Movement, formed in 1989 by some members of the World Evangelical Fellowship and the Lausanne Committee for World Evangelization drew a plan to mobilise all Christians and bring the gospel to all people by year 2000. The target of the movement was defined as "the world of those people who have never heard the gospel clearly enough to make a decision for Christ."

In India, the All Church Congress on Development held in 1989 was attended by some 1200 missionaries, church and mission leaders. It was organised by the Council on National Service (CONS), which claimed to have a "single vision of planting a church in every village and colony of every town and city of India by the year 2000 AD". Another major event 'Mission India 2000' was launched through a large conference in January 1992 and resulted in publication of the Mission Mandate. A compendium containing 56 articles calling for churches in India to involve themselves in the movement and to make Gospel of Jesus Christ with all urgency and disciple all the missions of responsive people as though this is our last and final chance.

Not all this went unnoticed by the Hindu leaders in India. They were alarmed at the language and aggressive tone of the document. An influential senior RSS/BJP leader who later was appointed Governor of a southern state told this writer "We

Hindus are ready for *shastrartha* (debate) over the true religion. Are Christians ready for it?"

Although some Indian Christian theologians pleaded for broader meaning of evangelization than the conversion of individuals including involvement in 'struggle for justice and peace', but the urgency of the evangelisation of 'unreached' peoples and their conversion by AD 2000 dominated the vocabulary in evangelical circles.

Meanwhile within the Catholic Church, the project, 'Evangelization 2000' was launched by charismatic groups within the church, it gained wide support. Its objective was similar to its Protestant counterpart, the mobilization of Catholics in cooperation with other Christians for the evangelization of the world with the year 2000 as the target date. To 'save the world for Jesus' by the year 2000 was described as the best birthday gift for Jesus.

This traditional attitude to other religions and calling for evangelization of the people of other faiths was most noticeable point of contention between Hindus and Christians.[5]

'O Bull Come and Hit Me': Arun Shourie and Christians Debate, 1994-95

Following the publication of *Redemptoris Missio,* discussion of Christian attitudes towards other religions continued to be the main agenda within the Catholic Church in India, particularly in relation to Hinduism, and there was increasing tension between the Vatican and Indian theologians on Indian Christian approaches to Hinduism. This prompted CBCI to organise a National Consultation on Mission in January 1994 at Pune in order to evaluate and reflect on Catholic missionary work in India since Vatican II and provide a forum for clarifying 'disturbing' and 'confusing' views and practices 'which caused contradictions and tensions'.[6] The CBCI invited newspaper editor Arun Shourie to present a Hindu 'assessment' of the situation.

Arun Shourie wrote a book *Missionaries in India: Continuities, Changes, Dilemmas* (1994) based on the papers presented at the Catholic Bishops Conference of India consultation.

The product of a Christian education himself, Shourie praised Christian missionaries for their dedication, exemplify lifestyle and study of the Hindu scriptures, but argued that in the process of their work, they had 'completely disgorged not only [the] self-confidence but also [the] self-respect' of Hindus and even made them 'feel ashamed' of their traditions.

Furthermore, Shourie insisted that the missionary's ultimate object had always been and continued to be to convert Hindus because they believed that their salvation depended on conversion, and that conversion was believed to be the keystone of the Christianity, and its principal preoccupation. This view also echoed in other RSS ideologues.[7] Shourie was particularly critical of missionary work among *Dalits* and tribals in North-East India. He argued that Christians should not work where there is political unrest—as in North-East India—and that, to avoid any misuse of religion, conversion should be scrutinized through legislation.

Finally, Shourie concludes with the question of conversion:

> In view of the fact, now proclaimed by the Church, that salvation is possible in each religion, what is the ground for converting people to Christianity, in particular by the sorts of means which we saw are in use in the North-East to this day. The litmus test of the new ecumenism would therefore be the extent to which the Church brings its traditional zeal for saving souls through conversion in line with this new acknowledgement.

Sourie's extensive use of the argument of Vivekananda, Gandhi, the Niyogi Report, Ram Swarup, and Sitaram Goel shows that he stands in the long tradition of Hindu arguments against conversion. By using the Pune Consultation materials and connecting them, with colonial documents, he was able to convince Hindu readers that these objections still held, and call for a moratorium on Christian conversion activities.[8]

The organisers of Pune consultation were shocked with Arun Shourie's arguments and forceful presentation. Arun Shourie took the liberty of including in his book extra 48 pages of material distributed at the consultation that was intended only for internal discussion and not for public scrutiny. Some say that the organisers purposely "leaked" those papers, as they wanted to know the Hindu reactions through Arun Shourie. While the main organizer Fr. Kanjamala of CBCI wrote letters of objections, Shourie expressed that the documents in the consultation would "enable the readers to glimpse the conditions in which the Church is today as an organization."

The points raised by Shourie got wide publicity in Hindi and other vernacular press and the main thrust of news coverage was criticism that the missionary schools provide a kind of 'safety bulb' for conversion efforts and that other social services like medical services are ultimately to soften people's view on conversion efforts. We will touch these topics in this book elsewhere.

Father Augustine Kanjamala, the main organizer of the Pune Consultation, responded to Shourie in a series of articles putting forward Christianity as a 'legitimate alternative' to Sankratization for the Scheduled Castes and Tribes. He argued that much of their misery was due to unjust social structure legitimized by Hindu religious tradition, which compelled them to look to Christian missionaries for protection of their land and promotion of their human dignity. Therefore, conversion is a protest movement against the dominant castes as well as the acceptance of an alternative path to social progress and liberation and in this context, the conversion of the communities of Scheduled Castes and Tribes into a religious system that is 'rationally more tenable' was invincible.

In response to Kanjamala's arguments that *Dalit* see Christianity as liberation alternative, S.A. Godbole argued strongly that this is not true as Church in India practices caste system. Another writer Vinod Pawar also disputed Kanjamala claim of social justice and alleged that conversion is a spiritual motive and not a social justice. In addition, that *Dalits* were suffering not because of caste but due to poor governance.

Prajna Bharati, a Hindu forum, organized a public debate between Shourie and Fr. Kanjamala. The proceedings were published by the *Voice of India* (1995). Kanjamala, first to speak, alleged that Shourie's critique was of concept of mission belonging to 'another age'.

Kanjamala argued that Catholic church no longer see conversion as the primary motive of missionary activity, which is now directed not at the other world salvation of the poor but at liberation from social injustice.

Well-versed in latest religious developments Shourie tarred Kanjamala's arguments to pieces in his lengthy reply. Shourie agreed that the missionary movement had inspired social reforms, that it had been exemplary in education and medical field, and that everyone had the right to propagate their faith. Shourie rejected Kanjamala argument that the institutional church had not denounced the old doctrine and still expected conversion.

Shourie's argument was that contemporary missionary work was essentially continuous with the colonial mentality, the change was only in the circumstances, quoting the CBCI documents, he pointed out that the notion of salvation in other religions was 'a matter of concern' for many Christians precisely because it weakened the motive for conversion. The Church in India had not been able to accept these changes and continued with the same methods—though force was now disallowed—as evidenced in an intelligence report he had obtained on missionary working in the North East India. He dismissed Kanjamalas theory that conversion was a protest movement against Hinduism because large-scale conversions were not taking place. Shourie claimed that since Christianity had failed in Europe.

By focusing on conversion, Shourie succeeded in demonstrating a measure of commonality between colonial and contemporary missionary attitudes in India. Shourie was correct in arguing that if Kanjamala's 'personal belief that salvation is possible in all religions' were the practice of whole church 'there would be no problem at all'. However, Kanjamala could not convince Shourie and the Hindu audience that this was the case in the face of Catholic documents to the contrary, and by insisting on his own understanding of conversion as a protest, he failed to represent the multiple dimension of Christian understanding of conversion within the Catholic Church.[9]

Ordinary Christians were kept out of these discussions. On the whole inviting Shourie to CBCI Conference was like "*Aa bail mujhe maar*" (O Bull, Come and hit me). I had known Shourie for a long time and in very humble manner, I expressed my reservation to some people in the Catholic Church that it was not a wise decision to invite Shourie to such an internal meeting. Nevertheless, the CBCI officials as usual never cared for laypersons advice and went ahead.

The Christian respondents largely focused on Shourie's conspiracy theory and his use of historical material, which they thought was not properly interpreted or fairly treated. They tried to de-link colonial administrators from missionaries, to bring out the positive contribution of the missionaries and mission work, or to disconnect the past from the present as a 'bad dream' or 'mistake' of earlier missionaries.

However, it was a missed opportunity to engage in conversation for a better understanding on Christian mission and conversion not only for Hindus but also for Christians themselves. Careful examination of book and his public debate with Kanjamala shows that Shourie's arguments were, in contrast to what most Christian respondents saw, a theological one. He called for the church to espouse a Hindu understanding of truth, which he characterized as affirming salvation in all religion.

What seemed to be missing among the Christian leaders in the 1990s was intra-Christian discussion on conversion, and instead, there was a dismissive attitude towards those who held different understanding.

Violence against Christians

During the late 1990s, militant rightwing organisations diverted their hostility away from Muslims their usual targets, and launched a campaign of violence against India's Christian minority. Christian missionaries, they claimed, were using foreign funds to induce the ignorant poor to leave the Hindu-fold and convert to Christianity, a 'foreign religion'. A well-planned programme to "Hinduise" the *vanvasis* (not *adivasi*) tribals was chalked out by the Sangh Parivar in mid-1980s, but it was implemented after 1989 when the BJP noted that it could corner reserve seats by creating certain pressure in the tribal belt.

During the late 1990s, Indian news media and human rights groups drew attention to churches being destroyed, nuns assaulted or raped, priests hacked to death, and social relief organisations solemnly warned not to engage in 'conversions'. Dang district in Gujarat, Phulbani in Orissa, Jhabua in Madhya Pradesh were worst affected areas.

In 1996, there were seven cases of anti-Christian violence, in 1997, it went up to 24, and in 1998, there were more than 120 cases. These included attacking churches, burning Bibles, and intimidating missionaries. In 1995, a Franciscan Clarist nun Sr. Rani Maria was murdered in Madhya Pradesh for raising voice for the voiceless.

These attacks were spread in several parts of India: Gujarat, Maharashtra, Haryana, Uttar Pradesh, Karnataka, Manipur, and Orissa.

December 1998 saw the beginning of a series of communal attacks on Christians. They took the form of an escalation in attacks on Christian institutors and on church workers and members. News magazine *India Today's* article dated March 30, 1998, reported that no fewer than 30 clashes had occurred in Orissa in the preceding year. These attacks had been going on ever since the BJP-led government had taken over in March 1998. On September 23, 1998, nuns at the Clarist Convent in Baghpat (Uttar Pradesh) were sexually assaulted. Two men raped a house cleaner and looted a Salesian convent near Calcutta on September 24, 1998. On September 25, 1998, nuns were gang raped at a Christian convent in Jhabua (Madhya Pradesh). Although specific culpability for the incident remains unclear, it came in the wake of the VHP-BJP's anti-Christian campaign.

Between December 25, 1998, and January 3, 1999, in Dangs and neighbouring districts, over twenty churches were burned or destroyed, and scores of individuals were physically assaulted, in some cases tied and beaten up and robbed of their belongings while angry mobs invaded and damaged their homes. Rallies continued to take place in several districts for the sole purpose of intimidating and terrorizing Christian community members. According to an article in *The Hindu*, "The disturbances broke out only in [those] tribal-dominated areas where the BJP failed to make inroads in the last few elections, despite setting up a special tribal cell in the party. The division on religious grounds could ensure support to the BJP of the majority community voters among the tribals."

On February 2, 1999, a day after the National Commission for Minorities submitted its report to the President, the office of the Gujarat Director General of Police (Intelligence) issued a memorandum to all District Superintendents of Police and Police Commissioners of the Gujarat State Police seeking district-level information on, *inter alia*, the total population of Christians; the location of Christian missionaries; the amounts and sources of foreign funding they received; the addresses and telephone numbers of the "main leaders"; the number of Hindu-Christian conflict cases registered; the number and types of vehicles and weapon-owning licences possessed by Christian missionaries etc.[10]

Human Rights Watch investigated these attacks in Dangs district in south-eastern Gujarat. The events were preceded by escalating violence throughout the state in which many police and state officials were implicated. Of the 108 cases of attacks on Christian institutions reported in 1998, some 58 were in Gujarat alone.

Instead of taking action to protect Christian institutions and personnel, the police department of the BJP headed state government distributed a secret circular instructing its officers to find out where Christians lived, identify the leaders and the foreign countries that provided their financial support, ascertain if they had access to firearms, discover the "tricks" which they used to convert Hindus, and compile dossiers on any Christian with "criminal minds". It was apparent that Gujarat BJP movement regarded the Christian victims rather than those who attacked them as the culprits who were causing the trouble.[11]

The BJP-led Central Government did not condone the December attacks on the Christian community. Prime Minister Vajpayee condemned then and said they should stop immediately. He did not put the blame on the victims but he implied that the troubles stemmed from the churches' evangelic programme, by calling for a "national debate" on the practice of converting Hindus to Christianity. His call had the effect of giving a degree of legitimacy to the campaign that was being waged by the extremist elements in the Sangh Parivar, to convince the Indian people that such conversions should be outlawed. The Prime Minister's behaviour bewildered everyone.

While Vajpayee did not endorse their violent actions, he made it clear that in his view, the Hindu fundamentalist organizations had a case when they objected to the Christian Churche's conversion efforts, a case that merited serious consideration. This was a careful tactic to avoid taking a hard line against them because the core of the BJP's support came from their ranks.

Given the failure of the BJP led Central Government and State Governments to act decisively to deal with the problem, it was not surprising that attacks on Christians and their institutions continued in 1999.

On January 23, 1999, an Australian missionary and his two young sons were burnt alive by a militant Hindu mob that poured gasoline on and set fire to the van in which they were sleeping. Graham Staines had worked for thirty years in the areas and not involved in conversion.

The Vajpayee regime appointed a Supreme Court justice to act as one-man commission to investigate the Staines killings and to present within two months a report that would identify the individuals and/or groups that were responsible for it. For weeks, Justice Wadhwa was not given any staff nor an office. This go-slow policy of the government's indicative of sincerity of the government.

The Wadhwa Commission report was submitted on June 21 and it found that neither the Bajrang Dal nor any other Hindu fundamentalist organization had been behind Dara Singh's violent action. According to Justice Wadhwa, it had been carried out by an individual who had no organization affiliation. The Commission portrayed killing of Staines as an expression of a personal determination to do away with a religious enemy rather than an expression of a Hindu fundamentalist organization's opposing to the conversion of tribal Indians to Christianity. An editorial in the *Deccan Herald* argued that Justice Wadhwa had taken narrow view of the incident.[12]

In 1997, a Catholic priest Fr. Christudass was paraded naked in the streets of small town Dumka and another priest Fr. A.T. Thomas was murdered but these events were ignored by most human rights activists outside Bihar. They were seen as concern of Christians alone. The attacks on Christians intensified between March 1998. In July 1998, 11 Christian schools in Bangalore, Mysore, Mandya, and Mangalore were disrupted. Acharya Giriraj Kishore, Secretary General of VHP asked Christian missionaries to leave India.

The US State Department in its first annual report on religious freedom throughout the world in 1999 named India among the countries for the 'deterioration of religious tolerance in many states' and stated that at many places Hindu extremists had attacked Christian personnel and property and inadequacy of Central and State Government response. The Vajpayee government reacted sharply to the report and did not allow the officials of the Commission to visit India.[13]

Target North East

Much has been written about the growth and spread of the saffron influence in the tribal pockets of western and central India.

However, the campaign to saffronise the tribes of the North-East has gone almost unnoticed.

Historically, the north-eastern states have been cut-off geographically and culturally from the rest of India. Largely populated by tribes—many of whom continue to follow their ancient animist religions—the Seven Sisters of Assam, Meghalaya, Mizoram, Manipur, Tripura, Nagaland and Arunachal Pradesh have always attracted proselytizers, whether it was the Vaishnavites who influenced Manipur in the late medieval period or the Christian missionaries of the colonial period.

Although the RSS has been active in the north-eastern India since Independence, its presence was felt in the region only in 1995. By 1997, the RSS and its subordinate associates started concentrated work in the region. According to Seva Disha, a five-yearly RSS report on the activities of the Sangh Parivar, its presence has grown at a steady pace.

The *Parivar* in the North-East India runs Ekal Vidyalaya, Sewa Bharati, Vidya Bharati, Vanvasi Kalyan *Ashram*, Friends of Tribal Society (FTS) or Van Bandhu Parishad (VBP), Vishwa Hindu Parishad, Bharat Kalyan Prathisthan (a unit of the VHP), Bharatiya Jan Seva Sansthan (BJSS) and the Rashtriya Shaikshik Mahasangh are running both formal and informal education units including *Balwadis* (pre-schools), Bal Sanskar Kendras, hostels, residential schools, night schools, coaching centres and primary, secondary and senior secondary schools across the north-eastern states. The tension between missionaries and the *Parivar* escalated in 2000s.

In 1997-98, thousands of Bru tribals had fled Mizoram following ethnic clashes with Mizos. They had taken refuge in the bordering areas of Tripura. At that time, the Vanvasi Kalyan *Ashram* (VKA), an RSS affiliate in tribal areas provided relief at the camps, saying that the Bru tribals are Hindus. "We consider every tribe to be a part of Hindu or Sanatana Dharma. We consider all Vanvasis a part of this larger Dharma", Rajesh Das, Sangathan Mantri (Organisation Secretary) of Vanvasi Kalyan *Ashram* (VKA) told this writer during his visit to the North East. The VKA runs a growing network of schools, hostels, and temples in the North East.

In 1990s, the battle for the hearts and minds of the North East seems set to intensify with the growing presence of the Rashtriya Swayamsevak Sangh (RSS) and its affiliates in the region, who are working to further the *Hindutva* agenda in that area.[14] Indeed, the saffron bodies seem to have learnt a good deal from the Christian missionaries and their message is being successfully propagated through education.[15] Since the late 1990s in India, the frequency of what can be called "everyday" acts of anti-Christian violence has increased dramatically.[16]

Pope John Paul II—Visit to India

Pope John Paul II visited to India in 1999 November (from November 5 to 8) created tension throughout the country.[17] The VHP had threatened countrywide agitation and appealed to the Prime Minister Atal Bihari Vajpayee to cancel Pope's visit to India.[18] The Sangh Parivar demanded that the Pope apologize for the Goa Inquisition and 'forced conversion' in Goa during Portuguese period and that he should withdraw the claim of salvation only through Christianity.[19] Vajpayee was keen to present a more moderate face both to preserve the ruling coalition and to consolidate international ties and investment. Moreover, Vajpayee could not very well cancel the visit as the invitation to the Pope had been issued some time ago—in 1995 by former Prime Minister I.K. Gujral. A huge police presence was mobilised in the Indian capital of New Delhi to ensure tight security. "All the avenues of the Papal visit stand converted into virtual fortifications with police cordoning off the area and keeping vigil all day", one report noted. In addition, the government initiated a widespread police crackdown against some of the Hindu chauvinist organisations planning protests against the pontiff's visit. However, in order to prevent a backlash within the party itself and the opening up of internal divisions, the government's reception for the Pope was decidedly muted—almost a snub.

On November 6, 1999, the Pope released the document Ecclesia in Asia released in a meeting of Catholic Bishops from Asia and said, "the church will reap a harvest of faith in the Asian Continent in the new millennium." He reasserted the traditional view of evangelization was priority. In Ecclesia in Asia issued during his visit, Pope insisted that Christ is the only Saviour for all people. Pope stated that the third millennium is for conversion of Asia.

Ecclesia in Asia was very much criticized by the secular media. The Indian media complain that, according to the document, conversion remains the 'cardinal objective of the church', and that inter-religious dialogue promoted by the Indian theologians was discarded in favour of 'motivated dialogue'. The Sangh Parivar vowed to take up more hardliner attitude towards religious conversion. The Hindu writers declared 'Pope has silenced the secularists as well missionary apologist' (Arun Shourie, 1999). The only reference to conversion in the document was the phrase 'a call to conversion', which was much quoted by Hindus but was in fact a call to Christians to become worthy of God. However, the content of that document made it more than clear that there was a continuing call by the church hierarchy to the explicit preaching of Christian gospel in the Asian continent with a view to conversion of non-Christians.[20]

Although Pope John Paul's previous visit to India in 1986 had also met with ultra rightwing opposition but on this time the VHP campaign for an apology received much wider media coverage and triggered a wider public debate on conversion by drawing attention to the atrocities by the Catholic church under Portuguese rule, the VHP both embraced Christians about their past and also succeeded in awakening the religious sentiments of Hindus.

The Sangh Parivar on Religious Freedom

Throughout the debate on conversion during 1998-99, the Sangh Parivar consistently asserted that the root cause of Hindu-Christian tension was the Christian campaign of conversion. It is therefore, necessary to examine the truth of the claim. The prominent historian, Sumit Sarkar, located the root of the violence generally in the Parivar's aggressive campaign of *Hindutva,* which needed 'enemy' for their reaction to the threat of globalization and to spread of liberation theologies, which sought to empower the downtrodden in Hindu society against the interests of a dominant minority of high caste Hindus. Supporting Sarkar, K.N. Panikkar insisted that blaming Christian conversion was an 'afterthought, convenient pretext'. He added that the violence was due. First, to the Parivar's search for political support from tribal areas it was necessary to 'cut' considerable Christian influence on tribals; and secondly, as retaliation against the secular positions taken by several Christian organizations in the face of Parivar politics. This view was also shared in the report of the All India Federation of Organization for Democratic Rights, first published in April 1999 which saw conversion as 'a manufactured, deliberate division and a trap' and a justification for its attack on Christians.

However, though the arguments may have explained the socio-political dimensions of the situation, they neglected to examine the religious dynamics of this context in which the Parivar operated. In this case, the Parivar constantly expressed resentment towards Christian campaign of conversion in tribal areas, and argued that Christian missionaries actually 'targeted' the tribal areas with what seemed to be careful planning to achieve their goals of converting *adivasis*. Moreover, there were many examples of Hindus' objections to Christian conversions both in their writings and in their campaign of such *ghar wapsi*. Explaining the Parivar's resentment of conversion, Pran Chopra forcefully states, the Hindu argument:

> Historically, most conversions to Islam and Christianity took place under the shadow of the power of Muslim and Christian conquerors of India... the vast majority of Hindus, who had remained faithful to their religion despite defeat in battle... saw the converts as people who had betrayed the nation by going over to the other side of the conquerors, and they saw conversions as the converts device... for subverting Hindu society by dividing it against the higher Hindu castes, which had resisted what many Hindus saw as a religio-cultural invasion by foreign conquerors.[21]

It is apparent from the above discussion that the issue of conversion was a key issue for the Parivar to deal within the course of their campaign of *Hindutva*. In 1998-99, the Parivar used the national media to argue for the illegitimacy of conversion in a pluralistic society like India. They produced an unprecedented number of articles and books during the period, but some of their most forceful arguments are found in the writings of Ashok Chowgule, David Frawley, and Arun Shourie. These writings characterise conversion as violence against humanity, an attack on Hindu nationhood, and an inherent problem of Christianity.

The most important development in the Parivar's argument against conversion in 1998-99 website was the identification of conversion as the violence against humanity and therefore, evil and unacceptable. In the *Parivar*'s view, 'all conversions are wrong', therefore, 'social and religious violence' in this age. Swami Aseemanand Saraswati, the head of Vidhya Gurukulam, who wrote an 'open letter' to the Pope presenting Hindu point of view on conversion, presented the most vigorous argument. He contended that all should have the freedom to pursue their own religion, each of which has some beauty and something to contribute to the enrichment of humanity. However, he claimed:

> Religions that are committed by their theologies to convert...are necessarily aggressive, since conversion implies a conscious intrusion into the life of a person, in fact, into the religious person. This is a very deep intrusion, as the religious conversion is not merely violence against people; it is violence against people who are committed to non-violence.[22]

David Frawley, a Catholic who converted to Hinduism, offered a vigorous critique of 'organized conversion' by missionaries as perpetuating 'psychological violence' towards people of other faiths, and insisted that conversion is an 'illogical assault', a form of 'religious violence and intolerance', and an attempt of one religion to exterminate all others'. Conversion refuses to recognize the religion of another as valid. Above all, the organized conversion business undermines and discredits the natural faith of people."[23]

Similarly, Ashok Chowgule presented conversion as part of the destructive effect of missionary activities on the local people, exploiting and undermining the local culture and religion, as illustrated in the case of the Spanish and Portuguese conquest of America. He also argued using V.S. Naipaul's analysis that conversion is used as a tool to 'destroy a people's history', as it serves to prevent convert from returning to the past.

This identification of conversion with violence was echoed in a memorandum submitted by rightwing groups to the Prime Minister of India, which was not entirely new since the Sangh Parivar already connects conversion with perversion and colonial aggression. But, what was new in the late 1990s was the VHP's attempts to club the past history of the Inquisition and forced conversion by Christian and Muslim rulers with present campaign for the conversion of Hindus in the context of the global expansion and economic supremacy of the wealthy nations.[24]

The ideology of *Hindutva* strongly asserted that the rights of the majority Hindus must be respected as opposed to the Christians and moderate Hindu argument of the freedom of choice of individuals. From this perspective, Christian conversion was regarded as 'fundamental contempt for Hinduism' and force to 'sanitize Hindus'. 'Tolerance', Shenoy argued, 'is being preached to one section when other religions are teaching intolerance'. A.N. Dhar pointed out that, despite the difficulties, especially the birth of Pakistan, Hindus had kept India as a secular, not a Hindu state. For him, conversion was an attack on majority Hindu generosity, which had been able to uphold the rights of other minority religious communities and that the rights of minorities in India should be respected, but there were clear limits on this.[25]

Presenting this problem of conversion *versus* 'Hindu rights', Ashok Chowgule, the President of VHP Maharashtra, challenged Christians not only to accept the notion that the Hindus way of salvation is as valid as the way through Christ, and that salvation is possible in other faiths as well. Indian Christians have to determine their own place in the society in India.[26]

It is difficult, of course, to pinpoint the exact reasons why violence against Christians began to increase in the 1990s. The Sangh Parivar did suffer a disapproving public backlash after the destruction of the Babri Masjid in 1992, and some have claimed that Sangh affiliates believed their anti-Muslim rhetoric was bringing them increasing diminishing electoral returns. At the same time, anti-Christian propaganda was gaining political traction, in large part due to the political rise of Sonia Gandhi. In 1998, Sonia Gandhi became President of the Congress Party (the main opponent of the BJP). Her foreignness was perennial issue, raised repeatedly by her nationalist critics and opponents, and her Christian faith was seen as a symbol of her non-native status. The stoking of anti-Christian sentiment not only helped the BJP burnish its nationalist credentials but also implied a critique of the Congress Party and reinforced the BJP's contention that the Congress was the party that pandered to foreigners and minorities.[27]

The most significant shift in India's political landscape has been the rise of the RSS and it is the BJP which took reins of the Union Government and the decline of the Indian National Congress in the 1990s. This rise of *Hindutva* radically altered the political discourse of India by challenging the court's secular structure as enshrined in the Constitution of India. In the 1990s, India witnessed a surge in the use of symbols in politics.

After demolition of Babri masjid in 1992, the rightwing forces focused on capturing power at the centre. The exodus of Hindu Pandits and rise of *Aazadi* movement in Kashmir made the BJP focus on Muslims. The exodus of Kashmiri Pandits and emergence of the *aazadi* campaign went mostly un-discussed in conversion debates in India but Hindu experiences in Kashmir largely shaped their reactions to conversion.

In later half of 1990s, suddenly the *Sangh Parivar*/BJP shifted their focus on Christians.

Why attacks on Christians at this point of time, is the core question? Why is *Hindutva,* which has spent most of its energies in attacking Muslims at various levels, targeting Christians now?

In 1998, Sonia Gandhi, Italian Catholic widow of Rajiv Gandhi, a relative new-comer was elected President of the Congress Party. In November 1998 her stature rose ever further as the Congress Party under her leadership and campaign fared extremely well, defeating the incumbent BJP state government in two states and winning election for the incumbent Congress government in a third state. After 1998 elections, the BJP was able to form the government at the centre with the help of other parties but it collapsed within 13 months. The BJP blamed it on the Congress Party. The BJP raised several objections to Sonia Gandhi and made her foreign origin an electoral issue in 1999 elections.

In the Sangh Parivar analysis rise of Sonia Gandhi in Indian politics was obstacle for the BJP's growth so it propagated that by voting Congress under Sonia Gandhi would be like handling the country back to a foreigner. It was around this time the violence against Christians in several parts of country took place. According to an Indian weekly newspaper, the real provocation that rattled the saffron brigade was the rise of Sonia Gandhi.

The Hindu Christian debate in 1998-99 helps us to see that that the interpretation of religious conversion requires more than an examination of personal changes of religious commitment or the socio-political changes at a personal in a community. Study of the debate exposes the religious complexity of the problem of conversion in India and suggests that it is also due to clash of two radical different religious frameworks of Christianity and Hinduism. The religious dimension is of vital importance to Parivar's pursuit of *Hindutva* ideology, which is described as a 'desire to restore the centre of faith of the Hindus'.

The idea of India as a primordial composite Hindu nation and the notion of Handiness or *Hindutva* remerged and gained ground due to new definition of democracy as majoritarianism. The *Hindutva* agenda was revived in the 1990s when religious identity along with caste was enhanced as an instrument of political electoral manipulation in the elections that followed the disintegration of the "rule" of the Congress Party.

In 1990s, the RSS role in determining policies, leadership, and strategies of the BJP became clear. However, the BJP was electorally weak until the late 1980s, when it jointed the VHPs campaign to construct Rama temple in Ayodhya. The BJP and VHP both achieved unrecorded strength because of their alliance. In 1990s, the BJP claimed to be more ethical and religious than other political parties.

The events that took place in 1990s shaped future relations between minority and majority. After the Babri Masjid demolition in 1992, communalism got a new dimension and started playing greater role in the Indian setting. The vitality of religious fundamentalism and its impact upon public life in the form of riots and religion based political parties have been among the greatest challenges to Indian political institutions in 1990s.

Conclusion

The rise of Hindutva during 1990s has to be seen within ethno-religious mobilisation and introduction of economic liberalization and privatization along with emerging social issues. During this period, hate campaign against the minority Muslims was "facilitated and justified in the name of achieving security for the Hindu self at individual, community, nationalised as well as international level." The new discourse of security and insecurity that *Hindutva* set in motion enabled "extreme violence to be mobilized, systematized, and institutionalised." The politics of hate spawned by the *Hindutva* was a good example that fed upon, as well as shaped, local societies.

The 1990s was thus marked by the growing fear generated by

the Hindu right that the minority Muslims population was increasing its presence in India, challenging Indian sovereignty and rule of law, and controlling the politics of the country.

The Sangh Parivar argued that the state has failed to implement family planning programmes and pass uniform civil code for fear of offending Muslim religious sensibilities. It has unfairly denied majorities the rights that it accord minorities to establish and manage educational institutors of their choice. By opposing safeguards of minority rights, the BJP has in effect redefined democracy as majorities and minority rights as a case for special bargaining.

In the late 1990s, the Christians became the target of rightwing ultra organisations. This sudden development baffled many scholars. One reason why from late 1990s the Christians became the target is perhaps the overall Muslim response to the events surrounding at Ayodhya campaign has checked the further growth of the social movement dimensions of Hindu nationalism. The BJP can only polarize religious communities if it can provoke a militant response from Muslims. However, since mid-1990s most Muslims have distanced themselves from the opportunistic leadership and firmed secular principles. By 1998, large segments of the Muslim community opined that if the BJP built the temple, they would not resist, their priority was at to their real needs, particularly better, and more extensive educational facilities and better jobs for youth, meanwhile, they would lend support to non-Brahmanical parties, which provided the major opposition to the BJP. In 1998 election manifesto, the BJP dropped the issues of the temple.

Hindu nationalists transformed public discourse by making matters that are generally considered private into public concerns. Call for national debate on conversion by the Prime Minister Vajpayee was in a way to take the issue of religion from private sphere to public and justify the Sangh Parivar's demand that state should take a stand and introduce new regulation. It emphasized that religious is a political public question rather than private and enabled it to demand new forms of state intervention and regulations.

In 2000 K.S. Sudarshan became Sarsanghchalak (Supreme Chief) of the RSS. He succeeded Rajendra Singh, who stepped down on health grounds. RSS chief K.S. Sudarshan recalled the

Niyogi report on conversion of tribals and issued strong statement against Pope's call for "planting the church or open wide to Christ the doors of Asia became focus of protest." This set new tone for the Sangh Parivar's stand on freedom to choose. In the next chapter, we will see how new religious pathways developed in India.

Notes

1. Alagappa, Muthiah (2004). *Civil Society and Political Change in Asia: Expanding and Contracting Democratic Space*, Stanford University Press, p. 211.
2. Puniyani, Ram (2004). *Hindu Extreme Right-wing Groups: Ideology and Consequences*, Delhi: Anamika Publishers & Distributors.
3. Ruparelia, Sanjay, Sanjay Reddy and John Harriss (2011). *Understanding India's New Political Economy: A Great Transformation?*, London: Taylor & Francis, p. 191.
4. Singh, Kumar Suresh (2002). *People of India: Introduction* (Calcutta: Anthropological Survey of India 1992) 2011 (rev. edn.) New Delhi: Oxford University Press.
5. Romano, L'Obervatore, April 18, 1983.
6. Christopher, Jafferlot (1996). *The Hindu Nationalist Movement in India*, New Delhi: Viking.
7. Swaroop, Ram (1994). *Hindu View of Christianity and Islam*, New Delhi: Voice of India.
8. *The Vedanta Kesari*, Volume 83, Issue 2, Kolkata: Sri Ramakrishna Math.
9. Manuel, Paul Christopher, Lawrence C. Reardon and Clyde Wilcox (2006). *The Catholic Church and the Nation-State: Comparative Perspectives*, Georgetown University Press.
10. Kanjamala, Augustine (2014). *The Future of Christian Mission in India: Toward a New Paradigm for the Third Millennium*, Wipf and Stock Publishers.
11. Anti-Christian Violence on the Rise in India, *Human Rights Watch* https://www.hrw.org/news/1999/09/30/anti-christian-violence-rise-india, September 30, 1999.
12. Engineer, Asghar Ali (2003). *Communal Challenge and Secular Response*, New Delhi: Shipra Publications.
13. Dettman, Paul R. (2001). *India Changes Course: Golden Jubilee to Millennium*, Greenwood Publishing Group.
14. *Outlook* (1999), Volume 5, Issues 1-11, p. 25, https://books.google.co.in/books?id=-TNWAAAAYAAJ.
15. CBCI Consultations on Mission, Ishvani Kendra, Pune, 4-9 January 1994.

16. Bauman, Chad M. (2015). *Pentecostals, Proselytization and Anti-Christian Violence in Contemporary India,* Oxford University Press.
17. *VATICAN News,* November 5, 1999.
18. *The Chicago Tribune,* November 8, 1999.
19. *The Asian Age,* October 10, 12, 17, 1999.
20. Wilfred, Felix (2014). *The Oxford Handbook of Christianity in Asia,* Oxford University Press.
21. Chopra, Pran (1999), "Conversion and conspiracies", *The Hindu,* 5 February.
22. Saraswati, Swami Dayanand (1999). "Conversion as Violence", *Indian Express,* October 29.
23. Frawley, David (1999). *The Missionary Position* http:// www/bjp.org/news.
24. Goel, Sitaram (1996). *History of Hindu-Christian Encounter,* New Delhi: Voice of India.
25. Sengupta, Hindol (2015). *Being Hindu,* Penguin, India.
26. Georg, Samuel (2008). "An Appropriation and critique of Stanley J. Samartha's Christology in a religious pluralistic context", *Asia Journal of Theology* 22/1(April): 53-93.
27. Copland, Ian, Ian Mabbett, Asim Roy, Kate Brittlebank and Adam Bowles (2013). *A History of State and Religion in India,* Routledge.

PART III

THE TWIST WITHIN THE INITIATIVES

"[We] will free India of Muslims and Christians by December 31, 2021. Our target is to make India a *Hindu Rashtra* by 2021."

—*Rajeshwar Singh*
Uttar Pradesh Dharam Jagran Samiti,
December 19, 2014

"We cannot accept violence against any religion on any pretext and I strongly condemn such violence. My government will act strongly in this regard."

—*Prime Minister Narendra Modi,* February 17, 2015

8

From Camphor Flame to Saffron Tornado

Conversion Debates—2000-2014

Introduction

India witnessed increasing faith based community conflicts from the beginning of 2000s. For Indians, the first decade of the 21st century with all its grandeur and technological advancements would best be remembered for the revival of religion in politics. The issues related to religion in the light of growing terror activities in India took centre stage and questions involving religious freedom became more complex. The BJP came to power in 1999, and Atal Bihari Vajpayee became the Prime Minister of India. Series of incidences shaped the political scenario. Starting from highjack of Indian Airlines plane to Kandhar (Afghanistan) in 1999 to attack on Indian Parliament in 2001, and 2002 Gujarat riots that rattled the country. Although the BJP lost 2004 Elections, it strengthened its position in several states particularly in the cow belt of northern India during this period.[1] The most audacious attack on the financial capital of India Mumbai in November 2008 known as 26/11 helped emergence of a consensus emerged that India needs hardliner conservative nationalists rule at least for a time being. But such abstractions fail to do justice to the clashing values in today's pluralistic society.[2]

Restriction on religious conversion, efforts to penalise religious minority groups, increasing intrusion of state administrators into the internal affairs of religious organizations grew after 1999. The words like *lalach* (inducement), *pralobhan* (allurement) and *jabran* (coercion) were frequently used in the public discourse and vernacular media to defame even genuine religious conversion.

Demand for a national anti-conversion law grew louder and louder. Violence against Christian minority grew dramatically from 1999 onwards. So, would a national law help? Could it be precise and clear, thus giving force to the Constitution's provisions, both its rights and protections? Will it help overcome the current contradictions? Did religion make a difference in the 2014 Lok Sabha election? In this chapter, we shall try to review the situation of religious freedom between 2000-2014 and try to understand the religious violence in India.

BJP-NDA Government—1999-2004

In the 1990s the BJP—the political heir of the Jan Sangh—became the largest party in the Parliament: the ABVP the largest student union and the Baratiya Majdoor Sangh the largest labour union in India. After the BJP formed the government in 1999, all the Sangh Parivar decided to penetrate society in-depth, at the grassroots level, and to prepare opinion for the *Hindu Rashtra.*

Factors, which led to the BJP victory in 1999 elections, included perceptions of its abilities to manage the economy better than Congress. The Kargil war in May-June 1999 provided a huge boost to the campaign of *Hindutva* forces, and hereby the electoral future of the BJP. The war generated defining response of binding a nation together as never before.[3]

Before and during the elections there was also considerable controversy created by the BJP over the issue of whether the Italian born Congress Party leader Sonia Gandhi (widow of Rajiv Gandhi) could really understand India in the same way as the India born leaders of the BJP. The rightwing extremists accused Mrs. Sonia Gandhi of being a "Vatican spy."[4] Along with targeting Mrs. Sonia Gandhi, the Sangh Parivar and the BJP started harassing Christians all-over India and made strong demand for a national law to ban conversion.

The Sarsanghchalak who took over from Rajendra Singh in 2000, K.S. Sudarshan brought new energy in the Sangh. In 2000, the General Secretary of the BJP, Venkaiah Naidu declared that the party had no 'organic link' with the RSS, which was a cultural and social organization. He insisted that the very notion of Sangh Parivar was a creation of the media (*The Hindu*, February 13, 2000). However, in September 2002, the same person, who had just been appointed President of the BJP emphatically declared, "We are proud of our connections with the RSS", as if things could be told at last.

This turning point, in this process was the 2002 Gujarat riots. It then turned out that the NDA allies at the centre were prepared to remain associated with the BJP. The BJP could be frank about its core identity—linking the relationship with the RSS—since NDA, allies were not so much as concerned with secularism as those of the Janata Party 25 years ago: no one left the ruling coalition or even protested somewhat vehemently.[5]

During the tenure of the BJP, anti-conversion legislation became a focal point for the resolution of the Indian 'national question', particularly the purposes of establishing a more resolute and extensive Hindu cultural identity.

Terror Attacks on India (2000 Onwards)

A new wave of terrorism hit India barely after two months of the BJP taking over at the Centre. On December 24, 1999, an Indian Airlines plane with 186 people on board was hijacked on its flight from Kathmandu (Nepal) to Delhi and was taken by the terrorist to Kandhar in Afghanistan under the Talibans. Sharing information about the terrorists' demands, Foreign Minister Jaswant Singh confirms that the terrorists wanted $200 million (about Rs. 900 crore) along with the release of 36 of their men (terrorists) locked in Indian jails.[6] They were rescued after paying ransom and releasing some dreaded terrorists. It was moment of face loss for the BJP government.

After this series of attacks took place. These were New Delhi's Red Fort (December, 2000), J&K Assembly (October, 2001), and Parliament of India, New Delhi (December, 2001).

In **2002**, the focus of terrorist attacks was on transportation system and religious centres. This year also witnessed the acts of terror in eastern part of Uttar Pradesh. In May, a train near Jaunpur in eastern Uttar Pradesh was targeted. In September, bomb blasts were carried out in a train in Rafiganj in Gaya and another train was targeted in the same month at Kurnool (Andhra Pradesh). In September 2002, Akshardham temple in Gujarat was attacked.

2003: The concentration of terrorists' attacks was generally

Mumbai. The attacks took place in the month of January, March, July, and August. The blast near the Gateway of India in August 2003 was most deadly, which claimed 50 lives and more than 150 were injured.

2005: The attacks again started with targeting Jaunpur in eastern Uttar Pradesh in July 2005 in which 13 people were killed in a train bomb blast. In the same month, there was an attack on the Ramjanmabhumi temple at Ayodhya. The same year witnessed multiple bomb blasts in Delhi at the time of Deepawali in October, which left 61 dead and more than 200 injured. The religious connotation of the timing of the attack is significant. The emergence of eastern Uttar Pradesh as terror hub is also significant.

2006: The year began with the attacks on eastern part of India. Varanasi temple in the month of March in which 28 died and more than 150 injured. Three months later, the western part of India. Mumbai commuter trains were targeted in which more than 200 died and nearly 1000 injured. In the month of September two bomb blasts took place near a Muslim graveyard at Malegaon (Maharashtra) in which 37 were killed and 125 injured.

2007: The year was characterized by the bomb blasts in areas where there is high concentration of Muslim population. February—Samjhauta Express (68 killed, 49 injured); May attack on Masjid in Hyderabad (14 killed, 100 injured); in August Hyderabad bombing (44 killed, 54 injured); in October—Ajmer (three killed, 10 injured); in November, Varanasi, Lucknow and Faizabad (15 killed, 80 injured).

2008: In this year, frequency, intensity, spread and audacity of terrorism emanating from outside the country was unprecedented. The year ended with the most audacious attack on the financial capital of India, Mumbai in November known as 26/11 of 2008 attack. Foreign sponsored terrorist traversed the sea from Karachi to Mumbai and attacked the city at eight different locations including Hotel Taj Palace. Some 173 people lost their lives and nearly 327 were injured. Earlier on July 25, the IT capital of India, Bangalore witnessed nine blasts (2 killed and 20 injured). Two months earlier on May 13, explosions had racked the city of Jaipur at eight different places (63 were killed and more than 220 injured. Again, on July 26, a series of 17 blasts shook Ahmedabad in which nearly 50 people were killed and more than 150 injured. In September, blasts again rocked Delhi killing 30 people and injuring

100. Two low intensity bomb blasts in Malegaon (Malegaon II) 8 people were killed and 80 injured. After Malegaon II for the first time, involvement of some Hindu groups was raised.[7]

The word "saffron terrorism" also came into circulation.

Between 2001 and 2008 some 15 attacks, 12 took place during the Congress regime, which came to power in 2004 defeating the BJP.

In May 2008 the Dar-ul-Uloom madrassa in UP, the most powerful Islamic seminary in South Asia issued a *fatwa* against *jihadis* groups. Following the November 2008 terrorist attack in Mumbai, which killed 166 non-combatants, the seminary leadership called upon Indian Muslims to oppose religious fanaticism. As a community, the Muslims of India have shown exemplary moderation and rejected the nihilistic worldview of Islamic *jihadist* groups like Al Qaeda and its Pakistani affiliates.

Legal Barriers on Freedom of Religion

The issue of conversion came to the fore once again with BJP winning 1999 elections.[8] This time the focus was on passing effective anti-conversion laws keeping in mind the *adivasis* (tribal) in India. The RSS inspired activities to 're-convert' tribal people back to Hinduism were reorganised with new vigour and long term planning.

The BJP government strengthened excising legislation or passed new legislation against religious conversions.

As of March 2007, the BJP asserted its plan to bring anti-conversion laws to Uttarakhand State. While the BJP-ruled Jharkhand was debating a final piece of legislation in 2006, the Bill lost its support after the BJP failed to regain power. Moreover, during the tenure of the BJP governments in MP, Chhattisgarh and Gujarat in 2004, the states amended their laws in order to make the punishments for so-called 'forced conversions' more severe.

Several state governments introduced anti-conversion laws. When the state of Chhattisgarh came into existence in the year 2000, it adopted the Madhya Pradesh Act of 1968 by the name of Chhattisgarh Freedom of Religion Act. The 1968 Act, however, was amended by the Chhattisgarh Dharma Swatantraya (Sanshodhan) Adhiniyam, 2006. The Tamil Nadu Prohibition of Forcible Conversion of Religion Act, 2002 was passed by the Tamil

Nadu Assembly. Gujarat followed suit in 2003 with the Gujarat Freedom of Religion Act and the year 2006 witnessed two States adopting such legislations: Rajasthan with the Rajasthan Dharma Swatantraya (Freedom of Religion) Act and Himachal Pradesh with the Himachal Pradesh Freedom of Religion Act (2006).

Punishment that is more stringent was introduced in Gujarat Freedom of Religion Act (2003) and Rules (2008) that proscribed religious conversions by means of 'allurement', 'force', or 'fraud'. However, the definition of these words was open-ended making room for misuse.

Himachal Pradesh's state assembly passed the Freedom of Religion Act in 2006, and the Governor signed it into law in 2007. The law states, "No person shall convert or attempt to convert, either directly or otherwise, any person from one religion to another by the use of force or by inducement or by any other fraudulent means nor shall any person abet any such conversion." The law stipulated punishment of up to two years' imprisonment and/or a fine of 25,000 rupees ($625) and increased penalties if SC/ST members or minors are involved. The law also requires a Notice of Intention to be filed within 30 days before any act of conversion, except for acts of reconversion.

However, certain provisions in Himachal Pradesh law were struck down in 2012 by the High Court, which upheld banning conversions by force, inducement, or fraudulent means but struck down the rule that those planning to convert needed to give one month's notice to the District Magistrate. Gujarat law, which similarly requires advance notification, in effect, permission, from the government for conversion, is currently facing legal challenge.

The law passed in Gujarat in 2003 and amendments in Chhattisgarh, Himachal Pradesh, and Madhya Pradesh in 2006 made conversions that were deemed to have entailed force or allurement non-bailable and cognizable offence. They required individuals to inform the local administration about their intention to convert and allowed district magistrates to determine whether this conversion were not by force or coercion. They introduced harsh penalties for those who violated the law. Himachal Pradesh was the only state where the Congress Party rather than BJP governments introduced such legislations.

On the face of it, as the term freedom of religion Acts implies, the legislation sought to prohibit coercion and ensure individual's rights to choose their faith. But in fact, its intent and effects were just the opposite. It increased the state's authority to engage in surveillance and punishment undermining religious freedom.[9] By heightening scrutiny around conversions, rightwing activists popularized the notion that Christians and Muslims are ruthless foreigners who take advantage of gullible, passive victims.

In 2006, BJP leader L.K. Advani called for national and state legislation to control conversion with a typical argument for these laws:

> We strongly condemn the campaigning of proselytisation, which poses a grave threat to Hindu society and to the national interest as well. We demand stern action against those who indulge in such activities... It is bad enough that religious conversions are conducted in a systematic manner through inducement and coercions. But such activities require an extra edge of ominousness when they are facilitated by foreign funded organisations ostensibly under the grab of social service for poor and under-privileged families. (*Hindustan Times*, April 17, 2006)

With five states of the Indian Union making laws regulating religious conversions in a span of seven years, adding to existing three state laws, and palpable apprehension in the atmosphere could well be sensed.

Violence against Minorities—1999-2004

During 1999-2004, the VHP became increasingly active in large areas of several north Indian states. Communal tension grew in many parts. In June 2000, four churches around India were bombed. In Andhra Pradesh Christian graves were desecrated. A church in Maharashtra was ransacked. Although incidents of violence against Christians occurred in nearly all parts of India, it has largely been confined to north, central, and western India, in the states of Gujarat, Maharashtra, Uttar Pradesh, and Madhya Pradesh. One of the most referred violence took place in February 2002 in Gujarat.

The Gujarat Riots (2002)

Communal violence in India reached at its unprecedented level in 2002. The communal violence that occurred in Gujarat (2002) is considered as genocide of Muslims. It is alleged that violence in Gujarat began after a Muslim mob in the town of Godhra attacked and set fire to two carriages of a train carrying Hindu devotees. Fifty eight people were killed, many of them women and children. The devotees were returning from Ayodhya, Uttar Pradesh Between February 28 and March 2, 2002, a three-day retaliatory killing spree by rightwing extremists left hundreds of Muslims dead. The vandalism, looting and burning of Muslim homes, shops restaurants, and places of worship was also widespread.

Tragically consistent with the long-standing pattern of attacks on minorities in India, and with previous episodes of large-scale communal violence in India, scores of Muslim girls and women were brutally raped in Gujarat before being murdered and burnt to death. According to the official records, more than 850 people have been killed in communal violence in the state of Gujarat, 254 Hindus and 790 Muslims. Unofficial estimate put the death tolls high as 2,000. The state government ruled by Narendra Modi was accused of 'silent spectator' in the whole affairs.[10] The seriousness of this was such that right up his election to governments in May 2014 some foreign governments including the US government, had ban in place on Narendra Modi visiting their country due to issues surrounding his role in violence in Gujarat in 2002.[11]

Violence against Christians

In 2004, violence against Christians erupted in Jhabua district of Madhya Pradesh. Some fundamentalist groups from Gujarat launched an anti-Christian conversions campaign, distributing flyers, interrupting school lessons, throwing stones at buildings and burning images of Christ. The police remained silent spectator during entire violence.

Violent outbreaks also occurred in Alirajpur (29 km from Jhabua) and Amkhut. Fundamentalist groups in Alirajpur—composed of VHP and Baratiya Janata Party members—attacked churches and houses of Christians. A Salesian priest and headmaster of Alirajpur's Don Bosco School, Fr. Stanny Ferriera, was stopped, beaten, left bleeding and his Jeep was set afire. The group then started moving towards school, wanting to burn it down. Since they were not able to enter the school, the group went to a nearby farm of the Salesian community, uprooting its trees and destroying its pump and irrigation system. The arrival of police forces avoided the worst. The school had to be closed for repair. In Jhabua, with a population of 1.4 million, there are 30,000 Catholics, most of whom are *adivasi* Bhils who have been converts for several generations. According to some observers, the campaign launched by ultra rightwing fundamentalists was an attempt to pit local tribesmen against Christians and missionaries so as to stop conversions and get political mileage.

In early 2000, the Gujarat Government attempted to survey Christian families and agencies on a number of occasions. The police often carried out the surveys in the middle of the night. The surveys included questions about the number of converts in the household or a parish, their cumbrances of conversion, and the sources of funding received from abroad. The government discontinued the survey towards the end of 2003 only after human rights and faith based organisations appealed to the Gujarat High Court arguing that such surveys were illegal.[12] No such surveys were conducted thereafter.

The important holy days of India's major religious groups are considered as national holidays including Good Friday and Christmas (Christians), the two Eids (Muslims), Buddha Poornima (Buddhist), Gurunanak Jayanti (Sikhs), Dushera, Diwali and Holi (Hindus) and Mahavir Jayanti (Jains). In 2003, the BJP government in Goa proposed removing Good Friday from the list of official holidays but it withdrew the measures after widespread protests by the Christians.

The BJP government under Prime Minister Atal Bihari Vajpayee proved much more restrained than their rhetoric and agitation strategy of the early 1990s. However, violence against minorities continued. People feel that not enough has been done. The state apparatus seems to function to a certain degree extremely late, and slow action against particular law breakers.

The BJP and the 2004 Elections

The BJP approached 2004 elections with 'India Shining', with images of happy prosperous urban Indians who had benefited from the BJP government. There was widespread commentary in the press that this campaign failed to connect with the reality of the poor in rural India. Did the BJP lost because of *Hindutva* or because of its neglect of *Hindutva*? Ayodhya was not an issue in the 2004 elections and the defeat of the BJP, therefore, is not a vote for secularism. Possibly socio-economic reasons influenced the outcome of elections more than other factors.[13]

In compliance with the RSS, despite criticism from three NDA coalition members, TDP, the Dravida Munetra Kazhagam (DMK), and Trinamool Congress, the BJP overhauled educational policies and institutions. Minister of Human Resource Development Murli Manohar (MM) Joshi sought to "Indianize, nationalize and spiritualize Indian education." He recommended incorporation of Vedas and Upanishads into the curriculum, requiring Sanskrit for third through tenth grade, and making Saraswati Vandana compulsory at government functions. Joshi appointed BJP and RSS members to head major institutions of higher education. The UGC provided funding for university level courses in Vedic Astrology. In 2001, NCERT issued the National Curriculum Framework for school education, which rewrote school textbooks and removed essay by prominent left leaning Indian historians Romila Thapar, Bipan Chandra, and Harbans Mukhia.[14]

The revised books depicted Indian history as the valiant and glories struggles of Hindus to resist Muslim domination. They portrayed Muslim emperors as ruthless invaders and later generations of Muslims as nation's enemy. The NDA government increased budgetary allocations for military and nuclear research to the detriment of research in agriculture, health and medicine and general science.

India's first BJP government produced relatively little change, and certainly not much of a radical kind: no Ram temple, no uniform civil code, and no change in the status of Kashmir. Positive measures included the introduction of mobile telephony on a large scale and further dismantling of the licence raj, *but foreign investment remained sensitive area and is still resisted.*

When BJP won the state assembly elections of 2003 with flying colours (In Madhya Pradesh, Rajasthan and Chhattisgarh), Vajpayee thought it was the right time to call for early elections and recommended premature dissolution of Lok Sabha in early 2004 to utilize the mood, which he thought, was in the BJP's favour. General Elections were conducted in mid-2004 during which BJP left no stone unturned to glorify itself through the "India Shining" campaign, amidst some criticisms, but almost all the newspapers, analysts and opinion polls predicted a resounding victory for BJP. In the early 2000s, India had witnessed steady economic growth under Vajpayee, and BJP in general had become synonymous with progress due to reforms, infrastructure including Golden Quadrilateral, but the results of the counting came as a shocker because BJP had lost.[15] Three new states—Jharkhand, Chhattisgarh, and Uttrakhand were created, largely at the behest of their *adivasi* populations. This ran counter to classic *Hindutva,* which prize a unitary India above all but smaller states did promise better local governance. In 2003, the BJP Government unveiled of a portrait of V.D. Savarkar in the Central Hall of Parliament.

What the NDA government of 1999-2004 did better was to bring high annual growth rate. Taking credit for this whenever it could, the alliance sought to tap the positive national mood at the 2004 elections with the slogan India Shining. This, however, proved insufficient to counterbalance, a wave of corruption scandals that hit senior government figures, making the new, clean BJP look rather more like the older, grubbier parties it had chided while in opposition. Enough of the electorate also felt that India was 'not shining' sufficiently in their lives, and they would tell their rulers so.

Despite losing power, the BJP became established as the primary alternative to Congress in 2004 with large-scale sympathisers in white colour jobs.

Congress-led UPA Government 2004-2009, 2009-2014

The unheralded Congress-UPA victory in 2004 set off a burst of government vitality, with a succession of constructive measure to promote the welfare of India's poor. This was the result of an unusual conjunction in India affairs—a political willingness to implement such schemes and enough money to pay for them. The UPA had a strong Left component, and there were consistently high annual growth figures through the mid-2000s.

The UPA had campaigned as a loose coalition, without a set of programme like that of the NDA in 1999. This deficiency was remedied by adoption of a Common Minimum Programme by the coalition partners after the election.[16] The problem of premiership proved more contentious. Sonia Gandhi had been projected as a prime ministerial candidate, but opponents had made much of her foreign birth during the campaign. In reflection, she declined the post while remaining the Congress Party President and the eminent economist Manmohan Singh, who had served as Finance Minister in the Rao Government, took office as Prime Minister.

However, there was a downside too, in that the government was then effectively split into public and private sections, with a front office in full view at 7, Race Course Roads—the Prime Minister's official residence; and a back room team, titled the National Advisory Council at 10 Janpath, which was headed by Sonia Gandhi as being the party president. This arrangement struck some as cumbersome, while others considered it unconstitutional or even illegal. In the end, it proved to be hampering decision making to some degree. It did damage to the long-term standing of Manmohan Singh, who was never able to convince the public that it was really his government he was leading.

The new administration set out on a programme to alleviate poverty and enhance 'rights' a complex twin track project. It introduced a Citizens' Rights to Information Act (2005)—a measure that had long been in the offering—and it secured the Rights to Education (2010), first introduce as a Constitutional amendment in 2002. It passed the National Rural Employment Guarantee Act (2005) to relieve distress in the agricultural sector. The UID was introduced in 2010.

The UPA after winning 2004 elections began to 'de-saffronize' textbooks and curricular nationwide and to restore the secular character of the education.

The much criticised Sachhar Committee was appointed in 2005 to report on the status and disadvantages of Muslims in India.

Commission for "Minority Religion and Linguistic Minority" known as "Misra Commission" was set-up by United Progressive Alliance (UPA) Government in 2005 to study and report on socio-economic condition of Christians and Muslims converted from Scheduled Caste origins. The Justice Misra Commission report was submitted on May 22, 2007. The Commission Report has suggested to delink Religion from Scheduled Caste and *Dalits* who, irrespective of their religion, suffer caste stigma and Scheduled Caste status should be given to all *Dalits* irrespective of their religions.[17]

The UPA displaced identity demands by practising economic issues around both growth and social welfare. Its victory in the 2009 elections revealed the popularity of its agrarian debt forgiveness scheme and its effort to provide employment through the NREG Act. The UPA Government counteracted the "saffronisation" of education by launching programme to 'detoxify" textbooks after the three member committee of historians reviewed them and withdrew the most controversial textbooks. In 2005, it unveiled new curriculum designed to promote secular values, it issued revised textbooks, the following year. The government dropped funding for Ekal Vidyalayas because an Inquiry Commission found that government funds were being used to generate hatred towards minorities. In 2009 it took important step in promoting free basic education to all children between ages six and fourteen by adopting the Right of Children to Free and Compulsory Education Bill.[18]

The UPA Government established the Ministry of Minority Affairs, National Commission for Religious and Linguistic Minorities, and National Commission for Minority Educational Intuitions. It sought to enhance educational opportunities for Muslims by improving the quality of *madrasas* and establishing Muslim universities. Prime Minister Dr. Manmohan Singh adopted a Fifteen-Point Programme for the Welfare of Minorities, which called for bettering minorities' living conditions, employment opportunities, and access to resources. The Eleventh Plan endorsed these objectives.

The UPA government created a Ministry of Minority Affairs in 2006 and appointed Sachhar Committee (2005) and the Mishra Commission (2007).

The Sachhar Committee (2006) issued a damning report on Muslim's economic and social disadvantages. The Sachhar Committee Report galvanized public attention in a similar fashion as the Mandal Commission Report on OBCs. Based on the key suggestions, new initiatives were launched. These included pre- and post-matric and merit-*cum*-means scholarship schemes for minority students and Multi-Sectoral Development Programme (MSDP) for 90 minority concentration districts under the aegis of Ministry of Minority Affairs (MoMA). Ministry of Human Resource Development, too, came up with new schemes for modernization of madrasas education, infrastructure development of minority institutions and greater resources for teaching of Urdu.[19] This irked the BJP and the RSS, which started campaigning that this move of UPA Government would reduce reservation quota for *Dalits* and OBCs. The major campaign was that all this is 'Muslim appeasement' at the cost of majority Hindu population.

However, all this good work was lost as from 2011, ministers of senior rank began to find themselves behind bars including Sukh Ram for a telecom scandal dating back to the 1990s, Andimuthu Raja for his part in the 2G scam and Lalu Prasad Yadav in fodder scam.

The UPA passed the Food Security Act, 2013, which was a gigantic political stroke, intended to buy the votes of the poor at public expense. However, all the money that the UPA poured into countryside over a decade proved of no avail in the final result at the polls of 2014 as the BJP and its allies were successful in raising a question in the minds of the people that after election the reins of the government if Congress wins, is likely to be given to Rahul Gandhi, an immature.

Rahul Gandhi (RaGa) soft handed, privileged political apprentice found himself against Narendra Modi (NaMo), a self-made hard man with three terms as Chief Minister behind him. RaGa was no match for NaMo. Comparing himself to the then Finance Minister P. Chidambaram, who got a degree from Harvard Business School, Modi asked voters of Chennai whether India would be better run by 'Harvard or hard work'.[20]

Anna Hazare Movement Recap

Towards the end of 2010, a new social movement started in India, which reached its pinnacle in the mid-April 2013. By the beginning of 2011, the people of India came to know of large-scale corruption of CWG, 2G, 4G, and coal frauds. These cases shocked large number of Indians. The growth of social media, which allowed accumulation and aggregation of public opinion like never before, helped coalesce people's anger against missed all until it was very late.

People's agitation and anger erupted against poor governance or mis-governance in the beginning of 2011. On the death anniversary of Mahatma Gandhi, January 30, 2011, there were marches all-over India and Anna Hazare announced his hunger strike for Lok Pal and Lokayukta. Baba Ramdev joined the movement and on June 6, his rally was dispersed by the police at Ramlila ground. In 2011 anti-corruption movement by Anna Hazare shook the country. The massive anti-government sentiment of 2011 was amplified by the media and solidified by new social media. It led to rise of several phenomenon, one of these was the Anna Hazare movement, an anti-corruption drive that sought to have a Lokpal, an independent ombudsman in the country. Beyond all this, the Aam Aadmi Party (AAP) got off to a flying start taking control of Delhi as minority government and the elections in December 2013.

The Anna Hazare movement highlighted certain essential ingredients of political communication, not all of these were newly discovered. The primary issue neglected by the leaders in Delhi was that democracy essentially meant a participatory role for the people in shaping the affairs of society. People had a right to protest, demonstrate and agitate on issues apart from electing members for legislative assemblies and parliament periodically. But, in 2011 India, there was hardly any leader, be it in the government or in the opposition, who could enthuse the people. This vacuum helped Anna Hazare movement to succeed. Second, the credibility of the leader was critical. Anna had taken the Gandhian route of protesting against the corrupt systems from his village Ralegan Siddhi and had a clean image in public service. Apart from the leadership issues, the IAC movement illustrated how media could be used to create hysteria among the people across the vast country. Anna movement was a wakeup call.[21]

The movement succeeded in pressuring the government to involve its activists in an effort to formulate an anti-corruption Bill. Anna Hazara was key person in this initiative joined by Kejriwal and company. A section of India Against Corruption (IAC) launched the Aam Adami Party. While Anna Hazare withdrew from the political entity it gave birth to a new political star called Arvind Kejriwal. Smart, young, and from a humble background Kejriwal was seen by the people as one of the solutions to India's crisis. While people liked him, wanted him to have future in Indian politics, and knew that he could take on the Congress, they were not sure that he could be a viable alternative to it.

Hence, this created another gap and simultaneously led to the rise of another political star—Narendra Modi. He had been Chief

Minister of Gujarat for three times, and thus offered an alternative to the Congress. Modi had more experience and proven record of accomplishment in running a state successfully and keeping Muslims at bay. While the Congress lost touch with the masses, Modi and the BJP began to echo popular sentiments, 'Congress Mukt Bharat' which instantly became popular. Since Indians like personalities in politics, the entire campaign revolved around Narendra Modi. '*Ab ki bar, Modi sarkar*' was splattered across hoardings and newspapers in every city. Rest as they say, is history.

The Camphor Flame

Hindu nationalist movement activity declined in the aftermath of the 2004 elections in which the Congress led UPA defeated the BJP led NDA alliance by a wide margin. A VHP demonstration pledging to build a temple in Ayodhya, on December 6, 2004, the 12th anniversary of the mosque's demolition was small and uneventful. The RSS spokesperson Ram Madhav called an armed attack on the mosque temple complex in Ayodhya on July 5, 2005 'unfortunate' and asked people to shun violence and protest peacefully.

The VHP organised a lacklustre *bandh,* without the BJP's support. The BJP *yatras* opposing UPA government (the *Suraksha Yatra* in April 2006 and *Vijay Yatra* in March, 2008) were poorly attended. Rifts between party and movement and unsympathetic state and national governments contributed to the decline of Ayodhya movement.

The Sangh Parivar sought unsuccessfully to organize a mass campaign around the Ram Setu. It opposed the UPA government's decision in June 2005 to dredge a canal to enable a passage of large commercial ships between Sri Lanka and India. It contended that the dredging would destroy Ram Setu—an underwater causeway that features in the Hindu epic *Ramayana*. The RSS organised protests in various parts of the country in 2007 and a rally in Delhi on 30th December.

The NDA Government under pressure from its coalition partner, the DMK had initially authorized the project. Although some BJP leaders supported the Ram Setu campaign and attended a few rallies, the BJP as a whole and BJP state governments did not wholeheartedly supported it.

The DMK government questioned whether Rama, and Ram

Setu are historical reality or mythology. The VHP strongly opposed the DMK for questioning the historical veracity of Ram's life.[22]

As a result, the Ram Setu campaign did not take root either nationally or in Tamil Nadu.

The BJP suffered consecutive defeats in two general elections, despite its attempt to capitalize on Hindu nationalists appeals in 2009. Its election manifesto that year promised to explore all possible means of building a temple in Ayodhya and vowed to protect and promote the cow and its progeny. It took a strong stand on national security, promising within 100 days of coming to office to revive the "anti-terrorism" mechanism that the UPA Government had dismantled and reinstate an improved version of the POTA. It also vowed to launch a massive campaign to detect and deport illegal immigrants. The BJP-RSS combine also raised the issue of religious conversion and of insult to Hindu religious leaders such as that of "Sankracharya who was forced to deplane Indian Airlines flight in 2005 for carrying his religious *danda* (wooden stick)".[23]

In 2009 election, the BJP projected L.K. Advani as prime ministerial candidate and made Narendra Modi as its star campaigner. *Hindutva* proved to be electorally unpopular. The BJP suffered an even more significant defeat in 2009 than in the previous elections.

From 2010, the RSS and the BJP reverted to the strategy, they had pursued during the Emergency, of joining other political parties in an anti-corruption movement directed against the Congress Government. The Sangh Parivar also directed its energy in fighting social exclusions, which remain the most solid challenges to Indian democracy and development.[24] The BJP supported Anna Hazare and Baba Ramdev's movement against corruption.

In late 2010, the RSS was forced onto the defensive after one of its leaders, Indresh Kumar, was charged as conspirator in the 2007 bombing of a Sufi shrine in Ajmer. The organisation responded with massive protests in defence of Kumar and of Pragya Singh and Swami Aseemanand, two RSS linked activists charged in relation to the Ajmer blast and two other bomb attacks between 2007 and 2008.

In April 2011, the Vivekananda International Foundation organised a two-day seminar on "Black money". The attendees included Ajit Doval, Gurumurthy, Baba Ramdev, social activist Anna Hazare, the anti-corruption campaigner Arvind Kejriwal, the politician Subramaniam Swamy, the retired IPS officer Kiran

Bedi and the RSS *pracharak* K.N. Govindacharya. Soon afterwards, Anna Hazare and Ramdev began much publicised fast against corruption accusing the ruling government of having abetted it. These sparked a massive protest movement that proved disastrous for the government and provided the BJP, the electoral offspring, with a platform for issues useful for 2014 election campaign.

In 2013, a crucial decision was taken by the RSS that base for nation building cannot be done on diversity. Since then the Sangh Parivar started promoting a Hindu identity as Indian identity.

After losing elections in 2004, the BJP cadre was demoralised. They all looked to "Advani for leadership who was considered hardliner. But, after his visit to Pakistan in which he praised Jinna he lost support from the RSS as well as from the BJP cadre. The RSS promoted new face Nitin Gadkari.

This was also time when the RSS and the BJP realised that the media coverage always portrait them as anti-minority. Therefore new emphasis was added to *prachar vibhag,* which came into existence in RSS in 1995s. The old policy of away from media was abolished and the RSS infiltrated its cadre in the vernacular oppress as never before.

All these added in the run up to the 2014 general election.

New Definition of Minorities

103rd Amendment Bill 2004—Put in Cold Storage

In numerous judgments including the *Kerala Education Bill* Case (1957), the *DAV College* Case and *TMA Pai Foundation* Case, the Supreme Court have upheld the principle of safeguarding the educational rights of the minorities enshrined in Article 30(1) of the Constitution, and in *Bal Patil* vs. *Union of India,* it stated that "since reorganization of States in India has been on linguistic lines, therefore, for the purpose of determining the minority, the unit will be the State and not the whole of India."

In the *TMA Pai* Case, the Supreme Court held that "a minority either linguistic or religious is determinable only by reference to demography of the State and not by taking into consideration the population of the country as a whole." This also applies to Scheduled Castes and Scheduled Tribes. Under Articles 341 and 342, the President is empowered to draw up a list in consultation with the Governor of each State, subject to revision by Parliament.

In 2004, the UPA Government introduced the Constitution (103rd Amendment) Bill that seeks to have State-wise minority status rather than national status, in line with Supreme Court Judgments. As per the provisions of this Bill, minorities in the State would be decided through a Presidential notification in consultation with the State Government.[25]

The Constitution (One Hundred and Third Amendment) Bill, 2004 along with National Commission for Minorities (Repeal) Bill, 2004 was introduced in Lok Sabha on December 23, 2004. The National Commission for Minorities (Repeal) Bill, 2004 repealed the National Commission for Minorities Act, 1992. It proposed to dissolve the National Commission for Minorities. The Constitution (One Hundred and Third Amendment) Bill, 2004 proposed to establish a new National Commission for Minorities, with a constitutional status, in order to inspire greater confidence towards the effectiveness of the Commission.

As per the 103rd Amendment Bill, States would be asked for their view, on the basis of data available, as to who is a minority. They would be consulted by the President of India, who would then notify the minorities in that State. While the President is to consult the states, he would not be bound to act on their advice. The Bills were referred to the Department-related Parliamentary Standing Committee on Social Justice and Empowerment under the Chairmanship of Smt. Sumitra Mahajan, and the committee submitted its report on February 21, 2006 in which it recommended that the Supreme Court's directives in the case of *Bal Patil* vs. *Union of India* should be considered in its entirety.

The Bill was stiffly opposed by existing "minorities" on the grounds that implementing the Supreme Court judgments to notify Hindus as a minority community in states where the national minority was in majority, would amount to "obfuscating the issue." The BJP opposed it on the grounds that the country has already been divided enough on religious grounds. The 103rd Amendment Bill was not presented in the last session of the 14th Lok Sabha on February 2009 and was allowed to lapse and was not reintroduced during the rest of the UPA term until 2014.

Narendra Modi government stand on Minority Commissions and on tribals belonging to separate religion is quite different from the UPA government.

Mukhtar Abbas Naqvi, the Minister of State in the Ministry of Minority Affairs, in Lok Sabha on August 12, 2015 stated that the states of Arunachal Pradesh, Goa, Gujarat, Haryana, Himachal Pradesh, Meghalaya, Mizoram, Nagaland, Odisha, Sikkim and UTs of Andaman & Nicobar Islands, Chandigarh, Daman & Diu, Dadra & Nagar Haveli, Lakshadweep and Puducherry have not yet set up a Minority Commission in their respective States/UTs. He said that the NCM Act does not extend to state of Jammu & Kashmir. Tripura has passed a Bill in this regard on November 26, 2008, which awaits assent of the President.

In so far as the Central Government is concerned, he stated that Hindus have not been declared as a minority community under Section 2(c) of National Commission for Minorities (NCM) Act, 1992 and that setting up of Minority Commissions by the State Governments was a State subject and no time frame could be fixed for formation of Minority Commissions by State Governments as it was for them to decide.[26]

The stand taken by BJP on the 103rd Amendment Bill is contrary to the public demands of minority status for Hindus made by both the BJP and the RSS. Judging from Mukhtar Abbas Naqvi's statement and the BJP's opposition to the Bill in 2007, unless there is a major rethink, it is unlikely that the Narendra Modi Government will reintroduce the 103rd Amendment Bill in Parliament.

Communal Violence

After 2000, a new type of modernist politics, both secular and religious emerged in India, which can be seen in Kandhmal (Odisha) in 2008, and Muzaffarnagar (U.P.) 2013.

People intoxicated with politics as in Gujarat because the premium on political power is very high and as such leaders take extreme measures to win power. Implicit in the argument is the idea that the religion based communal discord is a lesser issue than the access to power.

- **2006 Aligarh riots:** Riots broke out on April 5 between Hindus and Muslims over Ram Navami celebrations. Five people were killed due to the violence.
- **2008 Dhule riots:** In October 2008, 4 people were killed as

a result of Hindu and Muslim communal clash. The incident left over 200 people injured that included 113 police officers.

- **Kandhmal Violence (2007-08)**: It all began on 24th December, 2007 while local Christians were preparing to Christmas they were attacked by a crowd loyal to Swami Laxmanananda a rightwing *sadhu*. Over 100 houses destroyed, six people killed, and thousands were rendered homeless. In 2008, eight months after this attack Swami Lakshmanananda and his four disciples were gunned down by the Maoist but the VHP accused local missionaries of having masterminded the murder of their leader and unleashed violent attacks on Christian centres from at the dawn of August 24, 2008. A priest and nun working at the Diocesan Pastoral Centre in Nuagaon block of the district were severely beaten up stripped and paraded semi-naked. On 25th afternoon a young nun aged 29, was gang raped in public view. Even a Hindu girl mistaken for a Christian was burnt alive. Many other priests were severally beaten up and suffered injuries: ninety Christians were killed including two pastors and three Catholic priests. Nearly 250 churches and prayer halls were burned. Over 4,655 Christian houses were either totally or partially reduced to ashes. Over 50,000 terrified Christians fled to into jungles to save their lives. Over 22,000 men, women, and children were forced to live in refugee camps for months without much facility.[27]
- **Karnataka Violence 2008:** In September 2008 twenty-four churches and prayer centres in Karnataka were attacked injuring nearly 100 persons. Priests and nuns were attacked including cloisters nuns who never go out of convents. After Odisha, the Karnataka Christians suffered maximum number of attacks since the BJP Government came to power there in June 2008, making history as the first saffron government in South India.
- **2010 Deganga riots:** The Deganga riots had begun on September 6 and continued for several days. About 24 people were hurt and several houses and properties got destroyed when clashes broke out between Hindu and Muslim communities in the Basirhat sub-division of North

24 Parganas, about 150 km from Kolkata.

- **2011 Bharatpur riots:** On September 14, clashes broke between Gujjars and Meo Muslims in Bharatpur, Rajasthan. Eight people killed and 23 injured.
- **2012 Assam riots:** Kokrajhar has sadly been witness to communalism even in the past. On July 20, 2012 riots broke out in Kokrajhar that later spread out to the lower regions of Assam. 77 people were reported to have been killed. Around, 79,000 people from about 500 villages had to take shelter in 128 relief camps. The riots took place between Bodo community and Bengali speaking Muslims of the region. The clashes have their roots in the mid-nineties and peace still evades the region as the tension continues even today.
- **2013 Muzzafarnagar riots:** During the months of August and September, riots broke out in Muzaffarnagar district of a Uttar Pradesh that resulted in nearly 62 deaths of which 42 victims were Muslims and 20 Hindus. The riot between Hindu Jats and Muslims was said to have been triggered by a harassment of a Hindu girl but several reports point out that it was an outcome of intensive communal campaigning in the State by right wing groups.

In the year 2013, 479 incidents of communal violence took place with 107 people dead injuring 1,647 people including 200 police personnel. In 2012, there were 640 incidents of communal violence with 93 deaths. The violence left 2,067 people injured. The ruling Congress Party failed to take action. The UPA Government, in its dying days, was perceived to be afflicted by administrative paralysis.

While out of power during 2004-2014, the BJP again renewed its approaches to garnering power through mass campaign based on religious feelings and re-designing its election strategies. Critical in this was a generational change in which first A.B. Vajpayee and then L.K. Advani stepped down from their leadership roles, and in 2013 the RSS focused attention on Narendra Modi as a potential leader of the BJP.

Return of BJP 2014

Despite pro-poor policies and protection approach towards the minorities, the UPA lost the 2014 elections due to the decline of the Congress Party and the changing dimension of the state policies in India. Election results are not outcome of one-day affairs. The Congress-led UPA lost May 2014 election due to volcanic eruption of public anger against corruption combined with inability to check price rise. On the other hand, the rise of Modi was not instant magic; it was the outcome of a deliberate, well-crafted campaign that evolved over several years.

In December 2012, I was on visit to Gujarat to watch the assembly elections that was fought on development plank and much talked Gujarat model of development. On December 20, 2012, the news broke that Narendra Modi had scored a hat trick in Gujarat. That evening, Modi addressed a large meeting of RSS-BJP *karyakartas* in Ahmedabad. "Gujarat is a role model for elections", Modi said. This victory is not the victory of Narendra Modi but of the six crore Gujaratis and those Indians who aspire for prosperity and development. This is victory of all those who wish the country's good", he added.

This was a routine victory speech but I noticed that it was delivered in Hindi and not in Gujarati, designed for national audience way beyond Gujarat. In the frenzied crowd, posters had sprung up: "Modi Chief Minister 2012; Prime Minister 2014". In the evening over a typical Gujarati dinner with my Gujarati friend Brajesh Shah whose reaction was "I told you so". I had instant feeling that Modi is destined to assume greater role in national politics. The 2014 election shows that Modi was planning a long, single-minded journey to the top, not an overnight coup.

Narendra Modi's BJP came to power in a historic landslide victory in May 2014 with an absolute majority in parliament, winning 283 seats in the 543 seats.

Gujarat Development Model

For many people the period 2001-2014 when Narendra Modi held the office of Chief Minister of Gujarat was marked not so much by sectarian issues but by his efforts to promote the economic growth of Gujarat. This, which has often been called the Gujarat Model was based on paradigm of 'less government, more governance' and emphasis that business should be freed from government red tape and be allowed the freedom to develop. This model is to some degree similar to many neo-conservative models for development, which see the central problem has been the need to roll back big government and allow the private sector the freedom to develop a market economy.[28]

There has been considerable discussion of the degree to which the Gujarat model was successful. Like the central BJP government during 1999-2004, it was a model that seemed to promote urban middle and upper class prosperity rather than seeking to promote the welfare of all, including rural areas. The figures are open to dispute but it is possible to present Gujarat's development during this period as very successful economically but at the same time failing to improve the lot of the poor throughout the State and in particular in rural areas.

Analysis

Contemporary Hindu nationalism has been shaped by several important events between 2000 to 2014 period. The period saw rapid rise of the BJP and loss of power in 2004 in the height of India shining. The UPA rule from 2004 to 2014 was marked by several ups and downs. The UPA government appointed Sachhar Committee to study the socio-economic conditions of the Muslims community. But electorally, it proved wrong step. The BJP started campaigning that the Congress Party was pro-Muslims and cannot protect Hindu interests. This contributed to the downfall of Congress. During the period 2004-2014, when the BJP was out of power, the issue of Ramjanmabhumi was kept alive with the help of the VHP and a strong anti-minority campaign was launched throughout the country. Violence against minorities grew during this period.

The BJP suffered consecutive defeats in the 2004 and 2009 general elections. The 2009 defeat revealed its weakness in key federal states. These elections also revealed lack of popular support for *Hindutva*. This may be the reason why the BJP down played its *Hindutva* nationalist plank in 2014. The BJP's impressive victory in 2014 was propelled by a promise to renew India's economic growth and promise development. In practice, the BJP ran elections by combining themes of *Hindutva*, caste politics, promise of progress for all Indians and good performance.[29]

New religious politics took definite shape by 2000 with the

rise of Hindu revivalist movement in India, which was to some extent in response to the fundamentalist movements in all Muslim countries. Advocates of the new religious policies have found a fertile ground in the Gujarat. The main contention of their analysis is that the Hindu-Muslim riots have been the result of the revivalist cultural aggression.

The Gujarat riots in 2002 were transformation of local incident into statewide violence to institutionalised riot system to drive gains in elections.[30]

Communalism Entrenched

The BJP's political validation through the 1998-2004 NDA resulted in a further substantive normative change within domestic politics, namely the entrenchment of communalism and communal politics. The BJP's advantageous electoral positioning within a modernising, globalising and media-dominated middle class additionally strengthened their mainstream acceptance. Commentators also talked of a commensurate shift of "the centre of gravity of Indian politics to the right" (Vanaik, 2002: 322), especially concerning capitalism and positive secularism. These shifts questioned the legitimacy of Congress' normative secular basis but also seemingly demanded that Congress and India's leftist parties become less socialist in orientation (Momen, 2005: 254).

Reflecting their emergence as a political tool in the 1980s and their proto-normalisation as the BJP rose to prominence in the 1990s, under the NDA communal (and therefore anti-secular) politics therefore became an accepted part of politics for all parties. Thus, something that had been a trend before 1998 became legitimised by a communal party (the BJP) as they entered India's political mainstream and served a full term in government. As one senior academic said in an interview with the author in September 2009, that in post-2004 period there has been greater leaning of the Sangh Parivar to the media-influenced and expanding middle class who were beneficiaries of economic growth underpinned by neo-liberal policies.

Significantly, the electoral rise of Hindu nationalism "altered the balance of power between Hindus and Muslims that had persisted since Partition" (Nasir, 2005: 193). Furthermore, the 1998-2004 BJP led NDA allowed those groups associated with it to firmly establish their political positions. Thus, even post-NDA, Sangh Parivar activists spread their influence through the national and local institutions of government across India. In particular, Jaffrelot (2009) noted how "the saffronisation of the state and society has made progress in the last 15 years... the *Hindu Rashtra* is in the making along the societal lines the RSS has always valued." Through their active discrimination against Muslims, Christians and the lower castes (they becoming a bigger target in light of electoral success of the BJP and the wider Sangh Parivar entrenched communal norms.

During the BJP-led NDA period, the core norms underpinning the BJP's *Hindutva* ideology competed with, and at times successfully challenged, the 'secularism' prevalent in domestic politics. This process produced two significant modifications to the practice of Indian politics: ascendancy of multifaceted majoritarian democracy and the entrenchment of communalism and communal politics. These were not new ideas and were present before the arrival of the BJP-led NDA government 1999-2004, but it was only during the NDA rule that they were assertively established, entrenched, and, in effect, mainstreamed into the topography of contemporary politics. This was achieved *via* the validation of the BJP's political legitimacy, India's political centre ground shifting to the right and the avowal of 'communalised commonsense'.

Concurrently, the BJP-led NDA saw the emergence of an acceptable political religious nationalism capable of successfully questioning the secular origins of the Indian state. Despite losing power post-2004, the BJP became established as the primary alternative to Congress. India under BJP rule (1999-2004) indicates both the possibilities and limitations of using religious soft power as an analytical variable in relation to governmental policies including foreign policy.

Strategic Approach

After the BJP came to power at Centre in 1999, the Hindu nationalists introduced their most significant policy initiatives within federal states. As regional political parties and governments have become stronger, the BJP and RSS become greater proponents of federalism. In 2000, the NDA government recognized Uttrakhand, Jharkhand, and Chhattisgarh, where the BJP had performed well in the 1998 elections as new federal states. The

RSS has supported the creation of new states and called for the division of other states like Maharashtra, Andhra Pradesh, Karnataka, Gujarat, Rajasthan, West Bengal, Assam, and Jammu & Kashmir.[31]

The BJP governments, in close collaboration with the VHP and RSS, have doggedly pursued three Hindu nationalist commitments—educational reforms, cow protection, and banning religious conversion. All three issues promote discrimination and violence against minorities.[32] They reveal the important party-movement-state government collaboration in pursuing an ideological driven agenda through legislation and population mobilization.

Despite their loss in 2004 and 2009 elections, the influence of the 1998-2004 BJP-led NDA was important as it had proved the legitimacy of a non-Congress-dominated coalition, which then validated future political possibilities for any other political groupings.

Religious Conversion

BJP government strengthened existing legislation or passed new legislation in Gujarat, Rajasthan, Madhya Pradesh and Chhattisgarh. The laws passed in Gujarat in 2003 and in Chhattisgarh, Himachal Pradesh, and Madhya Pradesh in 2006 made conversion that were deemed to have entailed force or allurement non-bailable and cognizable offence.

The Sangh Parivar's focus on tribal areas brought tension between Christian missionaries and Hindu nationalists groups. In many places RSS-inspired activists tried to re-convert, tribal people back to Hinduism. The complication here is that for the RSS, tribal people have always been Hindus despite many tribal people not regarding themselves as ever having been part of *Sanatana Hindu Dharma* and saying that their religious beliefs are not part of Hinduism but separate indigenous traditions. The contradiction here is that some state governments regard RSS inspired campaigns as legitimate actions to reconvert tribal peoples but Christian missionaries' activities as illegitimate. The problem that arose in the Dangs of Gujarat seems related to tension between VHP-RSS inspired groups and Christian groups over attempts to convert tribal people.

The response of the Gujarat government to ban religious conversion appeared to be partisan as it only applied to Christian missionary activities and did not apply to RSS inspired activities as it regarded tribal people as being intrinsically Hindu, even if they regarded themselves as Christians and held that they had never been Hindu to begin with. This is another aspect of the interplay between Hinduism and politics in India: the question of whether tribal people are intrinsically Hindu, and whether freedom of religions belief includes the freedom for tribal people to choose a religion.[33]

These legislations inaccurately implied that all poor Hindus who had converted to Islam and Christianity wanted to convert back to Hinduism and that most were converted forcibly or trickery. The assumption that conversion out of Hinduism is coercive whereas conversion to Hinduism is voluntary underlies the BJP's mass reconversion ceremonies, named *ghar wapsi* in BJP ruled states.

Mainstreaming the Extreme

The BJP made trends that had been normalising prior to 1998 and mainstreamed them in Indian domestic politics. This mainstreaming created a lasting legacy comprised of two specific changes—the redefinition of Indian democracy along more multi-faceted and majoritarian lines and the entrenchment of communalism and communal politics. These changes persisted after the BJP-led NDA left power in 2004, continued into subsequent Congress-led United Progressive Alliances, and produced a long-term behavioural shift in Indian politics. Such normative changes threatened the tenets of secularism and inclusiveness that had been the long-standing benchmarks of domestic politics since independence.

In contrast, *Hindutva* is characterised by an inherent assumption of cultural superiority, a suspicion of outsiders (particularly Muslims and Christians but also foreign investment) and a desire to aggressively rebuild India as a *Hindu Rashtra*. The BJP referred to *Hindutva* as "cultural nationalism"—a unifying principle that represented a Hindu-dominated worldview based upon India's "timeless cultural heritage". In addition, the BJP called for "positive secularism", which represented "justice for all, appeasement for none", and contrasted with Congress' secularism, which was seen as discriminating against the Hindu majority.

While both parties supported a *swadeshi* (self-reliance) approach to economics, for the BJP this was returning to "economic sovereignty" based upon Indian primacy and Hindu nationalism.

Consolidation through Enmity

Through its *Hindutva* ideology, the BJP "attempted to provide an outlet for the religious and cultural consciousness of the people, one that was completely ignored and devalued by secularity" (Momen, 2005) and the policies of Congress. Therefore, in its emphasis on a *Hindu Rashtra,* the BJP shifted away from notions of an inclusive, secular India to one that was communal, Hindu-based, and Hindu orientated. The promotion of *Hindutva* domestically demanded the identification and targeting of suitable outsiders with whom to portray the *Hindu Rashtra* under attack. These outsiders were primarily the traditional Sangh Parivar target, which included not only the Muslim population but also India's law abiding Christian minority.

As such, the BJP promoted policies that had clear dissonance with Congress' secular norms, which were rejected as biased against Hindus and "pseudo-secular" (Noorani, 2011). Such policies led to increased violence and discrimination against India's Muslims and Christians during the BJP-led NDA period, often aided by the political involvement of Sangh Parivar elements (Ram, 2015). Promotion of the Hindu worldview also involved BJP attempts to rewrite history to compound their discrimination against these groups and to re-orientate the normative basis of the India state.

Ploughing the Same Furrow?

India's general elections held in April and May 2014, represented a tectonic shift in Indian politics. For the first time since independence, India elected a right wing Hindu nationalist party to power with an absolute majority. The Bharatiya Janata Party (BJP) became the dominant force of Indian politics, backed by a decisive and unprecedented, 'majoritarian' mandate, as Narendra Modi led the BJP to a sensational win. Its victory was so complete that it captured all or most of the seats in some states and reduced the Indian National Congress Party to 44 of the 543 seats in the Lok Sabha, a shocking comedown for a party whose history is integral to India's founding narrative. Coupled with the near obliteration suffered by parties on the left, it is easy to conclude that for now the centrist, secular and progressive voices have lost out. In immediate terms, the Indian polity stands redefined. With a BJP-led government in power, the Indian right now occupies centre stage and commands the national government.[34]

One important feature of 2014 election is that the BJP successfully consolidated the Hindu votes in a whole range of constituencies, especially northern and north-western India. The other side to Hindu consolidation is the political marginalisation and eclipse of Muslims. No political party has previously come to power by excluding Muslims so completely.[35] The BJP did.

Challenging Secularism

Since 2001, liberal democracy has increasingly come under attack in India. During its regime from 1999 to 2004, the BJP systematically attacked secularism and made 'pseudo-secularism' among India's educated middle classes particularly among under 30, many of whom are more concerned about career and consumeristic approach to life.

After it lost 2009 elections, the BJP has consistently identified itself as a Hindu nationalist party that seeks to promote the idea of India as an essentially Hindu nation and for the Hindu people. This was old dream but now put forward differently.[36] Followers of this ideology claim that India has been Hindu since time immemorial, and the edicts laid down by the ancient sages represent the core of Indian civilisation. A movement towards Hinduising society and advancing the political and social primacy of Hindus has continued to gain ground in India and Diaspora communities since the beginning of 2000s.

The real danger that Indian secularism now faces stems from the BJP's ability to transform the terms of political discourse within India. The right wing started a forceful move to convince people that Hinduism is not merely a religion but an entire cultural ethos that pervades Indian life and society. Consequently, it argues a secular order is impossible in India.[37] It also contends that secularism, as practised in India has amounted to little more than the "pampering" of minorities, and therefore "pseudo secularism".

During first phase of power from 1999 to 2004 the BJP, and the Sangh Parivar strengthened itself in the areas of institutional influence, and clearly exhibited that they have plan to change those Constitutional provision which gives freedom of religion and protection to the religious minorities. The BJP appointed Justice Venkatachalliah Committee to look into possible changes in the Constitution, which included issues such as reservation to the Scheduled Castes, minority rights to run institutions, right to propagate and convert and many more.

Freedom of Religion: New Parenthesis

Since 2001, one issue that the RSS/VHP brought to prominence in public discourse is that of the so-called connection between Christian groups, churches, and foreign funding.[38] Another striking aspect of this period is the manner in which the BJP leaders including the then Prime Minister Atal Bihari Vajpayee helped undermine the sense of collective horror over the burning of Graham Staines by suggesting a week after the grisly murder, a national debate on the matter of forced conversions. Vajpayee also pointed an accusing finger at the Muslim community, hinting that the 2002 ghastly pogrom in Gujarat against Muslims was a consequence of the Godhra incident. Earlier also during the attack on tribal Christians in Dang, Vajpayee has candidly suggested a national debate on *Dharmantaran* (religious conversion).

While the rise of communal tensions are linked to a complex set of social, political and economic factors it is also fact that overall an interdisciplinary agreement exists that the increase of communal riots over the last two decades corresponds to the Hindu nationalist movement in India. The effort has been to Hindu self-assertion and nationhood and involves requiting the nation's agenda to foist a *Hindu Rashtra* upon it, and reduce religious minorities to the status of second-class citizens (Mishra, 2012).

Many reports suggest that Hindu nationalist anti-minority violence is likely to be most extensive when an ideological driven, well organized Hindu naturalist political party, the BJP with close ties to VHP and RSS becomes weak and feel that reins of power are slipping from their hands.

Ever since the BJP formed government at the centre in 1999, the Sangh Privar has modified the definition of freedom of religion. Standing the Indian Constitution on its head, they now argued:

> "The Constitution clearly says (Article 25, Freedom of Conscience etc.) that "all persons are equally entitled to freedom of conscience and the right freely to profess, practice and propagate religion" but what is forgotten is that this right is "subject to public order, morality and health." If conversions or attempts at conversion lead to public disorder, the government has duty to sternly deal with Christian missionaries. If the government does not step in on liberal pretences, then violence can be predicted even justified by insulted citizens. It is time that Christian missionaries understand that India—and Hinduism—cannot be taken for granted."[39]

These lines were written nine months after the Staines episode in Orissa. In other words, violence could be justified against Christian missionaries if government did not introduce total ban on freedom to choose religion.

The rise of the BJP indicates that the Hindu fundamentalist movement is far less rooted in the forms of religious practices among Hindus than in the idea that India is a Hindu nation-state, with Hindu being defined mostly as non-Muslim and non-Christian. As Eck (2012) points out, *Hindutva* should not be confused with Hinduism. Moreover, she writes, a founder of the rightwing Hindu movement, the RSS-Vir Savarkar "was not interested in rituals expression or popular religiosity.... His vision was more political... more oriented to the language of communal identity than the reality of religious practices."

Conclusion

The political developments since 2000 onward show that in contrast to secularism the neo rich rural middle classes which largely come from upper castes and corporate Hinduism are at the helm of engineering religion based national collective who are aware that creating democratic Hindu majority would ultimately pave way for a *Hindu Rashtra*.[40] The implications of the Bharatiya

Janata Party's massive victory in the May 2014 general elections are far and wide particularly for the religious freedom, however, the assault of religious freedom started much earlier.

In the beginning of the twenty first century, it was assumed that sustained economic growth in India might be raising grand support butters for liberal democracy in the form of a new, more educated and cosmopolitan middle class which will be more secure, vocally self-confident, linked to a wider world of ideas and concerned about India's honourable reputation as a free country well on its way towards becoming an open, plural and tolerant society possessing considerable global influence directly concerned to these traits as well as to its sheer size and wealth. Alas, incidents since 2000 suggest that India is drifting towards religious majorities.

The BJP's stunning electoral success in 2014 because it managed to rally both social conservatives and those who favour a reduced role for the state in the economy has introduced new elements in Indian politics.[41] There seems to be a new approach in defining the meaning of religious liberty in the debates. From 2004 to 2014, India enjoyed the fastest economic growth within its history averaging eight per cent a rear. These boom years brought undoubted benefits to bring millions of people out of poverty. But, it also gave rise to the crony capitalism and inequality. In these new universe of realities what sense one would make of future of freedom to choose in India (T.N. Ninan, 2017). Will the onset of liberalizing of the Indian economy and the arrival of transnational capital create the much-needed political space for various communities in the Indian society? Whether India's increasingly inspirational society wills the communal politics survive and move towards *Hindu Rashtra* or will the new young India will stand for plural society ideas. Only time will answer these questions.

While the Congress and the other secular political parties were engaged in promoting pro-poor policies and reduce poverty, the Sangh Parivar was busy in convincing the masses to see the problem through religious blinkers. In 2013, the Sangh Parivar decided to influence the election with the express purpose of aiding their preferred candidate, Narendra Modi. The Sangh Parivar took advantage of democratic freedom using social media and agents of influence, deployed ex-bureaucrats, and *pracharaks* to spread propaganda. The purpose was to aiding their preferred candidate

Narendra Modi. The Sangh Parivar had one mission: use the democratic process to control the minds of the people and take over the system from within.

For the time being, the Sangh Privar has won the first round of battle for the minds. Such is the hold of ideology over the minds of men. The freedom to choose will remain at the heart of struggle for better India.[42] The extent to which the new political structure coupled with India's plurality will shape society, political and governance remains to be seen.

Notes

1. Adeney, Katharine, Lawrence Sáez (2005). *Coalition Politics and Hindu Nationalism*, New York: Routledge.
2. Haynes, Jeffrey (2016). *Routledge Handbook of Religion and Politics*, New York: Routledge, p. 76.
3. *Ibid.*, p. 77.
4. Maino, Sonia, a Catholic born and grown up in Italy met in England her future husband, Rajiv Gandhi the first son of Indira Gandhi, the then Prime Minister of India. While she was simply one of the daughters-in-law of the Prime Minister, nobody bothered to remark her origin and her religious connections. However, when Rajiv Gandhi became Prime Minister, after the assassination of his mother on October 31, 1984, then the Sangh Parivar started worrying about the possible religious connections of Sonia and her influence on Indian affairs. They called her the spy of the Vatican and saw in her the beginning of the conversion of the whole India. This aggressiveness made her over-conscious of the implication of her Italian and Catholic origin and she never appeared practicing any Christian devotion in public or making any religious statement. Also at the state funeral of Mother Teresa, when Communion was offered to all the Catholics, she abstained.
5. Adeney, Katharine and Lawrence Sáez (2007). *Coalition Politics and Hindu Nationalism*, New York: Routledge.
6. Singh, Jaswant, (2007). *In Service of Emergent India: A Call to Honour*, Indiana University Press.
7. Verma, Bharat (2011). *Indian Defence Review*, March, Lancer Publishers.
8. Osuri, Goldie (2013). *Religious Freedom in India: Sovereignty and (anti) Conversion*, Routledge.
9. Basu, Amrita (2015). *Violent Conjunctures in Democratic India*, New York: Cambridge University Press.

10. Human Rights Watch (2012). *India: A Decade on Gujarat Justice Incomplete*, New York accessed on May 21, 2017, https://www.hrw.org/news/2012/02/24/india-decade-gujarat-justice-incomplete).
11. Deshpande, M.D. (2014). *Gujarat riots: The true story—The Truth of the 2002 Riots*, Partridge Publishing.
12. Agnivesh, Swami and Valson Thampu (2002). *Harvest of Hate: Gujarat Under Seige*, Delhi: Rupa and Co.
13. Wallace, Paul (2015). *India's 2014 Elections: A Modi-led BJP Sweep*, Sage India Publications.
14. Basu, Amrita (2015). *Violent Conjunctures in Democratic India*, New York: Cambridge University Press, p. 46.
15. McGuire, John; Ian Copland (2007). *Hindu Nationalism and Governance*, Oxford University Press.
16. Wallace, Paul and Ramashrya Roy (2003). *India's 1999 Elections and 20th Century Politics*, Sage Publications.
17. Khanna, L.M. (2014), *Indian Social Justice*, Partridge India.
18. Saez, Lawrence and Gurharpal Singh (2011). *New Dimensions of Politics in India: The United Progressive Alliance in Power*, Routledge.
19. Chatterji, Angana P., Shashi Buluswar and Mallika Kaur (2016). *Conflicted Democracies and Gendered Violence: Internal Conflict and Social Upheaval in India*, New Delhi: Zubaan.
20. Guha, Keshava (2017), *Quartz India*.
21. Thakur, Pradeep and Pooja Rana (2011). *Anna Hazare: The Face of India's Fight Against Corruption*, Pentagon Press.
22. Jaffrelot, Christopher (2010), *Religion, Caste, and Politics in India*, Primus Books.
23. *Deccan Herald*, October 20, 2005.
24. Guest, Steven W., Varughese John and Nigel Ajay Kumar (2015). *Exclusion and Inclusion in Changing India*, Papers from the 3rd SAIACS Consultation, SAIACS Press.
25. Doniger, Wendy and Martha Craven Nussba (2015), *Pluralism and Democracy in India: Debating the Hindu Right*, Oxford University Press.
26. Press Information Bureau, Government of India, Press Release August 12, 2015.
27. Kandhmal, See for example Chad Bauman (2010). "Identity, conversion and violence: *Dalits*, adivasis and the 2007-08 riots in Orissa" In: *Margins of Faith: Dailit, and Tribal Christianity in India* ed. By Rowena Robinson and Joseph Marianus Kujur, Washington DC: Sage; PUCL (2009). Bhuvaneshwar Group and Kashipur Solidarity Group, *Crossed and Crucified: Parivar's War Against Minorities in Orissa*, Delhi; PUCL; Vrinda Grover (2010), *Kandhmal The Law Must Change its Course*, New Delhi: MARG; Angna Chatterji (2009). *Violent Gods: Hindu Nationalism in India's Present: Narratives from Orissa*, Gurgoan:

Three Essay Collective; Human Rights Organisations From Kandhmal to Karavali (2009).

28. Standing, Guy, Jeemol Unni, Renana Jhabvala and Uma Rani (2012). *Social Income and Insecurity: A Study in Gujarat,* Routledge.
29. *The Economic Times,* March 12, 2017.
30. *Asian Age,* September 25, 2000. Now RSS supports Smaller States, New Delhi.
31. Basu, Amrita (2015). *Violent Conjuctioures in Democratic India,* New York: Cambridge University Press, p. 43.
32. Subba, Tanka Bahadur, Joseph Puthenpurakal and Shaji Joseph Puykunnel (2009). *Christianity and Change in North-East India,* New Delhi: Concept Publishing Company Pvt. Ltd.
33. Friedlander, Peter P. (2016). "Hinduism and politics" In: Jeffrey Haynes, (ed.) *Routledge Handbook of Religion and Politics,* Routledge.
34. Sharma, Pratul (2014). "The Indian Right Arrives in Official Policy Prime," *The Sunday Standard,* December 7, 2014, http://www.new indianexpress.
34. *Ibid.*
35. Rajagopal, Arvind (2015). "Indian Democracy and Hindu Populism: The Modi Regime", *Social Text,* February 26, http:// socialtextjournal.org/peri.
36. Chari, Seshadri quoted in Saba Naqvi, "Numerocracy", *Outlook,* August 25, 2014.
37. RSS Chief Does it Again, Says "*Hindutva* is the Identity of Our Nation", http://www.ndtv.com/india-news/rss-chief-does-it-again-s..., Accessed April 17, 2015.
38. Doniger, Wendy and Martha C. Nussbaum (2015). *Pluralism and Democracy in India: Debating the Hindu Right,* Oxford University Press.
39. Kamath, M.V. (1999). "Mission Impossible: Putting An End to Conversion Activity", *Times of India,* October 13.
40. Flaten, Lars Tore (2017). *Hindu Nationalism, History and Identity in India,* New York: Routledge.
41. Nussbaum, Martha (2009). *The Clash Within: Democracy, Religious Violence, and India's Future,* Harvard University Press.
42. Ninan, T.N. (2017). *Turn of the Tortoise: The Challenge and Promise of India's Future,* Oxford University Press.

9
Religious Freedom
Modi Raj: 2014 Onwards

Introduction

The advent of Narendra Modi on India's political scene in 2014 heralded a new era of billionaires raj with stark socio-economic inequality. The Modi government completed four years of five-year office term on May 26, 2018. Many analysis and write up suggest that the economy is looking up and many reforms and regulations that the Modi government introduced have made India an easy place for doing business. With such measures, India can become one of the fastest-growing emerging global powers and ensure that the benefits of such growth reach all her people (Vimal Jalan, 2017). India attracted around US$ 60 billion in foreign direct investment (FDI) in 2016-17, making it one of the world's largest recipients of foreign investment (Uday Mahrukar, 2017). On the international level, Modi initiated new foreign policy and visited Israel—first ever visit by any Indian Prime Minister. In November 2017, India also pulled off a victory at the International Court of Justice by winning a seat against United Kingdom. Modi championed the adoption of an International Yoga Day at the UN. Indian takes pride in the fact that India is a 5000-year-old civilization even if its modern incarnation as a democratic state is only seventy years old. The Modi government brought forth the 'Jagat guru' role for India in the forefront (Aparna Pandey, 2017). The Bharatiya Janata Party (BJP) in 2018 is ruling at the federal level as well as in 21 out of 29 states.

Despite brightness all around, however, questions remain over the stridency shown by *Hindutva* outfits over cow protection, love *jihad, ghar wapsi* and other socially volatile issues. Since the beginning, Modi Raj is marked by controversies regarding secularism—especially between the freedom to choose a religion and goals of social-economic transformation.[1] So many questions arise: What are the prospects of India's democratic values as enshrined in the Constitution? What happens to India with Modi at the helm of the government? How enduring is the turning point in Indian politics that his victory has affected? Will there be a point of return? Can Modi give up his core agenda of Hindu nationalism, which has been the underlying ideology of his politics, or will he deliver a Hindu nation to his mentors? What roles have events outside the religion played in this new trend in India? What is the future of faith or religion based rights in India? It is against this background that we try to understand the implication of Modi Raj for religious freedom in India. As we discuss the freedom of religion in India, we should be mindful of a set of larger question such as how is this phenomenon connected to the overall political development of last decades.

2014-2018 Political Recap

India's sixteenth general election, held in April and May 2014, represented a tectonic shift in Indian politics.[2] For the first time since independence, India elected a right wing, Hindu nationalist, and party to power with an absolute majority. The Bharatiya Janata Party (BJP) became the dominant force of Indian politics, backed by a decisive and unprecedented, 'majoritarian' mandate, as Narendra Modi led the BJP to a sensational win. Its victory was so complete that it captured all or most of the seats in some states and reduced the Indian National Congress Party to 44 of the 543 seats in the Lok Sabha, the lower house of the Indian Parliament, a shocking comedown for a party whose history is integral to India's founding narrative. In immediate terms, the Indian polity stands redefined. With a BJP-led government in power, the Indian right now occupies centre stage and commands the national government.[3]

The saffron wave that hit India mid-2014 has all but reinforced the BJP's rising dominance in Indian politics. The results of the 2014 Parliamentary election and several other state elections particularly that of Maharashtra and Haryana in October 2014;

Jammu & Kashmir (J&K) in November-December 2014; Assam in April 2016; Uttarakhand and Uttar Pradesh in 2017; Gujarat and Himachal Pradesh in December 2017, Tripura and Nagaland in 2018—reflect unprecedented electoral growth of the Bharatiya Janata Party, indicating a fundamental ideological shift in Indian politics. The BJP has seen unprecedented political ascendancy by wresting back power in Uttar Pradesh in March 2017 after a gap of 15 years and expanding its electoral footprint to the North-East. Its victory in Gujarat Assembly elections in December 2017 possessed more features of its shortcomings as a ruling party than its strength. It not only showed how invincible but how vulnerable it could be as an instrument in the face of mounting resistance.

The first major setback to the BJP came in May 2018 when after the Karnataka assembly elections despite emerging as a single largest party it could not prove majority on the floor of the house and its Chief Minister Yeddurappa resigned before votes in the assembly. The Janta Dal(S) formed the government with the support from the Congress Party. Modi's effort to run a high voltage campaign akin to his 2014 run, the BJP lost quite a few elections such as Delhi in February 2015, Bihar in 2015, West Bengal in April 2016, Tamil Nadu in May 2016, and Goa in February 2017.

Nevertheless, the series of the BJP win represents a dramatic expansion of its electoral base, whose impetus could be traced to the 2014 electoral victory. Therefore, the regime change resulting from the 2014 Parliamentary elections is qualitatively different from the political transitions resulting from the other Parliamentary elections such as that of 2009 or 2004. The results of 2014 elections planted firmly the crude template of majoritarian politics in India's political landscape.

The political hegemony of the BJP seems near complete with installing their candidate as the President and Vice President of India.

Moreover, for the first time a party winning a majority in Parliament has not a single elected Muslim representative, in what is the world's second largest Muslim country.

The next test for Modi came during the assembly election in 2016 in states such as Assam, West Bengal, Tamil Nadu, and Kerala where the relevant parties with a regional following more explicitly invoking regional sentiments. Scripting history, the BJP stormed to power in Assam bagging a government in the North East for the first time dethroning Congress. Ms. Jayalalitha and Mamata

Banerjee retained power in Tamil Nadu and West Bengal with spectacular victories. Kerala kept with its tradition of voting a government out with the Left Democratic Front winning. Even then, the BJP not only opened account in Kerala assembly it also increased its voting percentage. The only consolation for Congress has been its winning the Pudduchery assembly elections.

Hence, as of the national success of the BJP did not appear to have undermined the propensity of Indian voters to support regional parties in state elections, even with single party rule at the Centre precluded the use of that support to exert a direct influence on Central politics.

In March 2017, Narendra Modi's BJP won Uttar Pradesh assembly elections with thunderous majority cornering 325 seats in the 403-member state assembly. The BJP had won more than 80 per cent of the seats. March 2017 assembly elections in Uttar Pradesh—India's most populous state with more voters–138 million—, proved to be turning point for the BJP and Narendra Modi. No party has ever registered such a mammoth tally, not even that of Indira Gandhi, whose best mark was 309 in 1980.

Uttar Pradesh was in the spotlight during these polls because the BJP won 73 of the 80 parliamentary seats in the state in 2014 and was instrumental in providing Modi with a clear majority. The party had been out of power in the state for 15 years after losing in consecutive elections to regional parties, and this election presented BJP with the chance to stage a comeback.

Results of five Assembly elections in five different States in April 2017 suggest the BJP has emerged as the national party of government.

Following Uttar Pradesh pattern, the BJP did not field any Muslim candidates in 2017 Gujarat assembly elections. The Bharatiya Janata Party—which has been in power in Gujarat for last two decades—has shown little interest in being inclusive towards Muslims.

Winning the trust and confidence of a majority of voters' election after election is no mean achievement, and there is no doubt the BJP should be commended for this. But at the same time, the uncomfortable question we must be asking is this—was this trust of voters won by the BJP fairly and squarely on the performance plank alone or whether a large part of it was also won through divisive innuendos, falsehoods, and fear mongering?[4]

As in May 2018, the BJP is in power in 21 states in India and the Congress Party is left with Karnataka, Punjab, and Pudduchery only. With such a figure and in terms of popularity, Modi now clearly matches Indira Gandhi, and if he remains on the same trajectory, will eventually overtake India's first Prime Minister, Jawaharlal Nehru, who was elected to three terms.

In fact, the 2014 Lok Sabha election verdict is nothing short of an unprecedented renewal of mandate for Modi's policies. All contentious measures undertaken over past several months and divisive statements made in the course of the electoral campaign were endorsed by more than 41 per cent of the people, which may be less than an absolute majority but is enough in India's first-past-the-post electoral system to claim majority approval.

One important feature of four years (2014-2018) is the assembly elections through which the BJP successfully consolidated the 'Hindu vote' in a whole range of constituencies, especially northern and north-western India. The other side to Hindu consolidation is the political marginalisation and eclipse of Muslims. No political party has previously come to power by excluding Muslims so completely.[5] The BJP does not have a single MP from the Muslim community; the representation of Muslims has fallen to an all time low, only four per cent of the members of the new Lok Sabha are Muslim, the lowest representation in the history of any Indian Parliament. The fact that India's largest minority community does not have an effective voice in its elected assemblies does not augur well for India's pluralism.

In the 2017 UP assembly elections, the BJP did not put up a single Muslim candidate. Modi's message is clear: the BJP is Hindu 'well wisher' party and that it is all set to establish a *Hindu Rashtra* through majoritarian rule policy. The surprise announcement that of Yogi Adityanath—a godman turned politician—as Chief Minister of Uttar Pradesh is the clearest signal that the 'religious politics' will be upfront for the 2019 general elections and beyond. Yogi Adityanath is posing new challenge to religious freedom. After the UP election victory, the balance of power in India has now decisively swung in favour of the BJP, and reinforces the party's position as the central pole in India's politics. Also, the party appears to have successfully forged a coalition of upper, middle-ranking, and lower castes to be able to manipulate the social arithmetic of Indian elections.

Modi's general election victory in 2014 helped the RSS to increase its sphere of influence in Christian dominated areas of North-eastern India. Today the BJP is in power in some North-eastern states.

To be sure, *Hindutva* has travelled a long way from the ideas of M.S. Golwalkar. While Modi has never pretended to proffer a new vision of *Hindutva* (much of his approach originates in the Savarkarite view of *Hindutva*), his politics has the ability of shaping the *Hindutva* rhetoric and the popular imagination about what *Hindutva* constitutes. Modi's *Hindutva* exhorts the followers to become Hindu politically. The conflation between nationalism and *Hindutva* has been the backbone of the new hegemony.[6] Any "anti-BJP" comments are now equated with the anti-national. The mixing of the registers of nationalism and *Hindutva* adroitly strengthens the BJP's new hegemony because while many people may not have any emotional connect with the idea of *Hindutva,* a majority certainly has emotional investment in the idea of nation. Because the BJP succeeded in converging these two the new recruits to *Hindutva* come from a cross-section of the society.

The two issues enabled Modi to build a majoritarian and pro-poor plank for the election and the verdict demonstrates that the strategy has been successful. Like all majoritarian leaders who assume office through democratic means, forcing the global community to accord respect, Modi has used India's demographic influence and is regarded as an international star.

Religious Freedom under Modi Raj, 2014 -2018: A Reality Check

On June 4, 2014, less than a fortnight after the swearing-in of the new government headed by Narendra Modi, 28-year-old information technology manager Mohsin Mohammed Shaikh was lynched in Pune, Maharashtra. (*The Times of India,* June 5, 2014). Shaikh's was the country's first death because of communally targeted violence after Narendra Modi assumed office. Since then many incident of intolerance have been reported across the country particularly from the northern part of the country.

In a number of cases, the cow vigilant groups (*gau rakshaks*) attacked Muslim men and women for 'allegedly' consuming beef or transporting cattle. Number of cases of beating Muslim men including a lynching case at Dadri, Uttar Pradesh.[7] *Ghar Wapsi* (reconversion into Hinduism) of Muslim families at Agra in December 2014 and Christians in Gujarat and in other parts the country.[8] The Modi government marked its first Christmas in office by asking government civil servants to work, despite it being an official holiday, to help rebrand the festival as Good Governance Day.[9] It reflects on the manner in which Indian politics is shaping up after the BJP and its close associates ascended to power. Although during the election campaign, Modi spoke of economic development and social progress as his priority, but the Sangh Parivar emphasised to pursue more radical *Hindutva* policies and raised the issues such as *dharmantaran*, 'love *jihad*', '*gau raksha*' (cow protection), and *ghar-wapsi* (reconversion) among others.

Different global surveys show different levels of religious freedom in India. But, all of them agreed that since 2014 after the BJP assumed power, freedom of religion and belief is increasingly under threat in India.

Beginning from US President Barak Obama in January 2015, to report by the US Commission on International Religious Freedom 2016, and Amnesty International Report 2017 along with *New York Times*, *Le Monde*, and *The Economists* coverage have criticised India for "broader rise of intolerance" towards religious minorities such as Muslims and Christians as well as "worrying developments" in Kashmir. Violence by cow vigilants increased in India in 2016. Limits on free speech and attacks on religious minorities, often led by vigilant groups that claim to be supporters of the ruling Bharatiya Janata Party (BJP), are an increasing concern in India. In 2016, students were accused of sedition for expressing their views; people who raised concerns over challenges to civil liberties were deemed anti-Indian; *Dalits* and Muslims were attacked on suspicion they had killed, stolen, or sold cows for beef; and non-governmental organisations (NGOs) came under pressure due to India's restrictive foreign funding regulations. In August 2016, during his India visit, US Secretary of State John Kerry emphasized the need to protect the rights to freedom of expression and peaceful protest.

India historically has been known for the land where all religions are recognized and can peacefully co-exist. However, of late situation seems to be changing, social data paints a grim picture of the current state of religious liberty in India. Many international research and human rights organisation have pointed out that since the Modi government took charge there has been continuous increase in attacks and violence on minorities. The U.S. Commission on International Religious Freedom, PEW, and Amnesty International in 2016 reports clearly pointed out growing deterioration of religious freedom in India.

US CIRF Reports

Three consecutive 2015, 2016, and 2017 reports of the US Commission on International Religious Freedom have pointed out growing religious intolerance and continued deteriorating religious freedom in India.

Covering 2015 period, the annual report of the U.S. Commission on International Religious Freedom released in Washington on May 2, 2016 said "religious tolerance deteriorated and religious freedom violations increased in India" in 2015, correlated it to the BJP's victory in 2014 and named Rashtriya Swayamsevak Sangh and Vishva Hindu Parishad for "numerous violent attacks and forced conversions."

The BJP President Amit Shah finds mention in the report for advocating a law against conversion.

The US CIRF report said: "In 2015, religious tolerance deteriorated and religious freedom violations increased in India. Minority communities, especially Christians, Muslims, and Sikhs, experienced numerous incidents of intimidation, harassment, and violence, largely at the hands of Hindu nationalist groups. Members of the ruling Bharatiya Janata Party (BJP) tacitly supported these groups and used religiously divisive language to further inflame tensions. These issues, combined with longstanding problems of police bias and judicial inadequacies, have created a pervasive climate of impunity, where religious minority communities feel increasingly insecure, with no recourse when religiously-motivated crimes occur."[10]

The report places India in the Tier 2 category of countries, which is defined as those "where the violations engaged in or tolerated by the government are serious and are characterised by at least one of the elements—'systematic, ongoing, or egregious.' If the situation in a country is characterised by all three features, it is designated a 'country of particular concern.' India has been a Tier 2 country since 2009.

"While Muslims, Christians, Sikhs, and other minority communities recognise that religious freedom issues in India predate the current government, these communities report that targeting of them has increased under the BJP government", the report said.

The Commission noted that during the past year, the Muslim community in India reported increased harassment, violence, and targeted hate campaigns. "Muslims often are accused of being terrorists; spying for Pakistan; forcibly kidnapping, converting, and marrying Hindu women; and disrespecting Hinduism by slaughtering cows", the report said. According to the Commission, there were "at least 365 major attacks on Christians and their institutions during 2015, compared to 120 in 2014."

The US CIRF recommended that the U.S. embassy in New Delhi must increase its attention to issues of religious freedom and the ambassador and other officials must visit areas where communal violence takes place. It also sought the U.S. government to press for the repeal of anti-conversion laws in several Indian states or to "amend them to conform with internationally-recognized human rights standards."

In the following year also the US CIRF report indicted the BJP government for continuously faulting on religious freedom and expression.

The annual report of the U.S. Commission on International Religious Freedom released on April 27, 2017 (covering events for the year 2016) said that religious tolerance and religious freedom continued to deteriorate in India in 2016.

"Hindu nationalist groups—the Sangh Parivar, and Vishva Hindu Parishad (VHP)—and their sympathisers perpetrated numerous incidents of intimidation, harassment, and violence against religious minority communities and Hindu *Dalits*", the report said, noting that these violations were most "frequent and severe" in 10 of India's 29 States. It said national and State laws that restrict religious conversion, and the foreign funding of non-governmental organisations (NGOs) helped create the conditions enabling these violations.

PEW Research Centre Report, 2017

In April 2017, the PEW Research Centre released report on 198 countries and ranked India as fourth worst in the world for religious intolerance. In the country of 1.3 billion, the incidence of hostility related to religion trailed only Syria, Nigeria, and Iraq, all places where sectarian violence is widespread.[11] India is now among the countries that impose "high restrictions" on religious freedom.

PEW analyzed cases that involved hate crimes, mob violence, communal violence, religion-related terror, and the use of force to prevent religious practice, the harassment of women for not conforming to religious dress codes, and violence over conversion or proselytizing.

Overall, the PEW study criticizes India for having "high" levels of government restrictions on religion, defined as interference in religion practice or proselytizing, hostility to minority religions and inaction on complaints of discrimination.

Amnesty International Report, 2016

Authorities in India failed to stop "incidents of religious violence" and often "contributed to tensions through polarising speeches", Amnesty International Report 2016 said. The Amnesty International Report released in February 2016 said that India's Hindu nationalist BJP government failed to prevent hundreds of incidents of communal violence, usually involving members of the Hindu majority pitted against Muslims or other minorities. Instead, ruling party law-makers and politicians were fuelling religious tensions with provocative speeches and justifications for the violence, it said. The authorities used repressive laws to curb freedom of expression and silence critics. Human rights defenders and organizations continued to face harassment and intimidation, and vigilante cow protection groups carried out several attacks (*Indian Express*, February 24, 2016). "In 2015, India saw several backslide on human rights. The government intensified restrictions on civil society organizations...", the Amnesty Report stated.

Human Rights Watch Report

Limits on free speech and attacks on religious minorities, often led by vigilante groups that claim to be supporters of the ruling Bharatiya Janata Party (BJP), are an increasing concern in India. In

2016, students were accused of sedition for expressing their views; people who raised concerns over challenges to civil liberties were deemed anti-Indian; *Dalits* and Muslims were attacked on suspicion they had killed, stolen, or sold cows for beef.[12]

"Some leaders of the ruling Bharatiya Janata Party made inflammatory remarks against minorities and right-wing Hindu fringe groups threatened and harassed them (minorities)... in some cases even attacked them", the report said.

Hate Speeches

Anti-Muslim rhetoric by several BJP leaders, including members of Parliament, further stoked insecurities among religious minorities. The authorities did not press robustly for prosecution of those responsible for violent attacks on minorities, and impunity for the assailants contributed to a sense of government indifference to growing religious intolerance.

Under the Modi Government, hate speeches by politicians increased almost 500 per cent in the last four years, according to a report by Association for Democratic Reforms. Communal, casteist statements of open calls to violence, or even instances of dog whistling was counted. After scanning 1300 articles, and 1000 most recent tweets of top politicians and public figures, it was found that there has been a meteoric increase.

From May 2014 until date, there have been 124 instances of hate speeches by VIPs. These comments were made by 45 politicians. Compared to this, during the UPA II government, there were 21 instances. 90 per cent of the comments were made. In some cases, such speakers were promoted in the political system.

As such Hate speech in India entered the political arena with the rise of communal streams in politics, like Muslim League on one side and Hindu Mahasabha and RSS on the other. These streams believed in the nation based on one religious community. These streams came from the sections of earlier rulers, proprietors, *Nawabs* and *Rajas* etc. The ideology of religion-based nationalism is narrow and it excludes 'other' from its notion of nationhood. These beliefs then are converted into Hate other, and later turn in to 'Hate speech'. This did form the basis of many a communal violence in pre-Independence era and during the last two decades.

Other Reports

Incidents of violence against religious minorities spiked in 2013 in the run-up to national elections. According to government sources, 133 people were killed and 2,269 injured in 823 incidents. A report issued in May 2017 by Alliance for Justice & Accountability endorsed by Indian American Muslim Council, *Dalit* American Coalition, and Organization of Minorities stated that human rights abuses against India's social and religious minorities have been on the ascendance since the BJP government came to power. Not all attacks on the minorities were by non-State actors. The U.S. Department of State report notes the police have "disrupted church services and arrested Christians on the false charges of forced conversions and disturbing the peace... Government officials at the federal, state, and local level [have] made discriminatory statements against members of religious minority groups."

A report entitled "Lynching Without End (2017)" has documented 24 incidents of lynching and vigilante violence, resulting in the murder of 34 persons and rape of two women, mostly from 2015 onward, almost all of the victims were mostly from Muslim community. According to the Report these attacks were not spontaneous expressions of mob anger, but the product of systematic incitement to violence and the consequence of long years of propaganda. In the event, both mobs and police have regularly treated victims of cow vigilantism as suspects in ways that marginalise and de-victimise these individuals rather than those indulging in violence.

Jharkhand Anti-Conversion Law, 2017

In September 2017 the Jharkhand Assembly passed Religious Freedom Bill, 2017 that seeks to put severe restrictions on religious conversions in the State. A conversion undertaken in exchange for "allurement", for example, would be illegal. Moreover, any conversion would require permission from the State Government. It contains stiff jail sentences and fines for converting people through "allurement" or "coercion". The intention of the BJP government can be gauged by this move.

Before passing this Bill, the Jharkhand government gave front-page advertisements with pictures of Mahatma Gandhi, and a toxic quote attributed to him attacking conversions by Christian missionaries.[13]

Jharkhand's Religious Freedom Bill, 2017, primarily targets Christians, and goes against the freedom of religion granted in India's Constitution. Christians constitute only 4.3 per cent of the population of Jharkhand. Other tribals follow animist Sarna faith, and some say they are Hindus. And left to themselves they all live in peace.

Christmas under Attack

There is general perception among minorities and liberal civil society groups that ever since the BJP government came to power in 2014, there has been a sharp rise in violence against minorities. This includes physical violence, stopping of worship in churches, attacks on churches, arrest of pastors and their companions, assault on Nuns, lynching of Muslim men in the name of cow protection and arrest of Muslim youth under the grab of love *jihad*. Forced reconversion back to Hinduism '*ghar-wapsi*' cases were reported from several parts of the country. There seems to be an effort to close the door of conversion from Hinduism in the name of freedom of religion and move forward towards a monolithic nationalism.

In 2014, within six months of Prime Minister Narendra Modi taking office, the Union Government had declared that December 25 would now be celebrated as "Good Governance Day". Rather than celebrate the Christmas holiday, schools, colleges, and government offices would need to stay open in order to mark this new government occasion. Facing a backlash, the Union Government played down "Good Governance Day" in 2015.

India December 2017 President Ram Nath Kovind refused to hear Carol singers on the eve of Christmas as has been the tradition with former presidents (*The Times of India,* December 24, 2017). The spokesperson of Rashtrapati Bhavan says a decision has been taken to have no religious ceremonies inside the building as India is a "secular state".

On December 21, 2017, a right-wing *Hindutva* mob reportedly barged into a community centre in Pratapgarh district to disrupt a Christmas event. Rumours were spread that, the event was a religious conversion programme. This came after a group called the Hindu Jagran Manch warned schools in UP's Aligarh against celebrating Christmas. A priest and four seminarians were reportedly thrashed by Bajrang Dal activists and handed over to the police for proselytising under the guise of a pre-Christmas event in Madhya Pradesh's Satna.[14] They were singing Christmas carols in the street.

On December 21st, the Madhya Pradesh police detained a group of Catholic seminarians and priests as they were out singing carols in Satna, booking six of them for outraging religious feelings and charging them under the state's draconian anti-conversion law. In the ensuing chaos, *Hindutva* groups set the carollers' car on fire and allegedly assaulted some of the singers. Eight priests who later went to the police station to inquire about the situation were also detained.

In Uttar Pradesh on 15th December, the Hindu Jagran Manch warned Christian-run schools in the town of Aligarh not to celebrate Christmas at all. In December 2016, three days after Christmas on the outskirts of Gorakhpur in eastern Uttar Pradesh more than a hundred, some wielding sticks, massed outside a church shouting, " We will not allow any conversions here." They shoved people, turned over furniture, and told Pastor Ritesh Joshua "You are the main culprit." Just at that time police arrived and saved the faithfuls. The men allegedly part of a religious activist group called the Hindu Yuva Vahini (HYV).[15]

In Maharashtra, Chief Minister Devendra Fadnavis' wife, Amruta Fadnavis was attacked on social media for simply supporting a Christmas-themed charity event. One prominent right-wing columnist accused Amruta Fadnavis of encouraging Christians in their alleged efforts at "harvesting souls". Amruta Fadnavis had to counter this charge by reaffirming that she was a "proud Hindu" and celebrated "every festival of the country".

Carol groups were under attack in Mumbai too. On 16th December, Ashish Shelar, a BJP MLA who heads the party's Mumbai unit, was trolled for inviting Mumbai residents to attend a Christmas festival in the city. Among Shelar's detractors was the chief strategy officer of right-wing magazine *Swarajya*, who criticised the event—which features a music competition, food stalls, and sand football on Mumbai's Chowpatty beach—as "a cultural war against Hindus."

Christian clergymen are a particular target of both *Hindutva* groups as well as the police under this law. In November, for instance, seven Christian children in Madhya Pradesh were detained by the police and their *Bible* reading teacher was booked under the accusation of converting them—an absurd charge given that the children were all born Christian, and were travelling with their parents' consent to attend *Bible* camp.

Today Christmas has become a secular celebration in India with people from all lifestyles and belonging to different faiths taking part. In that sense, such inclusive celebrations highlight the essence of India's unity in diversity.

Some leaders of the Bharatiya Janata Party made inflammatory remarks against minorities and right-wing Hindu fringe groups threatened and harassed them.

The million-dollar question is: Will *Hindutva* affects the Moditva principles. The answer will be unfolded in next general elections in 2019. Till then let us keep our fingers crossed.

Modi: Ideals, Ideology and Influences

A man with a vision can make a difference. Modi has a vision—to make India a better place and great nation. Narendra Modi neither was born great nor was greatness thrust upon him. He comes from a poor backward caste (OBC) family. After an episode of child marriage, which was against his principles, he courageously took bold risky step to achieve his destiny and to reach the pinnacle of fame. Rising from a *chaiwala* (tea boy) to the position of the Prime Minster of India was just being sheer dint of determination and dedication.

Modi's rise is a marvel of India's democracy. The entire literature on Modi is largely in the nature of personal or political biographies that chronicle the rise of the man from his humble beginnings in Vadnagar, Gujarat, to the highest political office in the world's largest democracy. To readers I would recommend three books on Modi: *Narendra Modi: The Man, The Times* by Nilanjan Mukhopadhyay; *Narendra Modi: The Game Changer* by Sudesh Verma, and *Modi: Leadership, Governance and Performance* by Vivian Fernandez.[16] They make fascinating reading. At the same time, there are also accounts that paint him in the most negative terms, charging him with perpetrating a pogrom in Gujarat and having fascist tendencies, which could pose a threat to the survival of a same Indian democracy that promoted him. Modi evokes strong and indeed extreme responses from both, his supporters and opponents, who have his image, whether positive or negative, cast in stone.

This prevents a real understanding of insight into what drives Modi. It is clear from a review of his writings, speeches, and blogs that Modi's exclusive driving ideology comes from the RSS would be incorrect. It will be even more misplaced and indeed too early to portray him as a fascist as some have done. Having been a full time political worker for his entire adult life, Modi has absorbed a range of influences other than the RSS. However, unlike in the case of Nehru who found his inspiration from Western thoughts, including Marxism and Fabian Socialism, Modi has been influenced exclusively by Indian symbols. These have included among others, Swami Vivekananda, Mahatma Gandhi, and B.R. Ambedkar, Sardar Patel and of course, RSS luminaries like Dr. K.B. Hegdewar, Guru Golwalkar, Pt. Deen Dayal Upadhayay, and Lakshmanrao Inamdar.

Modi has, of course, adopted RSS worldview which very briefly in my understanding are: (i) regaining India's prime position in the world as it was during the Maurya and Gupta period that marked the golden age of Hindu society (*Jagat Guru*); (ii) Establishing the right place of Indian history for Hindu traditions and glory which according to them have been minimised if not omitted from Indian historiography due to initially Muslim administration and subsequently British colonial rule (Wonder that India was); (iii) Rebuilding Hindu society to elicited the slavish mentality on the one hand and eliminating social evils like castes that divide and fragment this society; (iv) Build Hindu self-esteem to check conversion to other religions; and (v) the cessation of religion based preferences and concessions, which are seen as working against the interest of Hindu majority.

These views have been anathema to Indian secularist and RSS has suffered over the decades for espousing them publicly. It was banned three times and the RSS was marginalised from mainstream public discourse. But Modi's electoral victory in 2014 resulted in a historical shift in the Indian political scene, and hitherto marginalised RSS is now thoroughly well entrenched in the mainstream of Indian politics. Modi is influenced by Vivekananda who like him is not from Brahmin background but from OBC. Modi has internalised three messages of Vivekananda: need for reawakening and resurrecting the Hindu society; serving the Hindu society for leading position in the global intellectual community; and importance of executing a task in time bound manner. All the three have visibly become part of Modi's personate and work ethic.

Modi is committed Hindu nationalist. In *Jyotipunj*, a book he authored in 2001 in which he pays tribute to RSS leaders who shaped him. Modi says "what is best in me, is due in large part to my training in RSS." During the Lok Sabha elections, however, he refrained from making communal appeals. Modi is unlikely to dilute the RSS core vision of "India first, religion second."

At 63, Modi became Prime Minister of India. He is a marathon player, he will not be satisfied with one term, and will want to be remembered as a leader who prefixed 'India' with 'great'.

It is beyond doubt that Modi's remarkable victory, irrespective of the longevity of his leadership, has changed the very nature of Indian politics.

Modi government is plagued with thorny issues like construction of Ram Mandir at Ayodhya, uniform civil code, national level anti-conversion Bill, cow protection, checking love *jihad*, repeal of Kashmir's special status, which are on the billboard of RSS for optical reasons, as items on the agenda when the party is in clear majority. [17]

In an interview to PTI Modi had said, "I would like to see myself as an Indian first and foremost. I am a Hindu by faith and I am proud of the faith I belong to. I love my country. So you can say I am a patriot, but the government has only one religion—India first, as the government is run according to the Constitution and not by the ideology of any organization."[18]

Modi and the Hindu Diaspora in West

The 2014 BJP Manifesto stated that: The NRIs (Non-Resident Indians) and PIOs (Persons of Indian Origin) and professionals settled abroad are a vast reservoir to articulate the national interests and affairs globally. This resource will be harnessed for strengthening "Brand India." Modi exactly did this after becoming the Prime Minister.

Several years ago in 1995 I wrote that India's Diaspora, more than 20 million worldwide, is another source of economic strength and international influence for the homeland. For years, Indians viewed their fellow citizens who emigrated abroad for better opportunities with suspicion—as if they had somehow betrayed the motherland. However, Narendra Modi is changing contours of diplomacy and looking at new ways of strengthening India's interests abroad. No other prime minister earlier paid attention to the Indian Diaspora as Narendra Modi did. With roughly 25 million people of Indian origin now scattered across the globe—including more than 3 million in the US—attitudes about the Indian Diaspora are changing dramatically. Modi government is looking at the huge expatriate population as a valuable component of India's foreign policy.[19]

Since Modi became the Prime Minister he has repeatedly urged the community abroad to contribute money, time, and technical expertise to his signature programmes, including cleaning up the Ganges River, making India garbage-free and building rural toilets. Moreover, the Foreign Ministry is not hesitating in showing its leaning towards *Hindutva* ideology and has made a concerted effort to harness the energy and assets of Indian communities around the world. The RSS wants the NRIs to support *Hindu Rashtra* concept and convince the host countries that it is natural process. That is the long-term goal behind the Diaspora diplomacy.

In the relation between politics and religion there is growing influence on internal Indian politics of Hindu Indians living abroad. There are millions of people of Indian origin who settled in the nineteenth century in areas such as East Africa, South Africa, the West Indies, South America, and Pacific Islands like Fiji. The influence of these Indians on India is to some extent limited due to their poor low caste rural background and the length of time they have spent developing distinct sense of being overseas Indians.

In contrast to this, more recent migrants to Britain, Canada and North America and New Zealand are mostly from upper caste urban Hindu families. One impact of this has been that some of the people living in the Diaspora have been attracted to the visions of *Hindu Rashtra* and have consequently supported the BJP. Another factor, which has influenced this development is the role that temples and religious identities can play in helping people make sense of their lives as immigrants.[20]

It seems that as some Hindus outside of India have become more affluent they are increasingly involved in devotional activities, which includes temple building, sponsoring religious events such as teachings by different *gurus*, and fostering a sense of communal identity. Here is the case of modernity instead of leading to a decline in the influence of religion on daily life activities, the opposite is happening and religion is becoming more and more influential.

The RSS has Diaspora branches in forty-seven countries. It is in this "transnational configuration of the Sangh Parivar", that is seen as the "key reason for the importance of a multi-arena engagement". Many scholars believed that transnational criticism has a key role to play in the aftermath of Gujarat riots 2002, and have called for "a multi-sided and multilevel engagement with the local, national and international agents and structures" that have been implicated in Gujarat.

How did *Hindutva* come to span the subcontinent and its Diaspora. Chetan Bhagat has shown that the "highly active Hindutva presence" in Africa, the US, Canada and Europe, is largely the result of a conscious ideological strategy to cultivate Diaspora Hindus. The role of Hindu Diaspora in building a united, strong, and exclusive *Hindu Rashtra,* was articulated by Golwalkar whose views about the Diaspora are 'central' to the curriculum of the ideological inculcation session in the UK and the US and reflect how contemporary Diaspora *Hindutva* movements visualize their goals in the West. The VHP is also as aspirant on a global power nexus as it is anchored in nation state.

These organisations receive substantial social and financial support from its US based wings: Hindu Swayamsevak Sangh (HSS), Vishwa Hindu Parishad of America (VHPA), Sewa International USA, and Ekal Vidyalaya Foundation-USA. The BJP has close links with these organisations, a relationship that helped the party to raise funds for Modi's publicity in the U.S. While they differ in tactics and strategy, they all embrace majoritarianism, and are grounded in the philosophy and the pursuit of *Hindutva* ('Hindu-ness'), and feature prominently on the national political scene since the BJP's 2014 victory. They support the assimilation of Hindu culture and traditions into state policies and institutions, and generally oppose the secular agenda of the Congress and other non-BJP parties.

The importance of this can also be seen in the ways that Narendra Modi on his various visits to countries outside of India since his election has focused on the ways that Indians living outside can contribute to India's development. These appeals are about seeking new sources for investment in India, but in part, they also show the ways in which Diaspora voices are now listened to in Indian politics and are seen as being part of Indian polity.

The sense of an overlap between Hindu conceptions and of conception of India more broadly could also be seen at an event in Gujarat in 2015 aimed at Diaspora Indians, the Pravasi Bharatiya Divas where Narendra Modi spoke of Indian development and the importance of River Ganga. On purely material level, the river Ganga is the main support for livelihood for the millions of people who live in the Ganga basin. However, the Ganga is also a Hindu symbol and is revered by millions of Hindus as a sacred river. In some senses, though, what is evident is how Narendra Modi is handling this convergence of Indian and Hindu symbolism is that, he is skilfully balancing rhetoric that appeals to Hindus in particular and to the broader Indian community including Sikhs, Jains, Buddhists, Muslims and Christians.

Indian Diaspora is considered as a "model" Diaspora group in the West. Many large companies like Microsoft, Nokia, and PepsiCo are being run by Indian-origin CEOs. As the Indian community in the West comes of age in terms of both numbers and financial capabilities, financial remittances have started flowing to India in a big way.

Slowly but steadily under Modi Raj, the Indian Diaspora is primarily taking the shape of Hindu Diaspora, because most Hindus, no matter where they live, possess a deep, symbolic, special relationship to a spiritual homeland. Rashtriya Swayamsewak Sangh (RSS) has been directly involved in mobilising Indian Diaspora in different parts of the world for *Hindu Rashtra*.

Modi's affinity for the Diaspora is not just strategic, but also personal.

In 2005, the US government denied him a visa on the grounds that he had committed "severe violations of religious freedom" because he failed to stop violent attacks on Muslim minority in

2002 when he was the Chief Minister of the state of Gujarat. It was only after Modi became the Prime Minister in 2014 that he could visit the US. However, during the long years of visa denial, Diaspora Indians were his most ardent advocates.

The Hindu nationalist BJP has traditionally close ties with Indians abroad as part of its vision of a grand Indian civilization with global footprints.

Discussion

In May 2018, the Modi government completed four years of rule, much has been said and written about the key initiatives of the Prime Minister from Make in India to Skill India but freedom of religion or belief and related issues have not received the attention it deserves in a pluralistic society like India.

The year 2014 has proved to be a year of great significance to India as the BJP defeated the Indian National Congress Party in the general elections with an unobvious advantage, becoming the first ruling party in 30 years to govern by virtue of winning majority of seats in the Lok Sabha. After ten years of absence from political centre, the BJP resumed its reign, circumventing the frequent situation of a coalition government in India thus ushering in the "Modi era."

During the 2014, election campaign, the *Hindutva* card, which had helped the BJP to capitalize in earlier elections, was kept aside; instead, the party promised an India that was committed to communal harmony as well as development.[21] The new government started functioning and soon got lost in superpower-India fantasies and other such patriotic topic, therefore, it is important to have a reality check.

An objective and dispassionate examination of Modi government's performance shows a mix of positive and negative trends. India has become global economic powerhouse that simultaneously houses one-third of the world's poor.

The freedom of religion and belief along with freedom of expression has been constantly under pressure since 2014. The Modi government has since faced accusations of suppressing civil society voices in a number of contexts. Among issues that caught world's attention, the *ghar-wapsi,* cow protection, love *jihad,* universal civil code, triple *talaq,* and tightening of foreign funds for NGOs and passing of anti-conversion Act in some BJP ruled states are prominent. The BJP not only eschews official state secularism but also is formally committed to the promotion of *Hindutva* as well as three key policy planks: the abrogation of Article 370, which gives special status to Jammu and Kashmir, the construction of a Hindu temple dedicated to the Lord Rama in Ayodhya, and the removal of Muslim Personal Law. How the government implements its agenda while politically not alienating religious minorities is a dilemma at the core of its policy making and implementation.

During this period India also witnessed rise of religious identity based political movement predominantly middle class character, which is bourgeois as well as with some of ideas and programmes, which include select recourses of bourgeois liberalism. It is supportive of identity based exclusion and "othering".

By December 2014, within six months of Narendra Modi taking over as the Prime Minister, the Sangh Parivar affiliates started a large-scale '*ghar-wapsi*' programme (reconversion to Hinduism). Members of Parliament belonging to opposition parties protested against Hindu nationalist groups for converting religious minorities to Hinduism. They accused Prime Minister Narendra Modi of doing little to stop his hardliner supporters from forcibly converting Muslims and Christians.[22]

The *Hindutva* groups denied the charges, saying the conversions have been voluntary. Hardliner groups like the RSS, Bajrang Dal, VHP, Dharam Jagran Samity, and others say that India's Muslims and Christians were all Hindus who have converted to other faiths over the last few centuries, hence, it is legitimate to carry out *ghar-wapsi* for them. The RSS chief Mohan Bhagwat vowed to continue with the *ghar-wapsi*. "We will bring back those who have lost their way. They did not go on their own... They were lured into leaving", he said.[23]

The *Ghar-wapsi* programme drew international attention so much so that even US President Barak Obama mentioned about it during his visit to India in January 2015 and urged Modi Government to protect freedom of religion and belief.[24]

Christian clergy, nuns, and churches were targets of mob violence in dozens of cases in Delhi, Uttar Pradesh, Madhya Pradesh, and Chhattisgarh. The NGOs reported more than 800 religiously motivated attacks from May 2014 through the end of the year 2014. The year 2017 has been one of the worst years for anti-Christian violence in India. An influential global charity that monitors the treatment of Christians worldwide to produce a list of the 50 most difficult countries for them to live in (carried by all Western media), writes that in the first six months of 2017, India's Christians were harassed or attacked in as many incidents as in the whole of 2016.

In 2015 during Delhi Assembly elections campaign one Union Minister Niranjan Jyoti used an abusive term to refer to non-Hindus, by asking people at a public rally to choose between *Ramzada* (children of the Hindu God Rama) and *Haramzada* (bastards). The BJP lost the Delhi assembly elections within one year of registering mammoth victory in May 2014. Modi did not approve of hate language but he did not reprimand the Minister responsible.[25]

Since then, there has been a marked shift in public discourse. There has been a relentless foregrounding of communal identities, a ceaseless attempt to create a divide between 'them' and 'us'. Hate statements by Union and State Ministers, threats by Members of Parliament, state politicians, and cadres in saffron caps or *Khaki* shorts resonate through the landscape. The hate campaign is well documented. Dr. John Dayal, a prominent lay Christian leader of India in association with the Evangelical Fellowship of India and Alliance Defending Freedom recorded 44 separate cases of hate speech by prominent politicians.[26]

Low levels of violence were witnessed in the prelude to state elections in Haryana and Delhi and the incidences of communal violence in UP have increased dramatically since the BJP's national victory. At the same time as this violence has increased, some of the more militant associated organizations of the BJP have launched *ghar-wapsi* campaign aimed at poor Muslims, Christians and tribal population. Although the thrust of these campaigns is to check the proselytizing activities of other faiths, most analysts agree that, in parallel with the practice of BJP led state governments; the objective is to prepare the ground for national level anti-conversion legislation.

Let us refer to what the BJP/RSS leaders say about freedom to choose a religion. RSS Supremo Mohan Bhagwat said, "They went away (to other religion) because of some allurement and thus there is nothing wrong in bringing them back to original fold... It is like a thief who steals our valuables. The thief is caught and we will get our valuables back. They are ours."[27]

"Is conversion necessary? Will any country allow changes in its demographic character?" Union Home Minister, Rajnath Singh signalling the Central Government's willingness for an anti-conversion law.[28]

"An aggressive campaign is required for *ghar-wapsi* of those Hindus who had converted to other religions in the past." BJP's Lok Sabha MP, Yogi Adityanath, (now Chief Minister of Uttar Pradesh) at a conference said *'Dharmantaran Rashtrantaran Hai'* (Religious conversion is the same as change of nationality) at Gorakhnath Temple in Gorakhpur. It was announced that BJP MPs Yogi Adityanath and Tarun Vijay would introduce private member Bills in the Lok Sabha and Rajya Sabha respectively to stop religious conversions and debate the issue in next session of the Parliament.[29]

Since Mr. Modi rose to power, emboldened hard-line Hindu activists have assaulted cattle traders and people suspected of eating beef, claiming to defend Hindu beliefs. In July, vigilantes stripped and flogged four *Dalits*, or lower-caste men in Gujarat for skinning a cow. Many *Dalits* earn their livelihood from skinning dead animals and selling their hides to leather traders.

A detailed examination of the situations in India suggest that the mere declaration of secularity—even in the Constitution—does not guarantee of full respect for the human rights of all on an equal basis. Indeed, one needs to gain an insight into the real human rights practices rather than the hortatory claim.

During the period under review, anti-conversion movements by the Parivar became a focal point for the resolution of the Indian 'national question', particularly the purposes of establishing a more resolute and extensive Hindu cultural identity. It is remarkable to note the high degree to which Hindu majoritarianism has come to the fore as a force in Indian politics. It seems that effect of RSS policies will remain in India for a long time.[30]

This is where the big BJP shift becomes important. Quite often, we underestimate the tumult and transformation that has happened within the BJP since 2014, which in many ways is crucial for religious freedom in India.

The BJP as a party has had to reconfigure itself into an efficient and ruthless power machine. The reinvention of the BJP under

Prime Minister Narendra Modi and Party President Amit Shah has happened along three broad contours where flawless party-government coordination has been at the core of the execution strategy.[31]

The first contour of reinvention has been the growing around unmatched popularity of Modi. He is the first right-wing leader with pan-India appeal, which at this point even rivals strong regional leaders. However, the BJP has never been used to structuring its political strategy around any individual leader's popularity at the national level. This has given birth to dilemma among the core supporters, which also happened to be RSS member. When a party seeks votes for a state election in the name of its supreme national leader and succeeds, one must concede that the party's biggest face inspires credibility among a large section of the Indian electorate.

Development is the second axis on which the new BJP is redefining its presence. Development, *'Sabka saath sabka vikas'*, does the political trick that secularism may have done for Indira Gandhi. This tag line is the inclusive message that counters the exclusionary import of the right wing's core ideology. So, regardless of ideology, governance will be value-neutral, guided by development priorities. The government and party leadership work hard to convey this message, which they believe is vital to staying in power.

The third vital axis in this new BJP paradigm is technology. The party has embraced technology to dissolve divisions of old vote-banks. This is not to say the BJP has given up caste politics. By using better data analytics, geospatial tagging and organising systemic central control, the Modi government has been able to define, locate, and target the poor better than any recent government of the past. And, as a result, its interventions have proved more effective, as has its schemes in the rural sector or *Ujjwala* and many others being constructed around this data.

This has provided a corrective to who will benefit from government schemes. By removing any particular preference, the government has created a new class of supporters for the party that felt left out for lack of political representation and influence.

It also works well as anti-appeasement strategy. In sum, the mix is quite potent: a hugely popular leader, inclusive development logic, and use of technology to avoid religious and social divisions.

But what's instructive is that it is centred on winning and

retaining power. This situation adversely affects freedom of religion and belief.

The conflation between nationalism and *Hindutva* has been the backbone of the new hegemony. That is why the BJP has been so happy with intellectuals trying to problematic the nation. That particular intellectual initiative simultaneously places the BJP in a position of immense advantage and ensures that "anti-BJP" would necessarily be equated with the anti-national! Independently, both ideas—*Hindutva* and development—are potent political discourses. By weaving them together with nationalism Narendra Modi has bound them into an arsenal of his political offensive. Therefore, the coming times would be less about electoral victories and more about the onward march of this hegemony in the realm of popular imagination about how democracy shapes up in Modi's new India

On May 8, 2018 just few days before the fourth anniversary celebration by the BJP Government in office, the Archbishop of Delhi Dr. Anil Thomas Couto issued a pastoral letter to the faithful about "the threat to the democratic principles enshrined in the Constitution and the secular fabric." The Archbishop emphasises the value of prayer and the importance of fasting as redemptive practices. In his view, what needs to be redeemed is India's political life in which Hindu nationalist radicals increasingly target Christian and Muslim religious minorities. Indeed, not only Christians but Muslims as well are victims of attacks. In fact, he is not alone in expressing concern about democratic values.[32] Several Hindus have also done so. In a way, Archbishop Couto's letter has once again brought freedom of religion and beliefs at the centre of assessing Modi government.

Assessment of Modi Era

For all his popularity, Modi remained a deeply unsettling figure in Indian public life, a place he held ever since the Gujarat riots 2002 in his earliest days as Chief Minister. In years after 2002 he pledged himself to the cause of economic development and denied any lingering, intellectual influence over the agenda to 'Hinduise the nation', in the words of Vinayak Savarkar, the *Hindutva* ideologue who had once been an important.[33] "Development is also solution to the tension that people talk about" as Modi put it, in an answer to the question from Arnab Goswami about sentiments stirred up by extremist Hindus.[34] "If we provide them with facilities and give them education, all the tension will end", Modi further added.

Fears that Modi's arrival in New Delhi would prompt an upsurge in sectarian savagery proved unfounded. Indeed, the richer India has grown, the less violent it has generally become, with steadily declining rates of communal rioting over recent decades.[35] Even so, since 2015 there has been a growing drumbeat of alarming episodes involving Hindu chauvinists almost all of whom are staunch Modi supporters. Some have involved symbolic strikes against secularism: removing Nehru's name from school text-books, for instance, banning works on Hinduism by some liberal Western scholars, whose ideas were said to offend mainstream sensibilities. Others have features jingoistic campaigns against anti-national elements from students to human rights activists.

There has been particular animosity directed at Islam, beginning with trumped up campaigns what was often called 'love *jihad*', in which Muslim men were accused of using superstitious marriage proposals as a tool for the conversion of Hindu women. In 2015, authorities in New Delhi changed Aurangzeb Road, remaining it after the country's revered former president Dr. Abdul Kalam. The decision swapped one Muslim icon for another, but still removed a prominent symbol of the capital's Islamic heritage under centuries of Mughal rule. More prominent still was a spade of violent campaign to protect cows, which are considered sacred by conservative Hindus. Some involved legal changes, for instance to tighten rules governing slaughterhouses, most of which are run by Muslims. But at their worst, they developed into Islamphobia, leading to a rash of murder those suspected of eating or selling beef.

None of this was caused directly by Monitor indeed condoned by him. But, almost all these incidents were linked in one way or another to a constellation of fanatical Hindu groups that had grown bolder after Modi's arrival, most notably the Sangh Parivar, whose leaders remained tied closely to his government. Sometimes, Modi spoke out against these forces of division, but he generally did so reluctantly and belatedly, as if unwilling to dress down his more fervent supporters. For all his undoubted rhetorical skills, he also almost never deployed them to win over worried liberals, or to reassure minorities fearful about the rise of newly partisan Hinduism. Instead, his speeches preached a gospel of economic growth. "Almost for 1,000 or 1,200 years we were slaves", he told a cheering crowd of well-heeled diaspora Indians at New York's Madison Square Garden in 2014. The implication was clear: India was subjugated not during the British rule but also under the various Muslim empires that preceded it. Only now under Modi were they—meaning the long-suffering Hindu majority becoming free.

This in a way promoted a radical ambition to reimaging India as a Hindu nation.

Modi's record of economic control is on the face it is impressive. Growth has surged along at level most world leaders would envy. Indian's historically rocky finances have grown stable, and inflation has fallen. Power cuts have come down. Foreign investment rules have been liberalised, and few costly subsidy programmes have been trimmed back. The Prime Minister has many initiatives: *Swachh Bharat Abhiyan*, to clean streets and build indoor toilets; 'digital India', to boost online access; and a new three $ billion schemes to clean the sacred river Ganga. Most importantly is 'Make in India' a programme to boost India's export. The GST has been brought in as a part to turn India into a single sub-continental economy. Foreigners are pumping in record investment, while big multi-nationals—Alibaba, Amazon, Apple, Wall Mart, Faxcon, Uber, and Vodafone—talk up their India of future.

In the midst of such rosy economic scenario, fact is that the tolerant vision of India is in retreat. In truth its decline began not with Modi but much during the Vajpayee's rule. The RSS rise in the Modi era represent a new and fundamental shift in attitudes towards the secular ideals India's founding fathers held dear.

India is firmly under the grasp of a majoritarian idea, and while constitutional rights—irrespective of religion—remain, social isolation has reached worrying propositions. This obviously has left a large number of secular Indians, including Hindus, with a sense of queasiness.

Conclusion

Under Modi Raj since 2014, India has made substantial progress on economic front and international diplomacy. Many welfare schemes such as *Jan Dhan Yojana, Swachh Bharat Abhiyan,* Housing For All, Gas Connections for the rural, schemes in education, Skill India etc., have made lives of common citizens easy. However, due to ultra rightwing supporters of the BJP religious freedom, one of the core human rights has shown a 'downward trend' in India. The fear of further erosion of Faith and Belief based Rights (FBbRs) is haunting India's minorities after the BJP's unexpected huge majority electoral victory in the Uttar Pradesh and Gujarat assembly elections in July 2017 and December 2017 respectively. These election results have caused sharp shift by bringing the rightwing Bharatiya Janata Party (BJP) to the controlling status in Indian politics.

In consequence, the Indian polity stands redefined with the Hindu right spearheaded by the Rashtriya Swayamsevak Sangh (RSS) and BJP as the pole around which national politics is now organised (Yadav, 2017; Palshikar, 2017).

The overall trend marks a shift away from large-scale violence to low intensity violence, which does not attract the same attention as big incidents do. The pattern of violence in the last three years clearly indicates a new strategy of lowering the threshold of violence with the shift towards vigilante violence often described as mob lynching. Lynching and vigilante attacks have become the chosen method of violence against minorities—particularly Muslims—in the name of the cow protection. There is a shuttle message to the minorities that in this "New India" they have a different status than before. Behind these issues is a re-imagination of the idea of India built around constructed theories of Hindu subjugation and victimhood.

The treatment of religious minorities in India has emerged as one of the key issues in the area of freedom of religion and faith and human rights. Increase and systematic plan of attack on the Muslim and Christian communities is an important demonstration of the deteriorating condition of religious liberties in India. The fundamentalist organizations like the Vishwa Hindu Parishad (VHP) and Rashtriya Swayamsevak Sangh (RSS) openly say that no one should choose another faith or religion even if the Constitution guarantees freedom of religion.

There is no denying that there is a shift in the larger mindset over the years, culminating in administration interpreting constitutional guarantee of freedom of religion and belief as per the political atmosphere.

Indications so far are that Modi's message to his detractors is clear that he is not spearheading a movement to turn India into the unified Hindu nation his supporters want to create. He certainly wants India to become 'great'. The rapid rise in the economic and geopolitical influence of India have propelled speculation that India is headed towards attaining dominant global power position, possibly even attaining super power status in the future.

Freedoms of religion or belief issues are constant items of analysis, debate/discussion in academies, policymaking, and the media. For India, protecting freedom of conscience, belief, and practice is the best perhaps the only means of navigating the crucible of the twenty-first century: living with your deepest differences in shrinking world. Religious liberty is vital than ever.

The accumulative evidence suggests that the way to navigate a world of religious diversity and fervour is to protect the freedom of conscience and belief and to nurture the peaceful competitor of religious communities in civil society. How to constitute such societies require a deep understanding of empirical relationship, political dynamics, sociological patterns, legal norms, and theological insights needs further contemplation and research.

Will this have negative impact on enduring economic growth and endemic social instability?

Modi has shown restrain and he said "I appeal to all religious groups to act with restraint, mutual respect, and tolerance in the true spirit of this ancient nation which is manifest in our Constitution and is in line with the Hague Declaration." The declaration, among other things, defines what constitutes freedom of faith and how it is to be safeguarded.

Modi declared that his Government stands by every word of the Hague Declaration. "We consider the freedom to have, to retain, and to adopt, a religion or a belief is a personal choice of a citizen", he said, adding that the world is at crossroads and if not crossed properly, "can throw us back to the dark days of bigotry, fanaticism, and bloodshed. This harmonious convergence among religions could not be achieved even when the world entered the third millennium."[36] "My government will ensure that there is complete freedom of faith and that everyone has undue influence.... Mine will be a government that gives equal respect to all religions". Prime Minister Narendra Modi while addressing the Christian community at the National Celebration of the Elevation to Sainthood of Kuriakose Elias Chavara and Mother Euphrasia in New Delhi on February 17, 2015.

The diversity of India's culture, peoples, religious traditions, and languages is legendary. As the "Hymn to the Earth", found in the *Atharva Veda* in the first millennium B.C.E., reveals, India's own recognition of this multiplicity of cultures is not new. Over the centuries, the philosophers, pilgrims, and peoples of India have explored the culture of earth. "Unity in diversity" is type theme sometimes seen as cloche, sometimes seen as an ideal betrayed by countless historical realities, sometimes seen as the hegemonic invention of India's elites to keep the diversity in its proper place. None the less, it is a theme thwart has been sounded in many keys for well over two thousand years. Modi is unlikely to disturb this tradition.

Majority of Hindus are liberal and the Indian state is secular, and freedom of religion is constitutionally guaranteed and generally practiced. However, this is under stress since during recent years and, but, the process began much before Modi took over as the Prime Minister of India in 2014. Majoritarian notion of democracy have acquired new acceptability in recent years and majority rule have been pushed to achieve a restructuring of the Indian polity and a stronger authoritarian system politically. India remains a vibrant democracy in most respects but there are strong elements of authoritarianism creeping in like narrow nationalism to deactivate opponents, and increasing measures to intimidate and control the free press and impose curbs on dissent.

Under the leadership of Prime Minister Narendra Modi, India has a great opportunity to influence scalping our global future and the country to pursue growth that is more inclusive: "together with all, development for all." Modi has to work hard on two fronts: one, check crony capitals, growing inequality, and second control fringe elements of the Sangh affiliates. At present, the efforts are falling short of meeting the vision of expectation from Modi. Nevertheless, given the timeframe of just four years, it is too early to judge Modi. The fears of nationwide violence that accompanied Mr Modi's ascent to office in 2014 have not been borne out. A combination of strong economic growth, Narendra

Modi's personal popularity, and relative social peace are indication that India will witness an era of peace and prosperity.

Historic opportunity and unique peril mark our era, and the quest for religious freedom lies at the centre of this strategic moment. Religious liberty, though violated by regimes and slighted by rights advocates, serves as a lynchpin of human progress and thriving societies. Protecting the freedom of conscience, belief, and practices are the best—perhaps the only—means of navigating the crucible of the twenty-first century. Living with differences in a shirking world is a challenge that India will have to face in the future.

Notes

1. Singh, Rajeshwar (2014). http://www.dailymail.co.uk/indiahome/indianews/article-2879597/ *Daily Mail*, December 19.
2. Palshikar, S. and Suri, K.C. (2014). "India's Lok Sabha elections: Critical shifts in the long term, caution in the short term", *Economic and Political Weekly*, Vol. XLIX (39).
3. Sharma, Pratul (2014). "The Indian right arrives in official policy prime", *The Sunday Standard*, December 7, http://www.newindianexpress....
4. "How Gujarat was won", *The Hindu*, December 19, 2017.
5. Rajagopal, Arvind (2015), "Indian democracy and Hindu Populism: The Modi Regime", *Social Text*, February 26, http://socialtextjournal.org/peri....
6. Jefferlot, C. (2015). "The Modi-centric BJP 2014 election campaign: New techniques and old tactics", *Contemporary South Asia*, 23:2, 1-15 May, 2015.
7. "Indian man lynched over beef rumours". *BBC News*, September 30, 2015. Retrieved April 11, 2017, "Dadri: Outrage after mob lynches man for allegedly consuming beef", *The Indian Express*, October 1, 2015.
8. *The Times of India*, December 14, 2014.
9. *The Times of India*, New Delhi, December 15, 2014.
10. USCIRF Annual Report 2016, Washington.
11. PEW Research Centre Report 2017.
12. World Report (2016). Human Rights Watch https://www.hrw.org/world-report/2016 and World Report 2017, Human Rights Watch, https://www.hrw.org/world-report/2017.
13. Why Jharkhand's Anti-conversion Bill, *Hindustan Times*, September 2, 2017 www.hindustantimes.com/...jharkhand...anti-conversion-bill.../story.

14. *The Times of India,* December 22, 2017.
15. Rise of Hindu 'extremist' spook Muslim minority in India's heartland, *The Guardian Sunday,* March 26, 2017.
16. Other sources on Narendra Modi include: *Narendra Modi: A Political Biography by Andy Marino,* Harper Collins, 2014; *Marching with a Billion: Analysing Narendra Modi's Government at Midterm* by Uday Mazurka, Penguin Random House India, 2017; *The Modi Doctrine: New Paradigms in India's Foreign Policy* by Anirban Ganguly, Vijay Chauthaiwala, Uttam Kumar Sinha, *Wisdom Tree,* 2018 and *War Room: The People, Tactics and Technology behind Narendra Modi's 2014 Win* by Ullekh N.P., Roli Books Private Limited, 2015.
17. Kumar, Rajiv (2016). *Modi and his Challenges,* Bloomsbury Publishing.
18. http:/ndtv.com ("I am a patriot: Narendra Modi" Posted on April 27, 2014.
19. Modi, Narendra (2015). *Social Harmony,* Prabhat Prakashan, 2015.
20. Hegde, Radha Sarma and Ajaya Kumar Sahoo (2017). *Routledge Handbook of the Indian Diaspora,* London: Routledge.
21. Health, O. (2015). "The BJP's Return to Power: Mobilisation, Conversion and Vote Swing in the 2014 Indian Elections", *Contemporary South Asia,* 23(2).
22. Daijiworld.com. January 13, 2015.
23. *BBC News,* December 22, 2014 www.bbc.co.uknews.
24. *BBC News,* January 28, 2014.
25. *The Hindu,* New Delhi, January 27, 2015.
26. Hindu extremists preparing to launch Religious Holy War, *Daily Mail,* December 15, 2014, https://dailymailnews.com/.../hindu-extremists-preparing-to-launch-religious-holy-war....
27. *The Hindu,* December 21, 2014.
28. *PIB,* Government of India, Press Release, March 23, 2015.
29. *The Indian Express,* September 27, 2015.
30. Mahurkar, Uday (2017). *Marching with a Billion: Analysing Narendra Modi's Government at Midterm,* New Delhi: Penguin Random House, India.
31. Anand, D. (2016). *Hindu Nationalism in India and the Politics of Fear,* Springer.
32. *Indian Express,* February 18, 2015, 'My govt won't allow any religious group to incite hatred against others', P.M. Modi at Vigyan Bhavan Function, New Delhi.
33. McKean, *Divine Enterprises,* University of Chicago Press, 1996.
34. *Times Now,* You Tube, June 27, 2016 (http: youtube://youth.be 892 N6hiRpUM) Accessed on May 23, 2018.).
35. Kapur, Devesh (2012). "And Now (Modestly) Good News", *Business Standard,* April 9.
36. Narendra Modi Breaks his silence ... *Indian Express,* February 18, 2015.

PART IV

CONTOURS OF CONTROVERSY

Gau rakshaks (cow protectors) are forced to come out on streets as authorities have failed to deal strictly with those involved in cow smuggling.

—*Yoga Guru Baba Ramdev,* August 12, 2018

Killing people in the name of '*gau bhakti*' is not acceptable. This is not something Mahatma Gandhi would approve.

—*Narendra Modi*

"No person in this nation has the right to take the law in his or her own hands."

—*Narendra Modi,* August 15, 2018

10

Holy Cow

The Beef Controversy

On November 7, 1966, the RSS invited thousands of *sadhus* to *gherao* (surround) the Parliament demanding an immediate end to cow slaughter all-over the country. Incited by the rabble-rousing Bharatiya Jan Sangh (BJS) MP, Swami Rameshwaranand, who represented Karnal in undivided Punjab, the huge crowd marched towards the Parliament House complex with a clear intent to storm it. The Prime Minister Indira Gandhi was just less than 10 months in office and she was unsure of her political position both within her own party and in the country. In fact, on that very day, a no-confidence motion against her was being debated and voted upon in the Lok Sabha. Indira Gandhi sacked her Home Minister Gulzarilal Nanda the next day. As patron of the Bharat Sadhu Samaj, he was widely seen to be sympathetic to the protesters, if not actually a co-conspirator in the agitation in the precincts of Parliament.

After the February 1967 elections in which the Bharatiya Jan Sangh more than doubled its tally, Indira Gandhi knew that she had to do something on the issue. She confabulated with her colleagues, and on June 29, 1967, the formation of a high-level committee under the Chairmanship of A.K. Sarkar, who had just retired as the Chief Justice of India, was announced. The committee was given a wide-ranging mandate that included examining the feasibility of a national law to ban cow slaughter by amending the Constitution. The composition of this government committee was unusual. Perhaps, it has been without parallel in recent Indian political history. It had M.S. Golwalkar, the head of the Rashtriya Swayamsevak Sangh, R.P. Mookerji, a retired judge and elder brother of the founder of the BJS, and the Shankaracharya of Puri as prominent members. Two Chief Ministers—Charan Singh of Uttar Pradesh and D.P. Mishra of Madhya Pradesh—were included as were some other anti-cow slaughter activists. Three non-politicians were also part of the Committee—V. Kurien of the National Dairy Development Board, Ashok Mitra, economist and then chairman of the Agricultural Prices Commission, and H.A.B. Parpia, Director of the Central Food Technological Research Institute (Ziya Us Salam, 2018).

The Committee was given six months to submit its report. It began actively, had numerous meetings, and met a large cross-section of society. But, it never actually submitted a report. Questions would keep being asked in Parliament and the answers would be of the usual "the matter is under examination" type. Finally, after 12 years of its existence, Morarji Desai wound up the Committee in 1979 when he was Prime Minister.

Earlier in 1952, the RSS collected about 17 million signatures on a petition demanding a national ban on cow slaughter, its first public action after Independence. This programme was carefully selected as part of an effort to rehabilitate itself after the devastating 1948-49 ban imposed following charges of its involvement in civil violence. The decision of the RSS to focus on cow protection after the ban brought many advantages to Golwalkar and itself: it strengthened Golwalkar's position with the RSS, established a rapport with the Hindu religious establishment, and gave the RSS popular appeal among parts of the population that revere the cow. The Bharatiya Jan Sangh (BJS) made cow protection one of its core issues in the wake of the poor performance in both the 1951-52 parliamentary elections and the simultaneously State Assembly contest (Andersen and Damle, 2018). It pursued this objective separate from two Hindu orated parties that also supported a national slaughter, the Ram Rajya Parishad and the Hindu Mahasabha. The RSS was disappointed with the election results, as the cow protection issue did not mobilize voters. Hindu *sadhus* having good rapport with the dominant Congress Party did not feel like having their own lobby to advocate banning cow slaughter. Eventually in 1964, the RSS would seek to organize the clerics for cow protection and for the cultural issues through one of its own affiliates, the VHP.

For most believing Hindus today, the cow is a sacred and more than animal: it is *gau mata* (mother cow). Since 1951-52 parliamentary elections cow protection has been on the RSS agenda. However, the intensity and spared seen today is phenomena that grew around 2014 and many violent incidents have been reported.[1] In the hands of the Hindu right, the issue has acquired the status of a key element of Hindu identity in Indian politics *vis-à-vis* Muslim. The issue of cow protection and beef has assumed constant conflict between Hindus and Muslims in India (Swaminathan S. Anklesaria Aiyar, *Times of India*, July 17, 2017).

Cow protection has remained a core issue of RSS, though has subsequently advocated a more nuanced approach to a policy which threatens the lucrative multibillion-dollar beef and leather industries employing several million workers, creates economic problems for many farmers and is unpopular among many Indians, especially in the north-east and the south. The question is what is being done to deal with challenges emerging with issues like beef consumption and cow protection? In this chapter, we make an earnest attempt to understand and analyse socio-legal and political ramification of various legislative instruments, judicial decisions, and the constitutional provisions regarding cow protection in a plural society.

A Very Brief Historical Account

Across the world cattle remain essential to civilization's survival as a source of food, clothing, and labour. We often think of the long and inexorable march of civilization as manifestation of a culture, its architecture, jewellery, paintings, religion, and literature. It is rare that we would think of animals, and probably not one particular animal, as crucial to a civilization. In case of India more than gold, weapons, settlement or artistic or literary condiments, the focal point has been cow.

Cow protection as a tactic to assert Hindu identity has deep roots, especially among Hindu reform groups like the Arya Samaj in the latter half of the nineteenth century. The cow slaughter issue gained momentum from 1890s and rose to prominence in the 1920s when caw protection societies had become the feature of the broader Hindu nationalist agenda in the country.

In the *Satyarth Prakash* published in 1875 and a later pamphlet *Gokarunanandini* (Ocean of Mercy of the Cow) written in 1880s,

Dayanand Saraswati, founder of the Arya Samaj, linked the protection of cows to his critique of Hindu society and making an appeal to Hindus to devote themselves to cow protection. Dayanand Saraswati also set up a cow protection society, the Gau Rakshini Sabha; it was aimed at mobilizing Hindus on a community basis.

Hundreds of *gaushalas* were built as part of its effort to drum up support for Hindu nationalism. The cow protection movement had its biggest impact in the towns of the Uttar Pradesh where nearly two fifths of the population was of Muslims.

The Hindu Mahasabha adopted the cow protecting campaign as part of *sangathan* narrative with one major effect, targeting the British and then most prominently Muslims in north India. The Delhi session of the Hindu Mahasabha, presided over by Raja Ramphal Singh on December 26-28, 1918, had passed a formal resolution for the first time against cow slaughter in the country. The Sabha urged the Congress to pass a resolution banning cow slaughter, stressing the economic necessity of increased agricultural productivity as the rationale. However, the Congress refused to incorporate cow protection in its programme as the basis of an anti-British struggle, ruling out the option of trading Hindu support with Muslim renunciation of cow slaughter during the non-cooperation Khilafat movement of 1919-1921.

Gandhi condemned the protectionists' calls for an end to the Muslim slaughter of cows in return for Hindu support. The Hindus' participation in the Khialfat, he explained, "is the greatest and the best movement for cow protection." As soon as the Muslims realised that for their sake the Hindus are ready to lay down their lives, they will desist from cow slaughter. The conservative Muslims press insisted that cow protection should not be made a condition for unity, and that Muslims could not be expected to give up what was 'enjoined by Islam'. To the Mahasabha, the cow had emerged as a symbol of Hindu unity in a drive to promote *sangathan* through the defence of Hindu religious practices in the country.

In the early 1920s, the Hindu Mahasabha focused chiefly on the state's failure to fulfil the Hindu demands for cow protection in north India. At its Banaras session, October 1921, it criticised the government for not bringing in legislation for the prevention of cow slaughter, demanding the import of beef for the army in the country. At the Gaya session under the leadership of M.M. Malaviya in 1922, the party had launched an appeal against the slaughter of cows for the military and the export of beef to other countries, resolving on 'non-cooperation' against British rule until cow slaughter ended.[2] By 1920s, the claims to ban cow slaughter had strengthened the battle lines, targeting Muslims as never before. The Hindu Mahasabha incorporated cow protection as a symbol of Hinduism.

Cow protection, which was supported by Mahatma Gandhi, also had the backing of a significant part of the Congress Party during the long period after Independence, when it dominated Indian politics.

Cow protection is advocated in India's Constitution under the Directive Principles of State Policy, which instructs the State to "take steps for cow protection." In addition, anti-cow-slaughter legislation has repeatedly emerged as an electoral plank of fundamentalist Hindu political parties.

Debate in Independent India

The cow protection issue resurfaced in 1960s with major arguments that the State was not fulfilling its duty of protecting cows. Cow has emerged as metaphor for a strong and powerful nation helping to homogenise Hindu society in a conflict with Muslims. The cow protection issue resurfaced in Indian politics with a new vigour and militancy after landslide victory of the rightwing Bharatiya Janata Party in 2014. In fact, since 1998 ban on cow slaughter has been high on the agenda with the extreme rightwing parties and organizations.

In April 1979, Acharya Vinoba Bhave often called the spiritual heir of Mahatma Gandhi, went on a hunger strike to pressurize the Central Government to prohibit cow slaughter throughout the country and ended it after five days when he succeeded in getting the Prime Minister Morarji Desai's vague assurance that his government would expedite anti-slaughter legislation. After that, the cow ceased to remain much of an issue in the Indian political arena for many years, though the managements of cattle resources as have been a matter of academic debate.

With the formation of BJP in 1980, the cow protection was again put high on the political agenda. Moreover, RSS, the VHP and the

Bajrang Dal and their numerous outfits started including ban on cow slaughter on their agenda.

The BJP Chief Minister of Gujarat Keshubahi Patel announced the setting up of a separate department to preserve cow breeds and manage Hindu temples. The Bajrang Dal leaders even threatened to launch massive anti-cow slaughter movement in 2002.

From mid-1970s, the ISKCON made cow protecting a worldwide movement. Swami Prabhupada founded two-*gaushala* farm for cow protection—one in west Virginia and another in Pennsylvania US. In 1985, the ISKCON organized a visionary programme that revolutionized cow protection around the world. Adopt a cow programme as it was called, began as the brainchild of Avatar Acharya Das (Arvind Singh) from Uttar Pradesh who made his home in Pennsylvania. The ISKCON devotees in India also started this programme in Maharashtra. Soon a retirement plan for cows started operating in Vridavan near Mathura. Now ISKCON has an international Society for Cow Protection.

The cow was back to grazing the political pasture in 2005, due to the Supreme Court's judgement upholding 1994 decision of the Gujarat government's order banning slaughter of cows, bulls, and bullocks over the age of 16 years. This marked shift in India's legal position on animal protection.

In 2009, the Sangh was involved in the *Vishwa Mangal Gau Gram Yatra* that went through villages across India and collected signatures for an agenda to save and protect the cow. There is a Sangh-related *Gau Vigyan Anusandhan Kendra* (Cow Science Research Centre) in Nagpur that conducts research on "cow science". In 2012, the BJP's Uttarakhand poll manifesto had promised encouragement to the use of filtered cow urine in the State, saying it could be used to cure many diseases.

In 2014 election manifesto, the BJP again promised ban on cow slaughter. By mid-2015, the cow protection movement resurfaced with a new vigour and militancy resulting in ruthless scrutiny of beef eating within the country and beef export from India. The pressure was so high that the rightwing BJP led Modi Government has to declare that it would investigate how India became second highest beef exporting country in the world.

The views of the RSS regarding cow slaughter and protection are rooted in the nineteenth century Hindu reform movement's sue of cow veneration as a symbol to create a boundary makers that would help unify the fractured Hindu community. The RSS leadership from the time of Hedgewar looked on cow protection as a Hindu duty and therefore as a core elements of *Hindutva*.

Debate in Constituent Assembly

Much before the debate in the Constituent Assembly by the end of 1947 Allahabad, Varanasi, Ghaziabad, Jhansi, Meerut, Mirzapur, and Mathura municipalities had all banned cow slaughter. Mysore, Uttar Pradesh, and Bombay banned cow slaughter. This resulted in large number of Muslims filing legal suits claiming that these bans were unconstitutional infringements on their rights to freedom or religion or, in the case of those in the tanning and beef trade, general constitutional right to livelihood.

During the framing of the Constitution, the subject of cow slaughter was one of the most fraught and contentious topics of debate.

In the debate in the Constituent Assembly, Pundit Thakur Das Bhargava and Seth Govind Das proffered economic reasons to demand the ban on cow slaughter. Bhargava said",To grow more food and to improve agriculture and the cattle breed are all inter-dependent and are two sides of the same coin. [...] The best way of increasing the production is to improve the health of human beings and breed of cattle, whose milk, manure, and labour are most essential for growing food. [...] From both points of view, of agriculture and food, protection of the cow becomes necessary."[3]

However, Das referred to the religious argument in his submission to the Assembly: "... Cow protection is not only a matter of religion with us; it is also a cultural and economic question."[4]

Seth Govind Das called for the prohibition of cow slaughter to be made part of the Constitution's chapter on fundamental rights, at par with the prohibition of untouchability. In this, he was supported by other members of the Constituent Assembly, such as Shibban Lal Saksena, Thakur Das Bhargava, Ramnarayan Singh, Ram Sahai, Raghu Vira, R.V. Dhulekar and Chaudhari Ranbir Singh. Proponents of a cow slaughter ban advanced a mix of cultural and economic arguments, invoking the "sentiments of thirty crores of population" on the one hand, and the indispensability of cattle in an agrarian economy on the other.

After much debate, the Constitution's Drafting Committee agreed upon a compromise that prohibition of cow slaughter would find a place in the Constitution, but not as an enforceable fundamental right. It would be included as a "Directive Principle of State Policy", which was meant to guide the State in policymaking, but could not be enforced in any court. Furthermore, in its final form, this Directive Principle (Article 48 of the Constitution) carefully excluded the question of religious sentiments. Nor did it require the state to ban cow slaughter outright. Instead, under the heading "Organisation of Agriculture and Animal Husbandry", Article 48 says the State shall "organise agriculture and animal husbandry on modern and scientific lines and shall, in particular, take steps for preserving and improving the breeds, and prohibiting the slaughter, of cows and calves and other milch and draught cattle."

Members of the Constituent Assembly found these incremental compromises both unprincipled and unsatisfactory. Shibban Lal Saksena objected to such "back door" tactics, and asked why the Drafting Committee was "ashamed of providing for [the prohibition of cow slaughter] frankly and boldly in so many plain words."

Syed Muhammad Sa'adulla, a Muslim member from Assam, was forthright in declaring: "I do not want to obstruct the framers of our Constitution... if they come out in the open and say directly: 'This is part of our religion. The cow should be protected from slaughter and therefore, we want its provision either in the Fundamental Rights or in the Directive Principles...' But, those who put it on the economic front... do create a suspicion in the minds of many that the ingrained Hindu feeling against cow slaughter is being satisfied by the backdoor."

Sa'adulla said there were thousands of Muslims who did not eat beef, and that cattle for the agriculturists among them were as useful for them as they were for their Hindu counterparts.

Loyalist's Hindu members of the Assembly then took up the matter by offering various amendments. The Article 48, a provision that was grafted out of a compromise left nobody satisfied, came into being with the rest of the Constitution, on January 26, 1950.

Thus ban, the only such in any national constitution, represent a compromise between loyalist Hindu and other beliefs. At the same time, it contains the seeds of further controversy in its very vagueness. Moreover, the loyalists were encouraged to take up the matter at other levels of governments.

Cow Protection Law in India

After Article 48 of the Constitution made cow protection a state subject in India's federal system, several Congress ruled states quickly passed law banning cow slaughter, and some form of cow protection now exists in a large majority of India's thirty-six States and Union territories. Various provisions in the Constitution of India extend protection to cow and its progeny like that in Article 48, which enumerates on organization of agriculture and animal husbandry on modern and scientific lines and ban on slaughter of cows, calves and other milch and draught cattle. Which is in the line of Article 51A(g) of the Constitution of India bestowing a fundamental duty upon every citizen to have compassion for the living creature.

Article 48 of the Constitution of India mandates the State to prohibit the slaughter of cows and calves and other draught cattle. Article 48 states that "The State shall endeavour to organise agriculture and animal husbandry on modern and scientific lines and shall, in particular, take steps for preserving and improving the breeds, and prohibiting the slaughter, of cows and calves and other milch and draught cattle."

While this does not make it mandatory for the state to impose a complete ban on cow slaughter, it does give the State the power to do so.

Article 51-A (g) states that "It shall be the duty of every citizen of India—(g) to protect and improve the natural environment including forests, lakes, rivers and wildlife, and to have compassion for living creatures".

This gives the state power to enact laws banning cow slaughter to help improve the fundamental compassion towards living creatures.

In addition to this, entry 15 of List 2 of Schedule VII gives power to the state government to frame laws for preservation, protection, and improvement of stock and preservation of animal diseases.

Article 246 (15th Entry in the State List) says about, "Preservation, protection and improvement of stock and prevention of animal diseases; veterinary training and practice." This means the state legislature has exclusive power in the enactment of laws banning cow slaughter. That is why there are different laws banning cow slaughter to various degrees.

Various committees were appointed to introspect upon intricacies of the cattle ban. The Cattle Preservation and Development Committee was the first such committee appointed in 1947 by the then Ministry of Agriculture, which strongly suggested prohibition on cattle slaughter for those below 14 years of age. The recommendations were taken on serious note by many state governments and they passed laws giving effect to this recommendation.

The laws governing cattle slaughter vary greatly from State to State.

Immediately after independence, several states passed laws for prevention of cow slaughter. In the 1950s itself the states of Assam (1950), West Bengal (1950), Bombay (1954), Bihar, 1955), Punjab (1955), Uttar Pradesh (1955), Tamil Nadu (1958), Madhya Pradesh (1959) and Uttarakhand (2018) legislated to ban the slaughter of cows. Laws of similar kind were enacted in most parts of India with more recent legislations in Karnataka and Gujarat, for instance imposing even stricter penalties for the violation of this law.

Currently 26 states in India have various regulations prohibiting either the slaughter or sale of cows. Goa, Kerala, West Bengal and all North-East states with the exception of Manipur and Assam have made no laws banning the slaughter of cows.

India's Supreme Court in 1958 upheld state laws banning the slaughter of cows and the calves of cows and of buffaloes, as consistent with Article 48 of the Constitution, but Article 48 cannot be sued to mandate cow protection as it is only guiding principle for legislative purposes. Three quarters of those states banning cow slaughter make it a cognizable offence while in half of it is a non-bailable offence. State laws currently very wickedly, from a total ban on slaughter and on the consumption of beef top permission from state authorities to slaughter cows depending on the issuance of differently defined 'fit to slaughter' certificates. Penalties also vary widely. Since the BJP's landslide victory in 2014 parliamentary elections and its subsequently state election victories several states have toughened their laws on this issue.

The BJP ruled Gujarat in March 2017 amended its Gujarat Animal Protection Act of 1954—which criminalizes cow slaughter as well as transportation of cow for slaughter and possession of beef as non-bailable offence—by extending the maximum sentence for cow slaughter from seven years to life imprisonment, making it the state with the strictest cow protection laws.

The Directorate of Forensic Sciences was empowered to run mobile units to test suspect beef in transit.

The BJP ruled Maharashtra, Haryana and Rajasthan have also toughened cow protection legislation. The new Haryana Gauvansh Sanrakshan and Gausamvardhan Act, 2015 also ban the sale of canned beef.[12] The Rajasthan government has proposed amendment to the present Act in 2016. The amendments will allow for seizure of any vehicle used for illegally carrying or smuggling cow progeny, besides making such an act punishable with arrest.

A common feature of these laws is placing on the accused the burden of proving that the slaughter, transport, sale, purchase, or possession of cattle flesh did not violate the statute.[5] In May 2017, the Modi government made a controversial regulatory move to hinder transportation of bovines for slaughter by introducing the Prevention of Cruelty to Animals (Regulation of Livestock Market) Rules, 2017.

The Ministry of Environment, Forest and Climate Change, Government of India issued new rules in May 2017 banning the sale of cattle, including cows, for slaughter at animal markets across the country. The list of animals included under these new rules included bulls, bullocks, cows, buffalos, steers, heifers, calves and camels. The new rules titled 'Prevention of Cruelty to Animals (Regulation of Livestock Markets) Rules, 2017', mandate the constitution of District Animal Market Monitoring Committee by the District Magistrate or Collector and Animal Market Committee at the local level in consultation with District Magistrate and the State Board for the management of animal markets in the district.

In addition, the rule bans setting up animal markets within 50 km of an international border and 25 km of a state border. The government has banned the sale of cows and buffaloes for slaughter through animal markets.

The Central regulation for cattle business notified allows only farmland owners to trade at animal markets. The notification covers bulls, bullocks, cows, buffaloes, steers, heifers and calves, as well as the camel trade.

After buying a cow, a trader must make five copies of proof of sale and submit them at the local revenue office, the local veterinary doctor in the district of the purchaser, animal market committee, apart from one each for seller and buyer.

"Take an undertaking that the animals are bought for agriculture purposes and not for slaughter", reads a directive to committees overseeing animal markets in the rule notified under the Prevention of Cruelty to Animals (PCA) Act of 1960 that gives the Centre powers over animal welfare.

Taking animal outside the state will require special approval of the state government

The rule also prescribes about 30 norms for animal welfare in markets, including water, fans, bedding, ramps, non-slippery flooring, veterinary facility and separate enclosure for sick animals. The rule says "young" and "unfit animals" cannot be sold.

No animal market will now be able to run without approval of district animal market committee to be headed by a magistrate and having two representatives of government-approved animal welfare groups.

The regulation makes it mandatory for veterinary inspector to certify proper loading and unloading of animals to ensure they are not cramped inside trucks. The inspector can mark any animal unfit for sale.

A statement issued by the Environment Ministry says that, "The aim of these rules is only to regulate the animal market and sale of cattle in these markets, and ensure welfare of cattle dealt within the market... Under these rules the seller and buyer have to ensure that cattle has not been bought or sold in the market for slaughter purpose and an undertaking to this effect has to be obtained by the member-secretary of the Animal Market Committee from seller and buyer."

The Union Ministry of Environment, Forest, and Climate Change May 23, 2017 Order was criticised by Praveen Togadia, the then working president of the VHP, who quickly issued a statement asserting that the order only partially addressed the issue of cow slaughter, arguing that it in fact only applied to the prohibition of sale of cattle for the purpose of slaughter and was not the national prohibit ban that the VHP advocates.

The decision, however, has seen mixed reaction from people. This order provoked outrage in the north-east and the south, and the Tamil Nadu High Court stayed the execution of the regulation in that state. On July 11, 2017, the Supreme Court ordered the Union Environment Ministry to revise its order, it extended the Tamil Nadu High Court ruling to the whole of the country until the Ministry came back with something that would pass constitutional requirements and also remove buffaloes and camels from the list that could be regulated. The then Supreme Court Chief Justice Jagdish Singh Khehar moreover noted that the transportation ban stuck a ruinous blow to the livelihood of many people.

Considering the widespread objection, the Central Government may revise the rules or keep it on the back burner. Many states who were contemplating to bring or amend laws of cow protection on the 2017 rule pattern are now having second thought.

As the debate continues, it is important to note that the right of religion being claimed by sections of society to whom the cow is sacred to support the anti-beef laws has not been recognised by any constitutional court in the country thus far, much less being recognised as a right that trumps the fundamental right of choice of profession and diet for others.

New Phase in Cow Protection

Cow Vigilant Groups

Considering the controversial nature and the court's direction the RSS has adopted attitude that is less confrontational. The official web site of Gau Vigyan Anushandhan Kendra, an RSS affiliated cow protection group that focuses on its attention on using science to improve Indian cattle and their economic usefulness as well as providing shelter to cattle quotes Golwalkar where he stated:

> As patriotic and sober citizens, we cannot indulge in acts of lawlessness and violence, the only language that unfortunately our Government seems to understand and bows down before...What then we can do? Under the present set up, agitation, demonstrations are apparently well-recognised means to achieve any objective... But there is one more very respectable and universally accepted means that of demonstrating our approbation or misappropriation ... [and] it is through the ballot box.

But the reality is that many are not willing to rely on the ballot box, choosing instead to pursue cow protection vigilante activity existed before Independence, but the associated violence has become much more of a political issue in this era of social media and digital networks. More people are now aware of what is a serious law and order question. What happened to ever set off the current debate on vigilante activity was the highly publicised lynching of a Muslim for allegedly storing and eating beef, in a village in Dadri some 50 miles from Delhi on September 28, 2014. There are dozens of example of vigilante have emerged calling themselves as *gau rakshak dal*. Although they have no legal entity but they command huge public support. This vigilantism is extra-legal group coercion by some citizens, against others they consider out of line, for a larger cause they believe in. It does not have time for the regular justice system, for law and courts and democracy; the evil it sees needs urgent avenging. The public attention on the cow vigilante activity presented the RSS and the BJP with a dilemma—how to support cow protection while distancing itself from the associated violence. The term '*gau rakshak*' has slipped into India's lexicon in step with rising activism by self-styled protectors of cows.

Brutal attacks against Muslims and *Dalits* over rumours that they sold, bought, or slaughtered cows for beef have increased many fold since 2014 according to a report published by the Human Rights Watch in June 2017. The Report state that instead of taking prompt legal action against the vigilantes, many linked to extremist Hindu groups affiliated with the ruling Bharatiya Janata Party (BJP), the police, too often, have filed complaints against the assault victims, their relatives, and associates under laws banning cow slaughter.

Many Hindus consider the cow to be a holy animal, and slaughter is forbidden in most states of India. Since May 2015, a violent vigilante campaign against beef consumption has led to the killing of at least 10 Muslims, including a 12-year-old boy, in seven separate incidents of mob violence. In July 2016, in Gujarat, vigilantes stripped four *Dalit* men, tied them to a car, and beat them with sticks and belts over suspicions of cow slaughter. In a number of cases, the attackers have also robbed their victims of cash and cell phones, and damaged their property.

In one case, on April 21, 2017, in the Jammu region of Jammu & Kashmir state, a mob brutally attacked five members of a nomad cattle-herding family, including a 9-year-old girl, on suspicion that they were taking their cows for slaughter. A video posted on social media showed a group of men chanting slogans commonly used by BJP supporters, breaking down the family's shelter, beating an elderly man with rods and sticks even as women begged for mercy, and finally setting the shelter on fire.

On April 1, 2017, a mob in the north-western state of Rajasthan brutally assaulted a 55-year-old dairy farmer, Pehlu Khan, and four others with sticks and belts. Khan died two days later from his injuries. The RSS chief Mohan Bhagwat condemned such violence, stating, "Nothing should be done while protecting cows that hurts the beliefs of some people. Nothing should be done that is violent. It only defames the efforts of cow protection."

Several months later in the wake of another incident elated to cow vigilant violence, the Prime Minister Modi, who also favours a national ban on cow slaughter, stated that most of these vigilante groups are not legitimate—many of them are 'antisocial' masquerading as protectors of the cow—though he was widely cruised for having wafted so long to condemn the violence. On April 27, 2017, the police chief of Uttar Pradesh ordered strict action against cow vigilantes as he had direct orders from Chief Minister Yogi Adityanath to crack down on anyone indulging in criminal activities including those in indulged in moral policing the name of cow protection.

The *Gaurakshak* issue has become problematic for the government. Day by day vigilante 'cow protection' groups taking the law into their hands to assault people for allegedly slaughtering cows is becoming a social as well as law and order problem in many states. At last the Central Government issued an advisory to the State Governments to take action against those 'vigilante' groups who take law in their hands.[6]

"No person can, under any circumstances, take the law into their own hands. Any person, or persons, doing so have to be dealt with strictly under the relevant laws, and brought to justice in the quickest possible fashion, for the strictest punishment", the Central Government conveyed to the States.

The advisory refers to the directive principles of state policy that provides for preservation of cows, Article 48 of the Constitution that requires state to take steps for prohibiting slaughter of cows and calves. It also invokes Mahatma Gandhi's statement that protection of cow "means protection of that (which) lives, is helpless and weak in the world." However, "that does not entitle any individual or group of persons to take action on their own to prevent the alleged slaughter or punish the alleged wrong doers", the advisory said.[7]

What has triggered these responses critical of cow vigilantism has almost certainly been a surge in public awareness of such attacks and the news that the motive behind such violence is often theft and extortion rather than the protection of cows. *India Today* news magazine reported on April 7, 2017, the activities of two large organised cow vigilante groups in the states of Haryana and Uttar Pradesh, noting that a common model of operation was to blockade a road, use intimidation and sometimes engage in violence to seize the cattle from the trucks, and to then distribute the cows among themselves—all in the name of protecting the sacred cow. In the wake of such continuing incidents, India's Supreme Court entered the discussion in late 2017; it recommended that all States take stern steps to stop violence in the name of cow protection by appointing a senior police officer in every district, and further directed chief secretaries to file a status report noting what action had been taken to prevent cow vigilantism.

The growing incidents of attacks on Muslims and *Dalits* have created as panic situation around the country particularly in BJP-ruled states of Rajasthan, Haryana, Uttar Pradesh, Jharkhand, Gujarat, Madhya Pradesh, and Chhattisgarh.

Due to increasing protest by the people and adverse publicity overseas few senior RSS and BJP leaders have even questioned whether the government should involve itself in the issue of beef consumption at all, other than to crackdown on offenders. On December 9, 2015, Manmohan Vaidya important functionary of RSS told the media that, "We [the RSS] don't tell society what to eat", adding that even people who eat beef could join the RSS." He had in mind north-east where some members of the RSS eat beef. According to the BJP leaders of the NE, "we do not want to be bogged down with the issue [beef eating] which has no economic, political, and cultural consequences here."[8] Union Minister Gadkari who is very close to the RSS leadership and potential candidate for Prime Minister post in future, in a statement criticizing the Dadri lynching, reportedly stated. "I personally believe that the government should not have any role in deciding what people should eat."[9] This remark was almost identical to the Supreme Court's July 2017 ruling that the Union Government did not have the constitutional mandate in its May 2017 regulatory action to determine what people can eat, even though some Indian states have had laws against cow slaughter, since Independence.

The dilemma for the RSS on the issue of cow slaughter is that while the cow has a special spiritual or emotional significance for many Hindus, a number of supporters in India's north-eastern and southern states and among low caste Hindus and Muslims do eat beef. Moreover, the regulatory ban on transportation for slaughter was a blow to a lucrative multibillion-dollar meat and leather industry. Several newspaper reports note that India's meat and leather exports alone in 2016 were worth more than $ 16 billion in sales. The Supreme Court's removal of buffalo, not considered sacred from the list is a major boon to the leather and meat industries as a large part of such export are from buffaloes. The Sangh Parivar's reaction to this criticism of tougher federal measures and to the issue of cow protection in the states is to emphasize the value of research that would make of cattle more important and to encourage placing stray cows in *gaushalas*, which are funded by the State Governments. However, there are hinders of thousands of stray cattle released by the farmers as they are afraid of transporting them to sale for fear of arrest. Thus large number of unproductive animals with the farmers—small or big have created financial burden on already non-remunerative farming. Large number of stray cattles is also threat to crops, forestry, and grazing land for productive cattle.

The issue of cow protection and slaughter is special challenge for the RSS in the north-east India where tribes consume beef regularly and it is part of their diet since time immemorial. The issue assumed special important since 2016 as the BJP made inroads in the north-eastern states of Arunachal Pradesh, Assam, Manipur, and Tripura. Forming governments in all the four, the BJP is also partner in Nagaland where consumption of beef is very common. All but the Manipur allows slaughter under some circumstances and the state BJP leadership in these states has remained virtually mute on the issue, the local RSS leadership has been equally discreet. However, the first cow vigilant case was reported from Assam on April 30, 2017, when a mob lynched two men for selling cows.

The RSS is active in north-eastern states to make its presence felt and save the area becoming hot bed of 'anti-national' activities. But in the north-eastern states tribes consume beef regularly. The BJP wants to gain electoral success in these states. The RSS and the BJP both are avoiding cow slaughter issue in their discourse in the areas. In fact, the RSS encourages local mores and indigenous religious beliefs. Guru Golwalkar is reported to have vegetarian meals with the tribal participants during his visit to Assam in 1967.

Besides states in the north-east, cow slaughter is also permitted in Kerala, and West Bengal, under certain conditions. The RSS and the BJP both are growing in these two states. In fact, in Kerala there are about 5000 *Shakhas,* which is higher than Maharashtra's 4000 *Shakhas*. Large number of followers in Kerala is from OBC. The RSS/BJP in Kerala are emphasizing on economic conditions rather than couture issues such as cow protection in Kerala. The BJP is beginning to register its presence politically, winning a seat for the first time in the 2016 Assembly elections with a cumulative total of slightly more than 10 per cent of the popular vote, about the same percentage it won in the 2014 parliamentary polls and up from the 6 per cent in 2009 parliamentary elections. Reflecting generally favourable popular views on eating beef, the party and the RSS in the state have taken a rather subdued stand on the cow protection issue. To clarify the party's neutrality on dietary restrictions, the state leadership of the BJP in early 2015 informed the press that the party does not object to what people eat. This came in the wake of protest in Kerala over raid on the Kerala House canteen in New Delhi to check on claims (false, as it turned out) that beef was being served the jurisdiction that ban the sale of beef.[10]

In West Bengal the BJP is registering tremendous growth and is hoping to make mark in 2019 parliamentary elections. The party President Amit Shah, responding to questions of the BJPs views on cow vigilant during a visit to the state, said, "No one should take law in their own hands, we have given them the message strongly and cases have also been registered and arrests have been made. When asked the politically sensitive question of whether the BJP would ban cow slaughter if it comes to power in West Bengal, Shah gave a very cautious answer that avoided taking a side. saying, "That is for the elected government to decide."[11]

Beside the religious sentiments and legal tangles the issue of cow bovine protection need to seen from environmental economics perspective. We today find ourselves facing a grave threat to civilization—the global emergency of climate change, desertification, and habitat destruction. Our top soil is being eroded by wind and water due to deforestation. Poor land leads to poverty, hunger, social unrest, cultural deprivation, inhumanity, and war. In our careless, destructive, and proprietary ways, we have ignored the biological requirements of the living planet and as a result our neglect and abuse ground has become, alternatively, a hot planet. Himalayan glaciers are melting, floods are taking top soil away from the farmlands, forest is dying, large parts of India face severe drought, and tree mortality is rampant. Yet we fail to make sense of it, because too few of us have an intimate relationship with the natural world. We have almost forgotten the function of soil in affecting climate.

The question is how do we heal the great wound which mother earth is suffering? Where do the cows fit in? Cattle, like all grazing creatures can, if appropriately managed, help build soil. When moved in large herds according to a planned schedule, livestock will nibble plants just enough to stimulate plant and root growth, trample the ground in a way that breaks apart caked earth to allow dormant seeds to germinate and water to seep in, and leave dung and urine to fertilize the solid or with organic matter. The result is a wide variety of grasses and moth deep-rooted plants and rich, aerated soil that acts like a great sponge to minimize run-off and erosion. The use of cattle in land restoration a practice called holistic management was developed and refined over the decades ago by Allan savory, a farmer, and rancher.

It is in this background a new form of Hinduism that is emerging around the world on the values of vegetarianism and going back to the 'golden past' needs evaluation.

Some say that Hindu beliefs, values, and practices built on a "utilitarian conservationism" rather than "protectionist conservationism" could play an important role in restoring a balance between environmental conservation and economic growth. I wish to add that such a utilitarian approach needs to incorporate not just the Hindu majority but also the other religious populations of the country. A utilitarian model of action need to draw on available symbolic resources to ground ecological awareness in a system of thought that makes indigenous sense to the people of India.

It seems to me that much of the literature on this controversy has taken on the air of personal vendettas. No longer is there any intent to solve the bovine puzzle, but rather to move to a level of scholarly discourse at which the existential problem becomes obscured in favour of academic discourse itself. In other words, it is not the object of the controversy that seems relevant anymore; rather, it is the method of argumentation through which opinions are being expressed that serve as the common ground for debate.

Given the fact that the sacred-cow controversy can never be resolved by legal approach alone. In the light of the current ecological crisis affecting upon India's environment, a reappraisal of the cow as a symbolic resource for an appreciation of nature is all the more necessary. Perhaps this would allow for the development of a non-sectarian approach to confront the ecological crisis that faces India at present. Of course, this predominantly Hindu symbol would still need to be translated in a way that would empower all Indians who share the same "ecological ethnicity" be they Hindus, Muslims, Jains, Parsis, Sikhs, Christians, Jews, *Dalits*, or indigenous peoples.

It is true that the cow alone cannot save India's threatened environment, but she may provide a focus for further musing on humankind's spiritual relations to nature.

Given the increasing incidents of violence under the grab of cow protection in the country, it makes sense to view the cattle economy in the country through the prism of religion. The strident campaign against cow slaughter will have an adverse impact on the leather industry, which employs close to 2.5 million people, mostly *Dalits*. Although the general campaign against cow slaughter targets Muslims, it is Hindus who will be most adversely affected if the *Hindutva* brigade has its way with a total ban on cattle slaughter.

It is well known fact that non-Muslims also eat beef in India, although Muslims account for the majority of beef and buffalo meat. Overall 80 million Indies eat beef or buffalo.[12] Majority of cattle owners are Hindus. Only 15 per cent of households own non-milch animals in India. Anyone can understand where non-milch bovine does end up. They are the supply for India's multibillion-dollar beef industry. Most owners sell their non-milch animals without asking question about end use of the animal. It has been unacknowledged but convenient arrangement. The trading is done at the local markets, which is crucial for India's livestock economy. The government ban on sale of animal for slaughter and vigilant mobs attacking transporting cattle in the name of *gau raksha* can destroy these arrangements. The ordinary farmers in rural areas are baffled at the disturbance of these age-old economic arrangements.

The cow protection issue has slowly but steadily become less important in the Sangh Parivar since 1990s, as the economic development rose to the top of the BJP's agenda but the VHP, the Bajrang Dal, and the Durga Vahini have taken the hardest line on cow slaughter. The VHP seems more willing than the RSS or its other affiliates to engage in agitation, and possibly violence, to enforce the bans on cow slaughter and consumption of beef. While the RSS has consistently called for legal action to end cow slaughter on a national basis. Mohan Bhagwat said that a ban on cow slaughter has to be carried out by the states while completely obeying the law and the Constitution. In short, he has repeated Golwalkar's earlier advise that persuasion and the ballot box—and not agitation—is the best routes to fundamental change. Prime Minister Narendra Modi also toes the same line when he said, "killing in the name of cow worship is not acceptable. No person in this nation has the right to take the law in his or her own hands in this country" (*The New York Times*, August 7, 2016). He added though that Mahatma Gandhi would not approve of killing people to protect cows. "Killing people in the name of *Gau Bhakti* is not acceptable. This is not something Mahatma Gandhi would approve of", the PM said in an address in Ahmedabad, to mark the centenary of the Sabarmati *ashram* in Ahmedabad and 150th birth anniversary of Shrimad Raichandraji, a *guru* to Mohandas Karamchand Gandhi.[13] That being said and understood it remains open to witness policies of government to protect the holy cow by providing safe shelters, healthy food and proper medical care, infrastructure for their safety.

Conclusion

The cow protection issue today, while still drawing the support of the RSS, is handled with greater caution than in the past, perhaps because the matter has unleashed violence from the radical right that undermines the efforts of RSS (and the BJP) to convey a moderate image of Hindu nationalism.[14] No serious effort has been made either by the national BJP governments of Vajpayee or Modi to change the Indian Constitution to shift this matter from states to the federal government, a Constitutional Act that would be needed to legislate a national ban, though the Modi government made a controversial regulatory move in MY 2017 to hinder transportation of bovines for slaughter (Ander and Damle, 2018, *The RSS*, Penguin India). India thus is left with patchwork of state laws on cow protection ranging from no bans to total prohibition. On how to proceed politically, there is a mixed response from many RSS interlocutors. Some argue that action at the national level must wait until the BJP controls both houses of Parliament and state governments that the stringent legal requirements of constitutional amendments will be met. However, there is also a contending view that the political energy required for an amendment could undermine the party's economic development strategy, and so it counties to have the issue to the states.[15]

Today cow protection has become controversial political issue in India. Apart from reservation for backward classes, no issue other than cow slaughter has engaged the Supreme Court's repeated attention in recent times. Cow is at the centre of the country's increasingly violent social upheaval. The shifting terrain of the meat industry reflects the volatile politics of religion and caste rather than a significant political debate about environment and climate change.

As the BJP has evolved politically, it has also become more sensitive to negative impact of vigilantism on its effort to portray Hindu nationalism as a moderate force. While continuing to support an end to cow slaughter, the issue is not near the top of its policy agenda. The RSS, however, is adopting tactical approach: it does not want the BJP to sideline the cow protection issue completely as some say has happened with the Ramjanmabhumi issue, so it supports the VHP behind the curtain. So in future, the aggressiveness of the VHP will be test for the BJP and the RSS both.

Number of moderate Hindus say that it is time to revisit advice given by Mahatma Gandhi that "cow slaughter can never be stopped by law. Knowledge, education and the spirit of kindness towards her alone can put an end to it." So a new secular consensus has to be developed by all faiths in India. To understand the problem one should not focus narrowly on the unquestioned economic utility but one must also consider religious faith or belief as a force that plays detrimental impact on the iconology and food nutrition. This row over the holy cow is neither new nor likely to go away.

Notes

1. In September 2015, the cow slaughter and beef eating caught international attention beginning with the lynching a Muslim man Akhlaq in Dadri (Uttar Pradesh) hardly 30 kilometres from Delhi (*The Hindu,* September 30, 2015, New Delhi). Since then several cases of attack on minorities and *Dalits* have been reported. In 2016 on July 11, *Gau Rakshaks* (cow protectors) in Gujarat's Una town tied up and beat four *Dalit* men with iron rods for skinning a dead cow. On June 28, 2016 two Muslim women were punched, slapped and abused by a mob incensed at the possibility they might be carrying beef at Mandsaur town's railway station in the Bharatiya Janata Party-ruled state of Madhya Pradesh. The assault occurred under the supervision of police officers, who stood by and let the beating take place. (*Indian Express,* July 29, 2016). Lynching to death a 20 year Muslim Youngman from Saharanpur, UP for alleged smuggling of cattle (*Indian Express,* Oct. 17, 2015); assault on four Kashmiri students at Rajasthan's Mewar University over allegedly consuming beef in their hostel room (*The Hindustan Times,* March 16, 2016); thrashing and hanging of two Muslims herding buffaloes in Jharkhand (*The Times of India,* March 19, 2016); and petrol bomb attack on 18-year-old Kashmiri truck driver Zahid Rasool Bhatt who died of burn injuries on October 18, 2015 are other such cases.
2. Gould, William (2004). *Hindu Nationalism and the Language of Politics in Late Colonial India,* Cambridge University Press.
3. Assembly Debates: Official Report, Volume, 1949, Manager of Publications, Government of India, New Delhi.
4. *Ibid.*
5. For more details on been ban laws *see* Mangaldas, Leeza (2017). "India's got beef with beef: What you need to know about the country is controversial 'Beef Ban'", *Forbes,* June.
6. *The Times of India,* August 10, 2016.
7. *Ibid.*
8. Dowerah, Simantik (2017). "Rise of *Hindutva* in North East: RSS, BJP score in Assam, Manipur but still untested in Arunachal", *Firstpost,* April 21.

9. Express News Service, "Dadri Lynching Government can't Decide What People should Eat", Nitin Gadkari, *The Indian Express,* October 4, 2015.
10. Rajesh, M.B., (2015). "The BJP, Beef and the Battle of Kerala House", *The Wire,* November 1.
11. Indo Asian News Service, "Action being taken against Cow Vigilantes: Amit Shah", *Zee News* April 26, 2017.
12. "Economic, not religion drives ownership of cattle in India", *Mint,* July 11, 2017, New Delhi.
13. *The Times of India,* June 29, 2017.
14. Graham, Bruce, (1990). *Hindu Nationalism and Indian Politics: The Origins and Development of the Bharatiya Jana Sangh,* Cambridge University Press, pp. 26-27.
15. *Ibid.,* p. 178.

Bibliography

Aiyar, S.A. (2017). "Those who sow Hindu terror will reap Muslim terror", *The Times of India,* New Delhi, July 9.

Human Rights Watch Report, April 2017, New York.

Knott, Kim (2016). *Hinduism: A Very Short Introduction,* Oxford University Press.

Lewin, Ellen and Leni M. Silverstein (2016). *Mapping Feminist Anthropology in the Twenty-First Century,* Rutgers University Press.

Linzey, Andrew (2013). *The Global Guide to Animal Protection,* University of Illinois Press.

Salam, Ziya Us (2018). *Of Saffron Flags and Skullcaps: Hindutva, Muslim Identity and the Idea of India,* SAGE Publications, India.

Sharps, Donald K. (2006). *Sacred Bull, Holy Cow: A Cultural Study of Civilization's Most Important Animal,* New York: Peter Lang.

"The cow is just a political animal", *Frontline,* September 2, 2016 www.frontline.in/cover-story/the-cow-is-just-a-political.../article8994397.ece Frontline accessed on July 11, 2017.

Wulf, Christophe (2016). *Exploring Alternatives in a Globalized World,* Routledge.

11

'*Ghar Wapsi*' (Homecoming)

Politics of Conversion

Within few days after organising a successful *ghar wapsi karyakram* (reconversion programme) of Muslims to Hinduism in December 2014 Rajeshwar Singh, an RSS *pracharak* heading the Dharam Jagaran Samiti, was relieved of his responsibilities and sent on "indefinite sick leave", as the Sangh felt the campaign in Agra had invited undue publicity "undermining the larger goal of *Ghar Wapsi*' by focusing critical media attention on it (Andersen and Damle, 2018). Singh told the press that, "Our target is to make a *Hindu Rashtra* by 2021. The Muslims and Christians don't have a right to stay here. So they would either be converted to Hinduism or forced to run away from here."[1] Singh was a functionary in the Dharma Jagran Samiti (DJS), a group established to convert non-Hindus in India to their original faith. The issue had threatened to stall Prime Minister Modi's legislative agenda in the first year in office with opposition raising up the issue in Parliament. However, such reprimand to Rajeshwar Singh did not stop *ghar wapsi* programme in other parts of India. In February 2018 the first public display of *ghar wapsi* in West Bengal occurred in Kolkata when 16 members of a Muslim family, who were "re-converted to Hinduism", by the right-wing organisation Hindu Samiti.[2] Many cases were reported from Uttar Pradesh, Madhya Pradesh, Chhattisgarh and even Kerala.

Ghar (home) implies all that we associate with our home—origin, lineage, safety, security, trust, faith and, of course, family. But here, the right wing Hindu nationalist define the *ghar* as the Hindu umbrella, which they conveniently call 'Sanatana Dharma' and '*wapsi*' characterises returning of certain people who were lost, strayed, misled, stolen or captured.

The right-wing Hindu organisations fear that at the current pace of growth of the Muslim population the Hindus will become minority by 2050. Muslims are estimated by the 2011 Census to make up 14.23 per cent of the total population and 19.26 per cent of the population of Uttar Pradesh—this compared to 11.7 per cent in 1991, a growth at the national level of about 2.5 per cent over the past three censuses, while the Hindu percentage over the same period dropped from 82.4 per cent to 79.8 per cent.

The average Muslim yearly population growth rate was 2.2 per cent in the 2001-11 periods, while the Hindu yearly rate was only 1.6 per cent in the same period.[3] Such situations fuel the fear among the Sangh members over the rise of Muslim population and they consider *ghar wapsi* and battling 'love *jihad*' as tactics to limit the spread of Islam in India.

Within the Sangh Parivar, two organizations take care of reconversion (*ghar wapsi*). One, a semi-autonomous group launched by the RSS, calls itself the *Dharma Jagran*; the other is referred to as Dharma Jagran Samiti, which is a part of the VHP. *Ghar Wapsi* in Hindi literally means, "to come back home". The RSS ideologues argue that all persons from the subcontinent were once Hindus, and should return to Hinduism. They further say that Hindus were forcibly converted to Islam and Christianity after these faiths reached India. *Ghar wapsi* programmes in different parts of the country are aimed at reconverting 'those Hindus' who have accepted Christianity or Islam as their faith. The Jains, Buddhists, and Sikhs have also been appropriated as part of this idea of *Sanatan Dharma* and are legally part of Hindu religion.

Although *ghar wapsi* efforts have been going on for a long time and is one of the major activity of the VHP exact number of *ghar wapsi* figures are not available. The former hardliner Praveen Togadia who was replaced as the international working president of the VHP in 2018 claims that his organisation has re-converted more than 7.5 million people (5 million Christians and 2.5 million Muslims) to Hinduism in the last ten years. He told press that the average 'return' had climbed from 15,000 to 40,000 in 2015.[4]

The central and north-eastern India is on the radar of VHP for *ghar wapsi* programme on priority basis. Tamil Nadu, Kerala, Karnataka, Madhya Pradesh, Odisha, Maharashtra, Gujarat, and Chhattisgarh have already witnessed substantial *ghar wapsi* programme—the reconversion mainly of Christians. Although

Telangana and Andhra Pradesh largely remain unaffected by the raging controversy over the Sangh Parivar outfits' re-conversion drive.

Several groups emerged in the late nineteenth century to reform Hinduism, with one of the major objectives being the consolidation of Hindu society. Among the more influential of those reform movements was Arya Samaj which viewed conversion, either by choice or coercion, as an important part of its mission (*shuddhi*).[5] The disciples of its founder, Dayananda Saraswati, spread the message of social reform and Hindu consolidation throughout the country and abroad, including all the aforementioned aspects of conversion to full Hindu status. It also vigorously fought against the conversion of Hindus to other faiths.

In the beginning of the twentieth century, Hindu reformist movements saw conversion as a solution in the alleged numerical decline of Hindus. Colonial laws and the Census operations made religious leader aware, from the second half of nineteenth century onwards, of the importance of their numerical strength. For example, *Hindus: A Dying Race* by Mukehrjee, published in 1909, pictured Hindus as a community with a dwindling members, use "some census data and predictions to develop a horrific vision of Hindu decline as contrasted to Muslim growth and strength." This led the Arya Samaj, a Hindu nationalist reform movement founded in 1876, to start a *Shuddhi* (Purification) movement in 1920s with group conversions of Muslims to Hinduism.

After independence *ghar wapsi* resurfaced again in the 1960s after Niyogi Committee Report on conversion. Nevertheless, for a while, it went underground particularly in the 1970s and 1980s when secularism prevailed. Nevertheless, the idea was always in the air and returned with big bang in 1990s when the rightwing political party—the BJP gained control power at the federal level.

The founding leadership of the RSS took its inspiration from the reformist philosophic tradition of Swami Dayananda—conversion to Hinduism was always seen as a valid activity, partly to counter-proselytizing activities of Christians and Muslims and partly to consolidate the Hindu community. Prior to Independence, the RSS had worked closely with the Arya Samaj on issues relating to Hindu consolidation, the geographic unity of India (*Akhand Bharat*) and the security of Hindus. After Independence, the RSS grew somewhat distant from the largely urban Arya Samaj, and directed greater attention to traditional rural Hindus less interested in the Samaj's social reform agenda and its position to the use of idols. In line with this new approach, the RSS under Golwalkar's leadership began to focus on such traditional cultural issues as cow protection and the restoration of historic temples (Ayodhya, Kashi, Mathura, Somnath), thus establishing a rapport with Hindu religious leaders.

The RSS views the conversion of Hindus to Islam and Christianity as a potential threat to the cultural pre-eminence of Hinduism in India and, by extension, a threat to national unity.

Regarding Muslim efforts to convert Hindus, the RSS tends to interpret such actions as an effort to increase the Muslim population in India to strengthen Islamic influence and even create movements aimed at carving out independent Muslim states. Such efforts have triggered period calls to make all forms of conversion illegal, taking as a precedent colonial laws limiting conversion, which existed in several princely states.

Perhaps best-known early case of a state limiting conversion in independent India is that of Madhya Pradesh which, in 1968, enacted the Madhya Pradesh Dharma Swatantra Adhiniyam, prohibiting conversion from one religion to another by use of force, of allurement or by fraudulent means.[6] It also required that the subject of the attempted conversion report it to the district magistrate within a set period of time or risk imprisonment.

India's Supreme Court upheld the Madhya Pradesh law and a similar one in the state of Odisha on the grounds of public order, and made a distinction between the legal right to preach and the right to convert on which there are permissible limitations. Other states such as Gujarat have enacted increased fines and jail terms for those involved in the illegal conversion of women, *Dalits* and tribals, the legislation in Gujarat requires advance notice to a district magistrate of the conversion and the magistrates' judgement that the conversion did not involve force or allurement.

So far, such laws have been passed only at the state level, though the RSS has called for legislation at the national level as well. A legal distinction to conversion from low caste Hindus is that low caste converts to Christianity and Islam lose the economic and political benefits granted to them as Hindus by the Constitution of India.[7] This legal record has provided a narrative in which the state seeks to protect the convert who is viewed as a victim.

The conversion to Islam in February 1981 of some 1890 Hindu *Dalit* families in the village of Meenakshipuram in the Tirunelveli district of Tamil Nadu was interpreted by the RSS and others as another sign not only of the growing vulnerability of the low caste Hindus, but also that of Hinduism generally. There were at the same time reports of immigration from Bangladesh into India and forced exodus of Hindus from Kashmir. This sense of Hinduism in peril was context for a national campaign by the RSS and many other groups to strengthen Hindu solidarity, part of which was to address complaints of the *Dalit* communities. The BJP leader Vajpayee who visited Meenakshipuram commented that "the conversion was part of a "sinister conspiracy ... to undermine the demographic and secular complexion of the country and turn it into a theocratic state like Pakistan and Iran."[8] Hindus feared that Muslims plan to convert millions of *Dalits* nationally to ensure that the Muslim percentage becomes sufficiently high to enable them to bargain political advantages.

As one RSS leader told me, Meenkashipuram was one of the major factors that led the RSS to support the revival of the VHP in the early 1980s with its convocation of the first *Dharma Sansad* in April 1984; this conclave focused on two goals of uplifting the social status of low caste Hindus and protecting them from the conversion efforts of 'alien faiths'. This conclave also suggested some strategies to make Hindu society stronger.

The Sangh/VHP combine started re-emphasising on *ghar wapsi* from 1991. The Sangh placed some of its best *karykartas* to counter Christians in trial areas and to boost the *ghar wapsi karyakram*: Swami Aseemanand in the Dangs in Gujarat, Swami Lakshmanananda Sarasvati in Kandhamal in Odisha, and Raja Dilip Singh Judeo of erstwhile Jashpur state in Chhattisgarh. Sarasvati was shot dead by Maoists in 2008, and Swami Aseemanand was arrested in 2010 and jailed on charges of conspiracy and bomb blast in Malegaon and Ajmer but was acquitted in March 2017. Judeo became Minister of Environment in Atal Bihari led BJP government and was exposed in a scandal died in 2013. He was the first one to organise a "*ghar wapsi*" or homecoming of people in the villages of his fiefdom Jashpur (Surguja), washing their feet and garlanding them after purification rites performed under the watchful eyes of his private army.

Dharmantaran (conversion) and *ghar wapsi* (re-conversion) issues are highly debatable. As arguments for and against conversions flow and the majority-minority complexities and fears play out, the issue threatens to become a flashpoint.

The BJP may deny it, but the '*ghar wapsi*' campaign's distinct assertiveness since it came to power has sparked controversy amidst fears of majoritarianism.

The argument given by supporters of the *ghar wapsi* (homecoming) campaign is that unless corrective measures are taken up urgently, there is a danger to the existing demographic profile of the country. Many leaders of the Sangh Parivar are of opinion that the way the population of some religious groups is growing, there is a possibility of Hindus being reduced to a religious minority in several states.

Rajnath Singh, Union Home Minister, said in April 2015 that "the unanimous enactment of an anti-conversion law would be the best way to put an end to repeated question on communal harmony and *ghar wapsi*." He added, "No country can countenance a change in its demographic profile through conversion" (*The Economic Times*, December 29, 2015).

An article on January 4, 2015 issue of the *Organise*, mouthpiece of the Rashtriya Swayamsevak Sangh (RSS) has offered some statistics in support of this argument. It says, "There was a 5.2 per cent decadal (1991-2001) growth in Hindu population of Manipur. However, at the same time, Christians grew by 36.6 per cent and Muslims by 43.1 per cent." It further adds: "North-eastern states, excluding Assam, recorded 50.6 per cent growth in Christians and 42.4 per cent growth in Muslims (in the same period)."

Justifying the *ghar-wapsi* campaign, a senior RSS functionary told this writer: "Just review the growth rate of the population of Muslims and Christians since 1951 Census. You will then realise why we will soon have five more states and Union territories—Kerala, Manipur, Goa, Daman, and Arunachal Pradesh—where Hindus will be reduced to a minority. How can we let that happen?"

Data review suggest otherwise. It is true there are variations in growth rates among communities, with some growing at a rate marginally higher than others grew. But, there is a distinct declining trend visible in case of all communities.

In the decade of 1991-2001, for which data is available, while the average annual growth of Hindus fell by 23 basis points (from 2.05 to 1.82%) from the previous decade, the decline was much sharper of 27 basis points (from 2.85 to 2.58%) in the case of Muslims. Incidentally, the fear of alteration in the demographic structure of the country resurfaced following publication of the 2001 Census data on religion in 2004.

Data suggest even the long-term trend is one of decline in growth rates of all communities. In the period from 1961 to 2001, while the population of Hindus grew at an average annual rate of 2.04 per cent, that of Muslims and Christians increased by 2.70 per cent and 2.02 per cent, respectively. What is noticeable in the same period is the decline in growth rates of all religious communities, some more and some less depending on the phase of demographic transition.

Even with regard to specific states, the review of data dispels concerns raised in some quarters. In Manipur, for instance, as per the Census 2001 data, the population of Hindus grew at 5.9 per cent between 1991-2001 while that of Muslims and Christians grew at 43 per cent and 17.69 per cent respectively. Census operations were not carried out in three sub-divisions of the state in 2001.

What is more, according to the detailed analysis available at the Manipur government website, in the said decade, the proportion of Christians in the total population of the state fell from 34.11 per cent to 34.04. It is true that in the same period, the share of Hindus in the total population of the state dropped by a whopping 11 percentage points. But that was partly because the share of the 'other' religious category rose from 0.77 per cent in 1991 to 10.85 per cent in 2001. According to the state government website, the category of 'other' consists of those who are distinct from the followers of Hinduism, Islam, Christianity, Sikhism, Buddhism, or Jainism.

In other north-eastern States, the rate of growth of Muslims and Christians has been much faster than of Hindus. But in most cases, that can be attributed to a low base effect. In Arunachal Pradesh, for instance, after a growth of 73.41 per cent from 1991 to 2001, the number of Muslims stood at 20,675. In Mizoram, the population of Muslims grew by a whopping 122.54 per cent in the same period. But in terms of absolute number, there were 10,099 Muslims during the period when census operation was carried in the state in 2001.

Demographers also point out significant regional variation in rates of growth of population for all communities. In an essay in the *Economic and Political Weekly* (January 29, 2005), P.M. Kulkarni and Manoj Agarajan wrote: "While discussing religious differentials in India, one must also note that fertility for a religion varies substantially across states. Fertility among Hindus of Uttar Pradesh is higher than that of Hindus of Tamil Nadu and the same holds true for Muslims. This suggests there is no 'Hindu fertility' or 'Muslim fertility' or 'Christian fertility' as such. Besides, even in individual states, there is heterogeneity within a religion."

In the whole of south India, for instance, the average annual population growth rate of Muslims at 1.66 per cent between 1991-2001 was way below the national average of 1.9 per cent in the same period. The average annual population growth rate of Muslims in Kerala and Tamil Nadu were even lower.

A completely different set of factors, illegal influx of Bangladeshi migrants being the most prominent one, could be behind the rise in proportions of Muslims in West Bengal and some north-eastern states. The country has witnessed a constant inflow of people from Bangladesh since 1971. In 1971, Muslims constituted 20.46 per cent of West Bengal's population. It reached 25.37 per cent in 2001. Similarly in Assam, the share of Muslims rose from 24.56 per cent to 30.92 per cent during the period.

Let us have a quick look at the statistics:

- Eight States and UTs have Muslim share of population in excess of National average of 13 per cent.
- Five of them registered population growth less than the National average for Muslims between 1991-2001.
- Two recorded growth rate of Muslim population less than the overall National rate.
- Spurt in growth rate of Muslim population seen in States where they are in significant minority (less than 13%).

(*Source*: *Business Standard*, "*Ghar Wapsi* Campaign: Is the Demographic Profile Changing", January 20, 2015.)

The BJP governments in the States have provided extensive economic, political, and legal support to the Hindu nationalists and facilitated their expansion into the tribal areas. The support from the State governments has provided moral and political confidence to the Hindu nationalists to "control" the activities of the so-called anti-national forces as well as to prevent the tribal population from being converted and to bring the already converted ones back into the Hindu social and religious fold in order to strengthen the political project of "making India Hindu".

The then BJP's All India General Secretary Muralidhar Rao asserted that the BJP led NDA government had nothing to do with *Ghar Wapsi* programmes being organised by Sangh Parivar outfits and it was a natural retaliation for organised conversions in the country. *Ghar Wapsi* was not a new thing that happened after BJP came to power. "It (reconversion) is there for many years. When organised conversions take place, in a society that is alive, there will be retaliation of reconversion", Rao said.

"*Ghar Wapsi* is a law and order issue and it is for state governments to take steps in this regard", he said.[9]

RSS leaders like Yogi Adityanath are projecting *Ghar Wapsi* as a great achievement. It is being labelled as a masterstroke by RSS ideologues.

The central point is that the RSS does not recognise Indian nationalism and holds to Hindu nationalism so the whole manoeuvre for this "forcible conversions being passed off as *Char Wapsi* while dubbing other conversions as forcible."[10]

The Sangh Parivar describes "*ghar wapsi*" as the "homecoming of those who have lost way" or the re-conversion of Hindus who converted to other religions. The ruling Bharatiya Janata Party says the government has nothing to do with it, but in reality the campaign is spearheaded by the Dharam Jagran Samiti, an affiliate of the Rashtriya Swayamsewak Sangh, and the VHP.

According to one ideologue of the RSS, they had been calling for a ban on conversions, which was being opposed by secular elements and religious minorities. This new conversion *Ghar Wapsi*, would bring to fore the debate to make a strict law against all kinds of conversion.

The *Ghar Wapsi* programmes organised by the Sangh Parivar are an attempted show of strength. They seek the state's connivance in administering a terrifying form of majoritarianism. The programmes no doubt carry enormous potential to incite violence and hatred between communities, and capable of producing dire consequences. To that end, we must certainly impose responsibility on the state to curb the creation of an even more fractured society.

Indeed, the BJP has already been quick to take advantage of the clamour for an anti-conversion legislation. In reacting to rhetorical pressure from the Opposition in both Houses of Parliament, then the Union Parliamentary Affairs Minister (Now Vice President of India), M. Venkaiah Naidu, suggested precisely such a law as a solution for the present unrest. Yogi Adityanath, then the BJP member of the Lok Sabha for the Gorakhpur constituency (now the Chief Minister of Uttar Pradesh), who was a star attraction for the Hindu rightwing in *Ghar Wapsi* events said, "This (*Ghar Wapsi*) has been happening for ages. It is an ongoing process and it will continue to happen". "If the Uttar Pradesh Government feels the reconversion programme is wrong then the way the State governments of Madhya Pradesh, Odisha, Rajasthan, Himachal Pradesh and Gujarat have a law... a similar legislation should be made in U.P." (*Economic Times*, March 4, 2015).

Since 2015, the 150th birth anniversary of B.R. Ambedkar, the Sangh Parivar has put forth new line of argument. They say when Scheduled Caste Hindus were forcibly converted, Ambedkar told converted Hindus that they would be welcomed back. In a way, he supported *ghar wapsi*.[11]

The *ghar wapsi* remains a controversial issue. After converting back to Hinduism to which caste will the convert return? The RSS and its affiliates are aware of the dangers that caste poses to the social unity it seeks, caste still a major factor in the lives of most Hindus, especially for the two-thirds who live in rural India. A practical problem posed by conversion/reconversion, therefore, is where the non-Hindu converts will fit into the pervasive Hindu caste system. A number of strategies have been suggested and adopted to ease this social transaction. Conversion may pose many problems in urban India where caste still poses many problems for reconvert in terms of marriage, name, and worship in temples, buying house or land in a particular area, friend circle and so on. But there is also problem of the social ladder would fit. Such a person would surely not want to be at the bottom of the rung of the Hindu social hierarchy. On way out which the Sangh *Parivar karyakartas* are suggesting to *Dalits* and tribals is to convert to Buddhism, where there is at least philosophically no caste system. This is under intense debate in the Sangh Parivar circle. This is posing a problem in the Sangh Parivar as the RSS does not believe in caste system and has many attempts to remove caste untouchabiliy through their programmes. So much so that a *Dalit* was chosen to perform *puja* while laying foundation stone of Ramjanmabhumi temple. The RSS also supports inter-caste marriages, and inter-caste dining. Many Sangh leaders have organised evening meal (*ratri bhojan*) with the *Dalit* families.

Most analysts say that, the objective of the *ghar-wapsi* campaign is to prepare the ground for a national level anti-conversion legislation. At this stage what will be the strategy in near future is perhaps too premature: Whether India emerges as an ethnic democracy (in which Hinduism functions as *primus enter parse* and the efficient secret of Indian statecraft that has enabled the BJP to rise to power) or maintain its current *sarva dharma samabhava* policy remains to be seen. For last nearly 100 years *ghar wapsi* has been an integral part of core *Hindutva* agenda and there are every sign that the fundamentalist force will keep it alive for long time to come.

In spite of spread of Hindu fundamentalism's mindset and operation across India over the past few decades, with Hindu nationalists in the driver's seat after 2014, there has been broad resistance to the hegemony of one religion at the expense of others. Drawing from the widely popular non-violent movement initiated by Mahatma Gandhi and Ambedkar (both of whom clashed with *Veda*-touting orthodox Hindus through different modes of mediation and rejection respectively), a plethora of pluralistic voices have sought to carve out a more generous form of Hindu belief and practice. However, this topic so far has not been researched well.

Ghar wapsi remains a controversial political issue that the RSS and the BJP wants to avoid bad publicity it received worldwide in December 2014.

The conversion debate among Hindu nationalists has two sides: Hindus converting to other religious and others reconverting to Hinduism—referred as *Ghar Wapsi*. The first aspect of conversion has been bitterly opposed by the Sangh Parivar, whereas the second tends to be viewed favourably as another step towards buttressing National unity. Conversion arouses very strong emotions as it speaks to basic issues of identity. The RSS seems to have decided to play a balancing and mediating role between political goals of the BJP, which seeks support of the India's religious minorities to gain political power and the VHP. The RSS walks a fine line, and is likely to act as it did in Agra case when publicity undermines its own activities and of those other members of the Sangh Parivar. Its preferred approach to these differences is holding quiet behind the scene negotiations among the leaders of the affected groups and creating compromises that are compatible with the basic objectives of the member organization. Now according to the new strategy, the RSS affiliates would avoid converting people in public functions as was done during its failed attempts in December 2014. The entire DJSS brass has been asked not to talk to the media in order to avoid fresh controversy. "The *Pracharaks* would convince individual families to come under the fold of Hinduism and once they agree they would be converted inside their homes as it saves us from lots of unnecessary trouble from the hostile state government", said a senior DJSS leader on condition of anonymity. "Why to court controversy when the work can be done in much more efficient way by being silent about it. We have been asked to strictly avoid taking media", added the senior DJSS leader told me.

If this is the case than the objection to *ghar wapsi* would loose sting as under the Constitution anybody has freedom to adopt any religion and right to convert or re-convert.

To this day, the more inclusive option represents the religious and political vision of the majority of Hindus in India. In fact, majority of Hindus are still liberal and non-violent and believe in respect for all religion. The current ephemeron of *ghar wapsi* cannot be understood adequately as a single social movement. Instead, it must be considered as part of a wider field of competing movements. However, in the globalised era with neo-liberal economy supported the right-wing BJP there is every possibility of the issue of *ghar wapsi* being dropped off, picked up as per the political convenience. Through *ghar wapsi*, the hard-core nationalists want to reduce sphere of freedom of choice.[12] In short, the freedom to behave within an acceptable norm and public acceptability. At the heart of *ghar wapsi* controversy lies the question about freedom of choice: Choice in faith, choice in belief, choice in thought, and choice in action.

Notes

1. Andersen and Damle (2018). *The RSS*, Penguin, India.

2. *Times of India,* February 2018.
3. Daniel, Frank Jack and Roberta Rampton (2015). "In parting shot, Obama prods India on religious freedom", *Reuters,* January 27, http://in.reut3rs.com/aticle/2015/01/27india-obama-idINKBNOLOOF720127.
4. Heimsath, Charles H. (1964), *Indian Nationalism and Hindu Social Reform,* Princeton University Press, Ch. v.
5. Pandey, Gyanendra (ed.) (1993). "Which of us are Hindus", In: *Hindus and Others: The Question of Identity in India Today,* New Delhi: Viking, p. 254.
6. Golwalkar, M.S. (1939). *Our Nationhood Defined or We,* Nagpur: Bharat Publications.
7. Mulul, Achaia (2006). "RSS officially disowned Golwalkar's book", New Delhi: *Times of India,* March 9.
8. Frank (2000). "The rise of communalism in Tamil Nadu", *Eastern Anthropology,* Vol. 43, October.
9. Rao, Muralidhar (2015). "*Ghar Wapsi,* a natural retaliation for organised conversion", *The Economic Times,* April 23.
10. Punyani, Ram (2015), *Ghar Wapsi: Conversions and Freedom of Religion,* New Delhi: Media House, p. 53.
11. *Economic Times,* April 10, 2015, *In New Light: Now, RSS says BR Ambedkar supported Ghar Wapsi.*
12. Pal, Ruma (Justice) (2001). "Religious Minorities and the Law in Religion and Personal Law", In: *Secular India: A Call to Judgment* (ed.) Gerald James Larson, Indiana University Press.

12

The RSS and Minorities

Muslim Rashtriya Manch and Rashtriya Isai Manch

On January 9, 2018, the National Council of YMCAs of India proudly announced presence of Indresh Kumar, member of RSS National Executive, at the United Christmas and New Year Celebrations held in New Delhi. While Kumar was the chief guest and Catholic Archbishop Anil J. Couto of Delhi was one of the guests of honour. But this was not the first time that such function had taken place. This was not the only time Kumar and the office bearers of the Council had been collaborating. In February 2017, the Council had organised an event with RSS affiliates—Gau Raksha Manch, Muslim Rashtriya Manch, Dharma Sanskriti Manch, Himalaya Pariwar, Rashtriya Ekta Mission, Jai Bharat Manch, and Yuva Abhivyakti Manch—to promote culture of oneness, peace, unity, and development. At this event, Kumar was the chief guest and Lebi Philip Mathew, President of the Council, was one of the special guests. The Annual Report of the YMCA states that in 2016 the Council had organised a session with Kumar at YMCA, in which they say, "history was created when an initiative was taken on the request of Indresh Kumar to facilitate an open session with the ecumenical and Christian organisations on May 16, 2016. The session began with an exquisite rendition of Vande Mataram. The RSS has been attempting to launch a Christian outfit since 2015, on the lines of Muslim Rashtriya Manch. But, it never took off. Now, through the regional outreach of YMCA, they are hoping to do so. The RSS has been trying to improve its "image" in the eyes of the minorities. Ever since formation of the Bharatiya Sikh Sangat in 1986, the RSS has been actively engaged in creating similar forums of Muslims and Christians.

On July 2, 2015, some Muslims in a press statement announced organising an *Iftar* party in New Delhi. It is usual in India for the political parties to announce *Iftar* parties during the month of Ramzan to appease Muslim community. But this *Iftar dawat* was different as it was organised by the Muslim Rashtirya Manch (MRM), which described itself as an organization established with the support of the RSS "to bridge the widening gap between Hindu and Muslim communities in India". This *Iftar* party soon became talk of the town as one of the invitee was Abdul Bashir, the then Pakistani High Commissioner to India. Because of grumbling from within the ranks of RSS over this invitation, several RSS leaders believed it necessary to clarify the Sangh's relationship with MRM. The RSS spokesperson M. Vaidhya clarified to the media that news about the RSS sponsoring the *Iftar* party were not correct, and that the MRM was an independent Muslim organisation. This announcement was surprising as it is known in the media circle that the MRM was established with RSS's assistance in 2002, and has been guided ever since by an RSS *pracharak* Indresh Kumar formerly in charge of Sangh in Jammu & Kashmir. Indresh Kumar's formal title in the MRM is *margdarshak* (guide). He has also served as a member of the very influential ABKM, the central executive committee of the RSS.

Despite denial the fact is that the RSS has supported MRM since its inception in 2002 and the then *Sarsanghchalak* K.S. Sudershân participated in its official launch on December 24, in the same year. Yet the RSS has faced a recurring dilemma regarding how far it should go in supporting the MRM and how openly it should acknowledge its association. On one hand, the Sangh does not want to offend those of its many Hindu members who have negative views of Indian Muslims and Islam. On the other hand, it genuinely wants to bring Muslims closer to what it considers the national mainstream both for the reasons of political stability and to help the BJP garner political support among Muslims, some 14 per cent of the population. At least for now, it has fixed on a course of supporting the MRM while also keeping it at arm's length by emphasizing the MRM's independence (Andersen and Damle, 2018).

In fact, in 1979 the RSS formally opened its membership to Muslims (and Christians). Muslims are now in RSS as well as virtually all its affiliates. There are even a few Muslims in the

RSS who have gone through the three-year training programme that produces the full time corps of *pracharaks*. However, there remains an undercurrent of suspicion throughout the Sangh regarding Muslims (and to a lesser extent Christians) which has history.

Muslims have been looked with suspicion is evident from the writings of Golwalkar who says in his book *Bunch of Thoughts*:

> It would be suicidal to delude ourselves into believing that they [Muslims] have turned patriots overnight after the creation of Pakistan. On the contrary, the Muslim menace has increased a hundred fold since the creation of Pakistan, which has become a springboard for all their future aggressive designed on our country.

The RSS believes that the 1000 years of Muslim domination in the subcontinent were the result of external invasion; likewise, the Muslim ruling classes are always portrayed as foreign imperialist, though not Muslim masses, which are acknowledged converts. This distinction enables the RSS to claim that Muslims are in fact "sons of the soil", a definition that conveniently justified opening membership to them. Nevertheless, Golwalkar in 1939 wrote that, "The non-Hindu people in Hindustan must adopt the Hindu culture and language, must learn to respect, and hold in reverence Hindu religion if they want to stay in this country."

Muslims have been looked with fear and sceptics regarding their loyalty to India and this can be traced back to the very formation of the RSS in 1925. The goal at its inception was to unite the fractured Hindu community to defend Hindus; with Hindu, solidarity additionally being perceived as a necessary precondition for independence—Muslims were seen as an obstacle to that larger national goal. Partition and the subsequent Hindu-Muslim communal violence that ravaged India deepened this popular perception of Muslin disloyalty. The horrible experience of Hindu refugees from Pakistan to India always crested barriers in accepting Muslims in the RSS. This posed serious challenge before the RSS to admit Muslims at RSS Shakhas. Golwalkar, in the wake of the 1948-49 ban, responded to those demanding that the RSS open itself to Muslims by arguing that the RSS had no problem with Islam as a religion or with Indian Muslims (who he claimed were ethnically the same as Indian Hindus), but that he doubted any Muslim would join a nationalist organization like the Sangh. It hints that there has always been resistance about accepting Muslims in the RSS and that still continue until date (Jorg Friedrichs, 2018).

After Independence, it took nearly 25 years that the RSS could think of admitting Muslims in their fold. Golwalkar's choice of Madhukar Dattatraya Deoras (Popularly known as Balasaheb Deoras) as the third *Sarsanghchalak* in 1973 signalled a significant shift from the introverted reconstruction phase following the devastating 1948-49 ban to a more extroverted activists phase by Balasaheb Deoras. During his last days Golwalkar did expressed about how much RSS should change particularly under new leadership. Just after the Independence, until the death of Golwalkar was reconstruction phase primarily with focus on rebuilding the Hindu membership base, and one part of that strategy was to add a Hindu spiritual elements to the militant focus of *Hindutva*.[1] Golwalkar's choice of Deoras proved boon for the organisation. When Indira Gandhi imposed Emergency in 1975, many organisations involved in the protest against Indira Gandhi, including the RSS, were banned, and many senior leaders, including Doeras were arrested. While in prison, Deoras and other RSS leaders interacted with prominent figures of the banned Jamaat i-Islami, an influential Muslim organisation that was also critical of Indira Gandhi's increasingly authoritarian regime. This is how the new Janta Party government in 1977 improbably came to be supported by both the RSS and the Jamaat i-Islami. To give a new outlook and its openness to other Indians several prominent Janta Party leaders pressed the RSS to open its door for membership to Muslims and Christians, thus providing the context for RSS leaders to finally move on opening their ranks to Muslims. Balasaheb Deoras when faced internal opposition quoted Hedgewar to justify an aboutturn who had said that "he would be happy to live with Muslims and Christians with the spirit of brotherhood as children of mother India."[2] K.R. Malkani, whom I met several times in the 1980s-1990s told me that one problem with Muslims is that they have yet to identify with India, its people and its culture." Let the Indian Muslims feel and say this is their country and all these are his people and the problem (of Hindu-Muslim tensions) will cease to exist. It is a matter of changing his (Muslim) psychology.[3] Deoras felt sufficiently confident, two years later after the end of the emergency in 1977, to officially open RSS Shakhas to Muslims (as well as to other non-Hindus) in order to enact this aforementioned change on the 'psychological' sentiment used by his successor, Sudarshan, twenty five years later to justify the RSS's support for the MRM. But this was not easy as there was fierce opposition from the more conservative elements of the Sangh.

The MRM was founded with the stated aim of bringing Hindu and Muslim communities in India closer together. It states that Muslim suspicions of the RSS and its affiliates are misplaced, and that the Indian National Congress is responsible for a lack of leadership within the Muslim community. The MRM has also expressed support for many of the causes espoused by the RSS, including the banning of cow-slaughter. Its national convener, Mohammed Afzal, stated that the organisation faced significant resistance in the days following the Godhra train burning and the 2002 Gujarat riots.

Due to continued doubts and opposition about attracting Muslins to the RSS or its affiliates, the RSS leadership turned its focus to the creation of an independent Muslim activist's organisation, one that would interact directly with Indian Muslims. This is the story behind the birth of MRM as an organisation tailored to propagate *Hindutva* ideology directly among Muslims. The first convention of the MRM in 2003 passed a resolution demanding a total ban on cow slaughter. The second national convention in 2004 added a demand that the Article 370 of the Constitution of India be abolished to further the cause of national integration, in addition to proclamations denouncing terrorism and demanding equal rights for Muslim women.[4]

In November 2009, the *Jamiat Ulema-e-Hind*, one of the largest Islamic organisations in India, passed a resolution describing *Vande Mataram* as an un-Islamic song. The MRM expressed opposition to the resolution. Its national convener, Mohammed Afzal stated "Our Muslim brothers should not follow the *fatwa* as *Vande Mataram* is the national song of the country and every Indian citizen should respect and recite it." The MRM stated further that Muslims who refused to sing it were opponents of both Islam and India. In August 2008, MRM organised a *Paigham-e-Aman* (message of peace) *yatra* from the Red Fort in Delhi to Kashmir in support of land allocation for the Amarnath pilgrimage. Led by the

Jharkhand Shahee Imam Moulana Hizb Rehman Merthi, some 50 activists of the *yatra* were initially stopped at the border of Jammu & Kashmir. They were later allowed to go to Jammu where they held meetings with the Shri Amarnath Sangharsh Samiti. In November 2009, the MRM organised a *tiranga yatra* (march in honour of the national flag) leading to the Gateway of India in Mumbai, protesting against terrorism. One thousand volunteers took a pledge against terror and vowed to campaign against it in their home districts.

At its tenth convention in 2012, after reporting that MRM activists had unfurled the Indian national flag in Srinagar—they submitted a memorandum to the President of India, with the signature of a 7,00,000 Muslims, demanding an end to cow-slaughter. The MRM contributed workers to the BJP 2014 parliamentary campaign, and lent similar aid to BJP candidates in subsequent State Assembly contests in Jammu & Kashmir and in Bihar.

When questioned about Modi's involvement in the Gujarat riots, Afzal stated: "Had Mr. Modi been involved in the riots, his police would not have fired 1,200 rounds and killed over 200 rioters. Every court has acquitted him. And there is not a single incident of communal violence in Gujarat in the past 12 years."

In 2015, the Muslim Rashtriya Manch published a book title "Yoga and Islam" on universal appeal and acceptance of Yoga. The Manch expressed its views that 'Yoga' does not have anything to do with religion, further stating that "Namaaz is one sort of Yoga asana." The move was supported by the Union Ministry of Ayurveda, Yoga and Naturopathy, Unani, Siddha and Homoeopathy (AYUSH) but Hindu groups expressed reservations.

There are many activities, which the MRM seems to perform to enhance the RSS agenda among Muslim community. The MRM website gives details of programmes, including a beef free *Iftar* party in Ayodhya to promote cow protection, flag hoisting on January 26, at mosques and *madarasas* nationwide, periodic meetings between RSS leaders and Muslim intellectuals, and a campaign for a uniform civil code. The website MRM also organised a dialogue between Muslims and Hindus religious functionaries on the Ram Temple controversy in Ayodhya. In line with the RSS's increasing involvement in-service activities, the MRM has started a campaign to promote education in Muslim communities. The MRM claims to have 10,000 members in twenty-two states. Its leaders are constantly in touch with the RSS office in Delhi.[5]

The MRM has constantly campaigned against beef eating. The MRM organised its first cow shelter meeting in Haryana on September 13, 2015, which was attended by Haryana Chief Minister Manohar Lal Khattar and All India Imams Council leader Umer Ahmed Iliyasi. The MRM extended open support to the BJP ahead of UP Assembly elections by reaching out to local Islamic clerics to correct misconceptions about the RSS in a state where Muslin form almost a fifth of the population. Thus the role of MRM has been important for RSS and it indicates a shift in RSS look about Muslims after independence.

It may look like the RSS had a new beginning with Muslims. But the fact is that the RSS's approach to Muslims started much before the formation of the MRM in 2002, and even before the RSS formally opened its door to Muslims in 1979. Golwalkar in 1951 supported the policy of Shyama Prasad Mookherjee, founder of the Bharatiya Jana Sangh, to open his party's door to people of all faiths. He also advised Mookherjee to avoid including Hindu name in the new party, so as to distinguish itself from the explicitly sectarian Hindu Mahasabha. Some Muslims contested elections on the BJS ticket. Few were successful and one even becomes Mayor of Delhi. The successor, BJP formed in 1980, also had a few Muslim candidates as he stated and central levels, and some were in the cabinets of Vajpayee and Modi. Among these ministers were Najma Heptulla, Arif Beg, Sikander Bakht, Mukhtar Abbas Naqvi, Syed Shahanawaj Hussain, and M.J. Akbar, all six members of the Rajya Sabha. The BJP 2014 manifesto stands out for its concession to Muslims, such as improving the quality of education in Muslim communities, greater power to Muslim charitable boards and the institution, of state sponsored interfaith dialogues. The part of that document addressing Muslims issues states:

> It is unfortunate that even after several decades of independence a large section of the minority, and especially Muslim community, continues to be stymied in poverty. Modern India must be a nation of equal opportunity.[6]

This seems to be counter salvo to the Congress Party's Sacchar Commission on Muslims.

No doubt, all such efforts have increased BJP support among

Muslim community. It is said that vote share for the BJP and its allies in 2014 parliamentary elections doubled from 4 per cent in 2009 to 8 per cent in 2014. But despite all such encouraging signs no Muslim was given party ticket in Uttar Pradesh and Bihar Assembly elections though each has a substantial Muslim. In Gujarat Bohras and Ismailis support the BJP but no ticket for parliamentary seat was offered to them and even in assembly elections of 2017. However, the BJP nominated some 450 seats (of a total 4778) to Muslims in the states 2015 local body elections.[7]

The RSS's focus on reaching out to Muslims directly deepened during the religious tensions of the Ram Janmabhoomi movement of the 1980s. Sarsanghsanchalak Sudarshan, when he served as head of the intellectual wing of the RSS, took the initiative to start a dialogue on the subject with Muslim religious figures, bypassing Muslim political leaders and academics entirely, he had probably concluded that these religious leaders had much more influence with the Muslim masses and had a better sense of their concerns. Among the leaders, he met with Maulana Jhameel Illiyasi, the President of All India Imam Council, Maulana Wahiduddin Khan, the Shahi Imam of Fatehpuri Masjid, and Mufti Mukarram Ahmed. These religious figures were all present at the birth of the MRM in the late 2002. Despite all such efforts there is reservation about Muslim participation in RSS activities among a section of saffron brigade thinks that Indian Muslims at best can be Hinduized and not Indianized. In their view, the activities of MRM discourages and impedes *ghar wapsi*. They argue that most Muslims as well as Christians in India retain their Hindu caste identity and ancestral customs, therefore, it is much better to have *ghar wapsi* programme rather than Indianizing them. Organisational solidarity of an increasing diverse membership. Due to mix reaction among its cadre and intellectuals, the RSS leadership has taken the middle ground: the Sangh patronizes the MRM, but will not accord it formal affiliate status. Sarsanghsanchalak Mohan Bhagwat who attended the MRM annual conclave for the first time during his tenure in December 2016 made statements about Indian Muslims.

The goal of MRM is to narrow the gap between Muslims and the RSS brand of patriotism, an objective strongly supported by the RSS national leadership, thus reaffirming that the RSS is prepared to accommodate Muslims—but only on its own terms. The MRM has to prove that it has made or is making considerable impact on Muslim communities and that it has ear of the top brass of the RSS.

Shridahr Damle, a well informed observer of the RSS, told me he had interviewed Indresh Kumar in 2015. Kumar told him most Muslims wanted a decent life and protection from radical Muslims. This, Damle finds is in line with a statement by the journalist Arun Shourie, who remains an authority in Hindu nationalist circles. He recalls that in 1994, Shourie suggested that, after two BJP victories, non-sunniets, and non-orthodox Muslims would "come to us for protection."

While MRM is perhaps a fringe phenomenon, there are other indicators that heterodox Muslims might be interested in accepting subordinate status. Regardless of 2002 carnage in Gujarat, the Ismaili Bohara community kept warm relations with Modi, who was then Chief Minister of Gujarat. During Maha Kumbh in 2015 the Boharas served 70,000 cups of tea to pilgrimage and were duly commended by Hindu nationalists as 'true nationalists' and ' real Indians" (Abbes, 2016).

The official view is that Hindu Muslim relations are good. As Modi was saying all Indians should move together. Of course, there are some key issues such as common civil code, Kashmir, Ram Temple in Ayodhya. The RSS and the BJP move with electoral arithmetic in these cases.

Rashtriya Isai Manch (RIM)

After forming the Rashtriya Sikh Sangat on November 24, 1986, the RSS has been working on creating similar forums among Muslims and Christians. In 2002, the Muslim Rashtirya Manch was formed under the guidance of Indresh Kumar, the RSS functionary incharge of such activities. Now the RSS is making effort to have similar front among Christians in India.

On January 4, 2016, quoting *Economic Times* the *Zee News* reported that Rashtriya Swayamsevak Sangh (RSS) is likely to set up an outfit—Rashtriya Isai Manch. It will be on the lines of RSS's Muslim Rashtriya Manch. According to a report in the *Economic Times*, RSS has held meetings with Christian leaders to establish an organisation on the lines of the Muslim Rashtriya Manch.

A senior RSS *Pracharak*, associated with the Muslim Rashtriya Manch since its inception, has confirmed the plan. However, RSS is yet to take final decision on the name of the RSS's Christian outfit. Sources said that while the nomenclature is not yet final, it is envisaged that a Rashtriya Isai Manch on similar lines be set up to build bridges of 'goodwill' with the community. According to RSS member Indresh Kumar, on December 17, 4-5 Archbishops, 40-50 Reverend Bishops from across 10 to 12 states met and it was decided to develop a movement.

Indresh Kumar's statement of an Isai Manch, however, has generated a storm, catching the religious leadership far out on the limb. According to Fr. Joseph Xavier, a Jesuit priest expert in human rights and criminology, and a former executive director of the Indian Social Institute in New Delhi, the claim is an attempt at "false propaganda" for electoral purposes. "There was no meeting for that purpose", he said: "there was a Christmas celebration", which the Catholic Bishops Conference of India organises every year (Nirmala Carvalho, *Asia News*, January 4, 2016).

The reports are wrong, Archbishop Kuriakose Bharanikulangara of Faridabad, the most senior among the Bishops who attended the meeting along with Bishop Jacob Mar Barnabas of Gurgaon, told the Catholic news agency UCAN, "There was absolutely no talk about such an organisation at that gathering. First, it was not a meeting. It was a Christmas celebration. According to reports, 5 archbishops and 40 bishops attended the meeting. But Archbishop Bharanikulangara said only three bishops attended—two Catholic bishops including him, and one Orthodox bishop."[8]

On behalf of the National Council of Churches in India (NCCI), the umbrella body of major Protestant churches in the country, its Delhi-based secretary, Mr. Samuel Jeykumar, issued a statement: "This is to clarify that NCCI was not involved on 17th December meeting. In fact, on an earlier occasion they were trying to reach us for the Raksha Bandhan programme. We refused to participate in that programme. I had also spoken to the few Church leaders who participated in this particular programme. They went because of the Christmas programme and not participated in any specific meeting. The media report is a mischief. There is clear attempt to divide the Christian community. Hence, we all need to be careful. We are having some other pre-planned programme on January 13. Hence, we could not participate."

Fr. Ajay Kumar Singh, a lawyer and social activist of

Kandhamal in Orissa, remembered: "Indresh Kumar could never be forgotten for his role in Kandhamal's anti-Christian violence." The Kandhamal Survivors Association had submitted a memorandum to Manmohan Singh, then Prime Minister, to unearth his (Indresh Kumar's) role.

Dr. Richard Howell, general secretary of the Evangelical Fellowship of India (EFI), said his group was not represented at the meeting.

A slightly different note was struck by Fr. Paul Thelekkatt, former spokesperson of the influential Syro-Malabar Church and Editor of Church-run publication "Sathyadeepam" who said: "Personally I do welcome the proposal.... I believe that the RSS is ready to dialogue with Christians and not to impose anything on the Christians but to listen to the followers of another religion and to create a better atmosphere of mutual respect and cooperation and thus to grow together as equal citizens of this country."

In the light of this controversy it is important to note that on December 6, 20016 first Christian-Hindu Conference in Italy took place in the main hall of the Pontifical Gregorian University, Rome, which was attended by Paramahamsa Swami Yogananda Giri, honorary president of the Italian Hindu Union, and Bishop Paul Gallagher, Secretary for [Vatican] Relations with States and inaugurated by Cardinal Jean-Louis Tauran, President of the Pontifical Council for Interreligious Dialogue. The Vatican is very keen on such dialogue after Pope John Paul II visit was opposed by the Hindu organisation in India in 1999. In similar exercises earlier Vatican had invited RSS ideologues to Rome.

The Catholic Bishops Conference of India (CBCI) has not issued any statement contradicting Indresh Kumar's claim. Denial by a priest who has no position with the CBCI gives rise to many doubts in the minds of laity in India that *"kuch khichidi pak rahi hai"* (something is being cooked). Otherwise human rights activist John Dayal would not have written in his blog on February 11, 2016 urging the church leaders not to engage in any such exercise.

The latest development has been gauged with the RSS strategy to convince minorities about its vision of a Hindu nation. Political strength now forms important part of achieving this goal. The RSS has been successful in making breach in the north-eastern states and has now influential political presence in the state assemblies of Nagaland, Meghalaya, Manipur, Tripura, and Arunachal Pradesh. The Naga People's Front (NPF) is an alliance partner of the BJP at the Centre. With 88 per cent of its population being Christians as per the Census 2011, it turns out to be one of the three Christian-majority states in India including Meghalaya and Mizoram.

India's North East is no longer an unknown destination for the BJP, which until a few years was almost akin to an alien in the region. With its victory in the Assam Assembly election that helped the party opened its account in the North East in 2016, the win in Manipur in 2017 makes it even more ambitious to capture Christian-dominated states like Meghalaya, Nagaland, and Mizoram besides the Hindu-dominated state of Tripura. The BJP won 2017 Assembly elections in Christian dominated Goa.

The RSS, which would include the BJP for that matter, have not tried to impose the beef ban in the North East seen otherwise in the rest of the country. Beef for many tribes living in the North East forms an important part of their diet. This approach by the two organisations has helped them maintain a cordial relationship with the people of the region particularly in a state like Nagaland. "Many people in Nagaland have turned vegetarian for one reason or the other. They have even started Yoga. This is influence of RSS."

Mizoram has the smallest Assembly in the North East (with 40 members) but it is a terrain on which the RSS and the BJP have failed to create much impact so far. The hilly state which is one of the three Christian-dominated states in India is not very open to the nationalistic ideals of the RSS which has an intermix of subtle *Hindutva* flavour. In a state, which has 87 per cent of its population following Christianity as per the Census 2011, the challenges for both the BJP and the RSS are obvious.

For, according to the 2011 Census, 34 per cent of Assam's population is Muslim, while five other North East States have large Christian populations—Nagaland (87.93%) and Arunachal Pradesh (30.26%).

Nevertheless, the RSS has grown steadily in the North East, demonstrating not just persistence but also adaptability and pragmatism. It has, for instance, put the issue of beef, which is part of the diet for a large section of the people here, on the back burner, even as it runs a virulent and vigorous campaign against its consumption elsewhere in the country.

Today, 72 years after its quiet beginnings in the North East, the RSS can claim that it has played a significant role in powering the BJP's recent electoral successes here, especially in Assam and Tripura.

Many individual Christians are members of the RSS.

In Kottayam during my visit to Kerala I met 65-year-old retired Professor of History who is connected with the RSS. He does not see any conflict between being a Christian and an RSS leader. Isaac joined ABVP in 1975 and *Shakhas* are as much a part of his routine as the Sunday mass at the neighbourhood church. "I was attracted to their commitment to national and social interest. I realised that they are more secular than those who claim to be secular. On one of the Sundays, an RSS man drove me to the Church for my prayers. My faith is not a problem for them." Isaac says his wife has also become an active member of the Sangh. The couple uses spare time and social events in the community to talk about RSS. "I tell them the values that RSS stands for. I tell them that there is no difference between Christianity and Hinduism—we believe in the oneness of god."

But such individuals are not welcomed by the organised church and their number is very limited. Overall, the RSS may not have been successful informing a forum among India's Christians but it has made inroads and penetrated in the Christian dominated North East and *Isai adivasi* areas of central India.

Conclusion

The RSS policy on India's minorities has been evolutionary rather than revolutionary. As an organisation that emphasises cohesion and consensus, the RSS evolves slowly in response to change social norms and economic circumstances. Minorities, but, there is clear signs of shifting stance in the RSS on Muslim minorities.

During past three decades, the RSS has developed greater sensitivity to the diversity of India. This dawned on me when attending the 2015 India Ideas Conclave, organised by India Foundation and conveyed by Ram Madhav, General Secretary of the BJP and intimately connected to the RSS. Among the participants, there were outspoken critics of contemporary Islam and Christian conversion activities. They all demanded that there is a need for strong government to move against such elements but they also agreed that there is a need to develop harmonious living.

Today 'Hindu' definition include most Muslims and Christians as long as they are willing to scribe to what Uppadhaya in Integral Humanism described as the 'national soul', that unique element that gives life to a people's culture and institutions and provides the boundaries of what it is to be a member of the Hindu nation. It is within this broader framework that the RSS is now approaching Muslims, Christians, and Sikhs to create an inclusive society. There is a growing effort within the Sangh Parivar to bring Muslims into larger Indian cultural milieu, motivated partly by the fact that Muslims and Christians are considered ethnically similar to other Indians and partly to the political need of the BJP to win their support. The BJP governments support to modernise *madarsas* and the decision in Goa to continue support for Roman Catholic schools to avoid antagonizing the large Catholic population are signs of changing mood in the RSS. The Sangh and the BJP are adopting moderate approach to non-Hindus. Somewhere a meeting ground is being prepared. But, its future is still not clear. The social drama of Hindu-Muslim relations arises from the complex interplay of divergent perspectives. At the same time different actors play different roles and pursue different tasks.

Notes

1. Garett, W. Brown, Iain McLean, Alistair McMillan (2018). *The Concise Oxford Dictionary of Politics and International Relations,* Oxford University Press.
2. Narayan, H. Palkar (2012). *Dr. Hedgewar,* Bharatiya Vichar Sangh, Pune.
3. K.R. Malkani (1980). *The RSS Story,* Implex Publication, New Delhi.
4. *The Caravan,* June (2017). Sat D. Sharma (2012). *India Marching: Reflections from a Nationalistic Perspective,* Universe, Delhi.
5. Sat D. Sharma (2012). *India Marching: Reflections from a Nationalistic Perspective,* iUniverse, Delhi.
6. Manifesto 2014-Bharatiya Janata Party, www.bjp.org/manifesto2014, An Abridged Version (English) accessed on July 17, 2018.
7. Prashant Jha (2017). *How the BJP Wins: Inside India's Greatest Election Machine,* Juggernaut Publication.
8. UCAN http://www.catholicnewsagency.com/tags/catholic-news)

13

New Agenda in Education

In July 2018, the BJP government of Uttar Pradesh mooted a dress code for *madarsas* students. Until now the Muslim *madarsas* students wear white *kurta-payjanma,* which reflects a particular faith. In 2017 tension prevailed in many *madarsas* school over Saraswati *puja*. In January 2018, the BJP government of Rajasthan issued a diktat directing all government and private schools to not only chant prayers but to install an idol of goddess Saraswati and convene prayers with rituals. The order said that, "Every school, private, and government has to celebrate the festival and its rituals. It is also noted that every school has to encourage and engage its students in the rituals." The order also said that it is mandatory for every school to deliver a talk on the goddess Saraswati. Rajasthan has 1.20 lakh schools including 85,000 government and 35,000 private schools. It is first time that such a circular has been issued for private schools.[1] The Gujarat government had also issued similar order in January 2018. These are not isolated incidents. In May 2015, the BJP Government of Chhattisgarh issued an official circular banning the use of world "Father" in Catholic Christian educational institutions. In some cases, the circular "approved by the Collector" was also copied to the branches of Vishwa Hindu Parishad.[2] Schools in Chhattisgarh were asked to install Saraswati statues and call principals 'pracharya' or 'Sir' and not 'Rev Father.' In 2014 December just before Christmas, the Union HRD Ministry instructed schools to be open on Christmas and observe December 25, the Christmas Day as Good Governance Day. All such incidences spread throughout the country are the Sangh Parivar's concerns about minority schools are part of its larger preoccupation with the inculcation of national identity through education system.

The RSS from its inception had an agenda to create certain notions of citizenship and national identify through mass education that starts from early childhood. RSS long recognized the centrality of education to any project of gaining power and representing the political arena. With education as its core mission and virtually all RSS affiliates are engaged in some form of it, some with the specific mission of managing schools at the primary, secondary, and tertiary levels—and on a mass scale. In the RSS's strategy, schools are one of the modes by which nation building and identity can be imagined and reproduced to control over all aspects of schooling system—availability, cost curriculum, language, pedagogical techniques—are at heart of patriotism, and national identity. The RSS notion of citizenship, nationhood, and patriotism has become critical focus of this debate.

Background

The Sarsanghchalak Golwalkar in 1946 laid the foundation stone of the Gita Mandir, at Kurukshetra in Haryana then part of Punjab. Following this up, Nanaji Deshmukh—a *pracharak* in Uttar Pradesh—established the Saraswati Shishu Mandir at Gorakhpur. It provided a model for similar schools within the large state of Uttar Pradesh. In the decades after the ban, when the RSS was still operating under a cloud of suspicion, these schools provided an alternative way to spread RSS's message of national unity and pan Hinduism. Teachers of these schools often insert nationalist narrative into the school science and history books prescribed by national authorities, as these texts are held by some RSS circles to be devoid of respect for country's distinct civilization. The RSS's decision to set up its own school system was motivated by what it viewed as the deliberate attempt of India's post-Independence Congress government to deny RSS members and their Hindu message any place in the educational system (Andersen and Damle, 2018).

Prior to this during the colonial period, RSS leaders did not seriously address setting up a separate school system run by individual or groups with a nationalist outlook acceptable to the RSS. Prominent among such groups was the Arya Samaj whose schools incorporated its message of the unity of a Hinduism found in Vedic literature.

Although the RSS had set up its own school system in 1940s, it was only after testing political power in the company of Janata Party that the RSS has encouraged its affiliates to engage in educational experiments in order to package its *Hindutva* message in ways that make it more relevant and thus more appealing to Indians. Its educational front Vidya Bharati is one of the largest network of private schools across the country. Other RSS fronts providing education include the Vanvasi Kalyan *Ashram* (VKS) which specialises in hostels for *advisi* children among other activities, Sewa Bharati for *Dalits*, and the Ekal *Vidyalayas* Foundation which runs single teachers preschool centres where children are taught basic reading, writing, Sanskrit and, *Sanskars* (good behaviour).

Immediately after the Independence, the RSS took direct interest in shaping education at the primary and secondary levels. This was an urgent priority on the part of the RSS's largely urban, middle class base and by the growing demand for education. First years after Independence, prompted both by the Sangh's conviction that national values were inadequately represented in curriculum, both in public school and in private Christian schools.[3]

In 1969, the RSS formed the Bharatiya Shikshan Mandal (BSM), essentially an organisation of teachers belonging to the RSS, which focused its attention on evolving a "*Hindutva* curriculum". According to an RSS publication, the BSM's objective was to "infuse a Bharatiya content to the educational system"; it even drew up syllabi for Classes I to X on moral education and tried to get acceptance from State and Union governments.

In 1977, when the Janata Party came to power, the BSM tried to get its curriculum accepted by the Union Government. A number of seminars were organised as part of this attempt. Although these efforts did not succeed, the syllabi became part of the curriculum in RSS-run schools.

RSS Affiliates in Education

It was after the BSM's attempt failed that the RSS recast its organisational structure to strengthen its school network in the education sphere. The school network grew rapidly in the 1960 and 1970s so much so that the RSS in 1977 established a separate affiliate Vidya Bharati that not only formulates and revises the *Hindutva* curriculum from time to time but also oversees the management of various RSS educational institutions. Vidya Bharati at that time included some 700 schools. As reported in 2016, it had 13,000 schools with some 32,00,000 students and 1,46,000 teachers, making it the largest school system in India. In addition to this, Vidya Bharati schools, another RSS affiliate Eklavya established in 1986, has about 15,00,000 students in some 54,000 one teacher one school facilities located mainly in tribal and remote areas.[4]

The objective of Vidya Bharti is, "To develop National System of Education which would help to build a generation of young men and women, that is committed to *Hindutva* and infuse with patriotic fervour." Other objectives include "building up a harmonious, prosperous and culturally rich Nation", and "service of those brothers and sisters who live in villages, forests, caves, and slums and are deprived and destitute, so that they are liberated from the shackles of social evil and injustice." Describing the "Indian National Ethos" taught at these schools, the Vidya Bharati places primary importance on an "integral approach to life", with other facets of the curriculum including "recognition of divinity in every form of life" and "blending of materialism with spirituality." These objectives are virtually identical to those used by other affiliates and even the RSS itself, predictably, their end goals are social harmony and Hind unity.[5]

With a commitment to 'Indianize', schools of India, its educational affiliate, the Vidya Bharati, announced on January 2, 2015 a plan to establish model schools in all of India's 9000-odd administrative blocks to serve as an example of excellence to be emulated by government schools (*Economic Times*, January 2, 2015). Vidya Bharati also now includes such institutions as colleges, teacher's training schools, as well as 9806 "Informal Education" units. The Vidya Bharati controls 60 colleges, which offer graduate and post-graduate education, and 25 other institutions of higher education. The organisation also runs two teacher-training colleges, in Jaipur and Ahmednagar.

In Shishu Mandir about 90 per cent of the teachers are women; all teachers are required to undergo "special training" in Indian tradition and culture and the "Hindu way of education." The Sangh Parivar considers this a necessity, because, as a State-level organiser told, "a majority of graduate teachers who pass out of mainstream education courses are Convent-educated or otherwise not properly acquainted with the Hindu way of life."

The course material used in the Vidya Bharati schools throughout the country is the same. The schools themselves are known by a variety of names, such as Saraswati Shishu Mandir, Bharatiya Vidya Niketan, Gita Vidyalaya and Saraswati Bal Vidyalaya. Significantly, the State and regional-level governing bodies of these institutions do not always go by the name of Vidya Bharati. These bodies use different names depending on the socio-political situation in each State. For instance, the governing bodies in Delhi, where the RSS and the BJP have a significant political presence, flaunt the title Hindu Shiksha Samiti; those in Odisha and Punjab operate under the less-strident names of Shiksha Vikas Samiti (Education Development Council) and Sarva Hitkari Shiksha Samiti (Education Council for Universal Benefit). In a supposed concession to local sentiment, in the Jharkhand the governing body is called Vananchal Shiksha Samiti.

Vidya Bharati schools operate even in Kerala, where the political influence of the RSS and the BJP is not as significant as in many other States. The first Vidya Bharati school in the State, the Vyasa Vidya Peetham, was established on 10 hectares of land in Kallekkadu, near Palakkad. The organisation has since established its presence in all 14 districts of the State; today it runs 174 schools. Of these, 120 are Saraswati Shishu Vidyalayas, imparting education only up to Class IV. The rest, called Bharatiya Vidya Niketans, have up to Classes VII or XII. There is a teachers training centre at the Bharatiya Vidya Niketan's Adhyapaka Prashikshana Kendram, at the Vyasa Vidya Peetham campus in Palakkad.

In the scheme of things of the Rashtriya Swayamsevak Sangh, the business of running schools that further the political, ideological and social agenda of the fountainhead of the *Hindutva* ideology ranks high, and the programme is described as the "task of educating and ennobling young minds." The RSS leadership from the beginning had identified early education of children as an important component of the plan to propagate "*Hindutva* philosophy" through initiatives on the ideological, organisational and cultural fronts.

All these tremendous growth of RSS affiliated school system

has turned tables on the concerns Sangh once had regarding Christian missionary schools educating Hindus, as it now controls a considerable number of Muslim and Christian students enrolled in their schools. In 2017 there were about 74,000 Muslim children in these schools. Within ten years, the Sangh network of schools is likely to become reason for 'endangering' of large number of missionary English medium schools, which have been opened up in small district level towns. The RSS is now focusing on English medium schools and argues that after all in most Christian schools the teachers are Hindus. The expansion of the network of RSS schools is a major pillar of 'nation building' through education, especially going against the traditional separation of education and religion. The RSS feel they can emulate the work of Christian missionaries in reaching members of SCs and STs, who are not part of the BJP's natural vote bank. In providing help and support, the RSS hoped to instil *Hindutva* in all segments of society.[6]

The RSS also concentrated on publishing books on history and ethics for use in the Shishu Mandirs and the other affiliated schools. The Shiksha Sanskriti Utthan Nyas lobby, the Ministry of Human Resource Development to ensure that textbooks recommended to the state include some with a value orientation they consider appropriate. However, the textbooks for schools have been subject of debate right after the Independence. A parliamentary committee appointed in 1966 reported that textbooks in some states were 'overweighed' with Hindu mythology and "Hindu beliefs are presented in a manner as if they are universally held by all Indians." The Kothari Commission in 1964 had recommended that "necessary for multi-religious democratic state to promote a tolerant study of all religions so that its citizens can understand each other better and live amicably together." However, such directives did not stop publications with biased approach.[7]

Controversies

When the BJP-led NDA government came to power under Atal Bihari Vajpayee (1996 and 1999-2004), the new Prime Minister selected party's most outspoken ideologue, Murli Manohar Joshi, to head the HRD Ministry, the ministry responsible for education. Joshi responded to the RSS complaints of excessive Marxist influence in scholarly research bodies under his control by removing left-oriented scholars from their positions. He appointed RSS sympathisers to positions in Indian Council of Social Science Research (ICSSR), National Council for Educational Research and Training (NCERT) and ICHR. The opponents charged that he was communalising the institutions and undermining the secular nature of the Indian state. The focus of the ideological onslaught was on history textbooks, since the heart of communal ideology was the communal interpretation of history. At that time efforts were made to ban school textbooks which the NCERT has persuaded some of the tallest historians of India, such as Romila Thapar, R.S. Sharma. Satish Chandra and Bipin Chandra, to write. A countrywide protest, including from within NCERT and other autonomous institutions, paid to this attempt and it had to be abandoned.[8]

The debate, which was labelled by the press as the 'saffronization' of education, became a national issue in the summer of 2001 when even the coalition partners of the NDA said that if the Human Resource Development Ministry insisted on the new agenda, states not ruled by the BJP would refuse the textbooks and the changes made to the syllabus. The criticism of the new education policy was based on two main arguments. First, that they were directed by the communal agenda of the Sangh Parivar and were contrary to the principles enshrined in the Constitution. Second, that the subject of education was the individual states' responsibility and changes could not be imposed unilaterally from the Central Government thus, no curriculum could become national policy without the mandatory endorsement by the states.[9] Through these debates, the BJP remained isolated in Parliament, not supported by its own coalition partners.

When the BJP returned to power in 2014 after ten years of gap it faced the challenge of again saffronizing the school textbooks which had been de-saffronzied during the ten year Congress rule (2004-2014). The RSS resumed the earlier dialogue with the HRD Ministry. Powerful woman orator Smriti Irani, who assumed charge of the HRD Ministry, met the RSS leaders to get idea of revamping of the Indian education system so that it reflects the essentials of Indian culture. Among those who attended the meeting was the influential RSS *sah sarkaryavahak* Hosbale, who had taken the lead in the RSS on the educational matters. One of the agenda pursued was to introduce uniform educational policy in the states. On

September 6-7, 2015, the Education and Cultural Ministers of the BJP ruled state met with Smriti Irani and RSS participants to talk about a uniform education policy in the state. Meanwhile, controversial Irani was replaced by young dynamic patient listener Prakash Javdekar as the HRD Cabinet Minister on July 5, 2016. Javdekar called a meeting on July 27, 2016 that included senior RSS and BJP officials and other reconstituted of the Sangh Parivar engaged in education to discuss education policy earlier initiated by Irani as well as suggestions to "instil nationalism, pride, and ancient Indian values in modern education."[10]

Policy

Today, the RSS and Sangh Parivar have expanded, especially in rural and semi-urban areas particularly *muffissil* towns, there is discussion over appropriate focus of their education efforts. One concern before the Sangh Parivar is how to address the needs of rural and urban students. Urbanites, largely middle class, advocates merits, and specialised education with emphasis on technology, whereas the rural masses want skill based education that would address the demand for jobs among the huge number of students from farming families who cannot make a living, as farming is becoming un-remunerative.

Considering these challenges, the BJP since 2008 is emphasizing on three points:

- The focus on Indian culture, heritage, and ethical values in syllabi will be strengthened. Character building and all-round development of the student's personality will be emphasized. Sports, physical training, and social services will be mainstreamed in the education system.
- The growing de-emphasis of Bhartiya language in schools and college education will be checked. Teaching in the mother tongue will be encouraged.
- Efforts will be intensified for the propagation of Sanskrit.[11]

As the RSS has historically been averse to publicity, asserting that the organisation's work speak for itself, these respected figures had the legitimacy to get RSS members to consider it explored the mechanism through which intellectuals will carry the message to the larger public. The major purpose of these think tanks was to provide a forum for RSS *swayamsevaks* to discuss the relevance of *Hindutva* in the modern era. As the RSS affiliates' policy activism has become more complex, several of them have established think tanks to support their policy positions.

After the surprise BJP defeat in the 2004 elections, the RSS adopted a strategy to create think tanks that may reflect its ideology and comment on various policy initiates. Today there are eight think tanks in the Delhi region alone. These have emerged as major players in influencing the BJP government policy in the wake of the BJP victory of 2014. The oldest of these RSS-affiliated think tanks in Delhi is the Vivekananda International Foundation, whose head, Ajit Doval, was selected as Modi's national security adviser. Ram Madhav, the RSS *pracharak* turned BJP General Secretary, has taken a leading role in making them a venue for policy debates involving a range of policy experts, both Indian and foreign. The influential and the most recent is the India Foundation established in 2014. The India Foundation hosts two international conferences each year: one in India that focuses on broad political questions, and the other overseas addressing strategic issues.[12]

The RSS currently publishes a vast amount of literature on what they do and there are several publishing houses which the RSS and its affiliates use to publish authorized books and pamphlets in English and most Indian languages, such as Suruchi Prakashan in Delhi, Rashtrotthana Sahitya in Bangalore and the Bharatiya Vichar Sadhana in Pune and Nagpur. One thorny policy issue, which bothers the RSS ranks, is reservations in education. Constitution of India provides for affirmative action to uplift Scheduled Castes (SCs) and Scheduled Tribes (STs) through public-sector employment and reservation of seats in educational institutions of higher learning. But, these beneficiaries are restricted to Hindus which include Sikhs, Jains and Buddhists. Christians and Muslims are not included as beneficiaries. Some states have extended affirmative action benefits to them in special circumstance if they can convince the relevant authorities that they belong to a historically disadvantaged group.

The RSS in its own operations ignores caste. The use of caste to identify state affirmative action beneficiaries is contrary to the RSS goal of unifying Hindus into a single ethnic category. Despite this philosophical aversion to caste as a basis for state benefits, the Sangh Parivar has remained largely neutral on the reservation issue even though the policy of affirmative action almost certainly strengthens caste identity and legitimizes caste as a basis for provision of state benefits.[14]

Nonetheless, the political arm of the Sangh Parivar, the BJP, for largely political reasons has defended reservations as a legitimate tool for social reform and has rejected a review of how it is implemented. The BJP, after some hesitation about the extension of the benefits to include OBCs in the early 1990s, did express public support for its expansion and has remained committed to that view. With over 45 per cent of the population in castes eligible for OBC status, the BJP has little room to manoeuvre on this issue, if it wants to stay competitive politically. The most explicit RSS resolutions on the reservation question, "Tactics of Internal Disruption" and "Issue of Reservation", were passed by the ABPS in 1981 and reflect the RSS's dilemma in shaping policy on this issue.[15] The major recommendation in these resolutions is the formation of a special committee of "non-partisan social thinkers" to evaluate who should be included and for how long, a stand that allowed it to avoid a specific statement on the merits of reservation.

The resolution say, "The ABPS affirms the basic truth of our national life being one and indivisible and endowed with rich diversity." But, that same resolution also states that, "The RSS considers it necessary that reservations be continued for the present with a view to bringing all these brethren of ours who have remained backward in educational, social, and economic fields over the centuries at par with the rest of society." These resolutions try to satisfy the conflicting stands on this issue, stating[16]:

> "The ABPS agrees with the Prime Minister's viewpoint (Indira Gandhi at that time) that reservations cannot be a permanent arrangement, that these crutches will have to be done away with as soon as possible and that because of this arrangement merit and efficiency should not be allowed to be adversely affected."

It says nothing, however, on the criteria for a timeline on ending reservations or how to measure the effectiveness of the benefits, or how to keep merit from being adversely affected by the reservation policy.

The RSS in 2015 found itself on the defensive regarding its stand on reservations after a twenty-five-year hiatus when it avoided the issue. The public debate over the RSS's stance was triggered by a September 20, 2015 interview RSS Chief Mohan Bhagwat had with the editors of *Organiser* and *Panchjanya,* two RSS-affiliated weeklies, where he used almost exactly the same words as the ambiguous 1981 ABPS resolutions on reservations, asserting that reservations have been used for political ends, and suggested setting up an apolitical committee to examine who needs reservation benefits and for how long.

The context for these remarks was the violence that grew out of the protests by some members of the Patel community in Gujarat demanding they be included as a disadvantaged group eligible for OBC reservations.[17] This was a sensitive time politically, as Bhagwat's remarks were made on the eve of elections to the Bihar Legislative Assembly, and the RSS, and by implication the BJP was attacked by the opposition, which sought to use those remarks to show that the BJP and RSS were seeking to end the policy of reservations.

Within weeks, the RSS *sarkaryavahak* Suresh 'Bhaiyyaji' Joshi issued a statement on behalf of the RSS stating that, "Reservation can continue as long as it is needed in society. That is our stand... Whatever was said (by Mohan Bhagwat) was not presented in proper words. Nowhere was it said that there should be a review of the reservation policy." The issue resurfaced when Dr. Manmohan Vaidya, then the RSS *prachar-pramukh* and now its Joint General Secretary, issued a statement at the prestigious Jaipur Literature Festival in January 2017 suggesting that reservation for OBCs encourages separatism. Almost immediately the *sah sarkaryavahak,* Hosbole, who was present at the festival, issued a statement that, "The Sangh's opinion is very clear that the constitutionally provided reservations for the Scheduled Castes, Tribes, and Other Backward Castes should continue. It is still needed and it should be implemented entirely. This is the authorized view of the RSS." Vaidya also issued a clarification using very similar language. Finance Minister Jaitly in a March 15, 2016 statement in the Rajya Sabha on behalf of the Modi Government assured the members that, "The government policy is clear: reservation will continue."[18]

The RSS has committed itself to the continuation of the Modi Government and, despite private concerns about the reservation policy by some members, it will try to avoid doing anything publicly that could embarrass the BJP Government or complicate its electoral prospects.[19]

The debate over educational goals has intensified within the Sangh Parivar, a development linked to the very rapid growth of the RSS and its affiliates over the past two decades and the accommodation of groups with differing interests (for example, rural *vs.* urban on what skills to emphasize, and high and low castes regarding reservation). Influencing the debate is the growing support for the BJP among low-caste voters in rural areas.

It is very likely that the demographic composition of the RSS and its other affiliates is also shifting in this direction. These developments make it highly unlikely that the BJP or the RSS would seriously tinker with reservations.

Marching Towards Saffron Agenda

The Rashtriya Swayamsevak Sangh's (RSS) plan to creep into the education system is nothing new (Achin Vinaik, 2017). With the BJP gaining control at the federal level in 2014 landslide victory The saffronisation of education once again has started with new vigour. In 2015, the RSS affiliates announced that they want to set up a model school in every block of the country to check the growth of Convent schools and educational institutions run by missionaries.

"A look at our recent data suggests we have managed to establish an RSS model school in every district in Uttar Pradesh. Efforts in Bihar and Jharkhand have been commendable but we are sprucing up efforts in West Bengal and Tamil Nadu", said Ramendra Rai, who heads the Vidya Bharati Akhil Bharatiya Shikshan Sansthan.

According to an *Indian Express* report, teachers from the RSS-run Saraswati Shishu Mandirs (SSMs) could soon get sanction from the BJP Government in Madhya Pradesh to teach *pro bono* in government primary schools. The plan to rope in RSS teachers for government schools is expected to be implemented in 1,000 schools in a few months.

The RSS organisation's proposal to loan its teachers to nearby government primary schools has been welcomed by the education department.

"Though the idea is to focus on mathematics and language, the traditional weak spots, we will also introduce cultural activities, if permitted, that are common in SSMs", Madhya Bharat Chief of VBABSS Ramkumar Bhavsar told *The Indian Express*. The government has welcomed the idea given by the RSS schools' track record.

The BJP Government in the state had made 'surya namaskar'—adulation of the sun—mandatory in all schools, rising heckles of opposition parties and social organisations.

In March 2017, Uttar Pradesh Deputy Chief Minister Dinesh Sharma announced that implementation of Sanskrit Board in Uttar Pradesh education system will enlighten students ethically and therefore, develop their mindset. "Yoga Guru Baba Ramdev said that, Sanskrit Board should be built up. He also suggested for the inclusion of *Yoga* which will be introduced as a different subject other than physical education", Sharma told media. He further said the matter will be discussed with Chief Minister Yogi Adityanath to conclude, as the education system of the country needs a change. "People will get to know about Sanskrit language. These steps should have been taken earlier", he added.[20] Meanwhile in Gujarat, demanding an independent "State Sanskrit Education Board", the State wing of Sanskrit Bharati has launched a campaign for the "development and revival" of the ancient language in Gujarat.

Sanskrit Bharati, the RSS-affiliated organisation dedicated to the language, has launched a "21-point" signature campaign and roped in general public and Sanskrit experts and educationists in each district.

Every year, the students who score the highest in their districts in Classes 10 and 12 of the Rajasthan Board of Secondary Education are given cash rewards. This is only meant for girl students and was started in 2002. The award is named 'Indira Priyadarshini Puruskar Yojana'.

Now, the government has decided to do away with the former Prime Minister's name and call it 'Padmakshi Puruskar Yojana', reports *Hindustan Times*. The strange thing the award was first initiated to commemorate the birth anniversary of Indira Gandhi on November 19, and was started in 2010.

In fact, it is not just the name.

The award will be given on Basant Panchami every year. Padmakshi is another name for Goddess Saraswati, the deity associated with knowledge. Therefore, the Education Department has decided to organise the award ceremony on the day when Hindus celebrate Basant Panchami.

In the scheme, an award of Rs. 50,000 was given to Class 12 toppers and Rs. 40,000 to Class 10 district toppers in four categories: Scheduled Caste, Scheduled Tribe, Other Backward Class and

Minorities. Later, general category girls were included in the scheme and increased the award money.

In 2016, the Social Science textbook for Class VIII in schools of Rajasthan erased Jawharlal Nehru from the pages of history. It does not mention who India's first Prime Minister was.

The ruling party's attempt to saffronise education in the states ruled by the BJP is not a new thing at all.

"There's a growing clamour for giving more space to India's ancient past even if it means erasing "Islamic" medieval history. Even key figures like Mughal Emperor Akbar, famous for his religious tolerance, are at a risk of being effaced from history books across various states", notes a blog on rewriting of textbook history.

And Rajasthan has been a witness to this for a while now. The new textbooks for Class 10 and 12 introduced recently, has a passing reference to Mahatma Gandhi, no reference to Jawaharlal Nehru. Meanwhile, RSS ideologue Veer Savarkar occupies a large space.

To promote the idea of 'nationalism' and 'patriotism', the Class 10 book has allotted space to Veer Savarkar who has been described as a great revolutionary and a great patriot. Meanwhile, the textbook for class 11th Political Science says that Congress was a 'nurture baby' of the British, established by the capitalists and representatives of the upper middle class.

Business Universities in the state have included excerpts from the *Bhagavad Gita,* the *Ramayana,* the *Vedas,* in addition to concepts by thinkers like Kautilya, Swami Vivekananda and Mahatma Gandhi as part of its commerce and business administration courses.

On May 23, 2015, Rajasthan based 'Shiksha Ka Adhikar' organisation issued a note for the media alleging that the new textbooks issued by the Government of Rajasthan are weak than the current textbooks by every parameter of content, knowledge acquisition, pedagogy and scientific temper. The review revealed many errors and limitations from the pedagogical point of view. The experts expressed their anguish and amazement at these flaws and felt very strongly that these textbooks should not be taught for the coming session. They also felt the need to initiate a state level campaign and decided that a public interest litigation will be filed in the Rajasthan High Court. The review was conducted under the leadership of Prof. Apoorvanand of the Delhi University and Prof. Rajiv Gupta from the Rajasthan University.[20]

Future Plans

After making inroads into school education, the Rashtriya Swayamsevak Sangh (RSS) is looking to strengthen its grip on higher education. The RSS currently has a wing—Shiksha Bharati—that suggests policy decisions related to school education to the Central Government. The party is now looking to have a separate wing that will suggest policy decisions related to higher education institutions, both technical and non-technical.

According to RSS sources, the decision to set up a separate wing for higher education was taken up at a national teacher's conference organised in Delhi in March 2017.

The need for a "real nationalist narrative" focusing on the Indian perspective in higher education was deliberated upon by over 700 academicians, including the vice-chancellors of 51 universities, during a two-day workshop hosted by an RSS-affiliated body in Delhi in March 2017.

The lack of "Indian-ness in the educational system of the country has been pointed out by various commissions and the Supreme Court too has called for incorporating Indian views into it", said J. Nand Kumar, national convener of Prajna Pravah, which hosted the event. The participants of the event, including vice-chancellors (VCs) of 20 Central and 31 State universities, also interacted with RSS head Mohan Bhagwat.

"The exercise is not an alternative to the present educational system which is aping the West, but it is a real nationalist narrative to imbibe Bharatiya perspectives in it", Nandkumar said, quoting the RSS chief.

The participants also presented their suggestions about creating a non-governmental and autonomous academic ecosystem in education during interaction with Mohan Bhagwat.

"This 'Gyan Sangam' (event) is an effort to provide a platform to academicians working on Bharatiya perspectives in various academic disciplines and to work for their capacity building", Nandkumar said.

The event was divided into three parts in which themes such as cultural onslaught on educational system, intellectual colonisation, and resurgence of nationalism in higher educational institutions were discussed by the participants.

S. Gurumurthy spoke on cultural onslaught in a session chaired by Banaras Hindu University (BHU) V.C. Girish Chandra Tripathi.

J. Nandkumar said cultural onslaught on the education system is having a "poisonous" effect on the students and added that those who did not believe oneness of India were its example.

Prof. V.P. Nanda of Denver University presented a comparison of resurgence in nationalism in the East and the West.

The academicians also explored possibilities of imbibing Indian perspectives in subjects of art and culture, political science, management, pure sciences, journalism and mass communication, archaeology, law and economics among others.

Delhi University professor and convener of 'Gyan Sangam', Prakash Singh said that similar events will be held at state capitals.

He also emphasised that the initiative had nothing to do with the government and it was a move to bring about a change in the "mindset" of the people.

"When we will say something and point out shortcomings (in educational system) with evidence, it will have to be accepted", he said, adding that this initiative was going on even before the BJP dispensation assumed office at the Centre.

The event concluded with an address by Mohan Bhagwat.

It was also attended by Indian Council of Historical Research (ICHR) Chairman Sudharshan Rao and senior RSS functionaries Suresh Soni and Krishna Gopal.

The meeting was presided over by RSS chief Mohan Bhagwat, called for a focus on how to include a more 'nationalist narrative' and Indian perspective in higher education.[22]

The new education wing for higher education, when constituted, would advice the government on key policy decisions and construction of new buildings for institutions. However, no name has been chosen for the new wing.

"The responsibilities of the new wing will be carried out initially under the Sangh. We plan to assign a name to the wing later", said a source that is closely associated with the new initiative.

RSS leaders working in the education field have been conducting meetings with the VCs of various universities to chalk out a comprehensive plan with regard to the new wing. The ABVP, the student wing of the RSS, is also likely to be part of the plan.

Analysis

India is fast moving in the globalised economy and business culture. Globalisation, with its evolving and growing complexity in social stratification of nations, technology and education systems, has a potential to generate further polarisation and social economic division in society, that are likely to create discontent and social conflict. Thus, there is a nexus between ideology, the state and education reform globally.

The complex nexus between globalisation, ideology and education reforms—where, on the one hand, democratisation and progressive pedagogy is equated with equality, inclusion, equity, tolerance and human rights, while on the other hand globalisations perceived, by some at least, to be a brutalising force that is widening the gap between the rich and poor and bringing power domination and control by corporate bodies and world organisations. Hence, we need to continue to explore authentic democracy, social justice and cross-cultural values that genuinely promote a transforming pedagogy. We need to focus on the crucial issues at the centre of current and ongoing education reforms, if genuine culture of learning, and transforming, characterised by wisdom, compassion and intercultural understanding is to become a reality, rather than rhetoric.

In terms of debating the nation's past or portraying contemporary society through state produced textbooks, the RSS agenda may seem not very different from that of conservative governments elsewhere ; for them social science, especially history is intimately connected with inculcating national identity and patriotism (Nash Crabtree and Dunn).

The 'nation' is identified with dominant groups in society and only narratives that value the role of these groups positively are seen as patriotic. Patriotism in this version, also means extolling the virtues of one's own country over that of others and glossing over its negative phases. Ideological conflicts over the shape and content of history of civics textbooks invariably involved debates over the emphasis given to certain people-dominant groups *versus* women and minorities—or certain periods in history over others.

Nation building as depicted in historical narratives of the more recent school textbooks are characterised by new ideological basis and omissions. Both the Indianization of history textbooks and political motivated reforms in history curriculum and textbooks demonstrate a new dimension of political socialisation, and the nation building process currently taking place in the global culture.

As India becomes increasingly involved in the globalised economy of the 21st century, we can be sure that education will remain a crucial reproduce in the transition to adulthood and that it would become even more contentious and competitive over-time.

There are two related problems caused by current educational policy that have had important implications for social movements. The first is the poor quality of government schools when they do exist and second is the fact that it was not until the 1990s that India made a serious commitment to universal, compulsory education. Both of these factors created a situation in which the demand for education outstrips its supply by the state on the one hand, and on the other hand, education is unevenly distributed, such that it reproduced existing inequities among regions, genders, class, religious groups, and castes.

To get around the problems of quality, and reliability of schools parents often prefer to send their children to private schools. These schools themselves suffer from quality control issues and most are run as profit business. This makes the RSS schools an attractive alternative for those with limited resources. Unlike the government schools, the RSS schools actually have teachers who show up and teach as it happens in Christian missionary schools. These schools do not charge the high fees that other private schools do and they are able to provide an employment network to graduates through their connection to the larger Sangh Parivar. These services are made available precisely in those city neighbourhoods and villages that do not have adequate state provided education. For many parents, sending their children to these schools need not be an ideological choice. It is a way of maximizing existing opportunities for their children.

For the individual child, learning a skewed historical narrative, religious songs, and *yoga* hardly seems a high price to pay for the literacy and numeracy taught in these schools. For Indian society as a whole, that child's attendance at these schools rather than those run by the secular state and or a progressive secular missionaries does have enormous consequences. The relationship between schooling and the development of a particular national identity is an established part of the scholarship on nationalism mass. There are significant debates among scholars as to the mechanism(s) by which mass schooling and the initial achievement of literacy effects the adoption of a national identity, but that, the two are connected is undisputed.

What is interesting to note is that, even in the run up to the 2014 General Election, the education issues did not make waves in the press. The discourse of the average middle classes had charged. for those who live in rural areas, the critical issues were roads, water, electricity and jobs and to a lesser degree access to education. The possible reason for this is that religion and its role in society has always been a complicated subject in India. Although India is a secular state, religion has been used in politics when it suited a particular politician. However, in principle, religion was a matter of private sphere and very separate with regard to education. Nevertheless, the coming to power of the BJP led NDA II has shown that in India secularism is to date still a contested concept.

In essence, this shows that the BJP is more confident than even that it could push its nationalist agenda through the education portal. While issues pertaining to the 'Ram Mandir' at Ayodhya and the Uniform Civil Code might still be seen as divisive within society, there was little or no resistance to changes on the education front. The silence on this issue needs to be lifted and the debate on what has been happening to education system needs to be made public.

Concluding Remarks

The RSS and the Prime Minister Narendra Modi's policy in education is essentially ideological as they continue to stress on nation building, nationalism, patriotism, and global competitiveness. With this educational objectives in mind, Modi addressed leaders of the Vidya Bharati school system on February 12, 2016 and the Ekal Vidyalaya on May 17, 2017 advising them to come up with ways to provide job oriented skills that would make Indians more competitive in Indian and foreign job market.

On completion of the four years of the Modi Government, a meeting was organised on May 27-28, 2018 in New Delhi to discuss policy issues including education policy. Amit Shah along with five Cabinet Ministers met top functionaries of the RSS on Monday to deliberate upon various policies of the Modi government including the formulation of the much awaited education policy. RSS Joint General Secretary Krishna Gopal chaired the coordination meeting of the Sangh, its affiliates, the BJP and the government. This meeting was held over several rounds between the ministers and representatives of the Rashtriya Swayamsevak Sangh, Sewa Samooh (social work wing), Shiksha Samooh (education wing), Samajik Samooh (social work wing), and Vichar

Samooh (ideological issues wing). The BJP was represented by Amit Shah, Vinay Sahasrabuddhe, and General Secretary Ram Madhav and Ram Lal. The government represented by five Ministers, Jayawardhana Rathor, J.P. Nadda, Maneka Gandhi, Mahesh Sharma and Prakash Javdekar. The RSS was represented by the Sava Bahrain, Arogya Bharati, Vidya Bharati, Rashtriya Sevaka Samiti and Sanskar Bharati among others. Shiksha Samooh debated the education status and new education policy.

The Rashtriya Swayamsevak Sangh has always kept its eye on the long strategy. The RSS, which has greater say in influencing policy of the BJP Government, is for a "modern education policy" with sprinkling of "Indianisation" and "Spiritualization". All this shows that the RSS will engage its affiliates in not only school and higher education level but policy reform intervention will remain one of the core areas of intervention for reform in the future.

Notes

1. Khan, Shoeb (2018). "Government and Private Schools to observe *Saraswati Puja* on *Basanta Panchami*", *Times of India*, Jaipur, January 22, http://timesofindia.indiatimes.com/articleshow/46001385.cms accessed on August 21, 2018.
2. Bhardwaj, Ashutosh, "District officer in Mahasmund in Chhattisgarh bans use of 'Father in Missionary Schools", *Indian Express*, May 15, 2015. https//indianespress.com.india. Accessed on August 18, 2018.
3. Jain, Manish, Archana Mehendale, Rahul Mukhopadhyay, Padma M. Sarangapani, Christopher Winch (2018). *School Education in India: Market, State and Quality*, Taylor & Francis.
4. *Our Schools–Ekal Vidyala*, https://www.ekal.org/our-schools, accessed on August 21, 2018.
5. Barthwal, Harish Chandra (2015). *Rashtriya Swayamsewak Sangh: An Introduction*, Delhi: Suruchi Prakashan, Delhi.
6. Esteves, Sarto (2002). *Freedom to Build, not Destroy Attacks on Christians and their Institutions*, New Delhi: Media House.
7. *The Saffron Agenda in Education: An Expose*, Safdar Hashmi Memorial Trust, 2001, New Delhi.
8. Chandra, Bipan (2008). *India Since Independence*, Penguin, UK.
9. Guichard, Sylvie (2010). *The Construction of History and Nationalism in India: Textbooks, Controversies and Politic*, Routledge.
10. *Indian Express*, 28 July, 2016.
11. Ayyar, R.V. Vaidyanatha (2017). *History of Education Policymaking in India, 1947–2016*, Oxford University Press.

12. This writer attended its first conclave at Goa from December 19-21, 2014. The range of issue discussed was many and there were frank discussions among the participants.
13. *The Times of India,* September 21, 2015, RSS Chief Mohan Bhagwat pitches for review of reservation policy...https://timesofindia.indiatimes.com/india/RSS-chief...reservation.../ 49041309.cms accessed on August 22, 2018.
14. *The Times of India,* September 21, 2015, RSS Chief Mohan Bhagwat pitches for review of reservation policy...https://timesofindia.indiatimes.com/india/RSS
15. *A Compendium of RSS Resolution from 1950-2007,* New Delhi: Suruchi Prakashan, 2007.
16. VHP Website 'Youth', http//vhp.org. Accessed on August 21, 2018.
17. *Business Standard,* January 21, 2017, RSS propaganda chief calls for ending caste based reservations...https://www.business-standard.com/.../rss-propaganda-chief-calls-for-ending-caste-bas...) Accessed on August 21, 2018.
18. *The Hindu,* March 15, 2016, *No Move to Review Quota Policy,* Jaitely Assures MPs.
19. Chaube, Shibani Kinkar (2016), *The Idea of Nation and Its Future in India,* Taylor & Francis.
20. Safforonisation of Education, HuffPost India, https://www.huffingtonpost.in/news/ saffronisation-of-education/ accessed on August 21, 2018.
21. The other members were Devyani, Mamta Jaitly, Himanshu, and Mihir who reviewed the Hindi textbooks from class 1 to 8. Social Science books were analysed by Dr. Rajiv Gupta, Dr. Lad Kumari Jain, Rajendra Saiwal, Dr. Pramod Gauri and Prof. Apoorvanand, Kamal, Ketan, and Pramod reviewed Environmental Studies while the Mathematics textbooks were reviewed by Shri Ravi Kant. Komal Shrivastava and Dr. Shomna Dutta reviewed the Science textbooks.
22. RSS now looks to 'saffronise' higher edu-DNA India, www.dnaindia.com/india/report-rss-now-looks-to-saffronise-higher-edu-2428082. Accessed on August 21, 2018.

14

National Register of Citizens (NRC)

Politics of Migration, Religion, and National Security

Introduction

On July 30, 2018, India effectively striped 4 million people, majority of whom Muslims, of their citizenship in Assam. This was result of the identification process of illegal migrants through national register of citizens which started in 2015 in Assam. Of the 32.9 million applicants, the names of 28.9 million have been approved and included in the draft according to the India's Registrar-General.[1] The Assam exercise has become focal point of political debate in India. Political parties in India are formulating their respective positions on National Register of Citizens (NRC) with an eye on electoral gain. This has once again brought the issue of immigration into focus.

Migration is not a new phenomenon. From the antiquity, people have been moving from one place to another, sometimes in search of better opportunities, when they see some of their needs and desires are not adequately fulfilled in their present location, sometimes just to maintain the *status quo* when they see their present situation seems to be a declining one. However, the fear that any mass migration can alter a country's religious, ethnic, gender, age, and cultural landscape within a much shorter time than can birth, and death cycles has always haunted the natives and the state.[2] Demographic change through migration is relevant to the state power and national security. So, how does migration affect social cohesion? Are inter-religious and intercultural conflicts more likely to occur now-a-days? Migration is generally defined as permanent change of residence by crossing of specified administrative or political boundaries. The person who fulfil these two criteria are regarded as migrants. While internal migrations change in the place of residence from one administrative boundary to another within the same country, international migration is a move over a national boundary. Is the Assam exercise a prefect to more widespread dog-whistle signalling? Will such an exercise create a new group of stateless people in India? Will the Constitutional basis of citizenship change to that of religion? How do we tackle problem of illegal migrants? What are the implication of religion based demographic changes for national security? One related concern is to what extent have international standards concerning statelessness in the international human rights law framework been implemented in the Indian legal system and how could they be strengthened?

There has been legal and illegal migration from erstwhile East Pakistan (now Bangladesh) into Assam and other north-eastern states and even Bihar.[3] Indeed, India is facing huge illegal migration in its eastern areas. This has not only altered human numbers in some areas but also has profoundly affected the political power balance.

Implications of Migration

The study of migration is one of the major branches of demography. It is the third demographic component of population change along with fertility and mortality. Migration can change the size of the population and the other compositions like age, sex, language, religion etc. It brings both quantitative and qualitative changes in the socio-economic and political pattern of a region.

Migration is not just about movement of people; it is about the movement of their interests, values, politics, religion, and customs. In some cases, migration can create major national security challenges. Migration, the movement of people across international borders, is the third pillar of demographic change but is the only population driver that can change the composition of a state and community within months, weeks and or even years. Fertility and mortality look glacier in comparison.[4]

The ability of mass migration to change a country's *status quo* means that it has the potential to instigate conflict, or at least create divisions. This conflict, in turn, drives migration. Ours is a time of rapid and pronounced demographic change. The unleashing of 'jihadi' forces and international terrorism, to which are connected the drugs and arms and ammunition trafficking, have further complicated the issue. Together, the resultant movements of people have serious implications on socio-economic and political developments in any country.

Locating the Problem

During campaigning in India's 2014 Lok Sabha elections, Bharatiya Janata Party's (BJP) Prime Minister-designate Narendra Modi said that illegal immigrants from Bangladesh would have to leave the country if his party is voted into power. Since, the BJP did in fact win the elections, and with a record majority, how will Modi actually address the issue of illegal immigration? Many previous governments, including those of the BJP, have tried to deal with the issue, with very little success.

Amongst the initiatives adopted by the Indian Government for recognizing illegal immigrants from Bangladesh, the most publicized is the Illegal Migrant Determination Tribunal (IMDT), which was established by Parliament in 1983. It was designed especially for Assam State, where the issue of illegal immigration has long been a cause of social and ethnic tension. Unfortunately, the IMDT did not perform as expected. From its inception in 1983 through to the 2000s, the tribunal identified a mere 10,000 illegal immigrants, and deported only 1,400. Considering its poor performance, the Supreme Court of India struck down the law in 2005 and required that the Foreigners Act of 1946 be enforced throughout India to deport illegal immigrants from Bangladesh.

In 2015 work on National Register for Citizens (NCR) started.

What is the National Register for Citizens ?

During the Census of 1951, a national citizen register was created that contained the details of every person by village. The data included name, age, father's or husband's name, houses of holdings belonging to them, sources of livelihood and so on. These registers covered every person enumerated during the Census of 1951 and were kept in the office of deputy commissioners and sub-divisional officers as per the Centre's instructions issued in 1951. In the early 1962, these registers were transferred to the police.

Why was there a demand to update Assam in NRC?

Since Independence till 1971, when Bangladesh was created, Assam witnessed large scale migration from East Pakistan that became Bangladesh after the war. Soon after the war on March 19, 1972, a treaty for friendship, cooperation and peace was signed between India and Bangladesh. The migration of Bangladeshis into Assam continued. To bring this regular influx of immigrants to the notice of then Prime Minister, the All Assam Students Union submitted a memorandum to Indira Gandhi in 1980 seeking her "urgent attention" to the matter. Subsequently, parliament enacted the Illegal Migrants (Determination by Tribunal) Act, 1983. This Act made applicable only to Assam, was expected to identify and deport illegal migrants from the State. The people were not satisfied with the government's measures, and a massive state level student agitation started, spearheaded by All Assam Students, Union (AASU) and All Assam Gana Sangram Parishad (AAGSP) ultimately resulted in the Assam Accord signed on August 15, 1985 between AASU, AAGSP and the Central and State Governments.[5]

Who are included in the NRC?

Persons whose names appear in NRC 1951 or in any of the electoral rolls up to March 24, 1971, and their dependents are to be included in the current NRC. Persons who came to Assam on or after January 11, 1966 but before March 25, 1971, and registered themselves in keeping with the Centre's rules for foreigners registration, and who have not been declared as illegal migrants or foreigners by the competent authority could register. Foreigners, who came to Assam on or after March 25, 1971, are to be thereafter detected and expelled as per the law, apart from this, all Indian citizens including their children and descents who moved in Assam post March 24, 1971, were eligible for inclusion in the updated NRC, but "satisfactory" proof of residence in any part of the country (outside Assam) as on March 24, 1971 would have to be provided.

What happened to those whose names are not in the NRC 2018?

The July 30, 2018 NRC list is a draft and not the final one. The authorities say that people whose names are missing can still apply.

The period to file such claims is from August 30 to September 28. Applicants can call toll free numbers to enquire with their application receipt numbers. Those left out are not yet being labelled as "foreigners" or being sent to detention centres. However, only those applicants who had submitted their applications in 2015 will be considered.

Assam is the only state to have an NRC, first prepared in 1951 based on the census of that year.

Conceptual Framework

Types of Migration

In general, the field of migration study can be divided into two parts—internal migration and international migration. Internal migration is when people migrate within the same country or region, also known as 'in-migrant'. While the international migration is when people migrate from one country to another country, also termed as 'immigrant'. There is another category: legal migration and illegal migration.

The area from which a migrant departs is termed as 'area of origin' and the area at which he arrives is termed as 'area of destination'. When a large number of migrants depart from a common area of origin and arrive at a common area of destination during a particular period, is known as 'migration stream'.

Citizenship

The issue of citizenship in India is incredibly complex. Apart from the Constitution, there exists a cache of laws like the Foreigners' Act, 1946, the Passport Act, 1952, and the Citizenship Act of 1956. The rules are bizarre. Until 1986, every person born in India automatically became a citizen.

Then the rules were changed and until 2004, at least one parent had to be a citizen for a child to be given citizenship, after which it would be denied to her if one parent were an illegal immigrant. Then there is the Illegal Migrants (Detection by Tribunals) Act, 1983, that puts the onus of proving the illegality of a migrant on the complainant, while the Foreigners' Act requires the accused to prove his or her right to Indian citizenship.[6]

The National Register of Citizens (NRC) was the first attempt to enlist all *bona fide* citizens of India and was prepared after the Census of 1951. It included the names of all residents. At that time, Assam's population was only 8 million.

Who are the Illegal Migrants?

Unlike a refugee, an illegal migrant is a person who crosses an international boundary and without any valid document, enters into another country for carrying on any illegal or anti-social activities in that country or for other economic or political purposes. According to Section 2(b) of The Citizenship Act, 1955, an "illegal migrant" means a foreigner who has entered into India:

(i) Without a valid passport or other travel documents and such other document or authority as may be prescribed by or under any law in that behalf; or

(ii) With a valid passport or other travel documents and such other document or authority as may be prescribed by or under any law in that behalf but remains therein beyond the permitted period of time.

Magnitude of Migration in India

As observed by the Group of Ministers Report, illegal immigration from Bangladesh has led to demographic upheaval and generated serious communal, political, social, and economic tensions and conflicts in several areas of the North East of India. The most affected states are West Bengal, Assam, Meghalaya, Nagaland, Bihar, and Tripura, although migrants "have spread too far off states like Tamil Nadu, Maharashtra, Gujarat, Rajasthan, and Delhi." Although the exact figure is not known, it is estimated that there are about 15-20 million Bangladeshis staying illegally in India. The illegal migration of Bangladeshis in fact triggered the agitation by the All Assam Students Union (AASU) in 1979-85. Despite the Assam Accord of 1985, the issue remains unresolved to this day and the "silent demographic invasion" persists. Due to vote-bank politics, the motivation to block illegal migrants from Bangladesh is absent. The gravity and scope of threats arising out of illegal migration was highlighted by the then Governor of Assam, Lt. Gen. S.K. Sinha in his report.[7]

India currently has over 20 million (two crore) illegal migrants. Since 1992, their numbers have increased by 67 per cent at a yearly growth rate of 4.8 per cent. West Bengal has close to 6.4 million illegal immigrants. In 2004, the Union Minister of State for Home told Parliament that the country had 1.2 crore illegal immigrants.

At present out of total 27 districts of Assam, the districts that have been facing mostly the crucial problem of illegal migration are—Dhubri, Goalpara, Barpeta, Morigaon, Nagaon, Dhemaji, Cachar, Karimganj and Hailakandi. Seven bordering districts of Assam have registered a growth of 36 per cent, affecting the electoral fortunes in 73 Assembly constituencies. Three of these districts have more than 75 per cent Muslims, hailing mostly from Bangladesh.[8] This has also been corroborated by statement by the Army Chief, General Bipin Rawat, when he argued that the influx of Bangladeshi migrants had substantially altered the demography of Assam and other states in the North East. While Hindu population in the State went up by 41.8 per cent, Muslims' growth leaped by 77.42 per cent. Consequently, Hindus recorded a 3 per cent increase in 18 Assembly constituencies, whereas Muslims registered a 23 per cent surge in 40 Assembly constituencies. In eight districts, Muslims have already formed a majority. The AIUDF, a party that draws its support from illegal migrants, has grown at a pace of 71 per cent, while the BJP, branded as a Hindu party, has gained a miserly rise of 4 per cent in its cadre.

Assam is not the only state in the North-East faced with this serious problem. Arunachal Pradesh has still to sort out the problem of the Chakmas. In Mizoram too, the presence of Chakmas from Bangladesh has become a major political issue. Both the ruling and the opposition parties vie with each other to score political points against each other on the Chakmas issue. Flow of refugees and economic migrants from Bangladesh has made Tripura a Bengali majority state, leaving its indigenous tribes feeling marginalised.

The more enterprising migrants have fanned out in all corners of India including Delhi (one million), Bihar (one million), Kerala (2.8 million), Madhya Pradesh (1.5 million), Maharashtra (3 million) and Karnataka (2.3 million). Colluding political parties have already started providing them legitimacy to vote.

The problem of illegal immigration from Bangladesh into

Assam and the other states of North-East India has been studied and analysed in recent years by a good number of social thinkers (Vergese et al., 1980; Goswami and Gogoi, 1984; Hazarika, 1992; Weiner, 1993; Taher, 1997; Saikia, 2001; Bezbarua, 2001, Bhuyan, 2001; Deka, 2010) and from their studies the depth and magnitude of the said problem can be well understood.

Historical Background of Migration

The British developed the tea industry in Assam. The Assamese people living mostly in Upper Assam and cultivating one crop per year were not interested in working as labour in the tea gardens. Therefore, the British encouraged Bengali Muslim peasants from present Bangladesh to move into Lower Assam for putting virgin land under cultivation. This set in motion a movement pattern which despite changed conditions, has been continuing to this day.

After the partition of Bengal in 1905, the over-populated Muslim peasantry from East Bengal started crossing over to the fertile lands of thinly populated Brahmaputra and Surma valleys in the North East corner of India. The formation of the All India Muslim League in Dhaka in 1906 encouraged the migration to increase the Muslim population in Assam for political reasons. The arrival of immigrants continued even after the creation of Bangladesh due to ethnic persecution of minorities.[9]

The unrelenting influx of illegal migrants from East Pakistan/ Bangladesh into Assam and the consequent perceptible change in the demographic pattern of the State has been a matter of concern. It poses a serious threat both to the identity of the Assamese people and to our national security. It threatens to reduce the Assamese people to a minority in their own State, as happened in Tripura and Sikkim. Migration from Bangladesh to the North East region of India has been continuous throughout the twentieth century due to the reason of historical links, geographical and physical proximity. The better employment opportunities and availability of fertile agricultural land in Assam act as a pull factor while the poverty, subsistence living, ravages caused by floods and other natural calamities in Bangladesh act as push factors.

Impact of Illegal Migration

Illegal migration has generated a host of destabilizing political, social, economic, ethnic and communal tensions. Politically, the Bangladeshi migrants are in a position to influence the results of the elections in a large number of constituencies in the North East (about 32% of the constituencies in Assam). Economically, increased pressure on land, resulting in depletion of forest wealth, undercutting of wages of unskilled jobs, forcible occupation of Government land by the migrants and a host of other such issues, generate a ripple effect in the entire North East.

There is a tendency to view illegal migration into Assam as a regional matter, affecting only the people of Assam. Its more dangerous dimension of greatly undermining our national security is ignored. The long cherished design of Greater East Pakistan/ Bangladesh, making inroads into the strategic land link of Assam with the rest of the country, can lead to severing the entire land mass of the North East, with all its rich resources, from the rest of the country.

Large-scale illegal infiltration has already reduced the indigenous people of Tripura into minority and is fast changing the demographic composition of more and more areas of Assam in their favour and is also aggravating the unemployment problem and tensions and conflicts over possession of unchanging land area, resulting in many agitation and law and order situations.[10]

This will have disastrous strategic and economic consequences.

- **Community tension**: The Commission on Integration and Cohesion found that tension usually exist with the presence of high levels of migration combine with other forms of social exclusion like poverty, poor housing etc.
- **Economic consequences**: Immigration has increased pressure on the part of state government, as the government has to increase the expenditure on education and health facilities to the immigrants.
- **Displacing native workers**: There is a fear particularly during a recession that immigrants take jobs, which would otherwise go to local people.
- **Decreases wage level with the increase of population**: Illegal immigrants in every year have been adding a good

number of people in Assam. It is one of the main reasons of population explosion. Due to this, there is a possibility of decreasing wage level.

- **Political consequences**: The failure of government to respond the issue of illegal migration led to the agitation by the Assamese under the leadership of All Assam Gana Sangram Parishad (AAGSP) and All Assam Student's Union (AASU). Assam witnessed governmental instability, sustained civil disobedience campaigns and worst cases of ethnic violence. Assam accord was the result of this agitation.
- **Illegal voters**: Most of the Bangladeshi immigrants have their names enlisted in the voting list illegally, thereby claiming themselves as citizens of the state. The immigrant's population act as a vote bank for the political parties in Assam. The recent initiative NRC (National Register of Citizens) is meant for the detection of illegal Bangladeshi migrants. However, success of such initiative will depend on the strong political will.

Discussion

In the contemporary global system, no state can act on illegal immigration unilaterally. Just because one state decides that a person is a citizen of another country, the other country is not obligated to accept that determination. One way in which governments act on deportation is to sign bilateral agreements for the readmission of nationals of the relevant country. Not only is there no such agreement between India and Bangladesh, by all indications India has ever approached the subject of deportation with Bangladesh.

The security connection has internal as well as external dimensions, both causational and consequential linkages. The external dimensions are even more serious than the internal dimensions. Out of the 29 States that constitute the Indian Union 17 have international borders. In the North East, 98 per cent of the border is international border. During the colonial period, the British policy in the peripheral areas was dictated by the requirements of security from external threats. The division of the country, especially the division of Bengal and the creation of East

Pakistan is responsible for the many cross-border migrations. It is directly responsible for the huge inflow of migrants from East Pakistan (Bangladesh). The issue of illegal migrants is one of the major issues responsible for the tension in bilateral relations between India and Bangladesh. Many senior Bangladeshi political leaders have openly talked about India's North East to provide living space to ease its population pressure. Moreover, India-locked Bangladesh feels threatened by India's size and its military and economic power.

Even after its creation in 1971, successive governments in Bangladesh have continued the Pakistan policy of supporting subversive and secessionist forces in the North East. One cannot deny the ground reality that anti-India sentiments today are no less strong in Bangladesh than in Pakistan. The growing Talibanisation of Bangladesh is a matter of great concern. Its collaboration with the ISI for spreading subversion in the North East and its support to the *Jehadi* forces, including *Al-Qaeda,* cannot be ignored. Bangladesh has undergone a big political and social transformation over the past three decades. Islamic nationalism has replaced Bengali nationalism, architect ideology of the creation of Bangladesh.

The Task Force on Internal Security in a report in 2002 noted with concern the spread of the ISI network in the Siliguri Corridor, an area that is so crucial for the security of the North East. Large-scale illegal immigration from East Pakistan/Bangladesh over several decades has been altering the demographic complexion of the states in West Bengal and the states in the North East. The many ethnic insurgencies flourishing in the North East have developed networking of the *jehadi* forces.

All these developments should have raised alarm bells in India. But unfortunately, the policy-makers have continued in a state of denial. It would be suicidal to ignore the rapid growth of Islamic fundamentalism in our neighbourhood; but it also needs to be stated that it would be equally dangerous to twist the facts in such a way to give them a religious colour to play communal politics. Doing so would be doing what the *jehadi* forces have not succeeded in doing so far, that is, to radicalise the Indian Muslims and build a strong base of the *jehadi* forces in India.[11]

Migrations and ethnic factors have further complicated the relations between India and its neighbouring countries. The faith based demographic factor plays a crucial role when viewed in this context.

In respect of cross-border migrations, the dimensions of the problem have been even larger. Ever since the partition of the country, according to some estimates, about 35 million people have been involved in cross-border movement in search of security of life, honour and property, and sometimes to escape from religious prosecution and other forms of discrimination. War and civil strife are other factors that have resulted in large-scale migrations. Economic hardships, a desire for ethnic, racial, ideological and religious homogeneity have also driven people to leave their homes and migrate to the neighbouring countries.

The unleashing of *'jehādi'* forces and international terrorism, to which are connected the drugs, arms and ammunition trafficking, have further complicated the issue. Together, the resultant movements of people have serious security implications. The security threat from these migrations has seriously undermined the bilateral relations and inter-state cooperation among countries in South Asia. It is not possible to understand the dynamics of the relationship between these countries without understanding the nature of movements. They affect very strongly on both internal politics and foreign policy.

Military threats are no doubt important and cannot be ignored, but equally important are non-military threats. The epicentres of threats could be in environmental, demographic, ecological, and economic domains. They get more serious and complicated when linked to internal displacements and external migrations. However, it is not possible to appreciate the seriousness of the situation without understanding the political dimension.

Security is a complex construct. Threat to national security can be interpreted in many ways. It is an action of sequence of events that could threaten the quality of life for its citizens, or it could significantly narrow the range of policy choices available to the government. Illegal migration causes politicisation of the issues leading to ethnic and religious conflicts in the host country with their natural fall-out on the bilateral relations. Drugs, guns and international terrorism coupled with growing corruption and criminalisation of politics convert this already volatile mix into a dangerous brew, which seriously impacts on India's national security.[12]

Many of the security problems that are viewed as political problems have demographic roots. Policy interventions that are proposed and implemented with the intention of dealing with the demographic problem often result in distinctly political consequences. The centrality of India, both in terms of geography and political development, in South Asia, further underlines the importance of demographic factor for India's national security. The paradox, however, is that while political rhetoric concerning immigrants and refugees has increased, political will to take practical measures to check infiltration of illegal immigrants has in fact decreased.

Population pressures can lead to conflicts in a number of ways: first, because of population pressure on resources, that may be already scarce, leading to expansionist tendencies; second, when the clandestine population movement affects the demographic balance of the host region to the detriment of the interest of the local political elite, the latter are forced to enter into a relationship with the country of origin of the migrants.[13]

Of all kinds of factors impinging upon politics, however, the most complex are the ones having religious and ethno-nationalistic roots. The inter-state conflicts rooted in ethnic and religious discords are the most intractable and most violence-prone of all the issues relating to international conflicts, because they draw their sustenance from human emotions, which can often be irrational. Most of the migrations from the neighbouring countries have ethno-nationalistic and religious roots.

Suggestions

The Central Government should appoint a national immigration commission to frame a national migration policy and a national refugee policy. The commission should examine ways of strengthening the Foreigners Act, 1946, as well as feasibility of identity cards for both citizens and non-citizens and work permits for migrants. Border fencing in Assam must be completed forthwith on a war footing. The existing Border Security Force posts and the BSF water wing should be strengthened. Improved surveillance and effective river patrolling is essential. An efficient network of police and revenue intelligence needs to be built up. Officer in charge of the local police posts should be made responsible for the detection of illegal migrants. His annual assessment report should contain a separate column about his performance in this regard. The Police Station should have a separate register for recording information about illegal migrants, the routes through which they infiltrate, the places of shelter, and employment.

It must be recognised that there is no way the Indian Government can forcibly send away the large number of illegal immigrants who are already here, if the Bangladesh government refuses to recognise them as their citizens and accept them into Bangladesh. In this situation, the only practical solution is to follow a strategy of strong physical and legal measures to ensure complete stoppage of any future inflow of illegal migrants, and to extend the government control over those who are already here. The suggestion of giving work permits based on length of their stay and suitability to those already here deserves serious consideration. The internal controls include raising legal barriers to their employment and making their stay in the host state more difficult. Anyone giving shelter or employment to the unregistered illegal immigrant should lose his or her work permit in addition to other legal punishments.

Presence of large number of stateless people is threat to any nation. Although India is not a state party to the key UN Conventions on Statelessness, it is bound to other international conventions, which creates obligations for India to cooperate in its prevention and reduction of the phenomenon. So India's nationality laws ought to be improved to bring it in line with the international legal framework on statelessness.[14] Without positive action by the State to change the discriminatory nationality laws, statelessness will continue being passed on from one generation to the next. Thus, it should be in the interest of India to accede to the UN Stateless Conventions and change its Citizenship laws as provided.

Conclusion

In country after country, the topic of immigration is provoking passionate debates over national identity, state sovereignty and territorial integrity. In the beginning of the twenty first century, it was prevalent thinking that coming times would herald peace, freedom, and prosperity. But during the last 15 years, this outlook has changed dramatically. India has witnessed increased illegal migration particularly in the north-eastern parts. A deep analysis of the problem shows that the issue is of international nature and that adds to its complexity. Evidently, any solution to the issue involves a two-pronged strategy: one, deporting the already existing illegal migrant's, and two, braining such cross border immigration to an end. Both are daunting exercises. As far as the deportation of the illegal immigrants is concerned, it entails a massive, political, social, and economic exercise. Also one major complication in the issue is that Bangladesh is yet to officially acknowledge that illegal immigrants are its people. Without such acknowledgement, it will be impossible for India to deport them back to Bangladesh.

The problem of illegal migrants in the North East and particularly in Assam is likely to increase due to climate change "refugees" from across the borders. The stress of changes in the environment will further weaken marginal states. India has neglected threats posed by climate change to our national security. On the whole, distress migration as well as illegal migration in Assam and other parts of North East India creates serious problems with far reaching implications.[15]

The Constitution of India provides for inclusive principle of citizenship by birth than by blood or decent. The Constitution strengthened this progressive impulse with universal and equal citizenship, the most appropriate conception for a plural society. From the mid-1980s after the Assam Accord the idea of citizenship by descent started creeping into the law on citizenship, diluting the shift away from the birth-based principle, which is a major constitutional deviation. If the law concerning citizenship does not remain religion neutral, the constitutional idea of citizenship will be dealt a bloody blow.[16] A rights-based approach, girded by law, holding Article 21 high, guided by common sense and sympathy, not abuse and prejudice, must win the day. This is potentially a humanitarian crisis and must be dealt accordingly. Amidst this larger debate, the fate of illegal migrants remains undetermined and likely to remain for a long time.

Notes

1. *The Times of India*, August 1, 2018.
2. Huynh, Truong Huy (2013). *Migration: Practices, Challenges and Impact*, Nova Science Publishers Incorporated.

3. Bhattacharyya, Hiranya (2018). *Operation Lebensraum: Illegal Migration from Bangladesh,* Bloomsbury Publishing.
4. Borjas, George J. (2014). *Immigration Economics,* Harvard University Press.
5. *The Times of India,* August 1, 2018.
6. Shamshad, Rizwana (2017). *Bangladeshi Migrants in India: Foreigners, Refugees, or Infiltrators?* Oxford University Press.
7. *See* Group of Ministers Report on Reforming the National Security System, Government of India, Chapter II, p. 6, para 2.35.
8. Bhushan, Amar (2018). "Former Special Secretary, Research and Analysis Wing", *New Indian Express,* March 10.
9. Hazariak, S. (1994). *Strangers in the Mist,* Penguin Books.
10. The Migration Conference (2017). Proceeding compiled by Fethiye Tilbe, Elif Skender, Ibrahim Skirkeci, London: Transnational Press.
11. Marwah, Ved, IPS (Retd.) (2010). *Demographic Imbalance and Implications on National Security—A Management Challenge for India,* United Services Institution of India.
12. Pickering, Sharon and Julie Ham (2017). *The Routledge Handbook on Crime and International Migration,* Routledge.
13. Ghosh, Partha S. (2016). *Migrants, Refugees and the Stateless in South Asia,* Sage Publishing India.
14. Ghosh, Partha S. (2016). *Migrants, Refugees and the Stateless in South Asia,* Thousand Oaks, California: Sage Publications.
15. Brauch, Hans Günter, Navnita Chadha Behera, Patricia Kameri-Mbote, John Grin, Úrsula Oswald Spring, Béchir Chourou, Czeslaw Mesjasz and Heinz Krummenacher, (2009). *Facing Global Environmental Change: Environmental, Human, Energy, Food, Health and Water Security Concepts,* Springer Science & Business Media.
16. Jayal, Neeraj Gopal (2018). "If Hindus are natural citizens, it is a blow to India's idea of citizenship", New Delhi: *Times of India,* August 5.

PART V
CONCLUSIONS

Hindustan belongs to all those who are born and bred and who have no other country to look to. Therefore, it belongs to Parsis, Jews, to Indian Christians, Muslims and other non-Hindus as much as to Hindus... Religion is a personal matter, which should have no place in politics.

—*Mahatma Gandhi, India of My Dreams*
(fourth reprint compiled by R.K. Prabhu)
Navjivan Publishing House, Ahmedabad,
1992 [1947] pp. 344.

15
Conclusions

India of twenty-first century is radically different from that of the past. India is now a remarkably globalised nation and on track to become world's largest economy (Alyasa Ayers, 2018). It was in the mid-1990s that India embraced the liberalisation, privatisation, and globalisation. Now, in quarter of century after liberalisation, a new system has grown in India: the Billionaire Raj.[1] The rise of India's billionaires mirrored changes that had swept through the world economy over recent decades, bringing with them new anxieties about inequality, uncertainties, identity crisis, and suppression of religious freedom in the name of combating terror. The benefits of the economic boom have also undeniably been shared unevenly, with the greatest portion of India's new prosperity flowing to its top one per cent, or more specifically, the top fraction of the one per cent. The richest one per cent own fifty eight per cent of wealth, one of the world's starkest gaps, up from thirty nine per cent at the start of the decade.[2] Meanwhile, the bottom half of the country owned a paltry four per cent. Modern India looks like an economy in the Latin America, with a weak social safetynet and yawning inequality. The primary concern is that the illusions generated by distorted perceptions of prosperity and rising majoritarianism nationalism may prevent India from bringing social deprivations in political focus and lose sight of human rights including that of religious freedom.

Contours of Religious Freedom

India is drifting on populism path. Indian identity began a new phase with the new century. Its salience and substance in this phase are being shaped by India's new vulnerability to growing threat of ethnic conflict and by a new turn to religious majoritarianism.

The Ramjanmabhumi temple movement that led to demolition of Babri Masjid on December 6, 1992, subsequent riots throughout the country particularly 'terror' acts in Mumbai and trans border terror attack 26/11, 2008 on financial capital Mumbai awakened India to the new vulnerability and identity crisis. This vulnerability is central to how Indians define themselves in the new phase in the evolution of their national identity. The rising tide of populism in the name of a perceived majority has propelled a new infatuation with strongman rule that was apparent particularly prominently during the 2014 Lok Sabha election campaigns and subsequent rise of Narendra Modi. There is a marked increase in the insertion and assertiveness of religion in public life (Hauss, 2018). There is marked increase in vigilantism and violence against minorities as well as other dissenting voices.[3] Religious freedom is now at the heart of India's great debate.

Is India inching towards a *Hindu Rashtra?* Too early to decide. However, this raises some core questions whose answers must be sought. They are: What is the role and place of freedom of religion in the projection and promotion of India as a super power? What happens to freedom of religion in India with *Hindutva* forces at the helm of the governance? How enduring is the turning point in Indian politics that his victory has affected? Will there be a point of return? These questions arise with special urgency in India today. In this concluding chapter, we shall summarise the religious freedom in contemporary India and the object of the saffron agenda.

Before we go further, I would like to apprise readers, very briefly, about global scenario and the need for religious freedom in the twenty first century.

Several researches have indicated that there are linkages between religious freedom and other human goods (Hertz, 2014). That positive contribution of religious freedom to democracy, civil liberties, press autonomy, women's status, societal peace, and economic development and even health services as a lynchpin of human progress and thriving societies. As such protecting the freedom of conscience, belief and practice is the best perhaps the only means of navigating the crucible of the twenty first century; learning to live with differences. In an age of explosive religiosity and pervasive pluralism, religious freedom is more vital than ever.

Despite such good benefits of freedom of religion, the twenty first century globalised world is witnessing growing conservatism and fundamentalism with hatred and rise of religion-based extremism as one like ISIS in Iraq and Syria. Since 9/11, religion has belatedly become a major focus in security circles, yet rarely in ways that put religious freedom *per se* into the foreground. All these have made freedom of religion or belief one of the most complex fundamental human rights.

In spite of UN recognition of religious freedom as a universal human right, only a minority of people today enjoy the kind of liberties of conscience and belief called for in International Covenants. According to a massive study by the Pew Forum in Religion and Public Life, some 70 per cent of the world's people live in countries with very high restrictions on religion from either government policies or social hostilities. Religious believers and communities routinely find themselves facing serious repercussions from practicing their religion, including fines, destruction of property and violence.[4] Fundamental political rights and civil freedoms, such as the freedom of speech and expression, association and peaceful assembly, and religion or belief are often violated in many countries of the world.

During recent decades, religion once consigned to the so-called private sphere, has moved into the political arena. Since the 2000s, religion and religio-political forces have become potent influences in the domestic politics of many countries. The growing importance of religion as a marker of identity and a tool of political mobilization is reshaping the political landscape in an unprecedented manner.[5]

Many countries have introduced laws restricting freedom of religion in contravention of the International Conventions and Treaties. This problem arises from the understanding that international law and international practice in human rights should be considered as norms and principles, rather than norms and rules. This is the realisation of fundamental principles in human rights and value approach. Without accepting such approach, which considers principles and values of human rights at the legislative level, it is impossible to provide basic rights and fundamental human freedoms and protect them from undue restriction by the state. Why, despite having ratified international agreements on human rights (pacts, conventions etc.) many member states' national legislation practically does not align with law enforcement or rights protection in practice, even in the judiciary.

In the face of such trends, it is clear that the fight against religious intolerance and discrimination must be a key political priority for the international community, and in particular the UN and its Human Rights Council.

The main UN global policy framework for combating intolerance, stigmatisation, discrimination, incitement to violence and violence against persons based on religion or belief is set down in Council resolution 16/18. Resolution 16/18 was adopted with much fanfare in March 2011 and hailed by stakeholders from all religions and faiths as a turning point in international efforts to confront religious intolerance together to agree a common, consensus-based approach and practical plan of action.[6]

However, rather than working together to implement the 16/18 Action Plan, states have returned to pre-2011 arguments over the nature of the problem, the correct role of the international community, and whether the solution to intolerance lies in strengthening the enjoyment of fundamental human rights or in setting clearer limits thereon.

Major challenges are emerging in the face of increasing manifestations of hatred, intolerance, and violence based upon extremism. Religious extremism may, in some cases, lead to situations that are difficult to control, even composing the right to peace.

Faster communication and transport have made spread of ideas much easier in a globalized world. Due to Internet, Facebook, Twitter, WhatsApp, mobile phones etc., today religious ideas travel much faster than few decades earlier. This has raised opportunities and challenges in protecting religious freedom. Rise of populism, growing terrorism, fundamentalism, and insecure feeling has affected religious freedom in number of ways. The global rise of populists poses a dangerous threat to human rights. The supporters of populism claiming to speak for "the people", treat rights as an impediment to their conception of the majority will, a needless obstacle to defending the nation from perceived threats and evils. Instead of accepting that rights protect everyone, they encourage people to adopt the dangerous belief that they will never need their rights against an overreaching government claiming to act in their name.

The appeal of the populists has grown with mounting public discontent over the *status quo*. Many people feel left behind by technological change, the global economy, and growing inequality. Horrific incidents of terrorism generate apprehension and fear. Some are uneasy with societies that have become more ethnically, religiously, and racially diverse. There is an increasing sense that governments and the elite ignore public concerns.

In this cauldron of discontent, certain politicians are flourishing and even gaining power by portraying rights as protecting only the terrorist suspect or the asylum seeker at the expense of the safety, economic welfare, and cultural preferences of the presumed majority. However, if these voices of intolerance prevail, the world risks entering a dark era. When populists treat rights as an obstacle to their vision of the majority will, it is only a matter of time before they turn on those who disagree with their agenda.[7] Such claims of unfettered majoritarianism, and the attacks on the checks and balances that constrain governmental power, are perhaps the greatest danger today to the future of democracy.

The rising tide of populism in the name of a perceived majority has paralleled a new infatuation with strongman rule. In such cases, the majority thinking seems to go, why not embrace the autocrat who shows no qualms about asserting his "majoritarian" vision—self-serving as it may be—and subjugating those who disagree.

India largely respects diversity and freedom of religion, which are mentioned in the Constitution. However, since mid-2000s, when the *Hindutva* (not to be mistaken with Hinduism) conservative forces renewed its campaign against human rights, religious freedom is under stress in India. After the 2014 election, victory of the Bharatiya Janata Party (BJP), under the leadership of Narendra Modi, there has been a climate of rising Hindu nationalism. This has in turn seen the promotion of an increasingly exclusionary environment, reflected in the advancement of policies and legislation—such as more stringent cow protection laws or changes in educational curriculum and so on. The BJP ruled Jharkhand state introduced anti-conversion law in 2017 and other states are interpreting existing laws to put barrier on freedom to choose a religion .

According to 2017 report of the Minority Rights Group, the failure of authorities to prevent or investigate attacks against religious minorities has created a climate of impunity, which, unless urgently addressed, is likely to encourage continued attacks. Consequently, the government must ensure existing legislation protecting the rights of all religious communities are enforced, and in some cases, strengthened, with the full commitment of police, judiciary, and other actors.

The government's continuing failure to rein in militant groups, combined with inflammatory remarks made by some BJP leaders, has contributed to the impression that leaders are indifferent to growing intolerance. The International Religious Freedom Report for 2016 (IRFR) released by the US Secretary of State said: "There was an increase (during 2016) in violent incidents by cow protection groups against mostly Muslim victims, including killings, mob violence, assaults, and intimidation".[8]

A new class of religious elites has emerged, stranding the social and political domain with the political class in the provision of services that some social actor consider important in navigating the affairs of state. Normally focus on armed non-state actors typically situates them in the context of internal security in India and religious groups belonging to majority religion are not considered threat to internal security. Since 2014, a phenomena of growing attacks on minorities by non-state actors in India has emerged as a cause of concern among the civil society worldwide. The database on such groups is limited.

The shift in method, from mass violence to low intensity individualised ones, being perhaps a deliberate strategy by those behind the violence to at once avoid too much public scrutiny, whilst also ensuring that the minorities are constantly under attack. Violent attacks on minorities in the name of cow protection, love *jihad, dharmantarana* using allurement, *Vandematram* singing, Saraswati *vandana* etc. are becoming common phenomena in the BJP ruled states.

Violence in the name of cow has become more common, covering larger areas of India (Milli Gazett, 2017). Emboldened by an ascendant Hindu nationalist movement, coupled with a controversial government ban on cattle slaughter, so-called cow-vigilante groups have been carrying out a ruthless form of mob justice, summarily executing those suspected of killing, trading, or consuming beef. India's embattled minorities, particularly Muslims, have endured the most of the violence (Amar Diwakar, *New Republic*, 2017).

These cases would not have been so frequent if it were not for the atmosphere of hate and suspicion created through a sustained political campaign and propaganda against Muslims (Apoorvanand, 2017). The strategic silence of BJP government works like unspoken approval to carry out the violent attacks. By allowing mob violence to continue unchecked, the ultra *Hindutva* Right boosts its image as the lone protector of Hindu religion and culture in India. These attacks are not spontaneous expressions of mob anger, they are the product of systematic incitement to violence and the consequence of long years of propaganda.

During last two decades, the freedom of religions has become one of the key issues attracting public attention. India after 2014 is radically different from that of the past and the influence of the RSS on the government is clearly visible. The RSS is no longer a political pariah perpetually operating under the threat of another ban, it is more willing to speak out, and be transparent. The rapid growth of its affiliate groups, penetrating almost all areas of society is awesome. Moreover, most importantly the RSS has emerged as key actor that can influence the public policy process in India today (Andersen and Damle, 2018).

RSS Modified

Under the leadership of *sarsanghchalak* Mohan Bhagwat, the RSS is changing and has become more powerful. The RSS has distanced itself from Guru Golwalkar's theory that Muslims are 'internal enemy' of India. It now says that all those born in India are Hindus and even Muslims and Christians can join the RSS. However, the RSS not changed its stand on inter-religious marriage (Hindu woman and Muslim man), *ghar wapsi*, cow protection and more importantly it is not in favour of granting any Indian right to choose his/her religion. The RSS is in favour of introducing stringent measures to check religious conversion.

Today, the Rashtriya Swayamsevak Sangh (RSS) is powerful and changing. Never before had the Sangh *karykartas* worked so hard and so enthusiastically on behalf of its political affiliate—the BJP—as they did during the 2014 Lok Sabha elections. The Prime Minister Narendra Modi comes from the RSS *Pracharak* background; the Vice-President is an RSS member while the

President is an RSS sympathizer. The BJP rules some 21 states where some two-third of India's population live. The RSS has made major gains in areas of the country where it had been weak (the north-east and the south).

Three speeches: one by the RSS chief Mohan Bhagwat at Vigyan Bhavan on September 17, 2018, another one also by Bhagwat on September 30, 2017 Vijayadashmi, and the third one by the Prime Minister Naredra Modi on August 15, 2018 from the Red Ford on the Independence Day; taken together gives ample indication of changes that are in the offering and the ones which are going to impact freedom of religion and belief in India.

During the three-day conclave (17-19 September, 2018), "Future of Bharat: An RSS Perspective", the RSS chief Mohan Bhagwat touched upon number of issues ranging from homosexuality to religious conversion, to Article 370, to cow protection.

Mohan Bhagwat said that for the RSS politics of quota is problem, not reservations. He pitched for cow protection but disapproved violence. Bhagwat emphasized that Articles 370 and 35-A must go. Bhagwat advised Ram Mandir be built at the earliest. He clarified that the RSS is not opposed to English. In addition, most importantly raising the issue of freedom to choose, Bhagwat asked, "What is the need for conversion?", thus making clear that anti-conversion laws are likely to be introduced in the future. Bhagwat favoured the Uniform Civil Code (UCC) and a national population policy. The RSS chief said the organization agrees with the Supreme Court, that homosexuality is not a crime and that the LGBTQ community is a part of society and should not be made to feel isolated. This is a marked different stand than earlier.

Speaking on Hinduism, Bhagwat said, "*Hindutva,* Hinduness and Hinduism are wrong words because 'ism' is a complex word. All Indians are Hindus by identity. *Hindutva* is the balance between all religions. A Hindu's true belief is unity. No one is an outsider in India." On cow protection issue Bhagwat said, "No one should take law in their hands to protect cow....The society needs to be made aware. Only then cows will be protected and the country would benefit. Cow protection should definitely happen. But it will not happen only through a law." Speaking on reservation, Bhagwat said, "RSS completely supports the reservation given by the Constitution to remove social stigmas. The decision regarding reservation continuity has to be taken by those to whom reservation has been granted. Whenever they feel it is not necessary, they will decide."

On several contentious issues, he was upfront. On building Ram Temple issue Bhagwat categorically stated that "the construction of a Ram temple in Ayodhya should start at the earliest. It will help end tension between Hindus and Muslims. If the temple is built in a harmonious way, then there will be no more pointing of fingers at Muslims." He also talked about Article 370 and Article 35A, on gender equality and on the elimination of Section 377. He spoke at length on the participation of women in the RSS and its affiliates, reservations for SCs, STs and OBCs, deplored lynching in the name of cow protection and at the same time, strongly supported cow protection. The Rashtriya Swayamsevak Sangh (RSS) *Sarsanghachalak* Mohan Bhagwat said he favoured a debate on the issue of a Uniform Civil Code (UCC). He said the Rashtriya Swayamsevak Sangh does not accept Article 370 and 35A of the Constitution, which give special status to Jammu & Kashmir.

The RSS chief in a bold statement even distanced the RSS from ideology of M.S. Golwalkar's view that Muslims are the 'internal enemy'. RSS chief Mohan Bhagwat's lecture series at Vigyan Bhawan Conclave in September 2018 has been the most significant event for the RSS since the 1974 speech by then chief Balasaheb Deoras. The RSS Conclave 17-19 September, 2018 compels us towards a new exploration of the troubled relationship between religion and democracy.

The RSS since early 2000s has grown into one of the world's largest private organisation, with an estimated nearly 2 million regular participants in its nearly 57,000 *shakhas* across the nation. In addition, there are 6000 *pracharakas*. The daily *shakhas* form the structural foundation of the RSS, as it is there that the Sangh aims to foster and inculcates its ideology of *Hindutva*—a brotherhood above caste, class, and regional identities.

There seems to be significant changes in the RSS along with the growth of its affiliates who carry different messages of the *Hindutva*. The changes seem to have occurred along with the liberalisation of economy during past two decades. The socio-economic changes have both transformed the RSS and led to its increased popularity in the Indian social milieu.

As per the available literature, the RSS considers loyalty to the nation as the essence of *Hindutva*. The mission statement of the RSS refers to the unity of Hindus as the organisation's guiding principle, though there is no formal RSS definition of what *Hindutva* is. Earlier narrow concept of exclusive approach has given way to inclusive thinking. Since the time of Balasaheb Deoras, the third head of the organisation, RSS leaders have used to term Hindu to cover all Indians, including Christians, Muslims, and other religious minorities. The one affiliate that has an exclusively Hindu religious base is the VHP, a group that works with the Hindu religious establishment on behalf of exclusively Hindu interests. This sectarian perspective has frequently put it at odds with the BJP that seeks the votes of all Indians, and tensions emerge on such issues as when to build the Ram Temple at Ayodhya, whether to provide financial support to Roman Catholic schools in Goa that use English as the language of instruction, whether to delay any action to abolish Article 370 of the Constitution (providing autonomy to Muslim majority in Kashmir), and how to handle the cow protection issue.

Though the RSS is supporter of strong federal centre it has established a pattern of accommodating regional, religious and cultural traditions by claiming them as elements of the larger Bharatiya cultuie. However, for the Sangh Parivar, more problematic than regional identity has been accommodation of Muslims and Christians. The RSS's nation-building effort has been almost exclusively focused on promoting a sense of unity among Hindus. There is a growing effort within the Sangh Parivar to bring Muslims into a larger Indian cultural milieu, motivated partly by the fact that Muslims and Christians are considered ethnically similar to other Indians and partly by the political need of the BJP to win their support. Hence, the alliance with the PDP in Kashmir whose support base is Muslim and the decision in Goa to continue support for Roman Catholic schools to avoid antagonizing the large Roman Catholic population. Largely, this more moderate approach to non-Hindus is driven, as Ashutosh Varshney has pointed out, by electoral considerations.

While there were coded *Hindutva* messages in the 2014 parliamentary campaign, the focus in that election was on economic development and creating jobs (*sabka saath, sabka vikas*). The BJP's 2014 campaign manifesto was largely lacking in Hindu nationalist themes while being explicit on enhancing the quality of life for Muslims.

Nonetheless, this more moderate face at the top is sometimes ignored in the lower ranks of both the RSS and BJP. The RSS leadership has repeatedly censured those engaged in violence against people suspected of consuming beef, the illegal transportation of cows, 'love *jihad*' and conversion as anti-socials who should be subject to legal action. Nevertheless, such admonition, often late in coming, has not substantially reduced the level of violence so far. How the BJP government responds to outburst of cultural intolerance will affect stability at home and the government's standing abroad.

One hundred and seventy one million people voted for Modi in 2014 elections. It is hard to know how many did so enthusiastically and how many were to some degree reluctant, viewing the BJP leader as their least bad option or feeling some degree of alarm at the company he kept. Modi's political family still included the RSS and its even more fanatical acolytes, all of whom campaigned openly for a Hindu society. Yet, it was Modi alone who took these ideas and remixed them with wider appeal. The Hindu nationalism of old was, if not entirely a fringe ideology, then at least a minority one. Before him, the BJP had held power in New Delhi on only a handful of occasions. The party's power base was restricted to particular stretches of Hindi speaking northern and western India, while its more militant adherents were viewed mostly as cranks. Modi was different: he took Hindu nationalism and fashioned it into something popular.

Many believe that the changes in the RSS something to do with the victories of the BJP, which could explain their firm support for the party, despite key differences on several significant policies. 'Cascading' might also account for the public's acceptance—especially outside the Hindi speaking heartland of north India. Reflecting its current willingness to accept this diversity, the RSS has virtually abandoned efforts to make Hindi the sole national language, reflecting popular support for English in the Dravidian speaking south and in the North East. Alternatively, for that matter even a rickshaw puller in north India wants to send his children to English medium school (Gathia, 2015).

The RSS's evolution, especially as it sought to expand outside the cow belt of the north India, has included the shedding of many age-old verities. Andersen and Damle in their book *The*

RSS mention that M. Vaidya, the former RSS spokesperson, has stated that the organisation was not interested in enforcing dietary practices and that those who consume beef can become its member. Sunil Deodhar, RSS *pracharak*, and the BJP's strategist for the 2018 Assembly elections in the north-eastern state of Tripura, declared that the BJP does not intend to impose a cow slaughter ban in the states where beef consumption is not a cultural taboo.

These shifts are only a few among many. The moot question is whether these shifts are temporary to facilitate BJP's electoral victory or are they genuine realisation of diversity. As Dattatreya Hosabale, an important functionary of the RSS, asserted, "We [the RSS] would want the BJP to win all the state elections because then only can significant social, political and cultural changes take place in this country...The 2014 election victory should be seen as the starting point of a long term mission."[9]

With the selection of Bhagwat as *Sarsanghchalak* in 2009, the RSS muted its comments on controversial economic issues like FDI and focused instead on building up the BJP, following the party's two successive defeats in the national parliamentary elections. While addressing a gathering of Indian business and intellectual elites in Delhi on November 2, 2013, Bhagwat suggested that the Sangh had moderated its once implacable opposition to liberalisation, privatisation and foreign investment. The Sangh, Bhagwat noted was 'not bound by dogmas'. Allying apprehension over the Sangh alleged antedivulian views; Bhagwat noted that the RSS understood that changes in the global economy meant that its views would need to 'evolve overtime'. Bhagwat's comments, coming as they did in the run up to the 2014 Lok Sabha elections where the RSS had decided to use its network to aid the BJP's election campaign, were an indication of a close alignment between the RSS's economic orientation and Modi's policy agenda. Prior to this, the RSS was consistently an outspoken supporter of economic self-sufficient.[10]

One may conclude that while the Sangh Parivar seems to be changing and becoming a dominant force seeking to influence the policy process, the RSS continues to view politics as only one of several factors shaping society, and not necessarily the most significant one.

The 2014 mandate has been interpreted by the BJP/RSS as a

green signal to make an aggressive push for implementation of its agenda of *Hindu Rashtra*. Encouraged by the 2014 Lok Sabha elections and particularly after 2017 Uttar Pradesh elections victory of the BJP the RSS desperately wants to change the power structure more forcefully than ever.

My observation is that the RSS would like the BJP to be in power for another term, only then RSS will go for its ideological programme. Whatever compromise BJP wants to do, the RSS would let them do. The Sangh Parivar first wants to spread its "Hindu-first" ideology to all corners of India by propelling the ruling party of Prime Minister Narendra Modi to power in as many states as possible. At the same time to lesser degree would pressurise minorities—Muslims and Christians—to accept that India is a nation of Hindus and wants to push for reconversion of minorities. The Parivar is not in a hurry to solve the Ram temple leave aside Kashi and Mathura. But, it would keep the pot boiling.

The Sangh Parivar may push for a nationwide anti-conversion law on the pattern of Freedom of Religion Act existing in many states. Attempts will be made to make a fine distinction between Article 25 of the Constitution of India—which guarantees all persons the right to freedom and conscience to profess, practice, and propagate their religion—and conversions by inducements that amount to force and coercion to entice individuals. The proposed anti-conversion law will bury debates of choice and conscience and constrain the exchange of ideas and opportunities. It will be an attempt to impose majoritarian norms, and a homogenous identity in a heterogeneous society.

The overarching 'test' the state-religion model is non-discrimination in the equal enjoyment of all human rights by all. The key indicators of non-discrimination 'test' are women's rights, minority rights, criminal punishment system, neutrality in education, and neutrality in resolving disputes between and within religious or belief communities and public manifestations of freedom of religion or belief.[11]

Establishing international network of Hindus who believe in *Hindu Rashtra* has been one of the dreams of the RSS since its inception. Around twenty-five million people of Indian origin had settled in the nineteenth century in areas such as East Africa, South Africa, the West Indies, South America, and Pacific Islands like Fiji. The influence of these Indians on India is to some extent limited as they are mostly not affluent *Pravasi Bharatiya* and their bonds with India is not that strong as that of recent immigrants who have settled since, Second World War in England, U.S. Canada, Australia, New Zealand etc., who come from urban educated professional communities which is why they are 'dear' in the eyes of the Sangh Parivar. This has led to the increased interaction between neo migrant communities around the world and India's ultra Rights. One impact of this has been that some of the people living in the Diaspora have been attracted to the visions of Hinduism favoured by the RSS and have consequently supported the BJP from outside of India.

The importance of the Hindu Diaspora can also be seen in the ways that Narendra Modi undertook various visits to countries outside India with the message that Indians living abroad can contribute to country's development as well as support *Hindutva*. These appeals are of economic in nature seeking new sources for investment in India, but in part they also show the ways in which Diaspora voices are now listened to in Indian politics and are seen as being part of Indian polity.

One of the strategy of the RSS is to influence Western countries particularly United States. The Indian *Hindutva* Diaspora (not to be mistaken with ordinary Hindus living abroad) is advancing this agenda in the West particularly in the United States.

A more self-confident RSS is now beginning to command an assertive presence on the world stage and wants India to be '*jagat guru*'. The RSS senior leaders now visit other countries, which have substantial Hindu population such as Fiji, Mauritius, Bangladesh, Sri Lanka, Myanmar, Surinam, and Jamaica to contact Hindus and bring them to the fold of *Hindutva*.

The electoral successes of the BJP perhaps indicate the growing acceptance of RSS views. Nevertheless, the RSS is not so much for bringing back the old Hindu Golden Age but for an economically strong Hindu nation on the pattern of United States. In his twelve years at the helm of the Gujarat government, Modi, as Chief Minister, used investment and economic development as key tools to make the state a laboratory to replace the traditional hierarchical Hindu caste order with a reformist *Hindutva* that inclined economic investment. The shifts are only a few along the many that demonstrate the willingness of some senior figures to modify the Sangh, ideologically and organizationally, to win mass appeal in a changing India. It is now the era of Bhagwat's *glasnost* in the RSS and Modi's *perestroika* in Indian economic sector.

India: Rising Economic Power

Today India is seeking its place under the global sun even as it strives at home to abolish large-scale poverty and achieve broad development goals. Its international heft has increased as its economic size and domestic market have grown. From being the twelfth largest economy at the time of the Western financial crisis, India was in sixth place in 2017, overtaking three developed economies (Spain, Canada, and Italy) as well as Russia and Brazil. Over a quarter century, the country has more than trebled its share of world trade, and multiplied manifold its foreign investment—inflows and outflows too, for that matter. The growth of its middle class has meant that some of its market has grown to world scale—the second largest market for mobile phones and for powered two wheelers (motor cycles, scooters, and mopeds) for instance. Martin Wolf of the *Financial Times* called it a "premature superpower"—a country that has gained in economic size while still being low income and struggling to deal with the most basic issues of poverty and the debilities that are mass poverty's side effects.[12]

India's extreme poverty has reduced in scope and scale by 2018 but retains widespread malnutrition, rural unemployment, and poor life quality among masses. Still there has been some progress. India has moved from the World Bank list of low-income countries to the lower middle-income category, where it will remain for the near future. It is more than likely that India would continue to account of the largest share of the world's poor. What India needs is "inclusive" economic growth. Large-scale unemployment in rural areas and small towns is serious challenge to peaceful coexistence as such unemployed youth can easily become fodder for religious fundamentalist forces.

The core question is whether India has any prospects of becoming next superpower, considering its restriction on religious freedom, discrimination against minorities, second-class treatment to women and *Dalits,* laws governing what people should eat, and adopting policies that are detrimental to the secularism and eventually to democratic functioning. Will 'majoritarianism' promoted by the Sangh Parivar bring lost glory and 'greatness' back to India? Not yet clear but India has to battle the debilities of widespread grinding poverty, diseases, hunger and other abysmal indicators of human development to the extreme extent. (Ninan, 2017). There is little doubt that India has not performed to its potential, even as other countries have. Much of the commentary on the subject looks at industrial, trade and currency policies—all of which are important, but few take note of the vital ingredients such as equality, freedom of religion, communal relations, violence, and discrimination against women, land ownership, and agrarian situation.

While setting up smart cities, industries, mines and power plants may be essential for the growth of the economy—and to provide seamless access to facilities to the ever-growing population of India, the human and environmental cost of this development needs to be considered before making decisions. India ranked 133 out of 188 on the Human Development Index in 2017. "For whom is the development and is it sustainable and ethical?" is an important question that the country needs to ask itself.

India seems to be fighting a losing battle when it comes to implementing and enforcing the laws that it has created. Legislation alone is never enough to reduce crime or stop it from recurring. Laws pertaining to violence against women, reducing environmental degradation, land rights, farmers' rights, freedom of religion rights etc. still face problems when it comes to actually going through with them. Apart from understanding the difference between making promises and carrying them out, not just during elections but otherwise, India needs to realise that a 'welfare state' ensures that its claims and legislation convert to action and implementation. According to the World Justice Project's Rule of Law Index, Netherlands ranks one globally when it comes to effective and timely enforcement of laws, whilst India ranks 66 out of 113 nations.

India is the fourth worst country in the world when it comes to religious intolerance. Be it the state or the people themselves, recognising equality in diversity is vital to ensure peace between people of different castes, religions, gender, and communities.

Many experts believe that a promising future and pluralistic society, the quality of Indian entrepreneurs, the country's demographic dividends, and social, economic, and political reforms cannot be achieved in an environment of fear, suppression particularly when the fringe force has enunciated the concept of "preference falsification". Simply to put, this means that people supportive of change refrain from expressing their true preferences for fear of punishment or social opprobrium. In the absence of any criticism of the *status quo*, this situation might become self-perpetuating. The deliberate amalgamation of the spiritual and temporal domains has serious implications for the future of liberal democracy.

India's super power status will largely depend on the future agenda of the *Hindutva* (Hindu–first) forces.

Which Way India Will Go?

Almost everyone today affirms the importance and merit of religious liberty but in India, it is under much pressure. Although India's Constitution guarantees freedom of religious belief, there is a gulf between the constitutional provisions and the practice. Religious liberty is being challenged by new questions (for example, *gharwapsi*, or killing in the name of cow protection) and new forces (such as globalisation and terrorism). Combined, these make the meaning of religious liberty in the twenty-first century India uncertain.

The election of May 2014 marked a sharp turning point in the history of India's democracy whose meaning is yet unclear. The electorate did not in any clear sense opted for Hindu Right politics.[13] One message that emerged loud and clear from the events since 2014 that religious freedom is in serious danger of becoming a second class right—in the sense that it can all too easily be trumped by other rights, claims and interest. It seems unlikely, however, given historical and current trend in Sangh Parivar guided politics that issues surrounding freedom to choose religion or *dharmantaran* will disappear from academic or public attention in the near future. It can be with near certainty that like the past one and half decade, the coming decade will also bring new threats to religious freedom as liberal secular democracy is besieged and its ideals are being challenged in India.

The near-term challenges to religious liberty in India are unique. The gravest challenges to religious freedom in most parts of the world bear little resemblance to those in India. They are sharply different from the dramatic and often heartbreaking challenges in rest of the world, where violent persecution and government intimidation are common. They are more subtly different from those in other democracies, such as U.S., the United Kingdom, Germany, and France. India's record of accomplishment on religious freedom is far better than Pakistan.

One thing is becoming clearer by the day: the BJP's contemporary political articulations and policy formulation cannot be understood if we do not view them as a paradigm shift driven by powerful ideological forces. It is not business as usual or a mere extension of old politics, it is an altogether new brand of politics. We may end up missing the bigger picture and fail to understand its implications if we continue to view the policies of the current regime using the usual analytical tools of politics.

India needs future literate intellectuals. So that we are better able to harness our imagination to grasp the potential of the present and create ways to act that are consistent with our values (Miller, 2015). Less remarked upon, but ominous for the future of religious freedom is the mounting evidence that less value is being attached to religion and religious freedom in the places where one might have expected it to be more secure—namely, in the minds and hearts of liberal middle classes of India. If that is so the greatest challenge facing defenders of religious freedom today may well be the task of convincing people that religious freedom is an important human right worth defending at home and abroad.

Narendra Modi's socially tolerant economic reformer image will be governed largely by the parenthesis of future re-election prospects. The RSS has larger ideological project: the destruction of Congress as apolitical force (Congress Mukta Bharat) and its left of centre, secular ideology along with it. In this context, Modi has proved strikingly successful. His victory in 2014 dealt Congress crushing and perhaps irreparable blow. Although the party has shown few signs of recovery in the years since its defeat as it staggers along under Rahul Gandhi's ponderous and diffident leadership.

Many in India are thrilled at the idea of India's fast economic growth. No doubt, that despite vast inequality India is set to grow in economic might and political power for the remainder of the twenty-first century. By some account, it has already overtaken China as the world's most populous nation: by others baton will pass during the next decade or two. Today, India's $ 2.3 trillion economy is slightly smaller than Britain's. Barring something unforeseen, it will surpass America in size by mid-century and then perhaps, China too.

The political and social rise since the late 1990s of formerly fringe Hindu nationalist organisations such as the RSS, the VHP, the BJP and numerous others RSS created organisations in Indian civil society has resulted in significant apprehension about long term future of India's constitutionally secular liberal democratic polity. The key political ideology of the RSS, the VHP and the BJP and of various other organisations is *Hindutva*, a strikingly untraditional synthesis territorial ethno-nationalism metaphysical penology, hierarchical religion and 'integration'. The aim of *Hindutva* nationalists is to turn India into an exclusive Hindu nation (*Hindu rashtra*).

The second rise of the BJP and violent communal incidents since 2014 have created a sense of un-certainties in the minds of the people at large. The fact that the BJP and the Sangh Parivar more generally have to argue at all about secularism is clear evidence of the entrenched genuinely secular pluralist sensibilities within the Indian polity. The BJP is subject to the parties of coalition arithmetic and the necessity of unguaranteed but regular electoral legitimization while remaining circumscribed by a flourishing, free democracy that is strong resistant to authoritarianism to consolidate as a national party. But, if the BJP has to become a hegemonic national popular party, it will have not only to court the OBCs vote bank but also appeal consistently to South non-Brahmin electoral , SCs, STs, or simply make token gesture towards India's (world's second largest) Muslim population.

Hence, one argument might run, irrespective of the context, of its *Hindutva* ideology, the BJP is a party characterized by political expediency and programmatize and can shift to centrist ground or move to religious extremism as the electoral situation demands. In the long run it has little choice but to transform itself into a centre—right party its political flavour residing somewhere between post-war Europe Christian Democracy and the American New Right of the 1980s, its policies comprising element of neo-liberalism and economic nationalism, social democracy and social authoritarianism and a patina of rhetoric *Hindutva*. From this perspective liberal democracy and the Constitution of India will be safe in the hands of the BJP.

While it may aim for economic liberalization, it is subject to internal economic constrains (ranging from resistance state bureaucracy to institutionalized corruption) and conflicting demands for state subsidies by rural producers or industrial sector. Economic globalisation driven from unfettered deregulation will alienate its relatively uncompetitive urban small business and rural middle class electoral constituencies.

Parsimony, pragmatic real politik and the consequences of the ruthless functional incorrigibility of the Indian social and political function, rather than ideological dogmatism and purposive ban will dominate BJP forces of political governance. Hindu nationalism may be here to stay but it will eventually manifest as ordering business within India's functioning anarchy. *Hindutva* will articulate—the aspirations of small middle class higher caste electoral constituency where 'historical' claim to represent the totality of Indian nationhood will seem increasingly inane and obsolete.

We can refer to this possibility as the 'robust liberal democratic constrain' as 'weak establishment' (which India's Constitution provides for) with the qualification that 'Hinduism' does not possess nor can it be represented by a 'Church' or corrigible ecclesiastical structure nor can the possible range of institutionalized relations between State and Religion in India be comprehended in terms of 'establishmentalism'.

This is relatively optimistic reading of the future of Hindu nationalism in India, one is in which constitutional and legal instruments, democratic processes and regionalism will curtail even weaken varieties of BJP religious nationalism. However, virtually all serious analysis of Hindu nationalism contain another strand, explicit to varying digress, that can 'imagine' a far bleaker future for India under Hindu nationalism governance.

Some scholars suggest an alternative scenario. A majority BJP government unconstrained by political coalition will aim to 'fundamentally' transform the spirit and substance of the Constitution, placing its organist, authoritarian, anti-minority *Hindutva* ideology at its core. Minorities will be under seize and without effective protection , it not under the threat of systematic pogroms by *Hindutva* movement acting with the complicity and support of the police forces and state bureaucracy. Aggressive and authoritarian legal protection of Hindu icons, deities, temples and sensibilities will be institutionalized. An aggressive ideology of Hindu race, broad culture and territory will become mandatory in state schooling. Articles 370 and 35-A of the Constitution will be recline. Authoritarian forms of governance will reverse affirmative action policy and *dalits* and *adivasis* groups will be coerced into Brahmanical ideologies. In the beginning the BJP rule may not touch tribals of the north-eastern India (majority of them are Christians) but the Christian tribals in plains (Odisha, Jharkhand, Chhattisgarh, MP, Rajasthan, and Gujarat) may lose affirmative action policy benefits. Repressive gender policy by self-appointed *Hindutva* activists will dominate urban lifestyles. Obscurantism reasoning will mould, an increasing aggressive and intolerant culture policies. Hate, xenophobia and Hinduism will define political discourses in the public sphere whereas liberal, secular and democratic sensibilities will be marginalised.

Contradictions seemingly serious ones between RSS and VHP and BJP will be ones of degrees within *Hindutva* political and ideological cluster that is otherwise constituent in its overall aims of activities. Political or strategic disagreements will be manageable family affairs dissections. The violent activism of the VHP and RSS in mainly north and western states aimed at polarizing *Hindutva* violence will be the precursor to the hasting of the Hindu vote by the BJP, these being extra-legal and legal component of a single Hindu nationalist strategy that can embrace without contradiction both electoralism and violent social movement.

Hindutva represents an uncompromising far reaching ideological project that can simultaneously in one and same move articulate tolerance and that, liberalism and a genocidal impulse, democracy and majoritarianim, universal humanism and forbidding xenophobia, and secular constitutionality under the rule of law and theocratic justified criminality.

Hindu nationalism represents a cluster projects, which seek to displace entirely the nature of, and associations between these terms. The Sangh Parivar aims to transform not only the content of the entire nation, Indian political culture but also the legitimate forms of that culture. This includes changing the nature of the public sphere and its forms of political discourse, the quality of relationship between legal and extra-legal sphere, the different layer of personal and civil society and the nature of civic association, solidarity and political and civil citizenship, while transforming the understanding of both through a long term aim to potentially but wholly transform 'body, mind, soul, and intellect' of each Hindu adult and child. This dislocates the fundamental understanding of family, community and civil society and nation in order to replace them with a vitality, organism and arguably quasi-eugenicist conception of society and nation.

The Constitution of India is secular and provides for existence of all religion with equal rights. According to the Constitution, the objective of domestic religious policy is to foster the creation of a tolerant society, peaceful co-existence and provide for freedom of conscience and worship. This "Constitutional nationalism" model is under pressure, challenged by the Sangh Parivar, and is increasingly being replaced by a new model of religious nationalism based on single religion Hinduism. This religious nationalism model wants to do away with religious freedom and impose *Hindutva* way of life on all and privileges a single language—Hindi.

Which way India will go ? There are number of social, economic, and international factors that will affect the future path for India.

First is demographic fear. Many times the Sangh Parivar has expressed this fear that due to increase in Muslims population Hindus will become minority in India by 2047 (when India completes 100 years of its Independence). However, such fears are unfounded. A Pew Research Centre report stated that India would have the distinction of having the largest populations of two of the three largest religions in the world—Islam and Hinduism. The Pew Research Centre estimated that by 2050 Hindus would make up 76.7 per cent of nearly 1.3 billion Indians. At the same time India is expected to have 311 million Muslims up from 14.4 per cent in 2010 to 18.4 per cent in 2050 (11% of the global total), making it the country with the largest population of Muslims in the world. Currently, Indonesia has the world's largest number of Muslims. Christian in 2050 is estimated to be still very small percentage 2.2 as today. Although the Muslim population will grow but Hindus will still be in majority even by 2050.

Due to high number of Muslims in future, the Sangh Parivar is waging a concerted campaign against all religious minorities in their efforts to Hinduise India. At the same time what is worry-some is that growing Arabisation of Indian Muslims is also pushing "liberal Hindus" particularly in rural areas and small towns towards *Hindutva* (Hindu first) politics and ideology. Thus, the onus of keeping peace is on both sides.

No doubt this demographic number do raise concern as India's social structure is intensely divided along myriad fault lines, which can take the forms of ethnicity, religion, language, region, caste, class etc. The challenge of social stratifications for the future of India is enormous but India with its historical experience will manage such differences.

Concluding Remarks

Hinduism is one of the world's oldest and greatest religious traditions. Hinduism cannot be represented by a 'Church' or corrigible ecclesiastical structure nor can the possible range of institutionalized relation between state and religion in India can be comprehended in terms of "establishmentalism". Hinduism believes in diversity and plurality. This pluralist depictive of Hinduism found its most eloquent exponent in the twentieth century in Mahatma Gandhi who propagated *sarva dharma sambhav* (equal respect for all religions). The diversity and India's culture, people, religious traditions and languages are legendary. A "Hymn to the Earth" found in the *Atharva Veda* reveals India's own recognition of this multiplicity of cultures is not new. Over the centuries, the philosophers, pilgrims, and peoples of India have explored the meaning of this celebrated diversity as any other culture on the earth. "Unity in diversity" is the theme that has been sounded in many keys for well over two thousand years. One verse of the ancient *Rig Veda* has become the signature of this theme: *Ekam sat vipra bahudha vadanti* (Truth is one the wise speak of it in many ways).The Vedic phrase crops up repeatedly in the rhetorical traditions of India. One truth, many paths, religion, languages, and traditions. Hindu, Sikhs, Muslims, Jain, Christianity, Zoroastrianism, all make today's India of diversities one complex and overlapping—regional, religious, linguistic philosophic. It is very complex and diversity of culture that shapes the distinctive civilisation that is India today. This diversity is under stress today.

Political dynamics in the past two decades, however, have introduced a new threat to the stability of Indian democracy (Behar and Prakash, 2018). Communal tensions—between Indians of various religious faiths and castes—have long plagued Indian society. Most Indians are at least somewhat concerned about these tensions. According to 2017 Pew Research Centre survey, almost four-in-ten Indians (37%) said "communal relations" are a very big problem in their country, while an additional 31 per cent named this as a moderately big problem.

The globalisation has led Indians to look for roots of their 'vibrant free democracy' in Hinduism. Aided by the new political economy, a new Hindu religiosity is being ever more deeply embedded in the everyday life, both in public and private spheres. Use of explicitly Hindu rituals and symbols in the routine affairs of the state and electoral politics has become so commonplace that Hinduism has become the *de facto* religion of the 'secular' Indian state, which is constitutionally bound to have no official religion.

Given India's growing visibility in the global economy, Hindu religiosity is being fused with feelings of national pride and dreams of becoming a superpower. The country's economic success is being attributed to the superiority of Hindu values, and India is seen as entitled to the Great Power status because of its ancient Hindu civilisation. Thus, the hard won achievements of all of India's many diverse religious traditions and culture are being absorbed into the religion of the majority community.

This scenario also raises many questions in our mind. Today, India stands at the crossroads of what sort of super power it will become. Will it evolve in a country, which has overcome inequality, corruption, and crony capitalism? Alternatively, will the appeal of Hindu nationalism grows in strength partly because of the RSS itself, but also because of the sense of identity crisis in the era of uncertainties of globalisation? India's rising prosperity offer no special defence against its slippage into majoritarianism. India is not a full liberal democracy, with public institutions capable of guarding in every respect of civil and political rights of its many people. Yet, it was never fully 'illiberal' democracy either in sense the likes of Turkey and Russia, which hold elections but then actively deny their citizens many important constitutional protections. With the RSS's saffron agenda India might drift towards full 'illiberal democracy' status with its secular foundation replaced by some kind of new Hindu majoritarianism vision and turned into a 'saffron tinged version of Russia'.[14] India's ambition to lead the second half of the Asian countries and the world's hope for a more democratic, liberal future depends on getting this transition right.

India matters now and will matter still more in future. It is a democracy; its economy is fast growing; and it will soon be the most populous country in the world. International and Western democracies should passionately desire India to be a successful model of democratic and market-led development and freedom to choose. An important question then is whether the government of Narendra Modi, in office since May 2014, has made a decisive difference to India's economic trajectory. The evidence is: not yet. Nevertheless, the reforms it has introduced might make a more noticeable difference in the years ahead.

The new culture of political Hinduism is likely to remain in one form or the other but the current phase is like a bubble, which will subside with the increasing realisation for the need for peaceful co-existence in globalised world economy.

The great crucible of the twenty-first century is learning to live with intense diversities. Significant elements of Indian elites are favourably disposed to Indian becoming cosmopolitan society. Some wish it to assume theocratic role. The overwhelming bulk of the Indian people are committed to a national alternative and to preserve and strengthen the plurality and co-existence *"Jio or Jine do"* (live and let live), Indian identity that has existed for centuries. The choices India makes will shape its future as a nation that aspires to be super power and the future of the world.

Notes

1. James Crabtree (2018). *The Billionaire Raj,* Harper Collins Publishers, India.
2. *Ibid,* p. 71.
3. Concerned Citizens of India: "Open Letters to Church Leaders", August 4, 2017.
4. Pew Research Canter, Ninth Annual Report, 2018.
5. Allen D. Hertzke (2013). *The Future of Religious Freedom: Global Challenges,* Oxford University Press.
6. United Nations Human Rights Council Resolution 16/18 of May 2011 https:// berkeleycenterr.geortownuniversity.ed.../unitednations-human rights-council-resolution

7. Nadia Marzouki, Duncan McDonnell, Olivier Roy (2016). *Saving the People: How Populists Hijack Religion*, C. Hurst & Company (Publishers) Limited.
8. US CIRF 2018 Annual Report, Washington DC.
9. Rupam Jain Nair, *et al.* (2015). "Special Report: Battling for India's Soul, State by State", Reuters, 13 October.
10. "FDI Reform: RSS economic wing SJM opposes P.M. Modi", *Financial Express*, 12 January, 2018.
11. Heiner Bielefeldt, Nazila Ghanea, Michael Wiener (2016), *Freedom of Religion or Belief: An International Law Commentary*, Oxford University Press.
12. Martin Wolf (2017), 'Chief Economic Commentator', *The Financial Times*, May 23.
13. Wendy Doniger, Martha C. Nussbaum (2015), *Pluralism, and Democracy in India: Debating the Hindu Right*, Oxford University Press.
14. James Crabtree (2018).

Epilogue

The Future of the Past

asato mā sad gamaya,
tamaso mā jyotir gamaya,
mṛtyor mā amṛtaṃgamaya,
shanti~ shanti~ shanti hi~~

This translates to:

From falsehood lead me to truth,
From darkness lead me to the light,
From death lead me to immortality,
Om, peace peace peace.

(Br. Up. 3.28)

As a young boy in the early 1950s, I was mesmerized by the vision of future—that far, far distant time at the end of the century—described with great fervour by scientists, sociologists, and spiritual *gurus*' writing in popular magazines. One scenario was that by that time, there would be no poverty, no hunger, and people would live in better houses, all children would get education, and of course, they would get nice jobs. Moreover, that people of different religion would live in peace and harmony. Sixty years later, I am living in the future that seemed so distant in the imagination of a small town boy. What is amusing irony is that millions of people go hungry everyday, live in shanties, numbers of street children have gone up, sexual abuse of women has become daily headlines in India, millions of children in India are malnourished and without proper education and many of them have to work to earn for living and feed their parents. On the top of all these, the ethnic conflicts, distrust and intolerance have grown many fold. The communal harmony is tattered and politics is seen through religious prism.

Indian and Chinese are two ancient civilizations that have survived so long because they respected diversity, non-violence, and peaceful co-existence through centuries. However, of late peaceful co-existence has been challenged by some fundamental forces and growing ethnic conflict has brought tension in India, which is threatening its future.

Recent writings suggest, communal conflict in India may be a product of the concept of a 'mainstream national culture' that is moving away from "salad bowl" culture to "melting pot" culture. As Ashish Nandy puts it, in a salad bowl culture, the ingredients retain their distinctness, but each ingredient transcends its individuality through the presence of others. In a "melting pot" model primordial identities are supposed to dissolve their identity. Those that do not are called nationalities or minorities; they are expected to dissolve in the end. Much of the recent violence in India can be traced to the systematic efforts being made to impose the "melting pot" model upon Indian realities.

India today is facing crisis of confidence in handling globalization. It is emphasizing on reasserting of cultural or civilization authenticity. Rapid economic growth during the last two decades and modern technologies far from erasing old rivalries and bitter experiences have enabled construction of a nature, more contemporary, more self-critical version of Indian traditions and have empowered the Hindu revivalist's forces.

Hindutva forces are making effort in India to discover masculinity or national consciousness in the past, which rendered "the golden age of Hinduism". Efforts are being made for violent emerge of a stream—rolling modern nation-state in which religious freedom is projected as threat to national security. The current communal conflict in India may be product of the concept of mainstream anneal culture that is fearful of diversities, intolerant of dissent unless it is cast in the language of mainstream, and panicky about any self assertion or search for autonomy by ethnic groups.

Growing inequality is posing threat to all kinds of freedom including religious freedom. Religious freedom is pivotal for all democratic freedoms. I believe the world today including India is in what I call a "healing crisis", which is very much the same as many of us are going through in our individual lives. A healing crisis in our personal lives is a time when we are really shaken up, usually because of some kind of challenge that comes in our lives, and we have to change in someway. May be the loss of a relationship, a financial crisis, loss of a job, or a health problem. When this is happening you feel like, "Oh, no! Why is this happening to me?"

Later, looking back at it, you see that something emerged from the experience that was very impotent. There was some kind of deepening, learning, growing or perhaps even a small change in your direction in life because of going through that experience.

Each one of us individually is in an evolutionary process. So is our country. So how can each one of us most effectively face the challenges in our own personal life, becoming as conscious as we can while also facing the issues in the world at large and have a healing effect?

Each one of us need to ask, "How might I best use my time, and talents to serve the larger world?" We have to take steps to transform our society and transform this planet. It is not for me or anyone else to tell people what to do. It is up to each one of us to do those things that we know in our hearts we should do. For some people it is getting sober, for others it is forgiving someone, and giving services or it is something else. For all of us, becoming more and more involved in the social and political issues of our day bears directly on what will happen in this world over the next twenty years. We have allowed ourselves to fall in line behind the gross delusion that economic principles are more important than humanitarian principles. We allow those in power to make balancing the budget more important than balancing the universe. We have witnessed the terrible social disruption that results from placing money before love on such a mass scale. We allowed this to happen, and it is our responsibility to change it. It is not enough to whine. It is definitely not enough to just tune out and throw up our hands.

Over the past two decades, opportunity—particularly economic opportunity—has tilted in the direction of the already privileged. The misinform of drifting is economic injustice. We give huge subsidies—billions of rupees—to wealthy corporate sector, while million of our rural and slum people, primarily *Dalits, adivasis*, poor farmers, *Dihadi majdoor* (daily wage earners), large number of abandoned women and children are living in social and economic conditions as desperate as those during the worst days of near famine like situation in 1966. This country is in major denial regarding critical violations of our own constitutional principles, not to mention the love of God.

Why should we be subsidizing our richest companies rather than India's poor children? We must repudiate the notion that the market forces alone fuels social good. It does not. Moreover, neither does government, by the way. Love alone.

India needs to wake up to the fact children who receive inadequate care of whatever kind—when cut off from societal compassion—become our main bearers of intolerance and religious hatred. The growing rage and despair in our children is the greatest threat to our future security and peaceful co-existence. The political system, as it now exists, fails to acknowledge that taking care of our children should be our top priority. This is not a matter of opinion. There is one principle that rules universe: Cause and Effect, or *Karma*. What goes around comes around. From a spiritual perspective, why farmers are committing suicide in a country which is the fifth largest economy in the world in 2018.

We must return to the principle of *Vasudhaiv kutumbakam* (entire universe is my home) and let noble thought come from all directions, upon which our great civilization survived for millenniums. Mahatma Gandhi said that to some generations much is given and from some much is expected. Our generation is the one to whom much has been given and one from whom much is now expected. Present people of India have a rendezvous with destiny. The question is whether we are going to sleep through the date or awake. Perhaps we are choosing to remain asleep. We are not awake.

That is why the social revolution of our time—and we do need a very social revolution—cannot be organised. It must be initiated by passion. It must be led as Gandhi said by the "small, still voice within". The power residing within the individual aligns with the basic democracy. To retrieve democracy, we have to start practising democracy. We cannot blame others for taking it away; if we, ourselves, abdicate all social responsibility because we are too busy tending our own gardens.

The tenets of higher consciousness can aid us in working for this transformation. The first higher consciousness principle to consider is that who we *are* is as important as what we *do*. Gandhi claimed the soul force is more powerful than brute force. Our current political system defines power in terms of brute force. We have the opportunity, if we are serious about it, to usher in an era in which power derives from soul force. Soul force is neither cheap nor easy to obtain. Many people pay lip service to soul force while avoiding its use as a social and political tool. It is easier to talk about than to practice. In fact, there is temptation to use spiritual seeking as escapism, an easy opportunity to avoid looking at, dealing with, or seeking to transform the suffering of the world. The mind plays an insidious game. We cannot resurrect a world whose crucifixion we have ignored.

We must be as committed to our spiritual goals as we are to our political goals. We marry the two by being awake. When you read that an innocent person is victim of communal conflict, that a girl drops out from school due to fear of sexual abuse, you write a letter to local authorities, newspapers, or Member of Parliament, make tweet about it or put it on social media. We need a healthy sense of moral outrage. Public pressure makes world go around, and that is how it should be, particularly in a democracy. Unfortunately too many people who have passionate feeling do not turn those feelings in action, we do not turn our energy into social force. Our idea of activism is to yell at television set.

Taking the energy in our hearts and transforming it into constructive social action is the next step towards our personal and political maturity. That is the essence of democracy, and it is the essence of spiritual power inherently in a democracy. Democracy means this country will go in whatever direction the people choose for it to go. Right now our democratic rights are being unravelled for no other reason than that we are not protesting enough.

Learning to love is the highest form of political training. Our love for people, particularly, children on the other side of town, must become a passionate commitment if we are to save this world. The children are bearing the weight of our insanity. Nevertheless, we must not allow anger to obstruct our effectiveness. It is our own fault that we have allowed this radical deterioration of social integrity. We must take personal responsibility and assert ourselves now. As Gandhi made clear that, the only way to eradicate institutionalized forms of injustice is by awakening the conscience of mankind. We must not attack the power structure; we must speak to its conscience.

None of this is to say that I am pessimistic about India's future, because I am not. I am as much a champion about what is right in this country as anyone is, and I am as blessed by what is right in this country as anyone is. I just want all of India's children including children belonging to *Dalit*, Muslim and Christian minorities, and *adivasi* communities, and to have same minimum level of opportunity that I had. We must seek to make opportunity universal accessible here, or this house will fall.

We need possibility thinking, not just in our private lives but in our public life as well.

In the words of Mahatma Gandhi, "We must have the innate respect for other religions as we have for our own. Mind you, not mutual toleration, but equal respect."

Love should come before money. The tug between the forces of suppression and demands of equality with religious freedom goes to the heart of modern life.

I also want to share with readers my inner feelings:

> *The purpose of this work is to awaken and challenge*
> *you to the next level of being human on this earth.*
> *It is to tune and tone you, cleanse and clarify you,*
> *so that the new ways of being will become available.*
> *It is to support you and encourage you*
> *so you have the heart and skill*
> *to leap into the unknown.*

References

Berry, Thomas, *The Sacred Universe: Earth, Spirituality, and Religion in the Twenty-first Century.*

Boo, Katherine, *Behind the Beautiful Forever.*

Chandy, Anna, *Battles in the Mind.*

Eck, Diana L., *India: A Sacred Geography.*

Kiš, Adam D., *The Development Trap: How Thinking Big Fails the Poor.*

Bibliography

Adcock, C.S. (2013). *The Limits of Tolerance: Indian Secularism and the Politics of Religious Freedom*, Oxford University Press.

Adeney, K. and L. Sáez (Eds.) (2006). *Coalition Politics and Hindu Nationalism*, London: Routledge.

Agarwala, Ramgopal, (2017). *Demonetisation: A Means to an End?*, Sage Publications, India.

Agnivesh, Swami and Valson Thampu, (2002). *Harvest of Hate: Gujarat under Seize*, Rupa & Company.

Akkara, Anto (2016). *Who Killed Swami Laxmanananda*? Bangalore: Veritas India Books.

Anand, D. (2011). *Hindu Nationalism in India and the Politics of Fear*, New York: Palgrave Macmillan.

Andersen, Walter and S.D. Damle, (2018). *The RSS*, Penguin Viking.

Annicchino, Pasquale (2017). *Law and International Religious Freedom: The Rise and Decline of the American Model*, Routledge.

Barua, Ankur (2015). *Debating 'Conversion' in Hinduism and Christianity*, Routledge.

Basu, Amrita (2015). *Violent Conjunctures in Democratic India*, Cambridge University Press.

Bauman, C. (2008). *Christian Identity and Dalit Religion in Hindu India, 1868-1947*, Grand Rapids: Eerdmans Publishers.

Bauman, C. (2013). "Hindu-Christian conflict in India: Globalization, conversion, and the coterminal castes and tribes", *The Journal of Asian Studies*, 72(3), 633-653.

Bauman, C. and R. Young (2012). "Minorities and the politics of conversion: With special attention to Indian Christianity", In: R. Robinson (ed.) *Minority Studies*, Delhi: Oxford University Press, pp. 185-204.

Bauman, C. and T. Leech (2012). "Political competition, relative deprivation, and perceived threat: A research note on anti-Christian violence in India", *Ethnic and Racial Studies*, 35(12), 2195-2216.

Bauman, Chad M. (2015). *Pentecostals, Proselytization, and Anti-Christian Violence in Contemporary India*, Oxford University Press.

Bennema, Cornelis and Paul Joshua Bhakiaraj, (2011). "Early Christian identity formation and its relevance for modern India", In: Cornelis

Bennema and Paul Joshua Bhakiaraj (eds.), *Indian and Christian: Changing Identities in Modern India*, Bangalore: SAIACS Press/Oxford: Oxford House, 59-76.

Berenschot, W. (2011). *Riot Politics: Hindu-Muslim Violence and the Indian State*, New Delhi: Rainlight.

Berger, P.L. (1969). *The Sacred Canopy: Elements of a Sociological Theory of Religion*, Garden City, N.Y.: Doubleday.

Bergunder, M. (2007). *The South Indian Pentecostal Movement in the Twentieth Century*, Grand Rapids: Eerdmans.

Bhatt, C. (2001). *Hindu Nationalism: Origins, Ideologies, and Modern Myths*, New York: Berg.

Bhattacharyya, Harihar and Lion König (2015). *Globalisation, and Governance in India: New Challenges to Society and Institutions*, Routledge.

Bielefeldt, Heiner, Nazila Ghanea and Michael Wiener (2016). *Freedom of Religion or Belief: An International Law Commentary*, Oxford University Press, p. 552.

Braithwaite, John and Bina D'Costa (2018). *Cascades of Violence: War, Crime and Peace building Across South Asia*, Australia: ANU Press.

Brass, P.R. (2003). *The Production of Hindu-Muslim Violence in Contemporary India*, Seattle, Wash.: University of Washington Press.

Bremborg, A.D. (2011). "Interviewing", In: M. Stausberg and S. Engler (eds.) *The Routledge Handbook of Research Methods in the Study of Religion*, Routledge.

Brewer, M.B. (2001). "Intergroup identification and intergroup conflict: When does in-group love become outgroup hate", In: R.D. Ashmore, L. Jussim and David W. (eds.) *Social Identity, Intergroup Conflict and Conflict and Reduction*, New York: Oxford University Press, 17-41.

Buckser, Andrew and Stephen D. Glazier (2003). *The Anthropology of Religious Conversion*, Rowman & Littlefield.

Burgess, S.M. (2001). "Pentecostalism in India: An overview", *Asian Journal of Pentecosta Studies*, 4(1), 85-98.

Burgess, Stanley M., Van der Maas and Eduard M. (eds.) (2002). *The New International Dictionary of Pentecostal and Charismatic Movements*, Grand Rapids, Mich.: Zondervan.

Campbell, D. (2006). "'Religious threat" in contemporary presidential elections", *Journal of Politics*, 68(1), 104-15.

Chan, S. (2000). *Pentecostal Theology and the Christian Spiritual Tradition*, Sheffield: SAP.

Chatterjee, I. (2012). "How they are othered? Globalisation, identity and violence in an Indian city", *The Geographical Journal*, 178(2), 134-146.

Chatterjee, Margaret, (2005). *Gandhi and the Challenge of Religious Diversity: Religious Pluralism Revisited*, Bibliophile South Asia.

Chaturvedi, Swati (2016). *I Am a Troll: Inside the Secret World of the BJP's Digital Army*, Juggernaut Books.

Chowgule, Ashok (1999). *Christianity in India: The Hindutva Perspective,* Mumbai: Hindu Vivek Kendra.

Coleman, J. (2008). "Authoring (in)authenticity, regulating religious tolerance: The implications of anti-conversion legislation for Indian secularism", *Cultural Dynamics,* 20(3): 245-77.

Condor, S. (1990). "Social stereotypes and social identity", In: D. Abrams and M.A. Hogg, *Social Identity Theory: Constructive and Critical Advances,* Great Britain: Harvester.

Copland, I. (2006). "Christianity as an arm of the empire: The ambiguous case of Indian under the Company c. 1813-1858", *Historical Journal,* 49(4): 1025-54.

Copson, Andrew (2017). *Secularism: Politics, Religion and Freedom,* Oxford: Oxford University Press.

Corvino, John, Ryan T. Anderson and Sherif Girgis (2017). *Debating Religious Liberty and Discrimination,* Oxford University Press, p. 288.

Crabetree, James (2018). *The Billionaire Raj,* Harper Collins Publishers.

Dayal, John (2007). *A Matter of Equity: Freedom of Faith in Secular India,* New Delhi, Anamika Publishers & Distributors.

Dombrowski, K. (2001). *Against Culture: Development, Politics and Religion in Indian Alaska,* University of Nebraska Press.

Doniger, Wendy, Martha Craver Nussbaum (2015). *Pluralism and Democracy in India: Debating the Hindu Right,* New York: Oxford University Press, p. 1.

Dreher, A., Gaston, N. and Martens, P. (2008). *Measuring Globalization: Gauging Its Consequences,* New York: Springer.

D'Souza, Dinesh (2018). *Death of a Nation: Plantation Politics and the Making of the Democratic Party,* St. Martin's Press, US.

Duesing, Jason G., Thomas White and Malcolm B. Yarnell (2016). *First Freedom: The Beginning and End of Religious Liberty,* B&H Publishing Group.

Durham, W. Cole, Tore Sam Lindholm and Bahia Tahzib-Lie (2013). *Facilitating Freedom of Religion or Belief: A Deskbook,* Oslo, Norway: NA Brigham Young University, p. xxxvii.

Evans, Malcolm, Peter Petkoff and Julian Rivers (2015). *Changing Nature of Religious Rights Under International Law,* Oxford University Press, p. 125.

Farrah, Ahmed (2016). *Religious Freedom Under the Personal Law System,* Oxford University Press.

Fernandes, Vivian (2014). *Modi Leadership Governance and Performance,* Delhi: Orient Publishing.

Fox, Jonathan and Shemul Sandler (2017). *Religion in World Conflict,* Routledge.

Freedom House (2017). *Freedom in the World 2017: The Annual Survey of Political Rights and Civil Liberties,* Rowman & Littlefield.

Froerer, P. (2007). *Religious Division and Social Conflict: The Emergence of Hindu Nationalism in Rural India,* New York: Berghahn Books.

Frykenberg, R.E. (2010). *Christianity in India: from Beginnings to the Present*, New York: Oxford University Press.

Frykenberg, Robert Eric and Richard Fox Young (2009). *India and the Indianness of Christianity: Essays on Understanding*, Wm. B. Eerdmans Publishing.

Ghassem-Fachandi, P. (2012). *Pogrom in Gujarat: Hindu Nationalism and Anti-Muslim Violence in India*, Princeton, N.J.: Princeton University Press.

Goldstein, Bjom, (2018). *The Political Psychology of Attitudes Towards the West: An Empirical Analysis from Tamil Nadu*, Routledge.

Golwalker, M.S. (1947). *We or Our Nationhood Defined*, Nagpur: Bharat Prakashan.

Gooren, H. (2010). "Conversion Narratives", In: M. Bergunder, A. Droogers, C. van der Laan and A. Anderson (eds.) *Studying Global Pentecostalism: Theories and Methods*, Berkeley: University of California Press, 93-112.

Grim, B.J. (2012). "Religion, law and social conflict in the 21st century: Findings from sociological research", *Oxford Journal of Law and Religion*, 1(1), 1–23.

Grim, B.J. and Finke, R. (2011). *The Price of Freedom Denied: Religious Persecution and Conflict in the Twenty-First Century*, Cambridge: Cambridge University Press.

Gujarat Freedom of Religion Bill (2003). Retrieved 05.03.2014, from http://www.emwd.de/fix/files/indien-religionsgesetz.pdf.

Gupta, C. and M. Sharma (1996). "Communal constructions: Media reality vs. real reality", *Race and Class*, 38(1), 1-20.

Hansen, T.B. (1999). *The Saffron Wave: Democracy and Hindu Nationalism in India*, New Jersey: Princeton University Press.

Hashemi, N. (2009). *Islam, Secularism, and Liberal Democracy: Toward a Democratic Theory for Muslim Societies*, Oxford: Oxford University Press.

Hastings, Adrian, Alistair Mason and Hugh Pyper (2000). *The Oxford Companion to Christian Thought*, OUP.

Haynes, Jeffrey (2016). *Routledge Handbook of Religion and Politics*, New York: Routledge, p. 76.

Hehir, Aidan and Robert W. Murray (2017). *Protecting Human Rights in the 21st Century*, Taylor & Francis.

Heredia, Rudol C. (2007). *Changing God's Rethinking Conversion in India*, Penguin Books India.

Hertzke, Allen D. (2013). *The Future of Religious Freedom: Global Challenges*, Oxford University Press.

Hurd, Elizabeth Shakman, (2017). *Beyond Religious Freedom: The New Global Politics of Religion*, Princeton University Press.

Jaffrelot, C. (ed.) (2007). *Hindu Nationalism: A Reader*, Princeton: Princeton University Press.

Jaffrelot, C. (1996). *The Hindu Nationalist Movement and Indian Politics: 1925 to the 1990s*, London: Hurst & Company.

Jaffrelot, Christophe (2005). *The Sangh Parivar: A Reader*, Oxford University Press.

Jalan, Bimal, (2017). *India: Priorities for the Future*, Penguin Random House, India.

Jha, Dhirendra K. (2017). *Shadow Armies: Fringe Organizations and Foot Soldiers of Hindutva*, Juggernaut Publications.

Johnson, Thomas K. (2017). *Global Declarations: On Freedom of Religion or Belief and Human Rights*, Wipf & Stock Publ.

Jones, A. (2009). "Faces of Pentecostalism in North India Today", *Society*, 46(6), 504-509.

Kaltwasser, Cristóbal Rovira, Paul A. Taggart, Paulina Ochoa Espejo and Pierre Ostiguy (2017). *The Oxford Handbook of Populism*, Oxford University Press.

Kim, S.C.H. (2003). *In Search for Identity: Debates on Religious Conversion in India*, New Delhi: Oxford University Press.

King, R. (2009). *Orientalism and Religion: Postcolonial Theory, India and 'The Mystical East'*, London & New York: Routledge.

Kinnvall, Catarina (2007). *Globalization and Religious Nationalism in India: The Search for Ontological Security*, Routledge.

Korostelina, K.V. (2007). *Social Identity and Conflict: Structures, Dynamics and Implications*, New York: Palgrave Macmillan.

Kumar, A.M. and R. Robinson (2010). "Legally Hindu: *Dalit* Lutheran Christians of Coastal Andhra Pradesh", In: R. Robinson and M.J. Kujur (eds.), *Margins of Faith: Dalit and Tribal Christianity in India*, New Delhi: Sage Publications, 149-169.

Kumar, Pravin (2017). *Yogi Adityanath: The Rise of a Saffron Socialist*, Times Group Books, New Delhi.

Latinovic, Vladimir, Gerard Mannion and Peter C. Phan, (2016). *Pathways for Inter-Religious Dialogue in the Twenty-First Century*, Springer.

Lobo, Lancy (2002). "Persecution of Christians", *Dialog: A Journal of Theology*, 41(2), 114-122.

Lobo, Lancy (2002). *Globalisation, Hindu Nationalism, and Christians in India*.

Lukose, W. (2013). *Contextual Missiology of the Spirit: Pentecostalism in Rajasthan, India*, Oregon: Wipf and Stock Publishers, p. 86.

Mahmood, Tahir, (2008). *Laws of India on Religion and Religious Affairs: Introduction, Text & Case Law*, Universal Law Publishing Company.

Majumdar, Uma (2012). *Gandhi's Pilgrimage of Faith: From Darkness to Light*, New York: SUNY Press.

Malhotra, Rajiv and Aravintan Nîlakantan (2011). *Breaking India: Western Interventions in Dravidian and Dalit Faultlines*, Amaryllis.

Mander, Harsh (2015). *Looking Away: Inequality, Prejudice, and Indifference in New India*, Speaking Tiger Books.

Maramreddy, Maria Joseph Reddy (2012). *Human Rights, Indian Legislation and Teaching of the Catholic Church*, Pontificia University.

Mehta, Pratap Bhanu (2017). *The Burden of Democracy*, Delhi: Penguin Random House India Private Limited.

Melanchthon, M. (2002). "Persecution of Indian Christians", *Dialog: A Journal of Theology*, 41(2), 103-113.

Menon, K.D. (2010). *Everyday Nationalism: Women of the Hindu Right in India*, Philadelphia: University of Pennsylvania Press.

Merrigan, Terrence and John Friday, (2017). *The Past, Present, and Future of Theologies of Interreligious Dialogue*, Oxford University Press.

Misra, A. (2011). "The Missionary Position: Christianity and Politics of Religion Conversion in India", *Nationalism and Ethnic Politics*, 17(4), 361-381.

Mounk, Yascha (2017). *The People vs. Democracy: Why Our Freedom Is in Danger and How to Save It*, Harvard University Press.

Mukhopadhaya, Nyanja (2013). *Narendra Modi: The Man The Time*, Delhi: Tranquebar Press.

Napel, Hans-Martien ten (2017). *Constitutionalism, Democracy, and Religious Freedom: To be Fully Human*, Routledge.

Narayan, A. (2003). *Home and the World: Inter-Religious Marriages in India*, Paper presented at American Sociological Associations Annual Meeting, Atlanta.

Ninan, M.M. (2009). *Life, Legacy and Theology of M.M. Thomas: An Anthology*, Create Space Independent Publishing Platform.

Ninan, T.N. (2017). *Turn of the Tortoise: The Challenge and Promise of India's Future*, Oxford University Press.

Noorani, A.G. (2011). *Challenges to Civil Rights Guarantees in India*, South Asian Human Rights Documentation Centre, Delhi: Oxford University Press.

Noorani, A.G. (2012). "Acts of bad faith: Anti-conversion laws", In: A.G. Noorani (ed.) *Challenges to Civil Rights Guarantees in India*. [online] Available from http://m.oxfordscholarship.com.ludwig.lub.lu.se/mobile/view/10.1093/acprof:oso/9780198 074144.001.0001/acprof-9780198074144-chapter-7 [Accessed 11.12..2017].

Nussbaum, Martha (2009). *The Clash Within: Democracy, Religious Violence, and India's Future*, Harvard University Press.

Osuri, Goldie (2013). *Religious Freedom in India: Sovereignty and (anti) Conversion*, Routledge.

Pew Forum on Religion and Public Life (2011). *Rising Restrictions on Religion*, Washington DC: Pew Research Centre.

Price, Lance (2015). *The Modi Effect: Inside Narendra Modi's Campaign to Transform India*, Hachette, UK.

Pruitt, D.G. and S.H. Kim. (2004). *Social Conflict: Escalation, Stalemate, and Settlement* (3rd ed.), New York: McGraw-Hill.

Puniyani, Ram (2005). *Religion, Power and Violence: Expression of Politics in Contemporary Times*, Sage Publications India.

Rambo, Lewis Ray, Charles E. Farhadiabn (2014). *The Oxford Handbook of Religious Conversion*, New York: Oxford University Press, p. 3.

Razdan, Nidhi (2017). *Left, Right and Centre: The Idea of India*, New Delhi: Penguin Random House, India.

Rehman, Mujibur (2018). *Rise of Saffron Power: Reflections on Indian Politics,* Philadelphia: University of the Pennsylvania Press.

Robbins, J. (2004). "The globalization of Pentecostal and Charismatic Christianity", *Annual Review of Anthropology,* 33(1), 117-143.

Robinson, R. (2003). *Christians of India,* New Delhi & London: Sage Publications.

Saeed, Abdullah (2017). *Freedom of Religion: Apostasy and Islam,* Taylor & Francis.

Sahoo, Sarbeswar (2018). *Pentecostalism and Religious Conflict in Contemporary India,* Cambridge University Press.

Sardesai, Rajdeep (2015). *2014: The Election That Changed India,* Penguin, UK.

Savarkar, V.D. (1969). *Hindutva–Who is Hindu,* Bombay: S.S. Savarkar.

Shaban, Abdul (2018). *Lives of Muslims in India: Politics, Exclusion and Violence,* Taylor & Francis.

Shani, O. (2007). *Communalism, Caste and Hindu Nationalism in India,* Cambridge.

Singh, K.S. (1992). *People of India: Introduction,* Calcutta: Anthropology Survey of India.

Sullivan, Winnifred Fallers, Elizabeth Shakman Hurd, Saba Mahmood and Peter G. Danchin (2015). *Politics of Religious Freedom,* University of Chicago Press.

Swamy, Muthuraj (2016). *The Problem with Interreligious Dialogue: Plurality, Conflict and Elitism in Hindu-Christian-Muslim Relations,* Bloomsbury Publishing.

Tajfel, H. and J.C. Turner (1986). "The social identity theory of intergroup behaviour", In: S. Worchel and W.G. Austin, (eds.) *Psychology of Intergroup Relations,* Chicago: Nelson Hall, 7-24.

Tajfel, H. (1981). *Social Identity and Intergroup Relations,* London: Cambridge University Press.

Thomas, M.M. (1971). *Salvation, and Humanisation: Some Critical Issues of the Theology of Masson in Contemporary India,* Madras: CLS, pp. 4-12.

Thomas, Pradip Ninan (2012). *Digital India: Understanding Information, Communication and Social Change,* Sage Publications, India.

Trigg, Roger (2012). *Equality, Freedom, and Religion,* Oxford University Press.

Zavos, J. (2000). *The Emergence of Hindu Nationalism in India,* Delhi: Oxford University Press.

Zavos, J. (2001). "Conversion and the assertive margins: An analysis of Hindu nationalist discourse and the recent attacks on Indian Christians", *Journal of South Asian Studies,* 24(2), 73-89.

Index